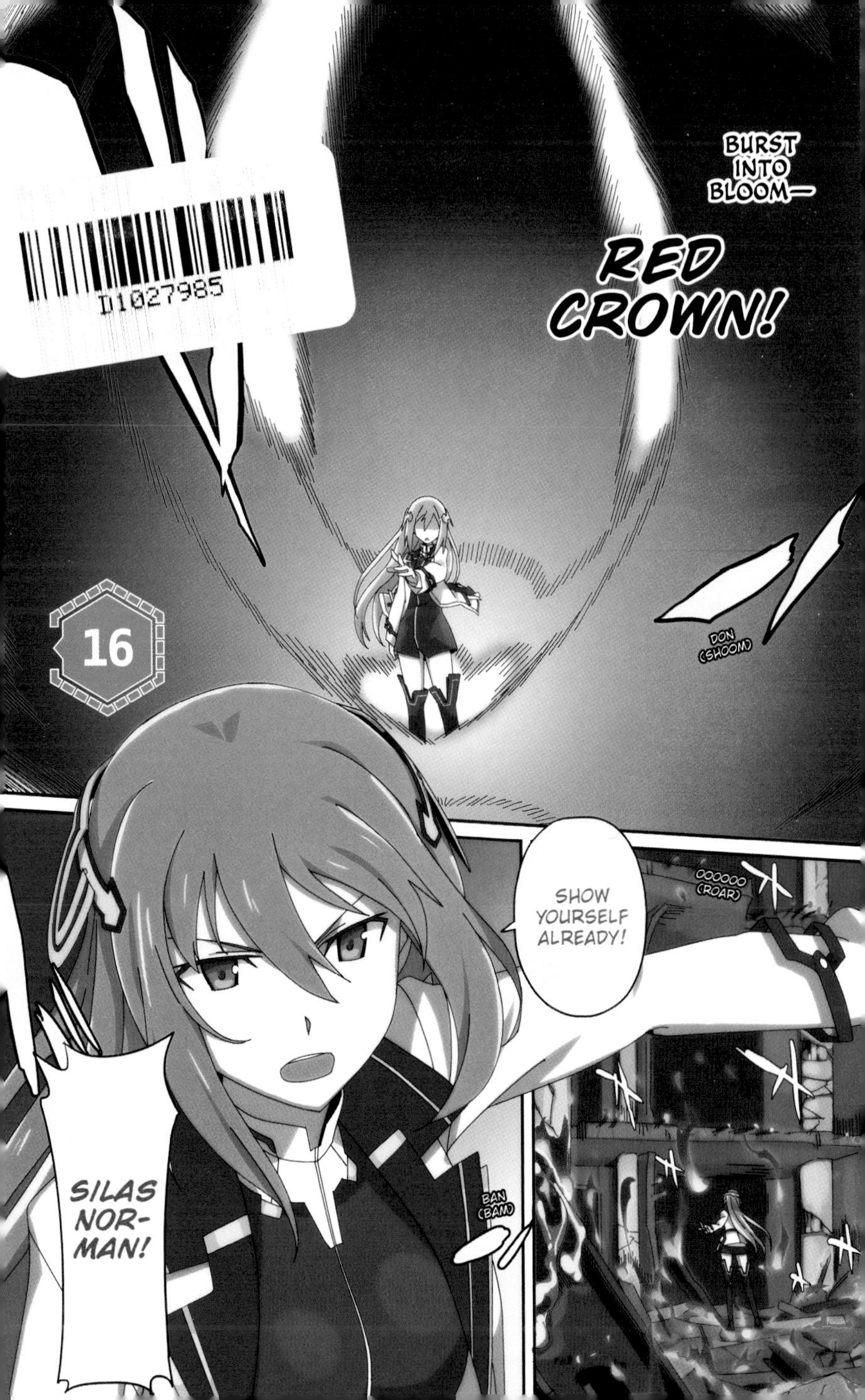
BURST INTO BLOOM—
RED CROWN!
DON (SHOOM)
16
OOOOOO (ROAR)
SHOW YOURSELF ALREADY!
BAN (BAM)
SILAS NOR-MAN!

ART:
Ningen

ORIGINAL STORY:
Yuu Miyazaki

CHARACTER DESIGN:
okiura

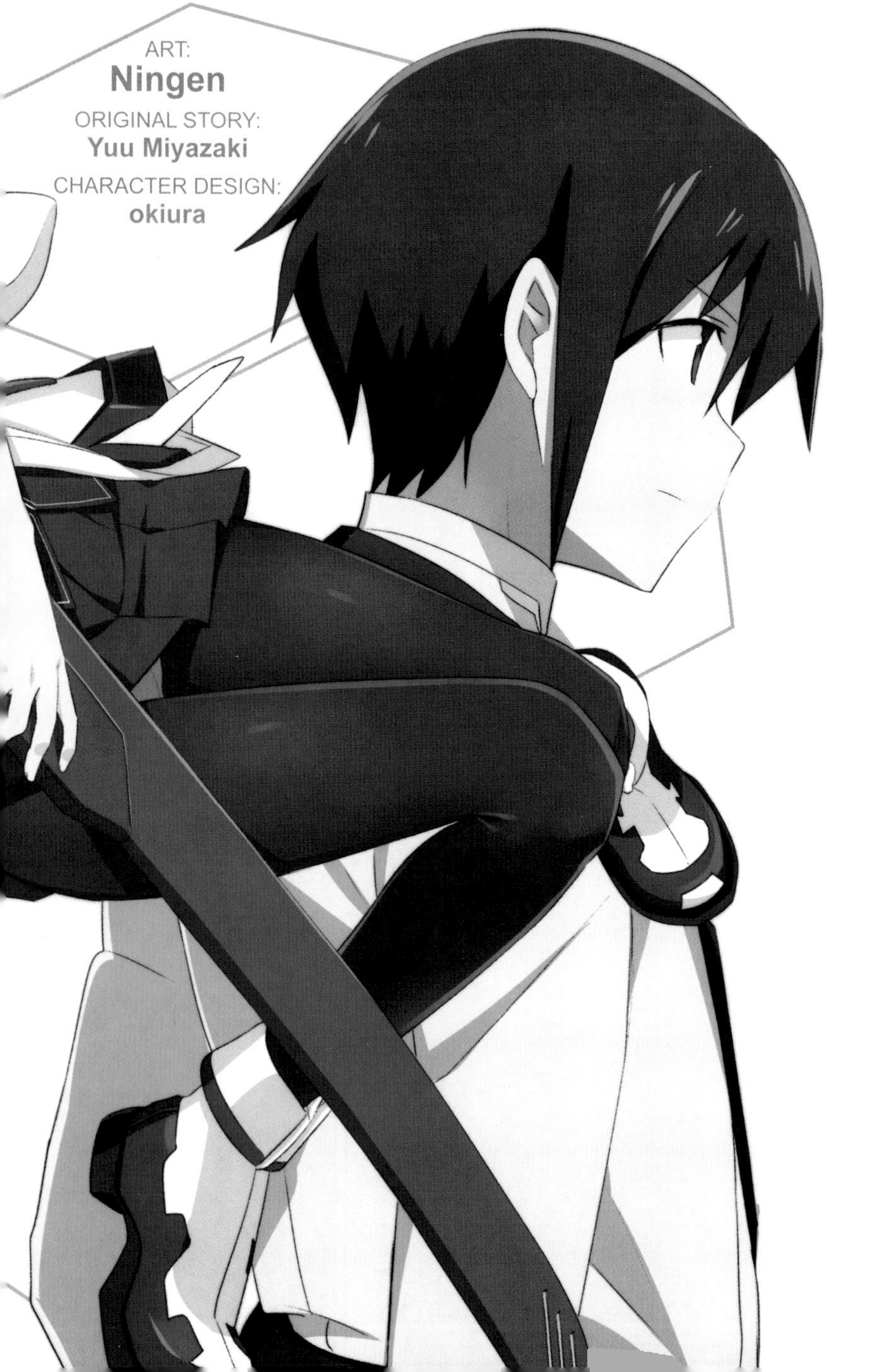

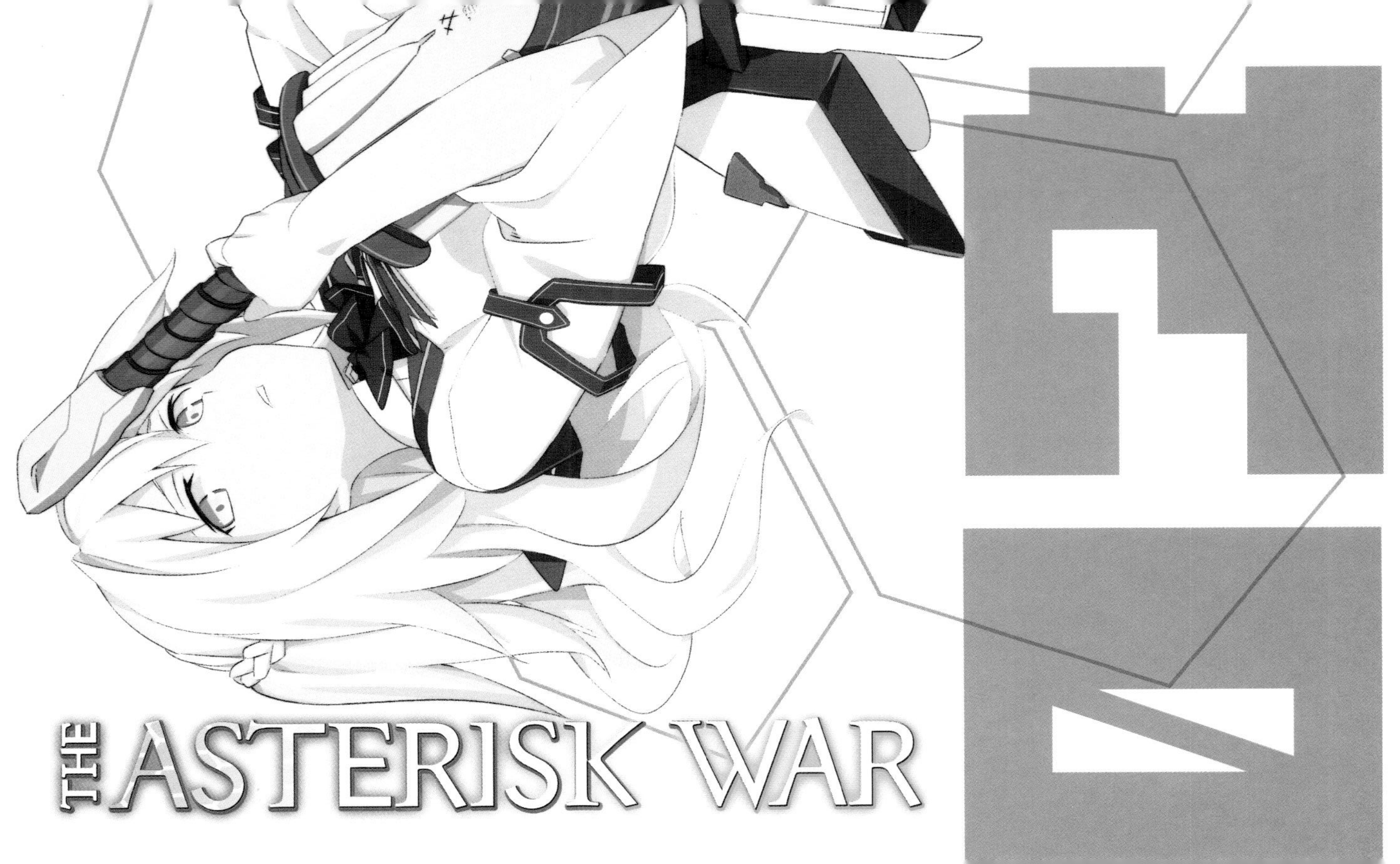
THE ASTERISK WAR
12

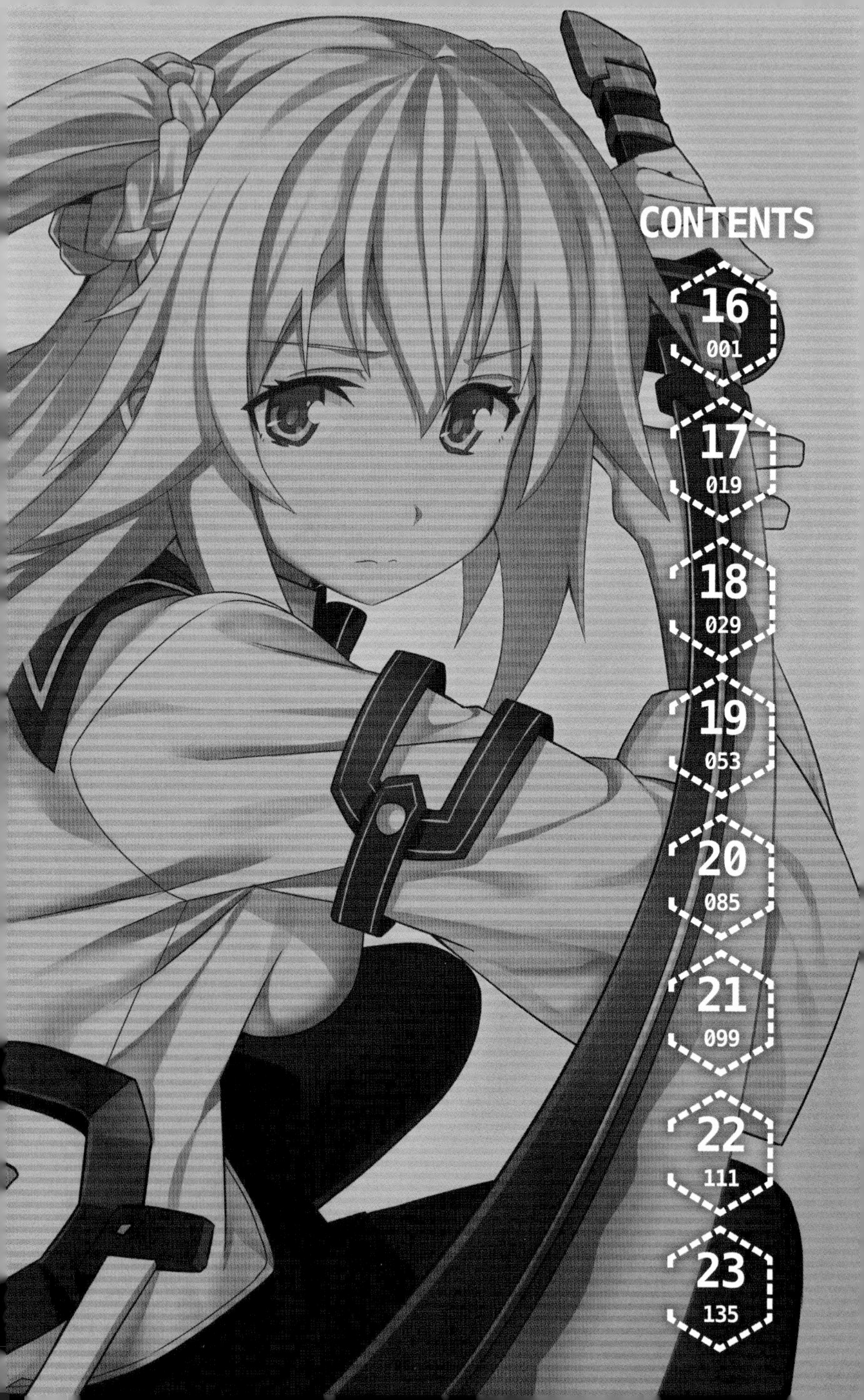

CONTENTS

THE ASTERISK WAR

03

ART: **Ningen**
ORIGINAL STORY: **Yuu Miyazaki**
CHARACTER DESIGN: **okiura**

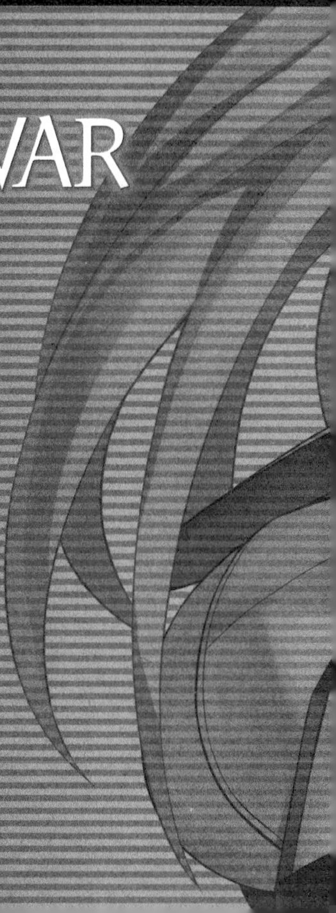

THE ASTERISK WAR

CHARACTERS

Ayato Amagiri

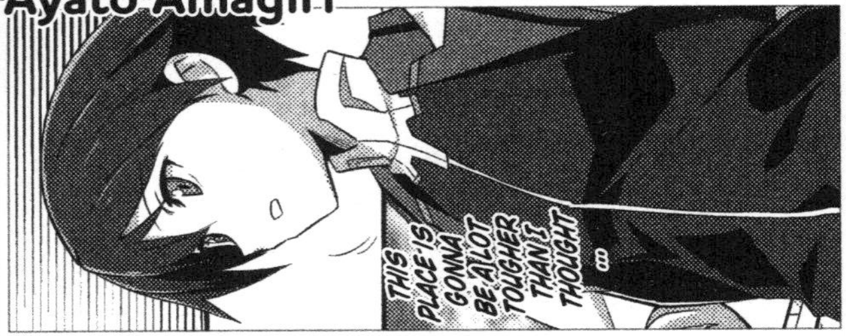
THIS PLACE IS GONNA BE A LOT TOUGHER THAN I THOUGHT...

Transferred into Seidoukan Academy High School on a special scholarship. A skilled swordsman who has been training since he was small in his family's Amagiri Shinmei Sword Style, but the enormous amount of prana he possesses has been sealed away.

Saya Sasamiya

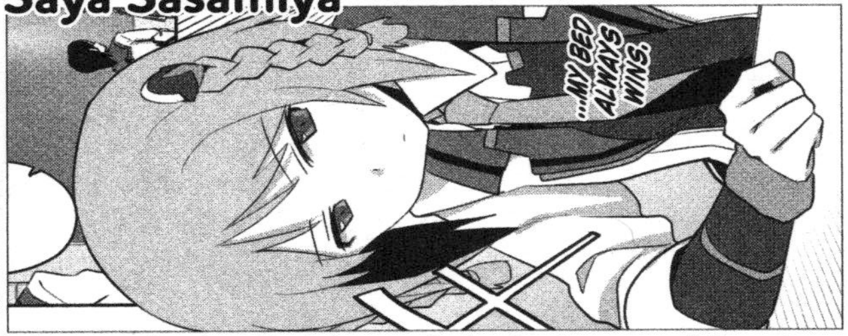
...MY BED ALWAYS WINS.

In the same grade as Ayato. They've known each other since they were small. Always sleepy due to bad circulation. At the request of her father, a scientist in meteoric engineering, she came to Asterisk to advertise the gun he invented. A firm believer that bigger is better when it comes to firearms and an expert in the subject.

Julis-Alexia von Riessfeld

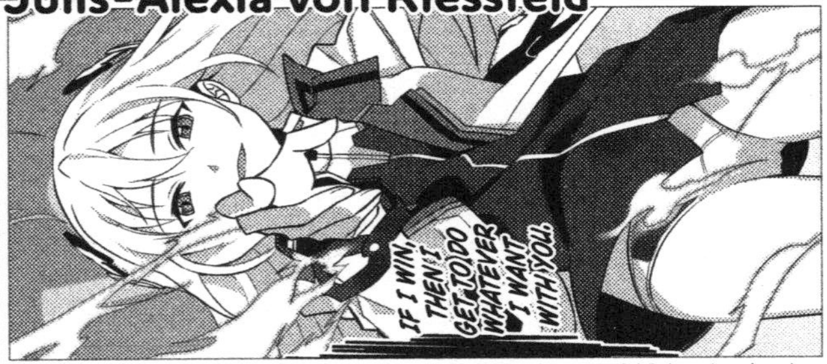
IF I WIN, THEN I GET TO DO WHATEVER I WANT WITH YOU.

A Page One student, ranked fifth at Seidoukan Academy, and a powerful fighter bearing the epithet "Glühen Rose—Witch of the Resplendent Flames." Proud and short-tempered but also conscientious and kind.

Claudia Enfield

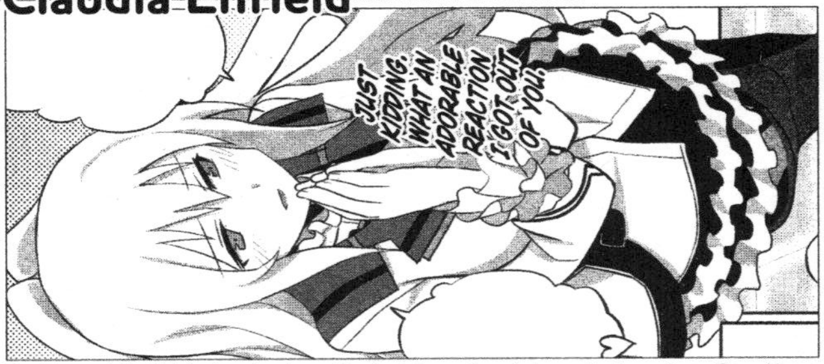
JUST KIDDING. WHAT AN ADORABLE REACTION I GOT OUT OF YOU.

President of the Seidoukan Academy Student Council and also ranked as a Page One. Always smiling, gentle, and polite—but describes herself as blackhearted.

THE WORLD OF ASTERISK

Rikka: the Academy City on the Water

A city that floats on the surface of the North Kanto crater lake, surrounded by six schools. Its hexagonal shape earned it the nickname Asterisk.

Seidoukan Academy

The school our main characters attend, ranked fifth in Asterisk. Seidoukan used to dominate in all three Festa events but has recently been in a slump. A campus culture that emphasizes students' independence attracts many Dantes and Stregas as students.

Queenvale Academy for Young Ladies

The only all-girls' school, Queenvale is consistently ranked last, and the matriculation requirement of "good looks" makes it an odd sort of academy. Students' beauty is on a level with top-class idols, and despite the rankings, they have plenty of fans, even from other schools.

St. Gallardworth Academy

One of the top-ranking schools ever since its founding, Gallardworth also boasts the most overall victories in Asterisk. The rigid culture there values discipline and loyalty above all else, and in principle, even duels are forbidden. Students are on poor terms with Le Wolfe.

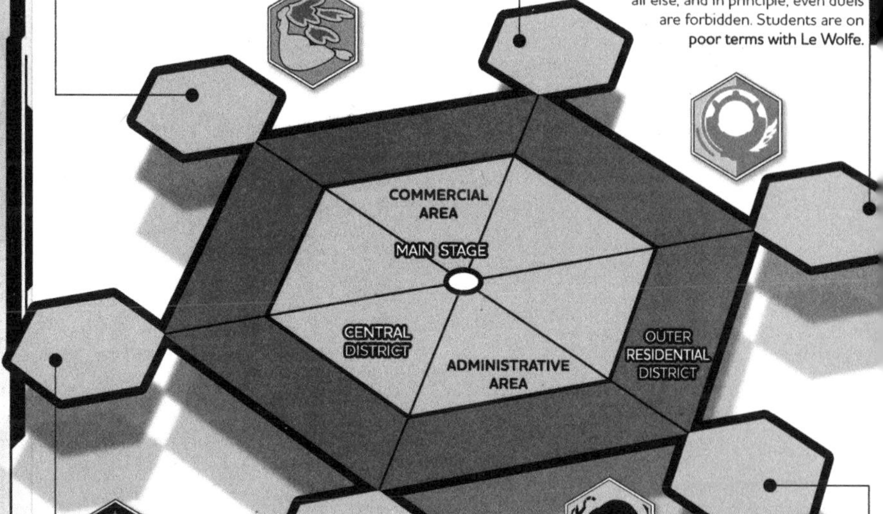

COMMERCIAL AREA
MAIN STAGE
CENTRAL DISTRICT
ADMINISTRATIVE AREA
OUTER RESIDENTIAL DISTRICT

Jie Long Seventh Institute

The largest of the six schools and the only school that has never once fallen to last place in the overall rankings. Bureaucracy clashes with a laissez-faire attitude, making the school culture rather chaotic. The atmosphere has strong Far Eastern leanings, and students boast their own martial art technique known as Star Xianshu.

Le Wolfe Black Institute

Ferociously strong when it comes to one-on-one battles, Le Wolfe has a tremendously belligerent culture, to the point of encouraging duels with students from other schools. The place is practically lawless, and more than a few students end up in mercenary or criminal activity. Whenever there's commotion in the city, Le Wolfe students are likely to be involved.

Allekant Académie

Specializing in meteoric engineering, Allekant is the only one of the six schools with an actual research department. Students' technological expertise shows in the quality of their Lux weapons, which far surpass those of the other schools. With a culture driven by results, they have rapidly progressed to the rank of second place in the last several years.

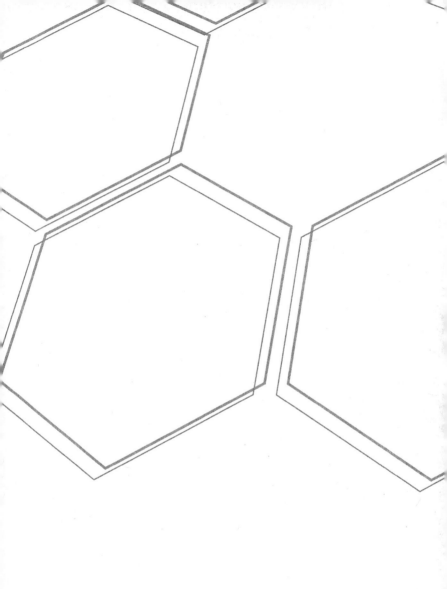

THE
ASTERISK WAR

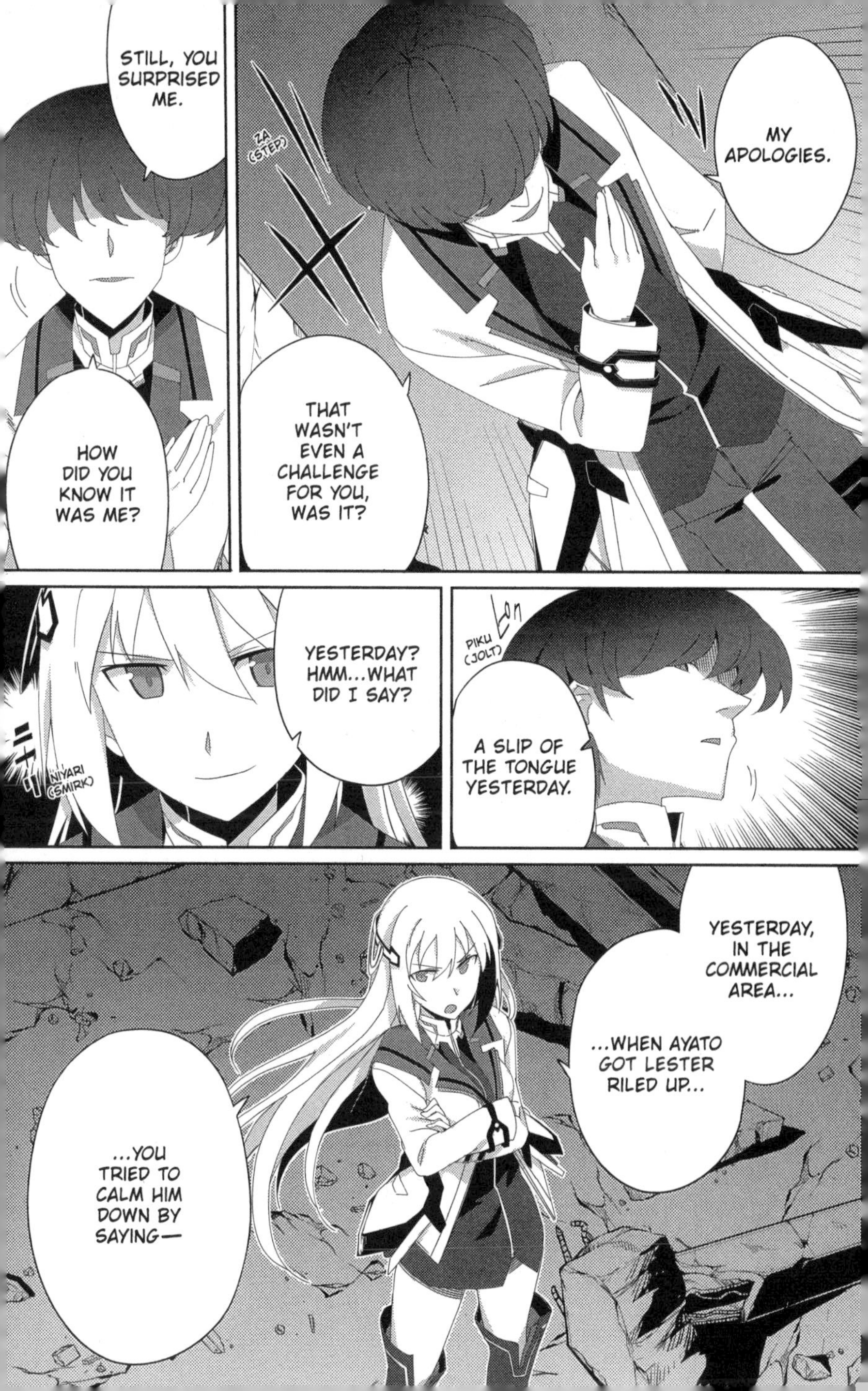
MY APOLOGIES.
ZA (STEP)
THAT WASN'T EVEN A CHALLENGE FOR YOU, WAS IT?
STILL, YOU SURPRISED ME.
HOW DID YOU KNOW IT WAS ME?
PIKU (JOLT)
A SLIP OF THE TONGUE YESTERDAY.
YESTERDAY? HMM...WHAT DID I SAY?
NIYARI (SMIRK)
YESTERDAY, IN THE COMMERCIAL AREA...
...WHEN AYATO GOT LESTER RILED UP...
...YOU TRIED TO CALM HIM DOWN BY SAYING—

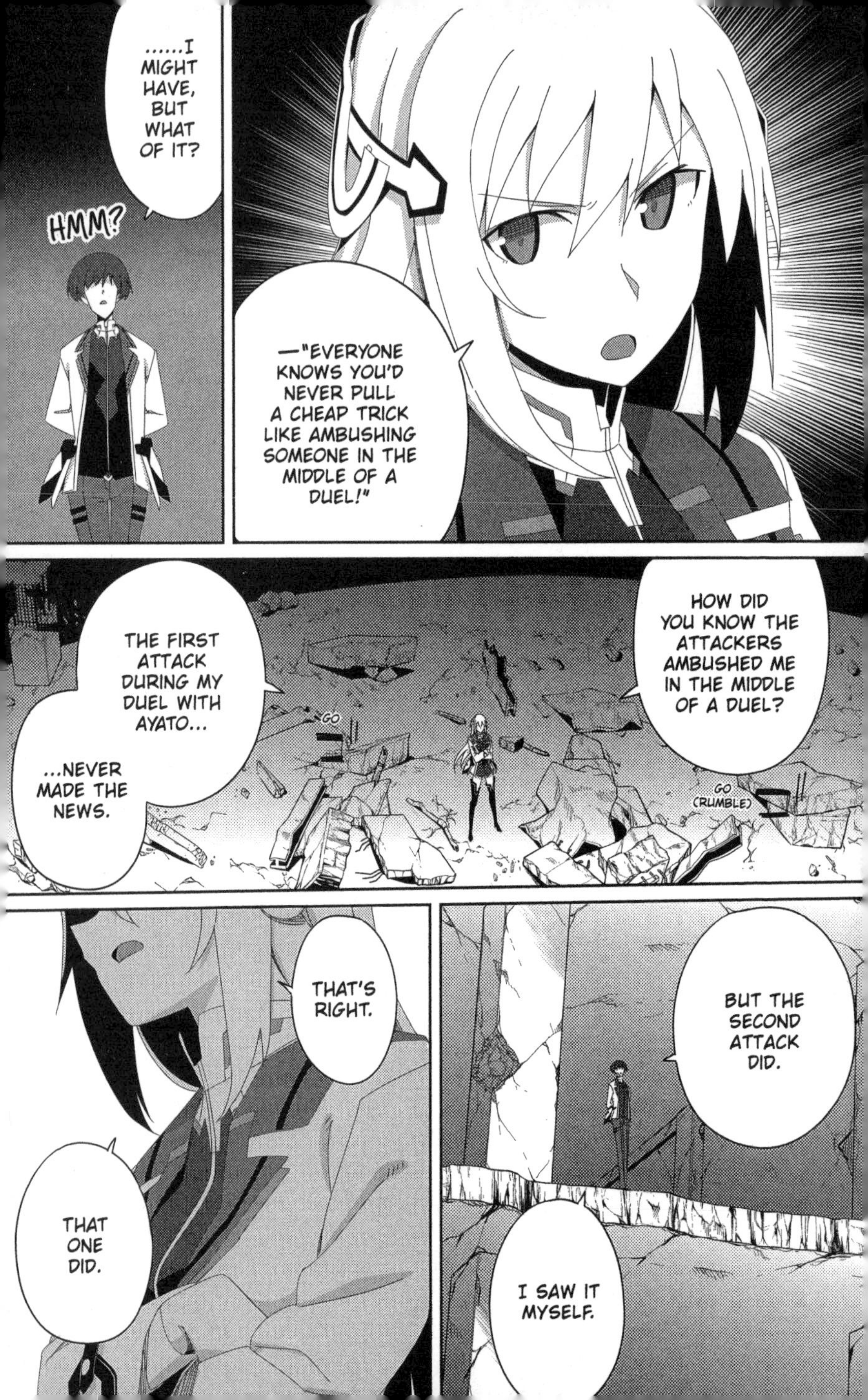
—"EVERYONE KNOWS YOU'D NEVER PULL A CHEAP TRICK LIKE AMBUSHING SOMEONE IN THE MIDDLE OF A DUEL!"
......I MIGHT HAVE, BUT WHAT OF IT?
HMM?
HOW DID YOU KNOW THE ATTACKERS AMBUSHED ME IN THE MIDDLE OF A DUEL?
THE FIRST ATTACK DURING MY DUEL WITH AYATO...
GO
GO (RUMBLE)
...NEVER MADE THE NEWS.
BUT THE SECOND ATTACK DID.
I SAW IT MYSELF.
THAT'S RIGHT.
THAT ONE DID.

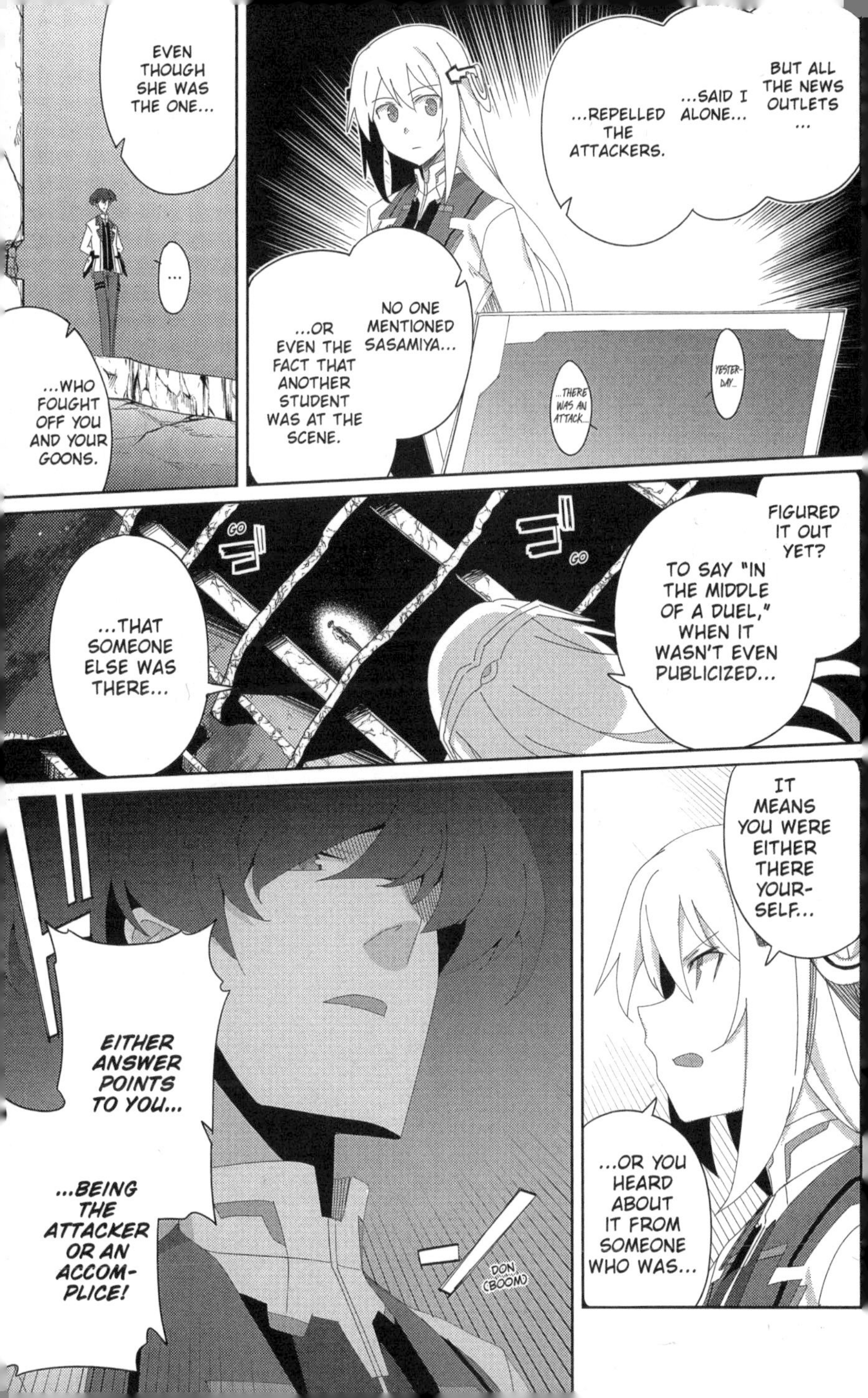
BUT ALL THE NEWS OUTLETS ...
...SAID I ALONE...
...REPELLED THE ATTACKERS.
YESTERDAY...
...THERE WAS AN ATTACK...
NO ONE MENTIONED SASAMIYA...
...OR EVEN THE FACT THAT ANOTHER STUDENT WAS AT THE SCENE.
EVEN THOUGH SHE WAS THE ONE...
...
...WHO FOUGHT OFF YOU AND YOUR GOONS.
FIGURED IT OUT YET?
TO SAY "IN THE MIDDLE OF A DUEL," WHEN IT WASN'T EVEN PUBLICIZED...
GO
GO
...THAT SOMEONE ELSE WAS THERE...
IT MEANS YOU WERE EITHER THERE YOURSELF...
...OR YOU HEARD ABOUT IT FROM SOMEONE WHO WAS...
EITHER ANSWER POINTS TO YOU...
...BEING THE ATTACKER OR AN ACCOMPLICE!
DON (BOOM)

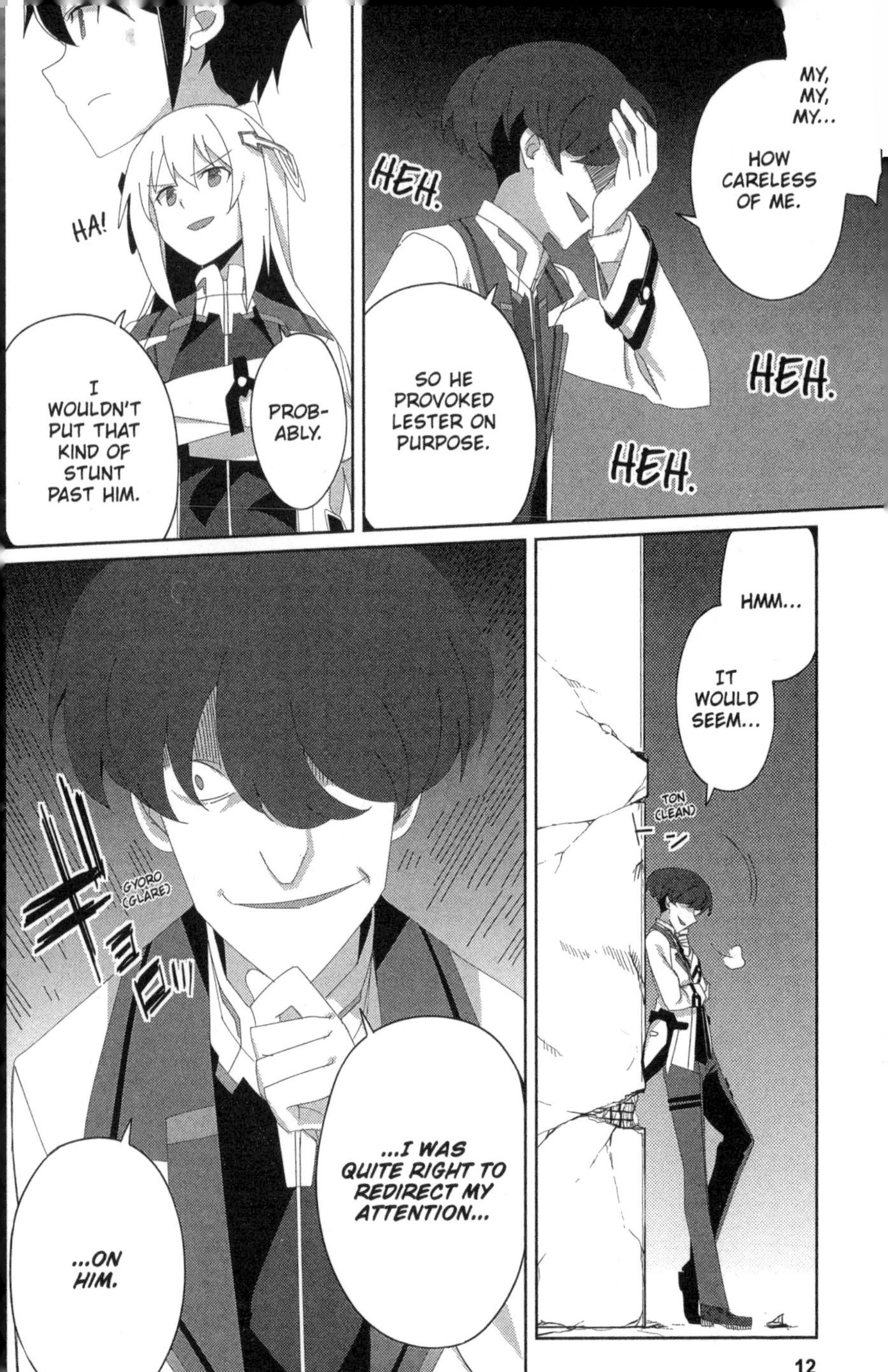
MY, MY, MY...
HOW CARELESS OF ME.
HEH.
HEH.
HEH.
SO HE PROVOKED LESTER ON PURPOSE.
HA!
PROB-ABLY.
I WOULDN'T PUT THAT KIND OF STUNT PAST HIM.
HMM...
IT WOULD SEEM...
TON (LEAN)
GYORO (GLARE)
...I WAS QUITE RIGHT TO REDIRECT MY ATTENTION...
...ON HIM.

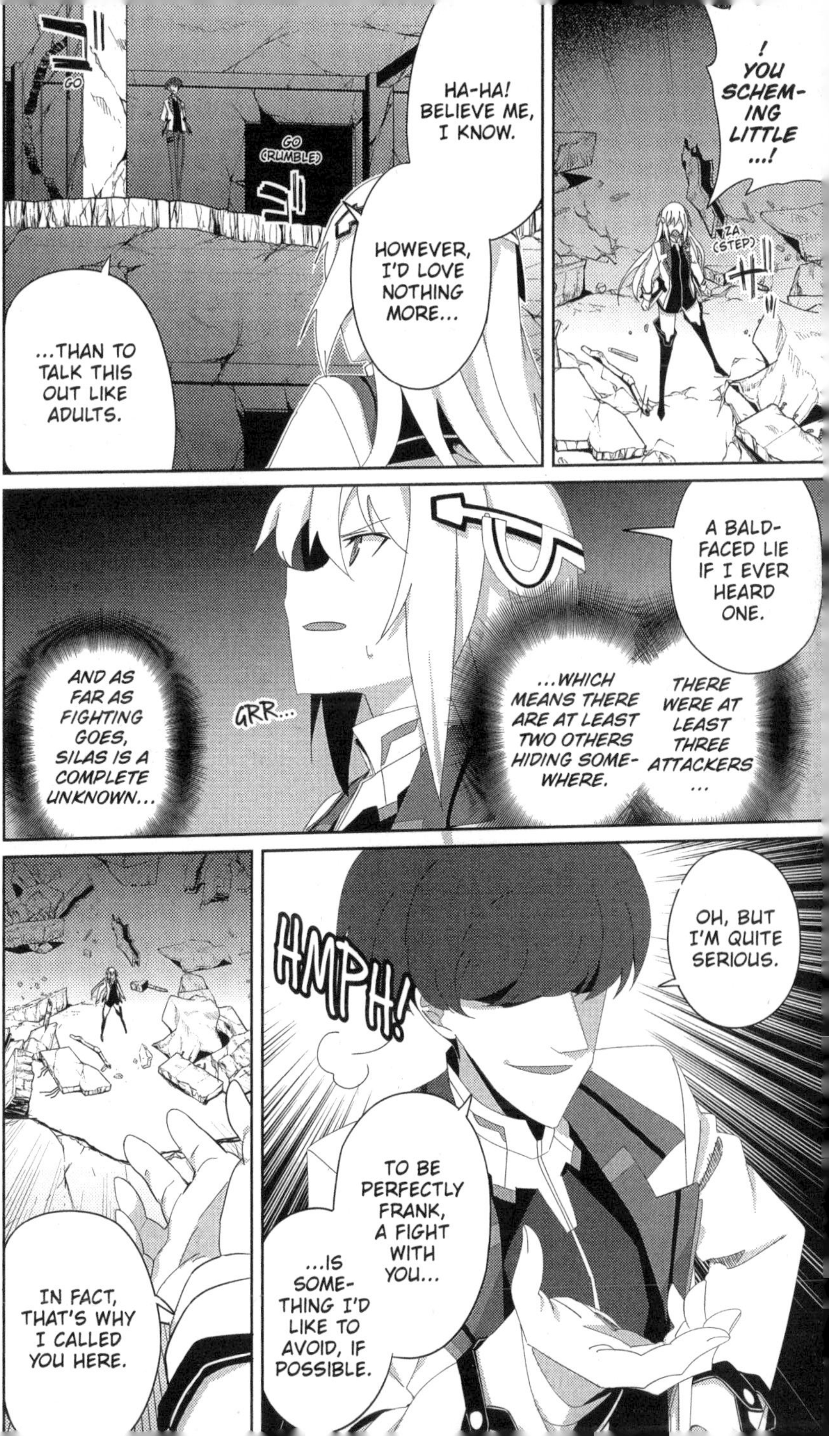
! YOU SCHEMING LITTLE ...!
ZA (STEP)
HA-HA! BELIEVE ME, I KNOW.
GO (RUMBLE)
GO
HOWEVER, I'D LOVE NOTHING MORE...
...THAN TO TALK THIS OUT LIKE ADULTS.
A BALD-FACED LIE IF I EVER HEARD ONE.
THERE WERE AT LEAST THREE ATTACKERS...
...WHICH MEANS THERE ARE AT LEAST TWO OTHERS HIDING SOMEWHERE.
GRR...
AND AS FAR AS FIGHTING GOES, SILAS IS A COMPLETE UNKNOWN...
OH, BUT I'M QUITE SERIOUS.
HMPH!
TO BE PERFECTLY FRANK, A FIGHT WITH YOU...
...IS SOMETHING I'D LIKE TO AVOID, IF POSSIBLE.
IN FACT, THAT'S WHY I CALLED YOU HERE.

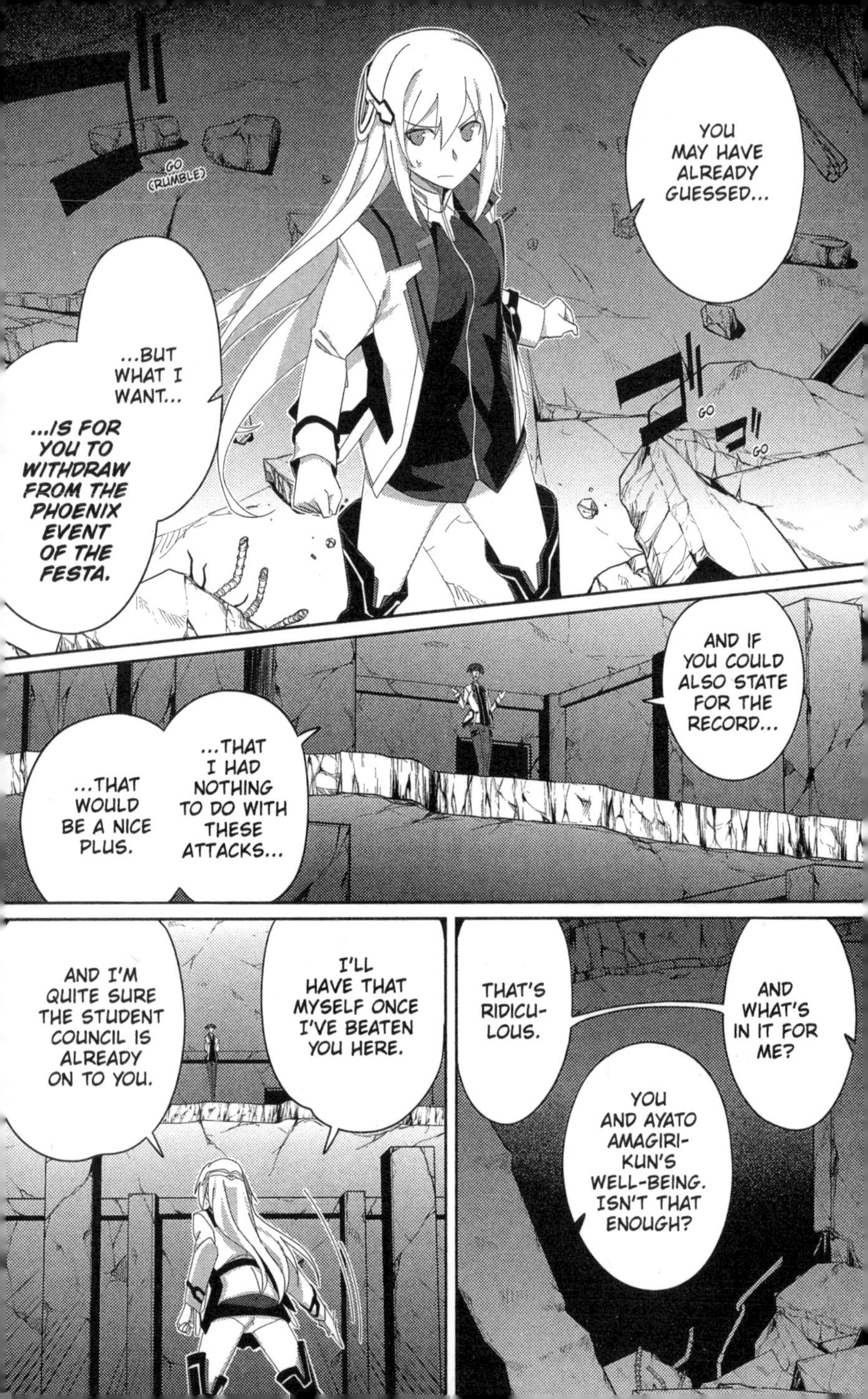
YOU MAY HAVE ALREADY GUESSED...
GO
GO
GO (RUMBLE)
...BUT WHAT I WANT...
...IS FOR YOU TO WITHDRAW FROM THE PHOENIX EVENT OF THE FESTA.
AND IF YOU COULD ALSO STATE FOR THE RECORD...
...THAT I HAD NOTHING TO DO WITH THESE ATTACKS...
...THAT WOULD BE A NICE PLUS.
THAT'S RIDICULOUS.
AND WHAT'S IN IT FOR ME?
YOU AND AYATO AMAGIRI-KUN'S WELL-BEING. ISN'T THAT ENOUGH?
I'LL HAVE THAT MYSELF ONCE I'VE BEATEN YOU HERE.
AND I'M QUITE SURE THE STUDENT COUNCIL IS ALREADY ON TO YOU.

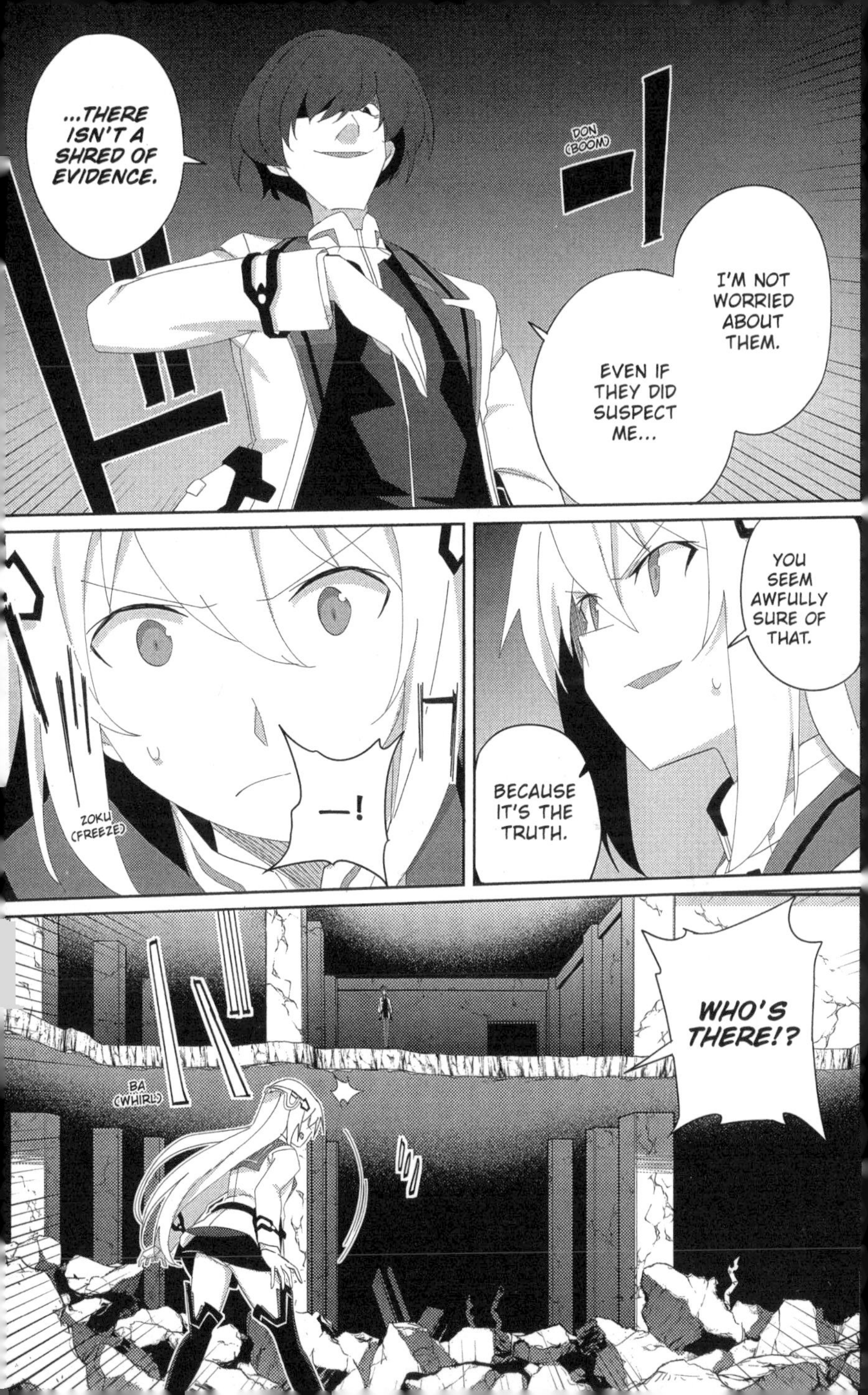
I'M NOT WORRIED ABOUT THEM.
EVEN IF THEY DID SUSPECT ME...
DON (BOOM)
...THERE ISN'T A SHRED OF EVIDENCE.
YOU SEEM AWFULLY SURE OF THAT.
BECAUSE IT'S THE TRUTH.
—!
ZOKU (FREEZE)
WHO'S THERE!?
BA (WHIRL)

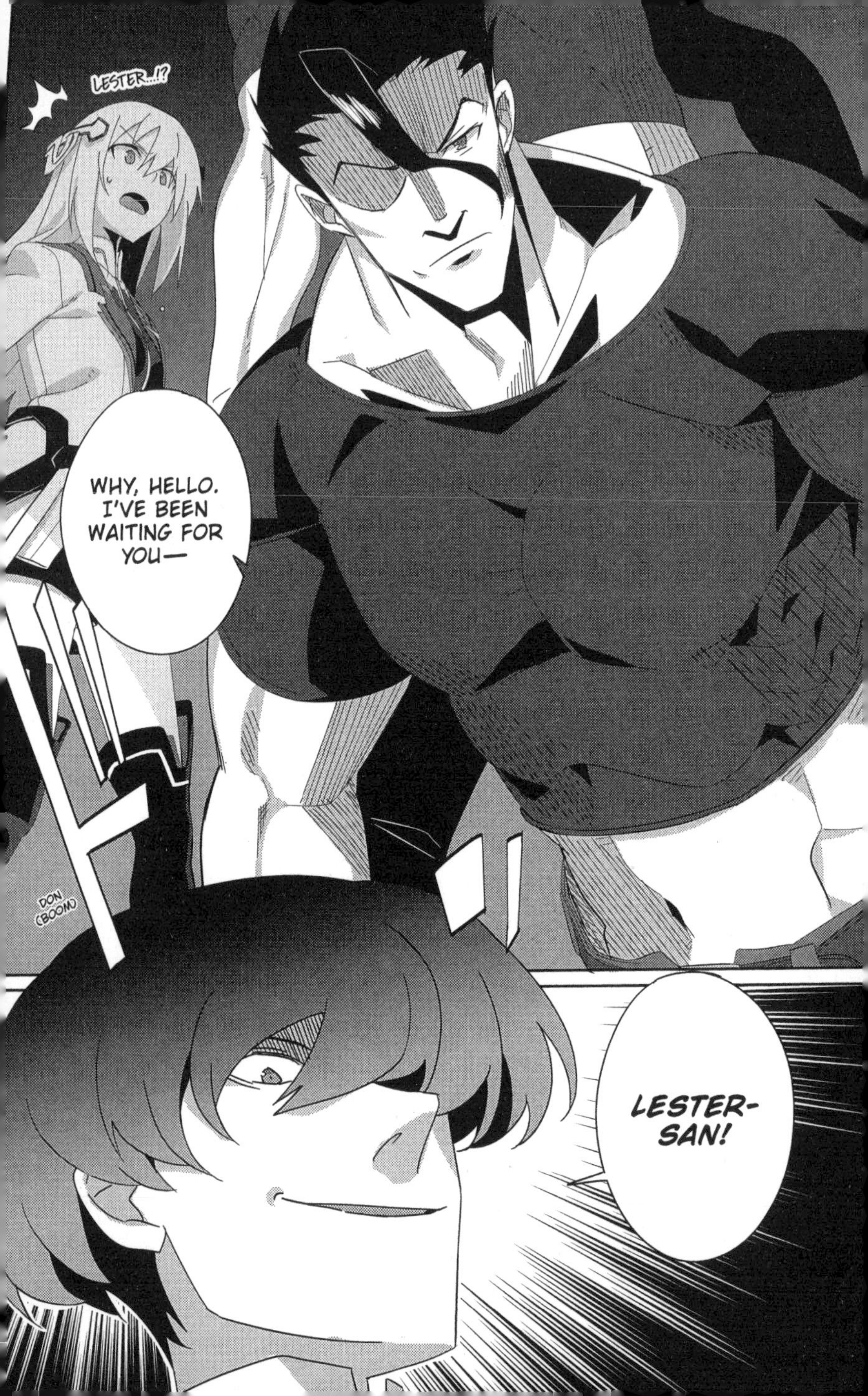
LESTER...!?
WHY, HELLO. I'VE BEEN WAITING FOR YOU—
DON (BOOM)
LESTER-SAN!

THE ASTERISK WAR

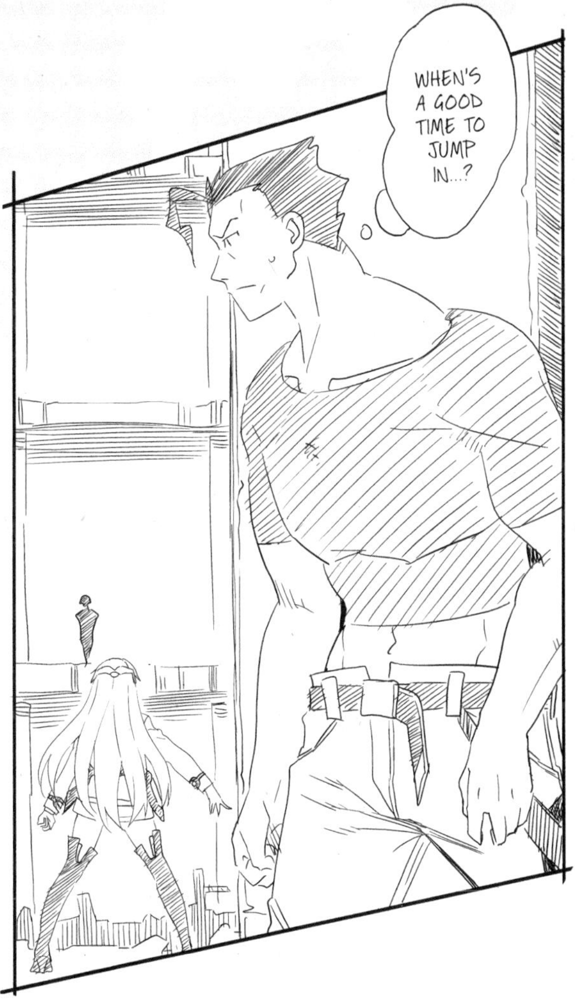
WHEN'S A GOOD TIME TO JUMP IN...?

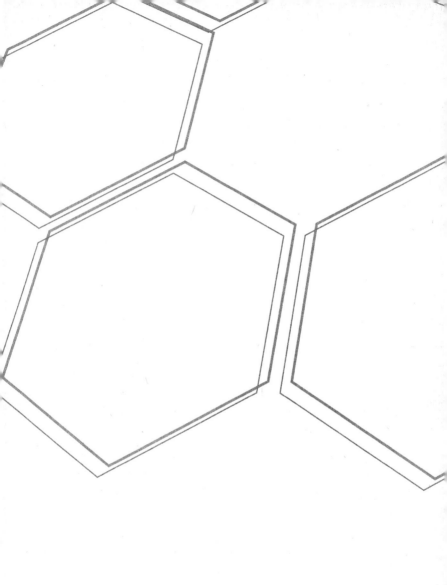

THE
ASTERISK WAR

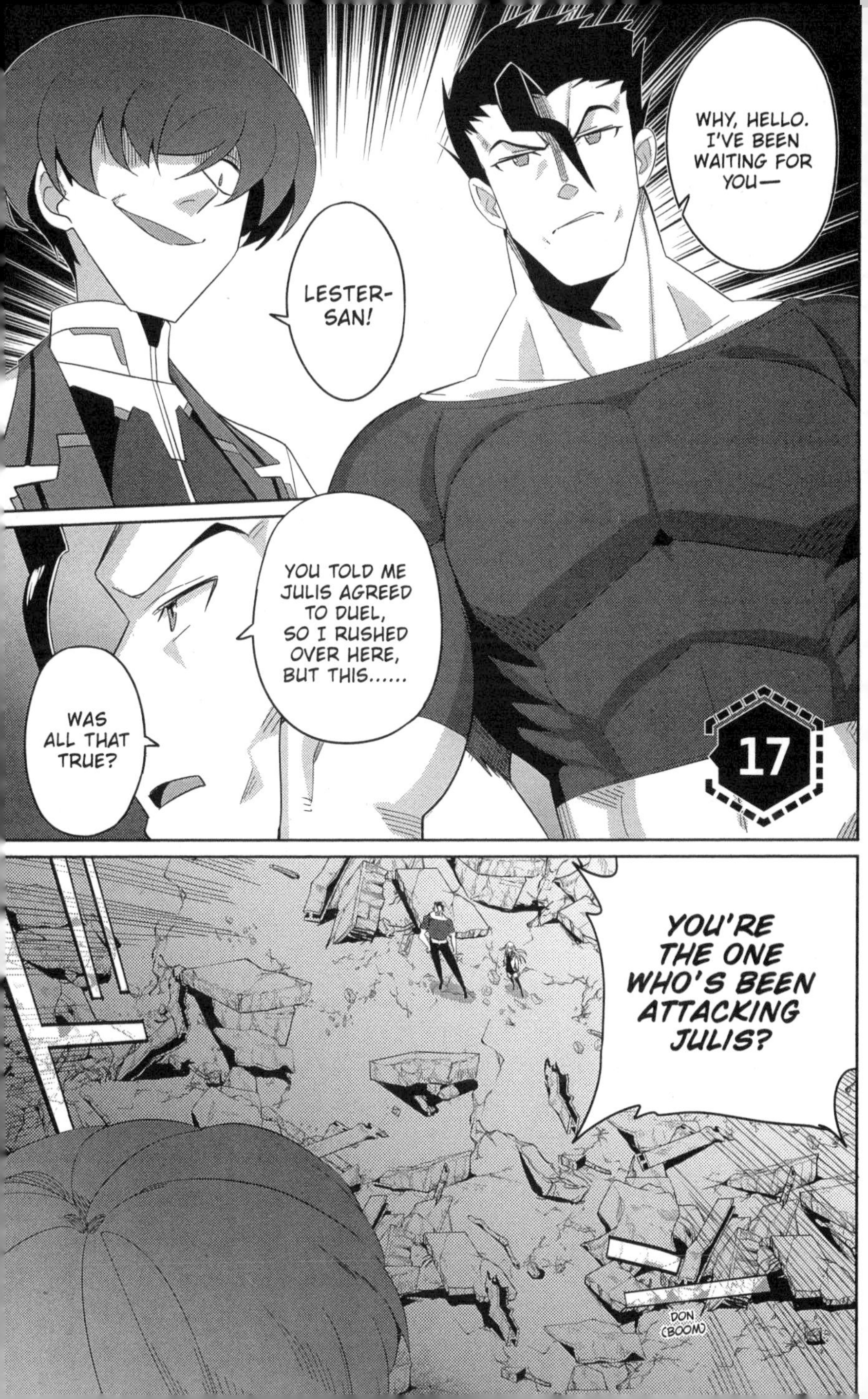
WHY, HELLO. I'VE BEEN WAITING FOR YOU—
LESTER-SAN!
YOU TOLD ME JULIS AGREED TO DUEL, SO I RUSHED OVER HERE, BUT THIS......
WAS ALL THAT TRUE?
YOU'RE THE ONE WHO'S BEEN ATTACKING JULIS?
DON (BOOM)

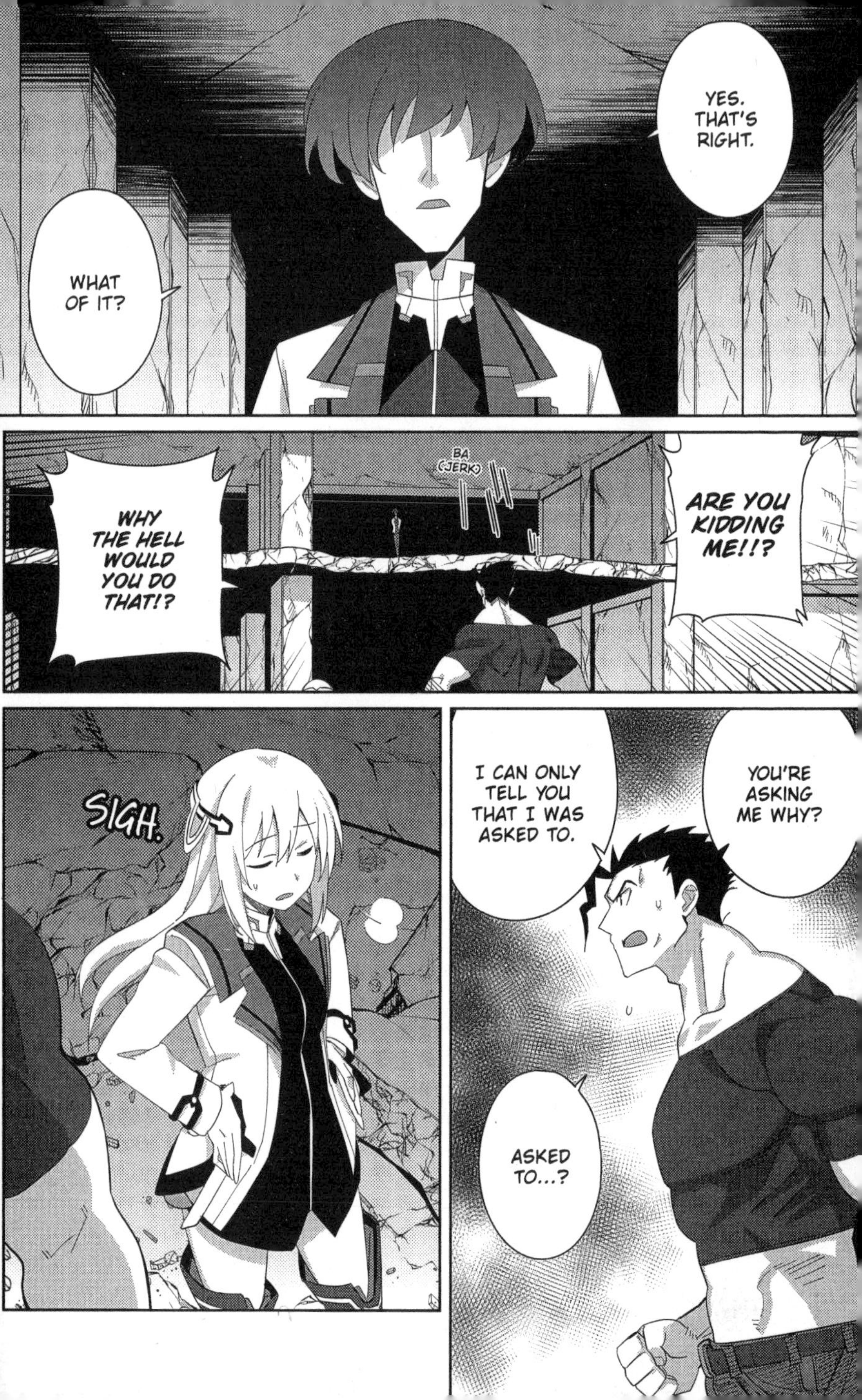
YES. THAT'S RIGHT.
WHAT OF IT?
ARE YOU KIDDING ME!!?
BA (JERK)
WHY THE HELL WOULD YOU DO THAT!?
YOU'RE ASKING ME WHY?
I CAN ONLY TELL YOU THAT I WAS ASKED TO.
ASKED TO...?
SIGH.

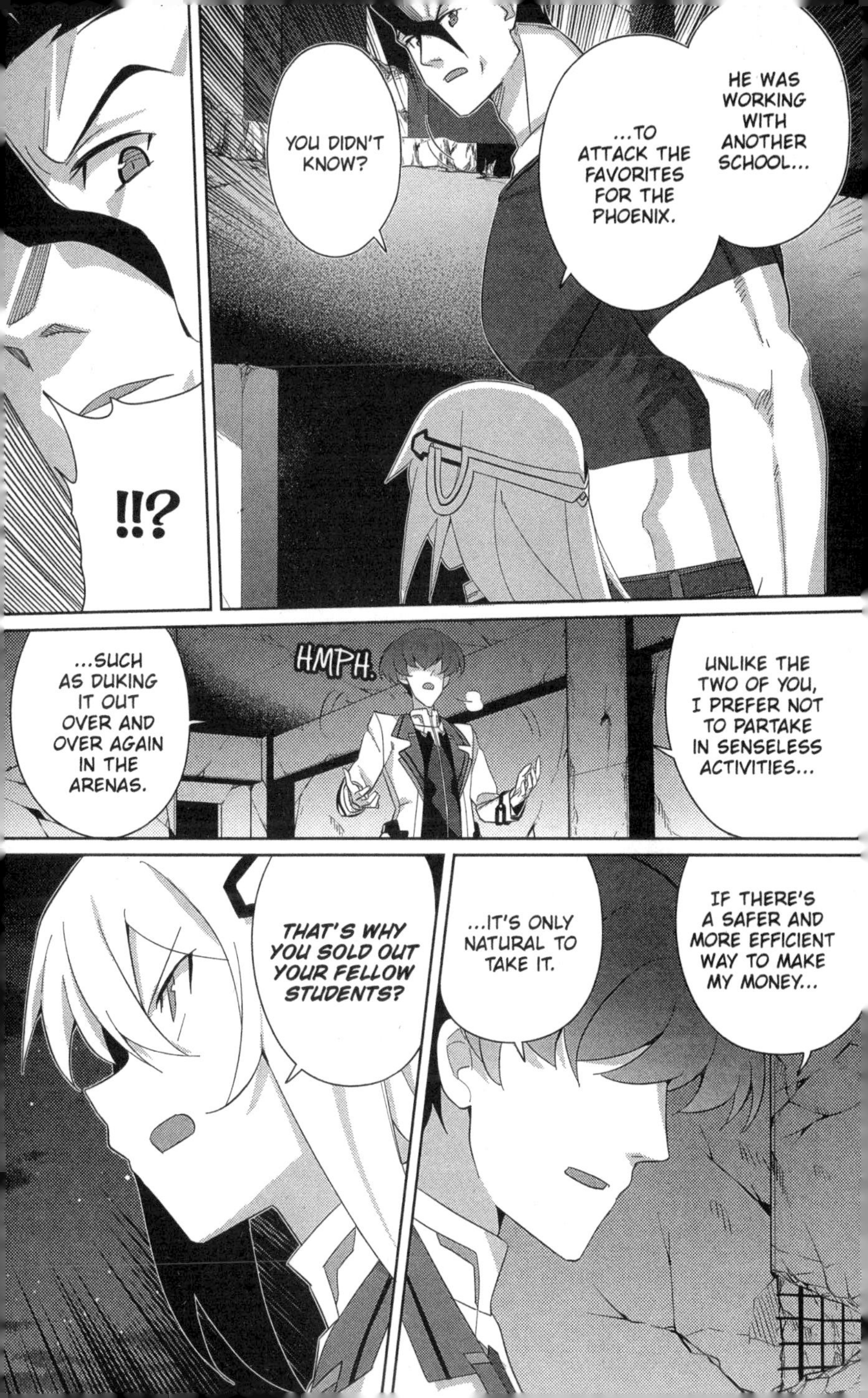
HE WAS WORKING WITH ANOTHER SCHOOL...
...TO ATTACK THE FAVORITES FOR THE PHOENIX.
YOU DIDN'T KNOW?
!!?
UNLIKE THE TWO OF YOU, I PREFER NOT TO PARTAKE IN SENSELESS ACTIVITIES...
HMPH.
...SUCH AS DUKING IT OUT OVER AND OVER AGAIN IN THE ARENAS.
IF THERE'S A SAFER AND MORE EFFICIENT WAY TO MAKE MY MONEY...
...IT'S ONLY NATURAL TO TAKE IT.
THAT'S WHY YOU SOLD OUT YOUR FELLOW STUDENTS?

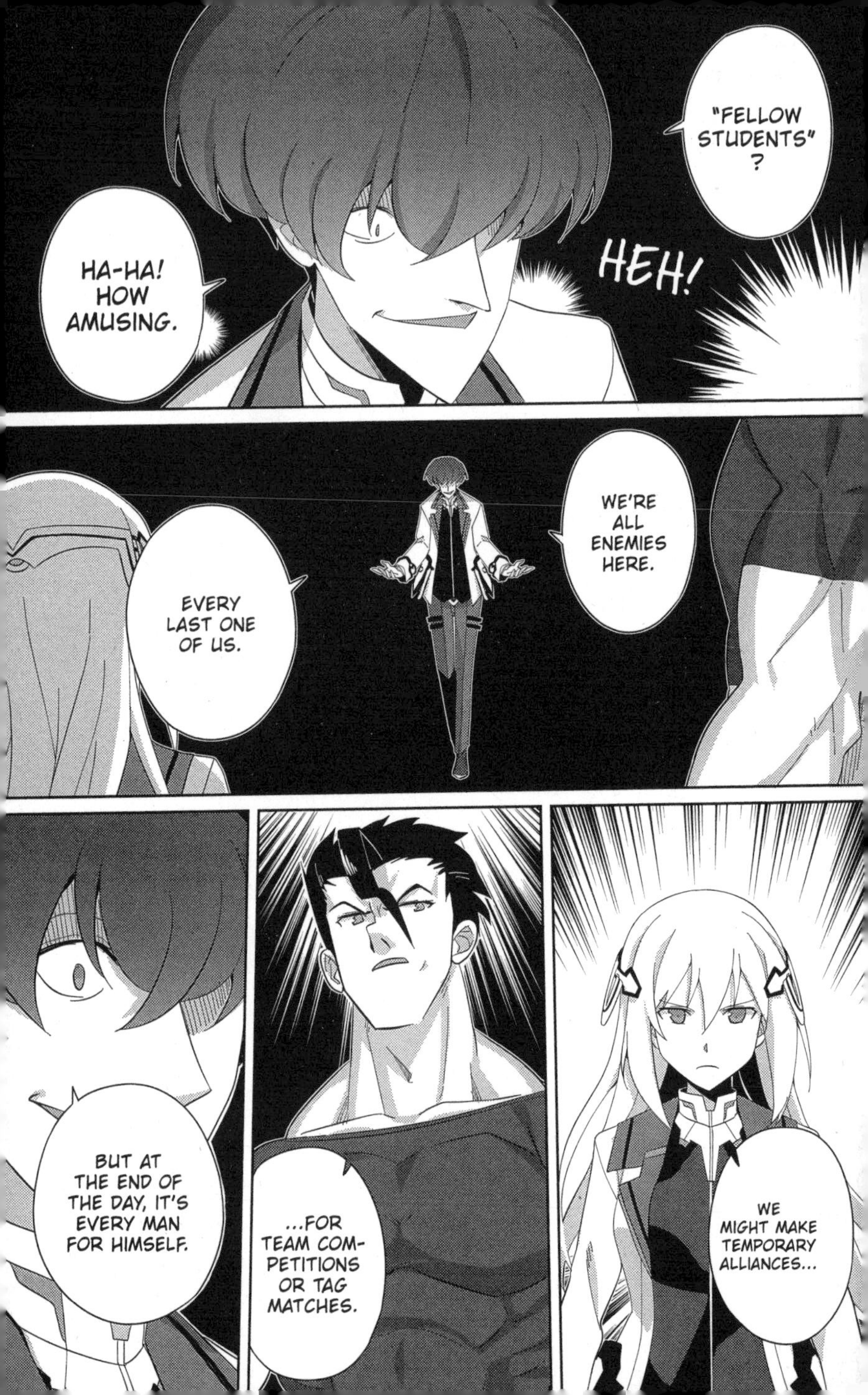
"FELLOW STUDENTS"?
HEH!
HA-HA! HOW AMUSING.
WE'RE ALL ENEMIES HERE.
EVERY LAST ONE OF US.
WE MIGHT MAKE TEMPORARY ALLIANCES...
...FOR TEAM COMPETITIONS OR TAG MATCHES.
BUT AT THE END OF THE DAY, IT'S EVERY MAN FOR HIMSELF.

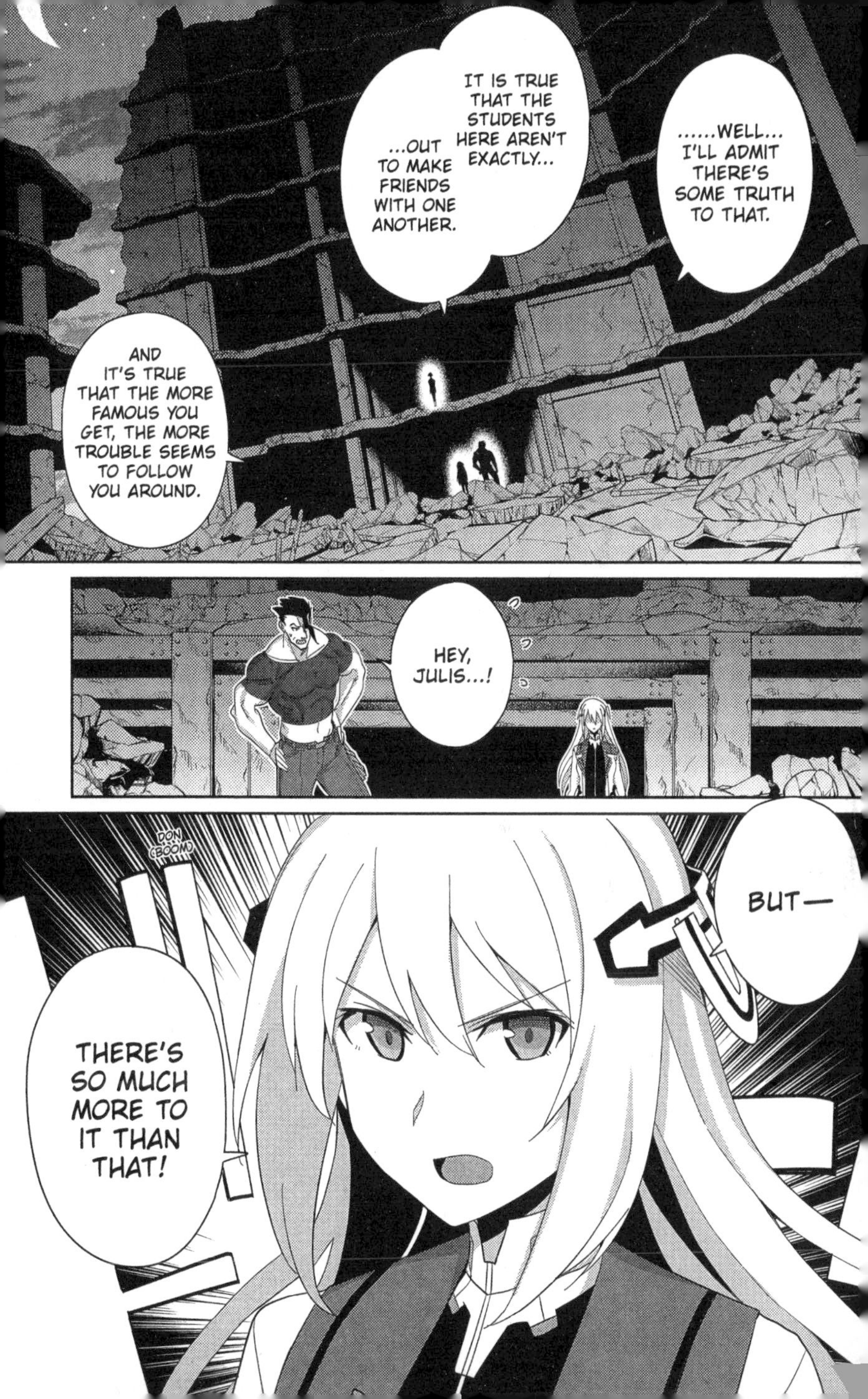
......WELL... I'LL ADMIT THERE'S SOME TRUTH TO THAT.
IT IS TRUE THAT THE STUDENTS HERE AREN'T EXACTLY...
...OUT TO MAKE FRIENDS WITH ONE ANOTHER.
AND IT'S TRUE THAT THE MORE FAMOUS YOU GET, THE MORE TROUBLE SEEMS TO FOLLOW YOU AROUND.
HEY, JULIS...!
BUT—
DON (BOOM)
THERE'S SO MUCH MORE TO IT THAN THAT!

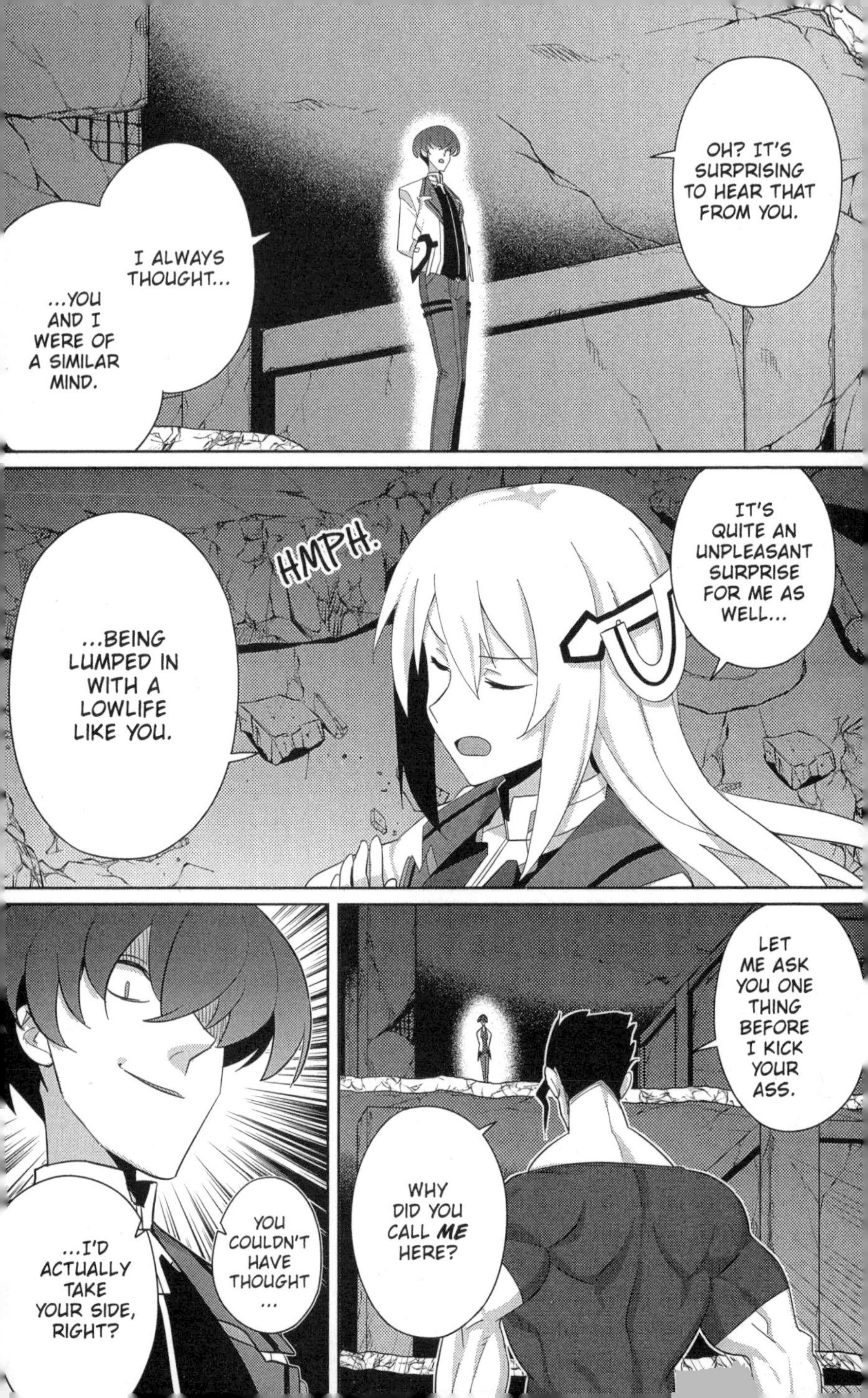
OH? IT'S SURPRISING TO HEAR THAT FROM YOU.
I ALWAYS THOUGHT...
...YOU AND I WERE OF A SIMILAR MIND.
IT'S QUITE AN UNPLEASANT SURPRISE FOR ME AS WELL...
HMPH.
...BEING LUMPED IN WITH A LOWLIFE LIKE YOU.
LET ME ASK YOU ONE THING BEFORE I KICK YOUR ASS.
WHY DID YOU CALL *ME* HERE?
YOU COULDN'T HAVE THOUGHT ...
...I'D ACTUALLY TAKE YOUR SIDE, RIGHT?

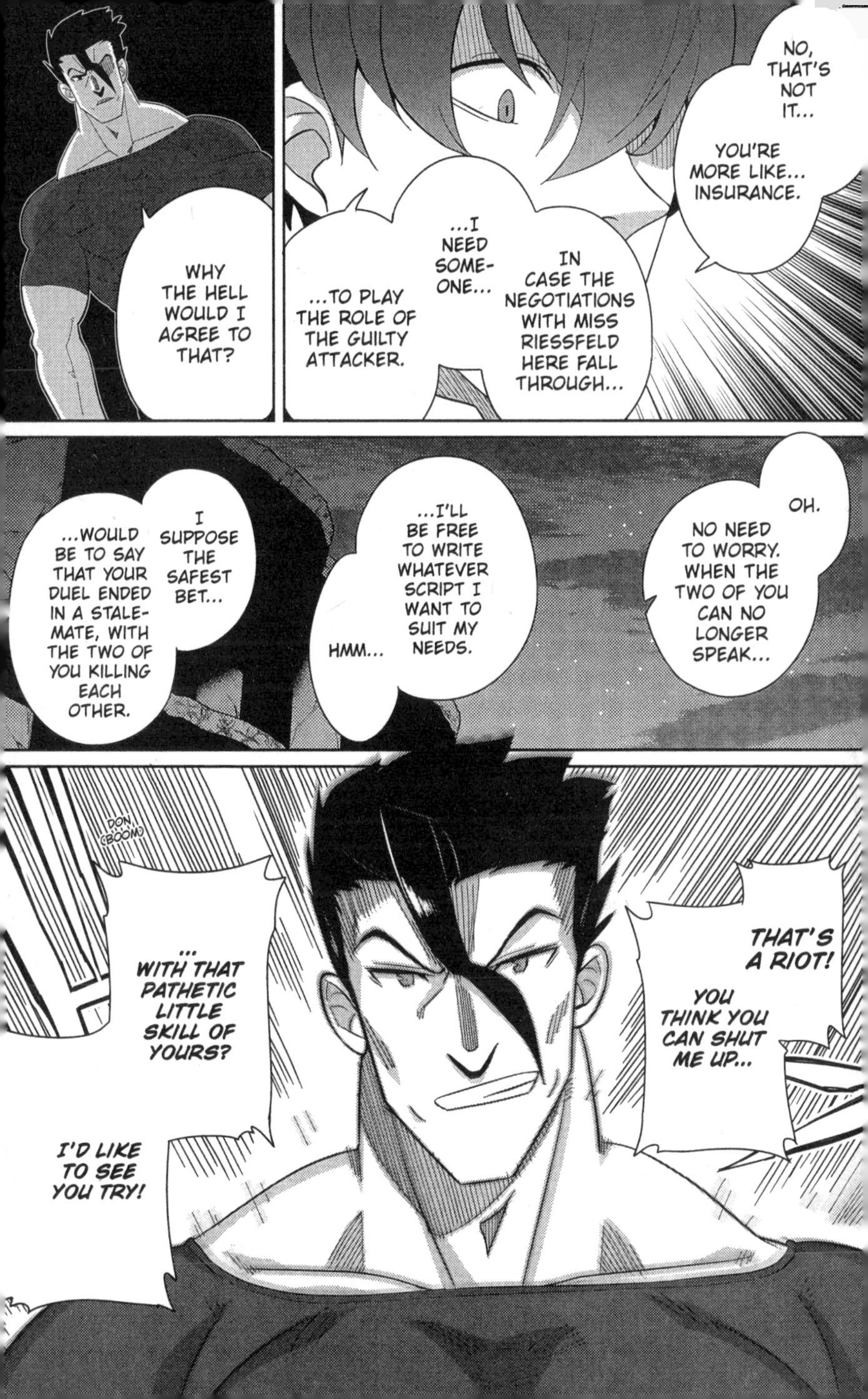
NO, THAT'S NOT IT...
YOU'RE MORE LIKE... INSURANCE.
IN CASE THE NEGOTIATIONS WITH MISS RIESSFELD HERE FALL THROUGH...
...I NEED SOME-ONE...
...TO PLAY THE ROLE OF THE GUILTY ATTACKER.
WHY THE HELL WOULD I AGREE TO THAT?
OH.
NO NEED TO WORRY. WHEN THE TWO OF YOU CAN NO LONGER SPEAK...
...I'LL BE FREE TO WRITE WHATEVER SCRIPT I WANT TO SUIT MY NEEDS.
HMM...
I SUPPOSE THE SAFEST BET...
...WOULD BE TO SAY THAT YOUR DUEL ENDED IN A STALE-MATE, WITH THE TWO OF YOU KILLING EACH OTHER.
DON (BOOM)
THAT'S A RIOT!
YOU THINK YOU CAN SHUT ME UP...
...WITH THAT PATHETIC LITTLE SKILL OF YOURS?
I'D LIKE TO SEE YOU TRY!

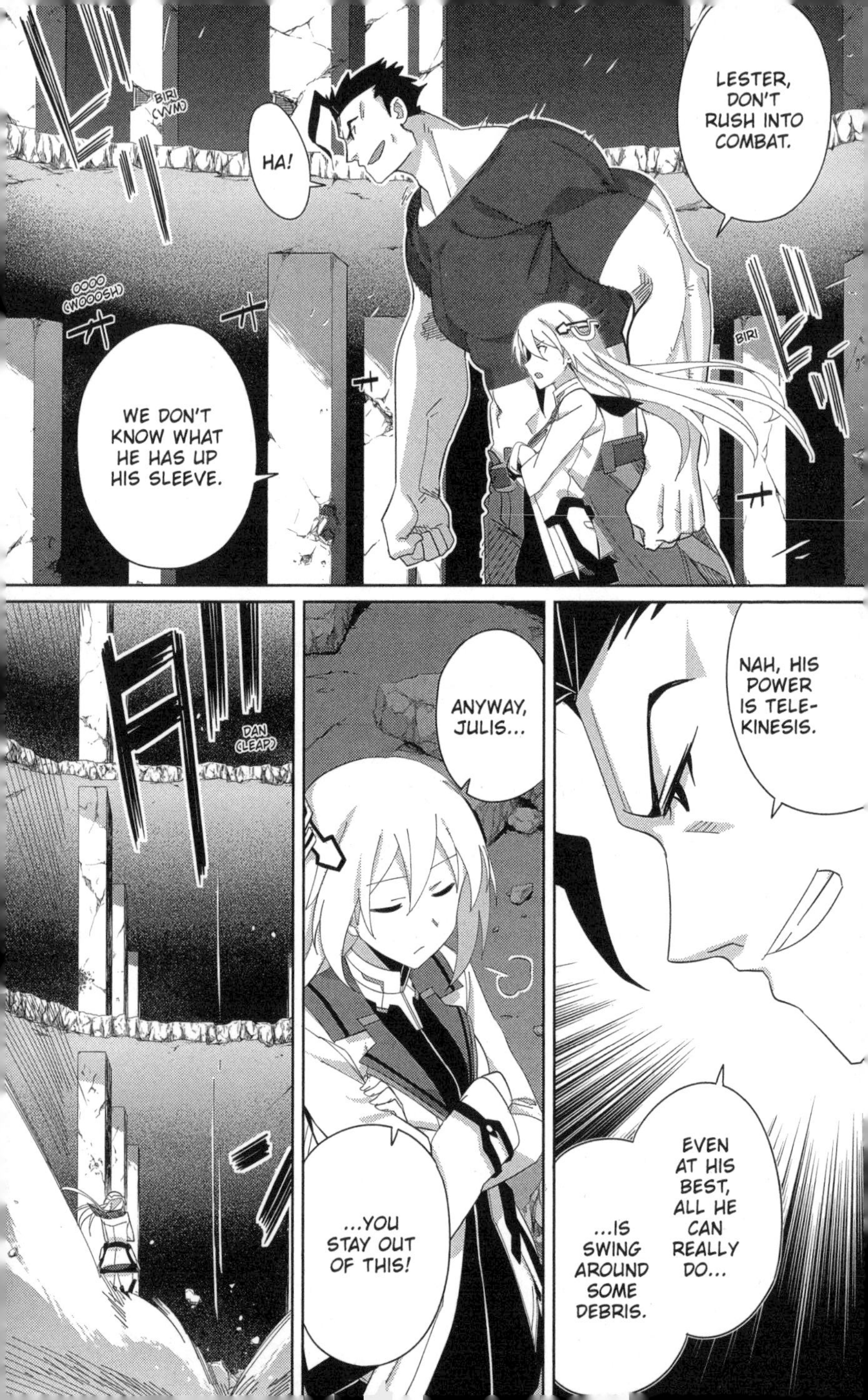
LESTER, DON'T RUSH INTO COMBAT.
BIRI
HA!
BIRI (VVM)
OOOO (WOOOSH)
WE DON'T KNOW WHAT HE HAS UP HIS SLEEVE.
NAH, HIS POWER IS TELE-KINESIS.
EVEN AT HIS BEST, ALL HE CAN REALLY DO...
...IS SWING AROUND SOME DEBRIS.
ANYWAY, JULIS...
...YOU STAY OUT OF THIS!
DAN (LEAP)

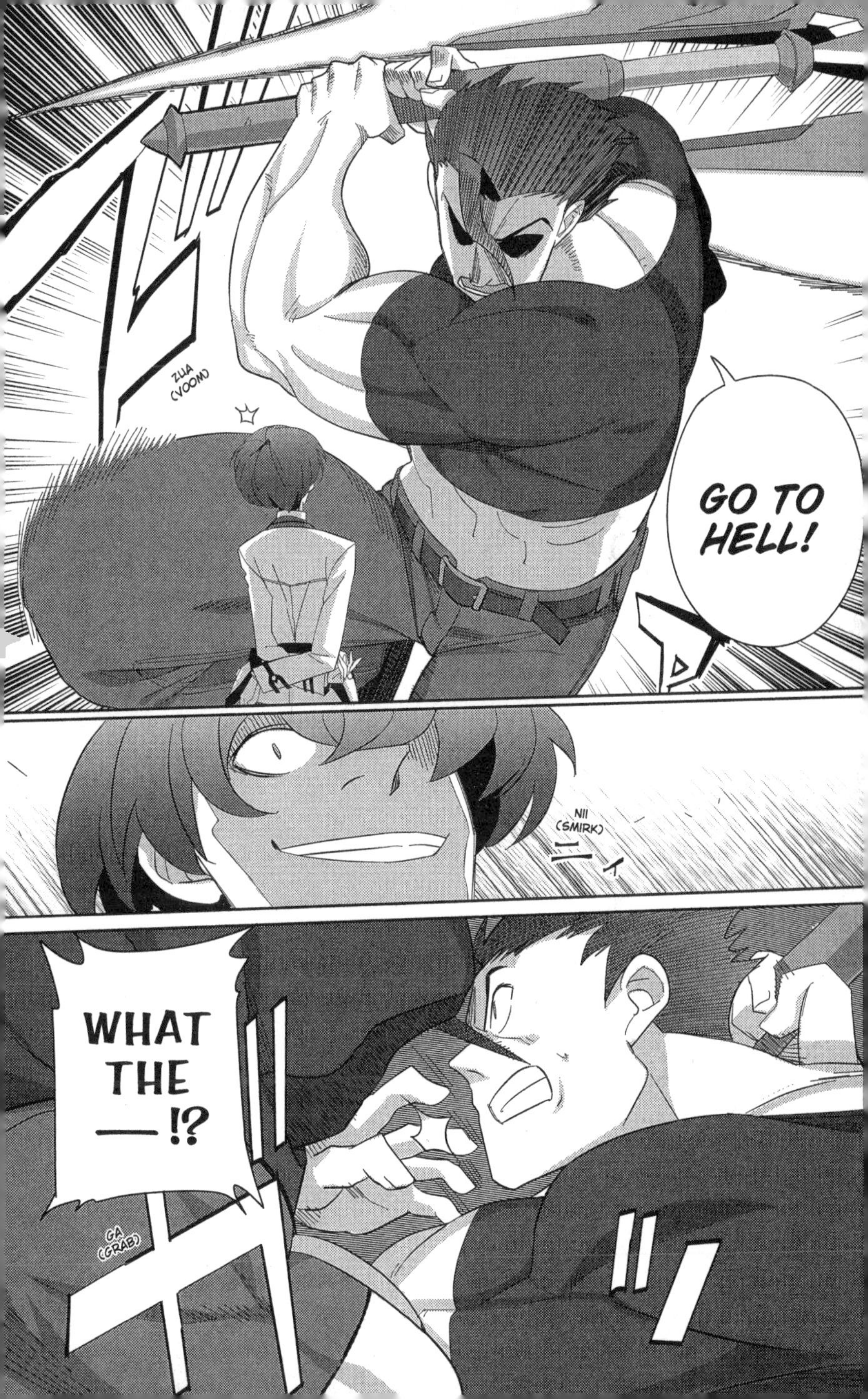
GO TO HELL!
ZUA (VOOM)
NII (SMIRK)
WHAT THE —!?
GA (GRAB)

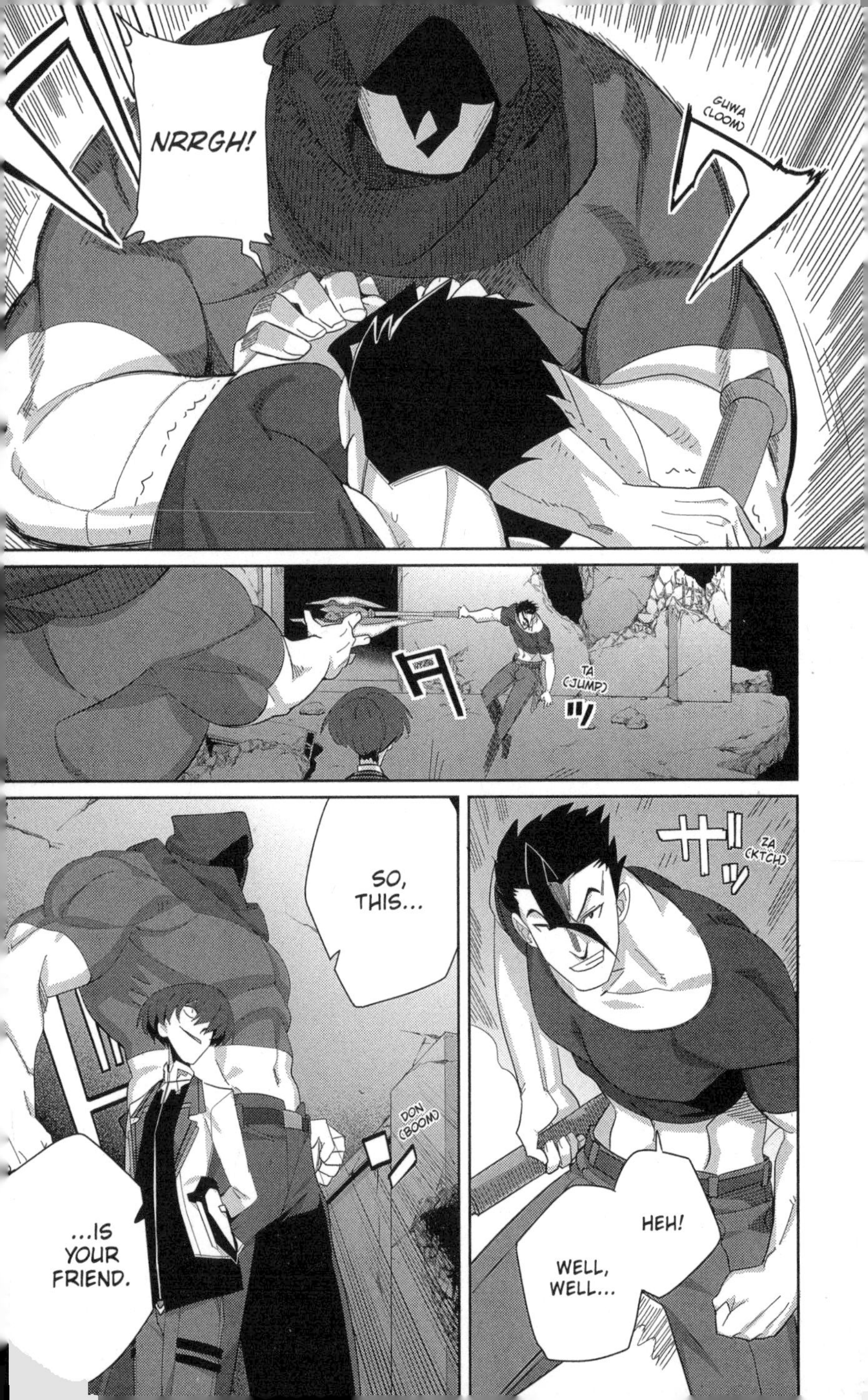
GUWA (LOOM)
NRRGH!
TA (JUMP)
ZA (KTCH)
HEH!
WELL, WELL...
SO, THIS...
DON (BOOM)
...IS YOUR FRIEND.

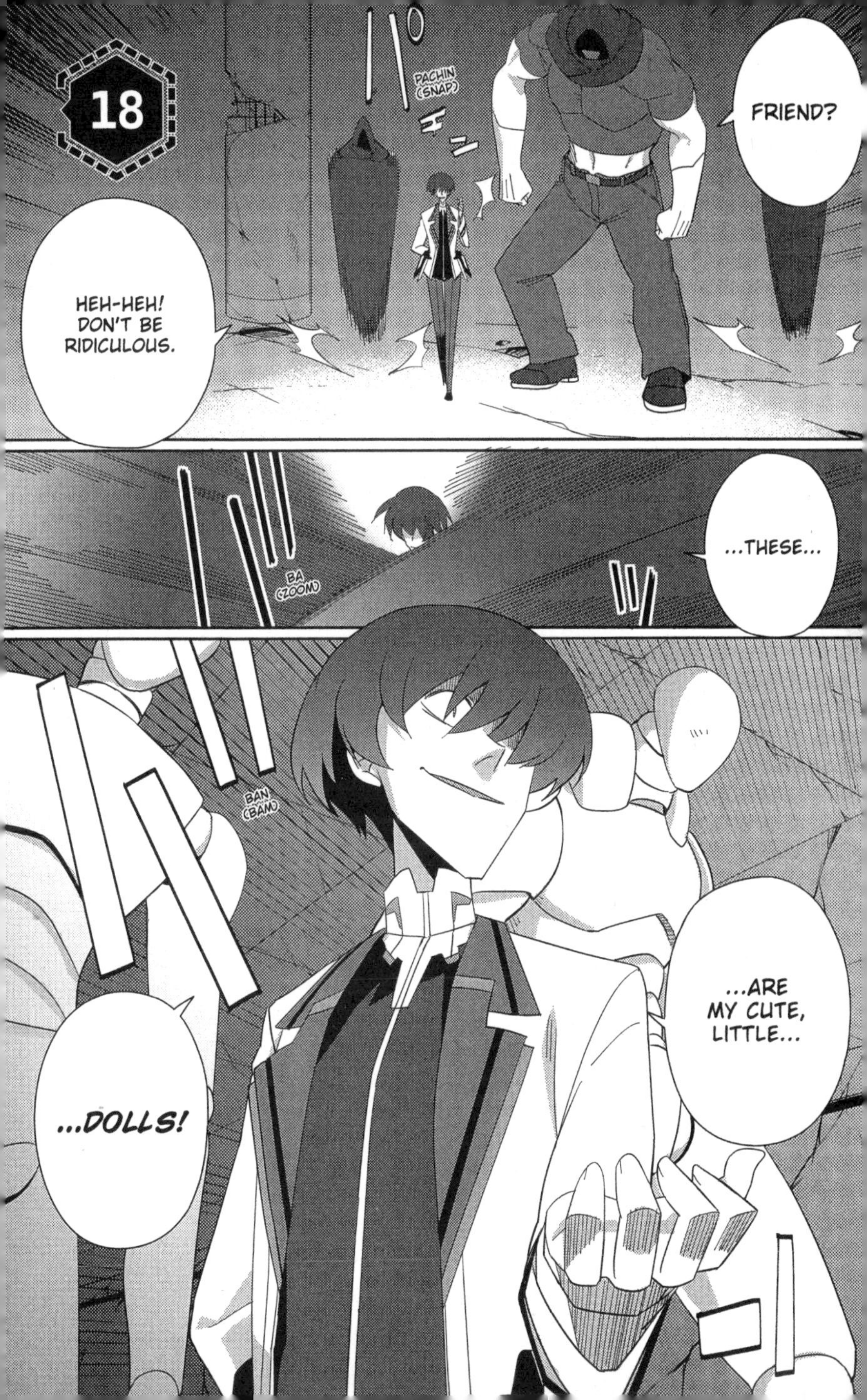
FRIEND?
PACHIN (SNAP)
18
HEH-HEH! DON'T BE RIDICULOUS.
...THESE...
BA (ZOOM)
...ARE MY CUTE, LITTLE...
BAN (BAM)
...DOLLS!

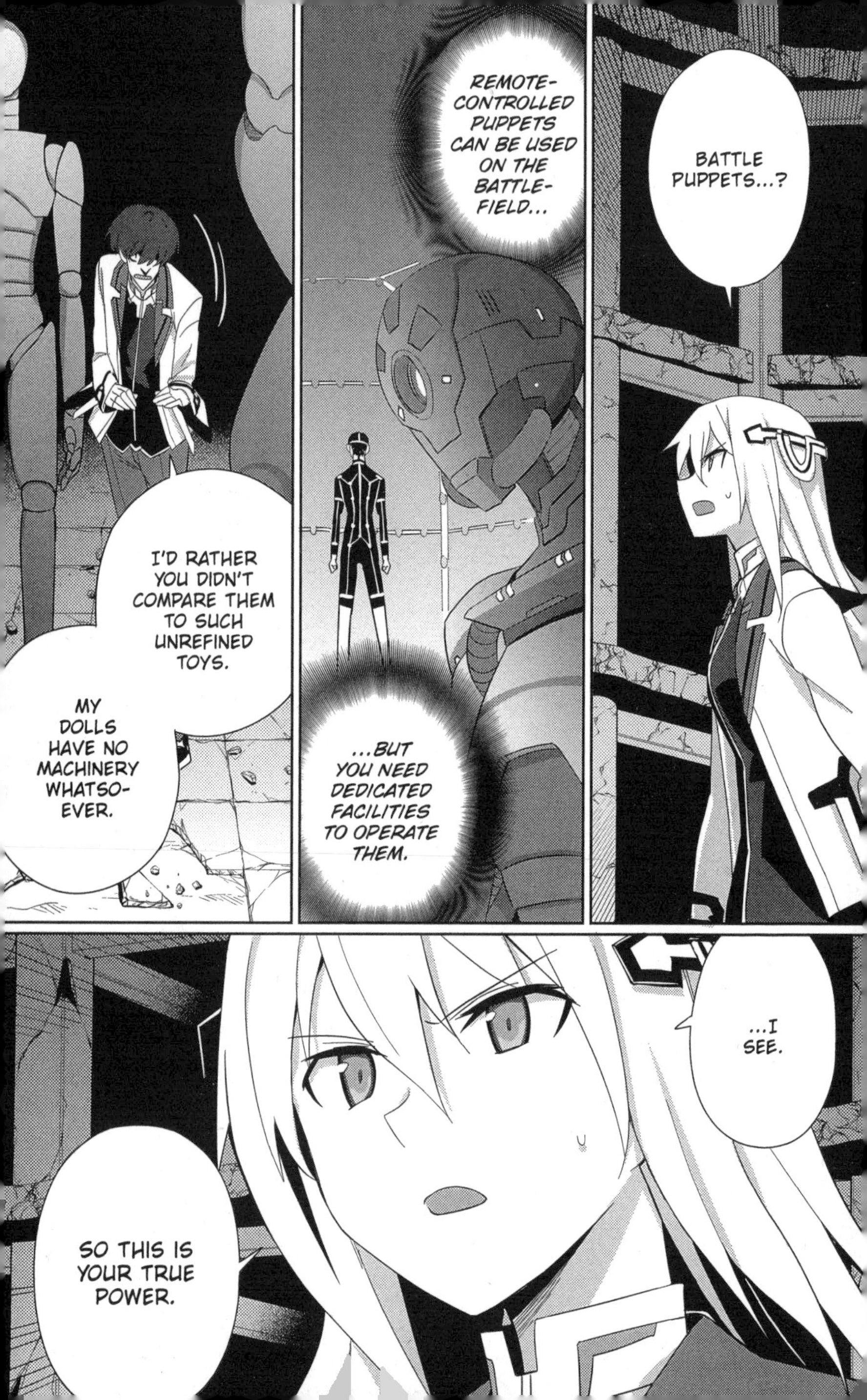
BATTLE PUPPETS...?
REMOTE-CONTROLLED PUPPETS CAN BE USED ON THE BATTLE-FIELD...
...BUT YOU NEED DEDICATED FACILITIES TO OPERATE THEM.
I'D RATHER YOU DIDN'T COMPARE THEM TO SUCH UNREFINED TOYS.
MY DOLLS HAVE NO MACHINERY WHATSO-EVER.
...I SEE.
SO THIS IS YOUR TRUE POWER.

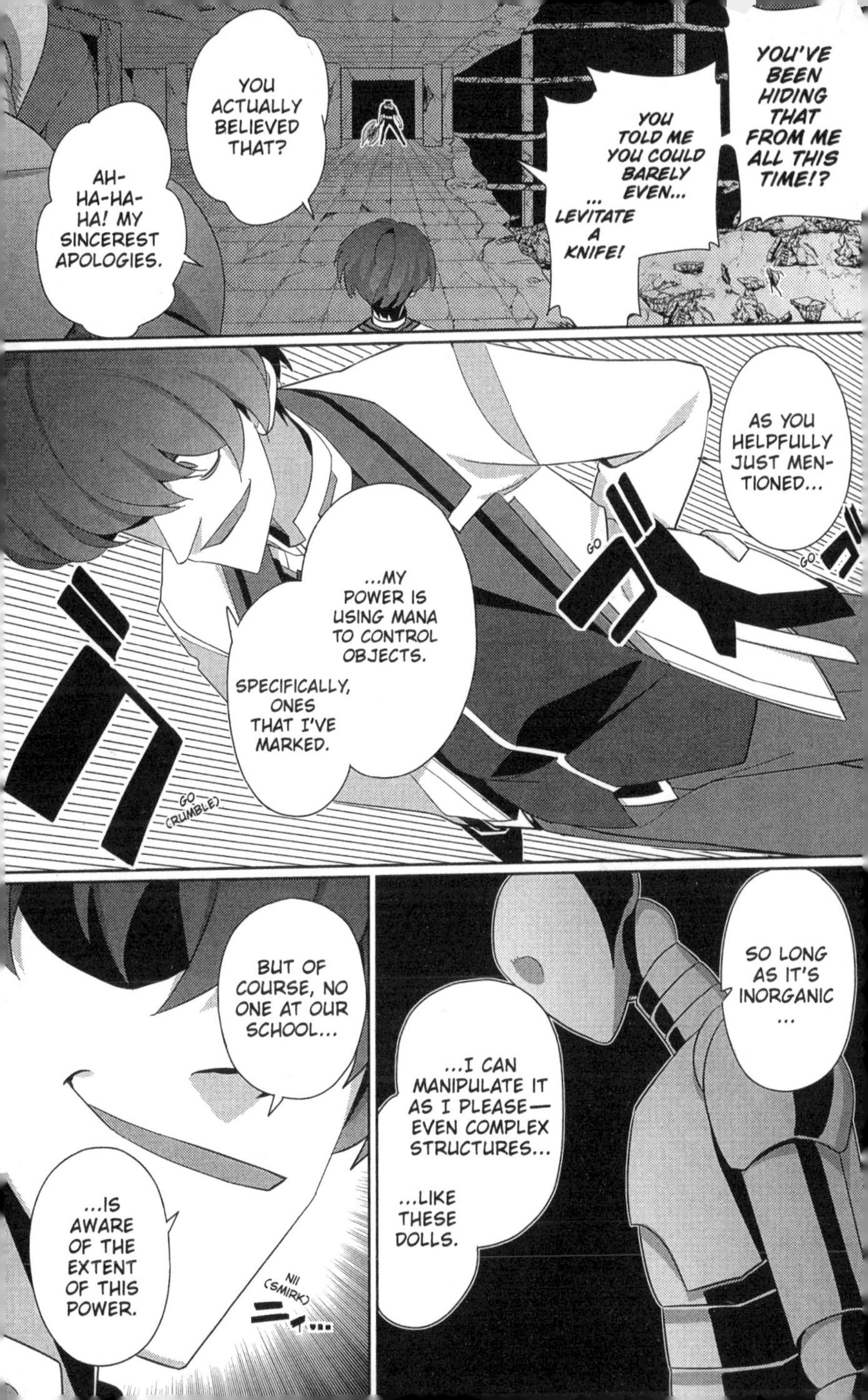
YOU'VE BEEN HIDING THAT FROM ME ALL THIS TIME!?
YOU TOLD ME YOU COULD BARELY EVEN... ...LEVITATE A KNIFE!
YOU ACTUALLY BELIEVED THAT?
AH-HA-HA-HA! MY SINCEREST APOLOGIES.
AS YOU HELPFULLY JUST MENTIONED...
GO
GO
...MY POWER IS USING MANA TO CONTROL OBJECTS.
SPECIFICALLY, ONES THAT I'VE MARKED.
GO (RUMBLE)
SO LONG AS IT'S INORGANIC...
...I CAN MANIPULATE IT AS I PLEASE—EVEN COMPLEX STRUCTURES...
...LIKE THESE DOLLS.
BUT OF COURSE, NO ONE AT OUR SCHOOL...
...IS AWARE OF THE EXTENT OF THIS POWER.
NII (SMIRK)

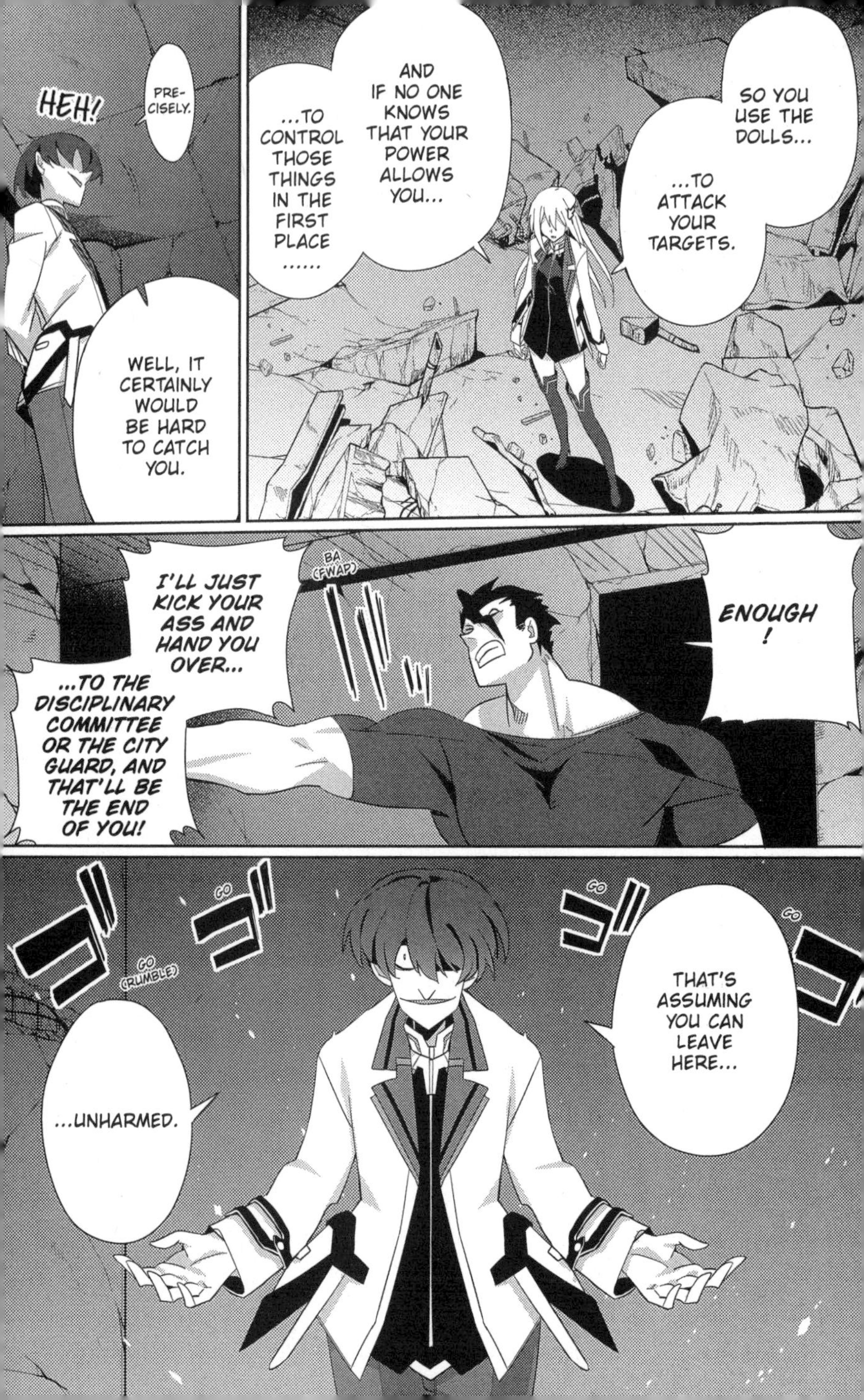
SO YOU USE THE DOLLS...
...TO ATTACK YOUR TARGETS.
AND IF NO ONE KNOWS THAT YOUR POWER ALLOWS YOU...
...TO CONTROL THOSE THINGS IN THE FIRST PLACE ......
PRE-CISELY.
HEH!
WELL, IT CERTAINLY WOULD BE HARD TO CATCH YOU.
ENOUGH!
BA (FWAP)
I'LL JUST KICK YOUR ASS AND HAND YOU OVER...
...TO THE DISCIPLINARY COMMITTEE OR THE CITY GUARD, AND THAT'LL BE THE END OF YOU!
GO
GO
GO
GO (RUMBLE)
THAT'S ASSUMING YOU CAN LEAVE HERE...
...UNHARMED.

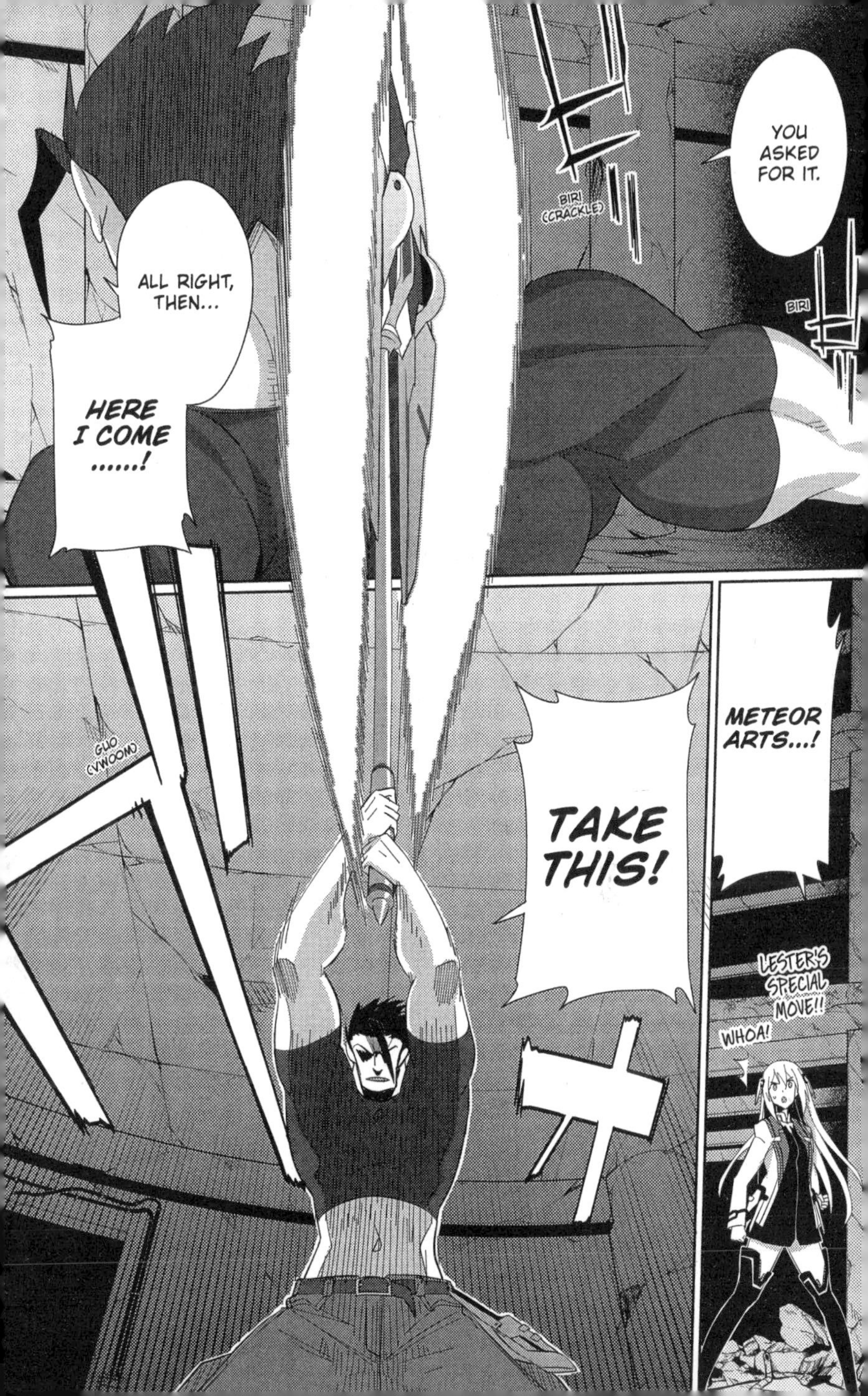
YOU ASKED FOR IT.
BIRI (CRACKLE)
BIRI
ALL RIGHT, THEN...
HERE I COME ......!
METEOR ARTS...!
LESTER'S SPECIAL MOVE!!
WHOA!
TAKE THIS!
GUO (VWOOM)

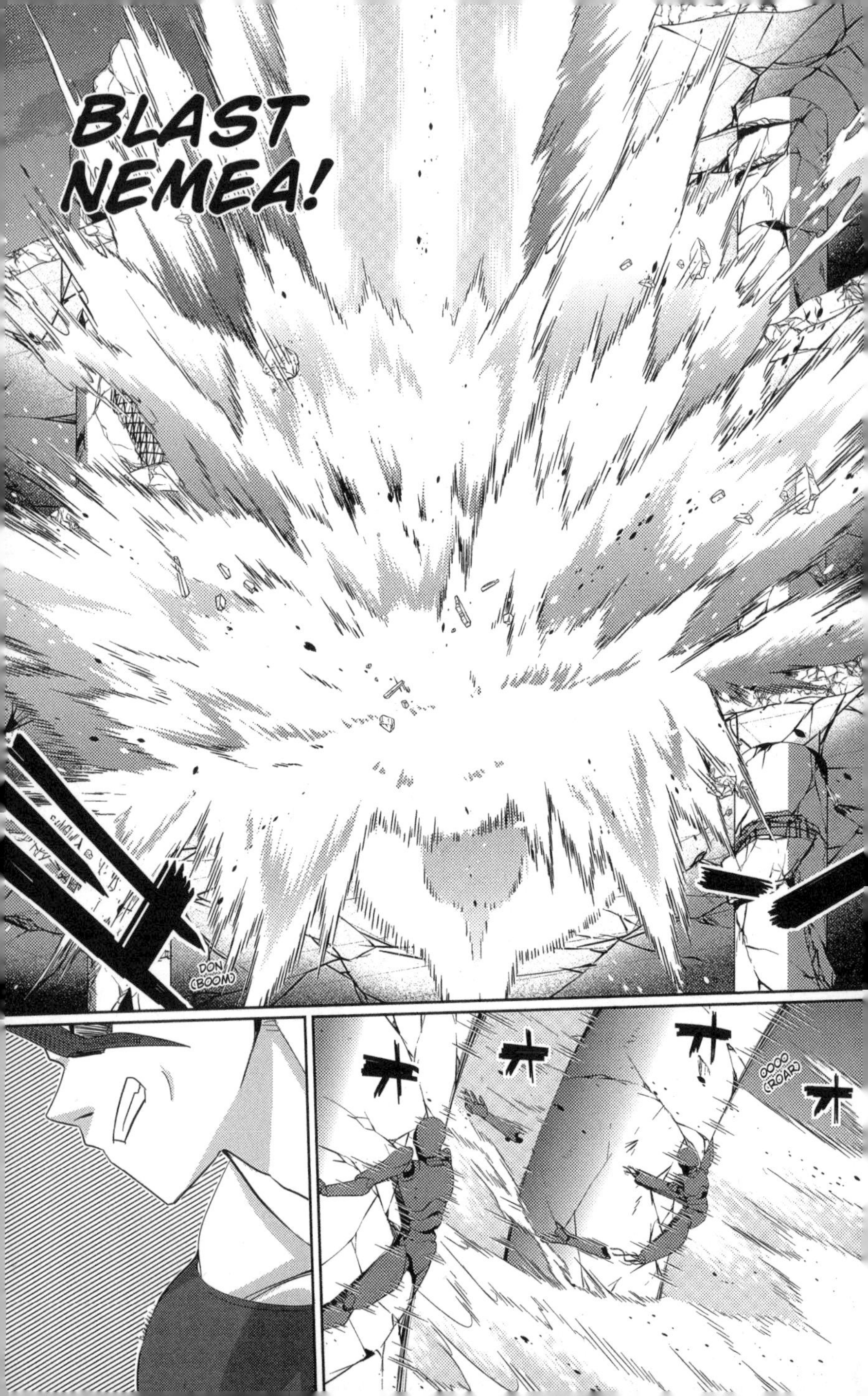
BLAST NEMEA!
DON (BOOM)
OOOO (ROAR)

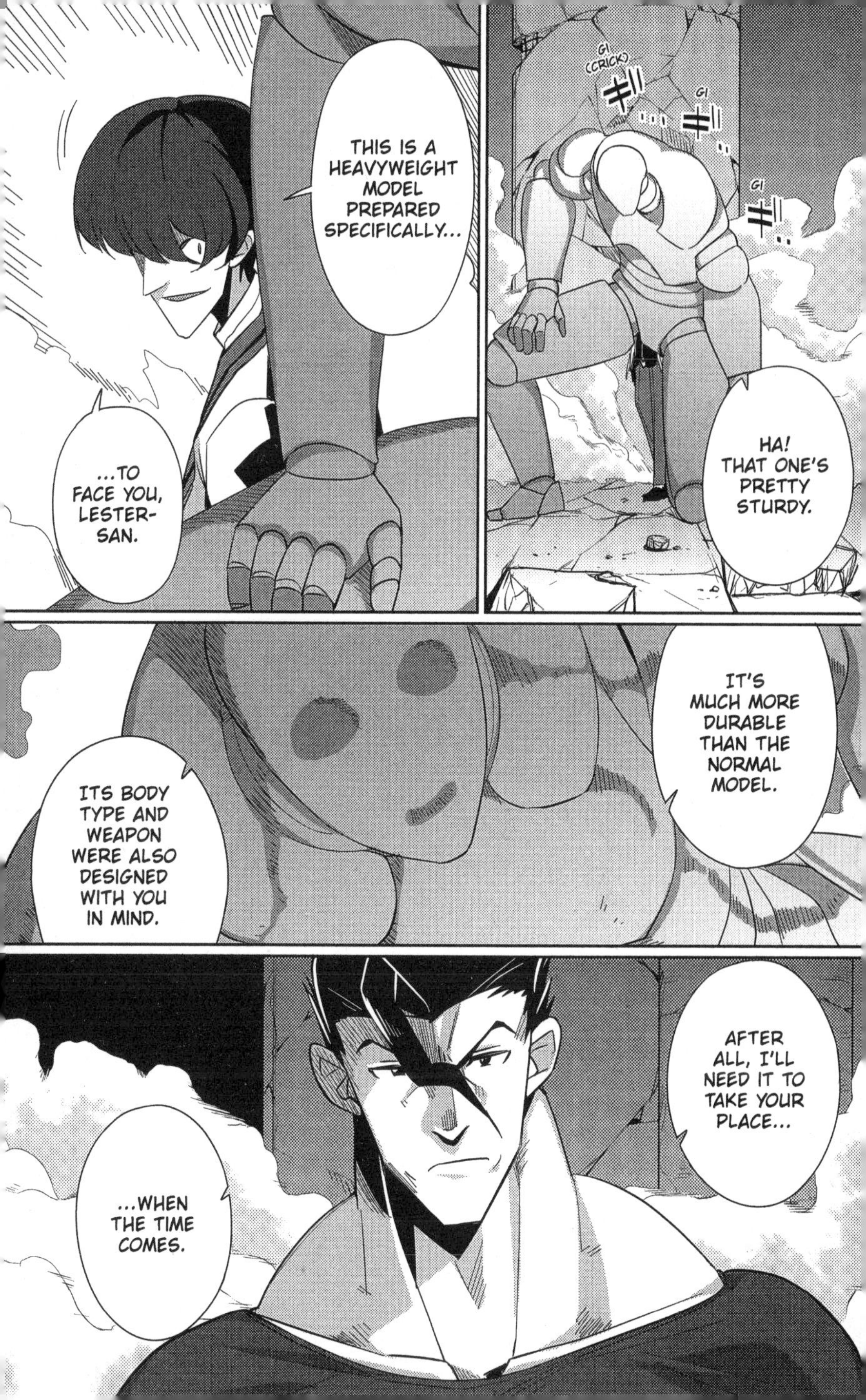
GI (CRICK)
ギ
GI
ギ
GI
ギ
HA! THAT ONE'S PRETTY STURDY.
THIS IS A HEAVYWEIGHT MODEL PREPARED SPECIFICALLY...
...TO FACE YOU, LESTER-SAN.
IT'S MUCH MORE DURABLE THAN THE NORMAL MODEL.
ITS BODY TYPE AND WEAPON WERE ALSO DESIGNED WITH YOU IN MIND.
AFTER ALL, I'LL NEED IT TO TAKE YOUR PLACE...
...WHEN THE TIME COMES.

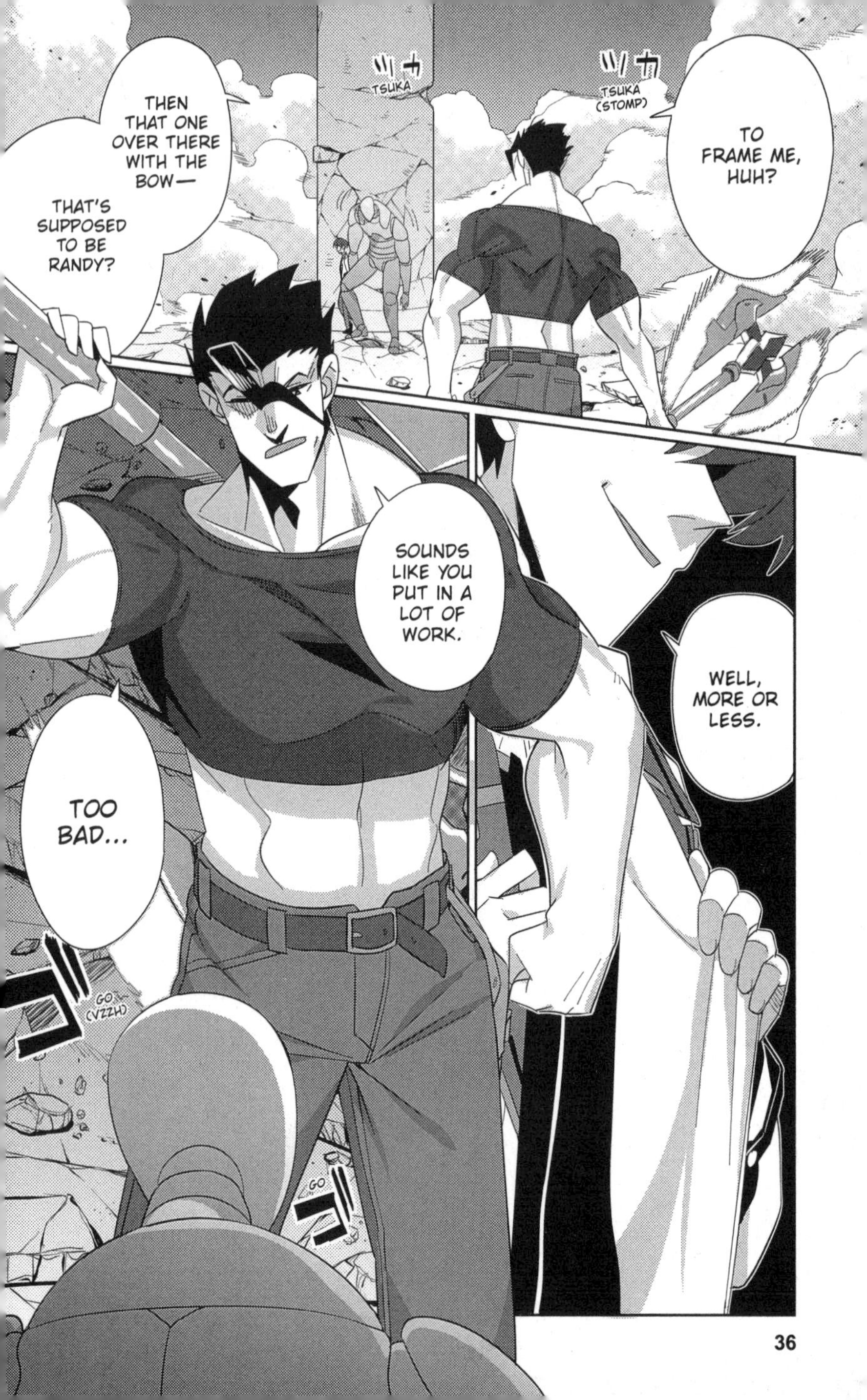
TO FRAME ME, HUH?
ツカ TSUKA (STOMP)
ツカ TSUKA
THEN THAT ONE OVER THERE WITH THE BOW—
THAT'S SUPPOSED TO BE RANDY?
WELL, MORE OR LESS.
SOUNDS LIKE YOU PUT IN A LOT OF WORK.
TOO BAD...
ゴ GO (VZZH)
ゴ GO

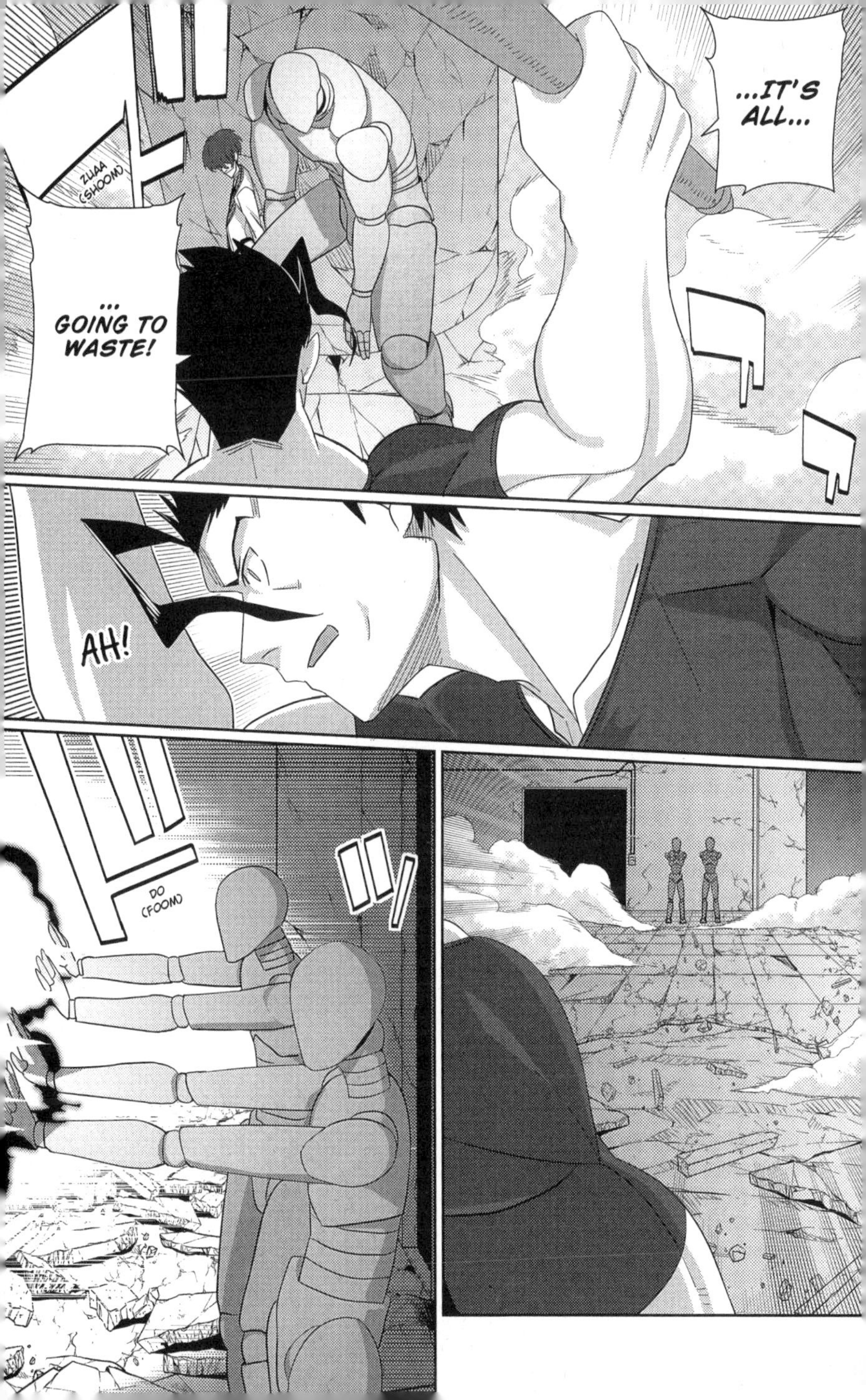
...IT'S ALL...
ZUAA (SHOOM)
... GOING TO WASTE!
AH!
DO (FOOM)

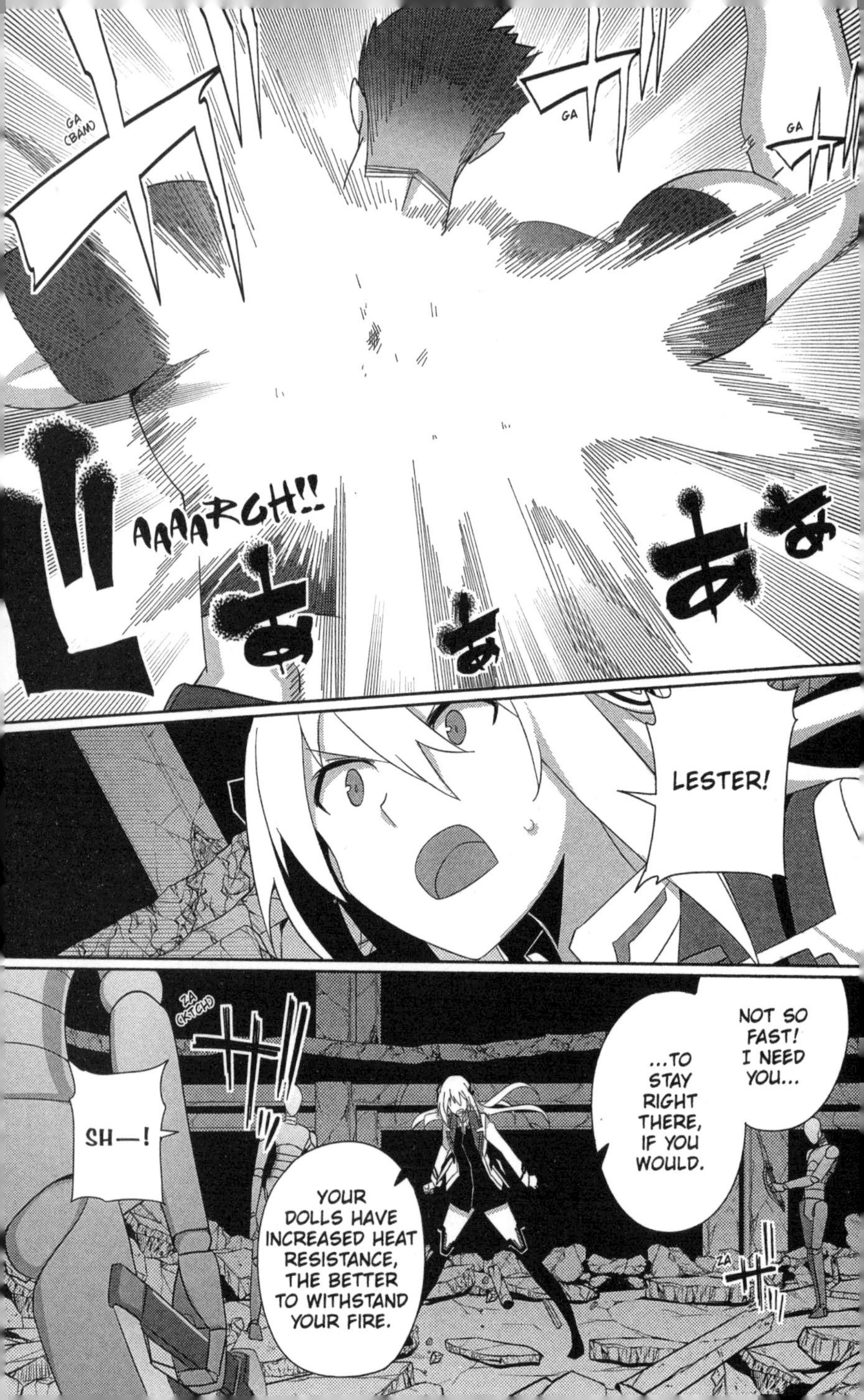
GA
GA
GA
(BAN)
AAAARGH!!
LESTER!
NOT SO FAST! I NEED YOU...
...TO STAY RIGHT THERE, IF YOU WOULD.
ZA
YOUR DOLLS HAVE INCREASED HEAT RESISTANCE, THE BETTER TO WITHSTAND YOUR FIRE.
ZA
(KTCH)
SH—!

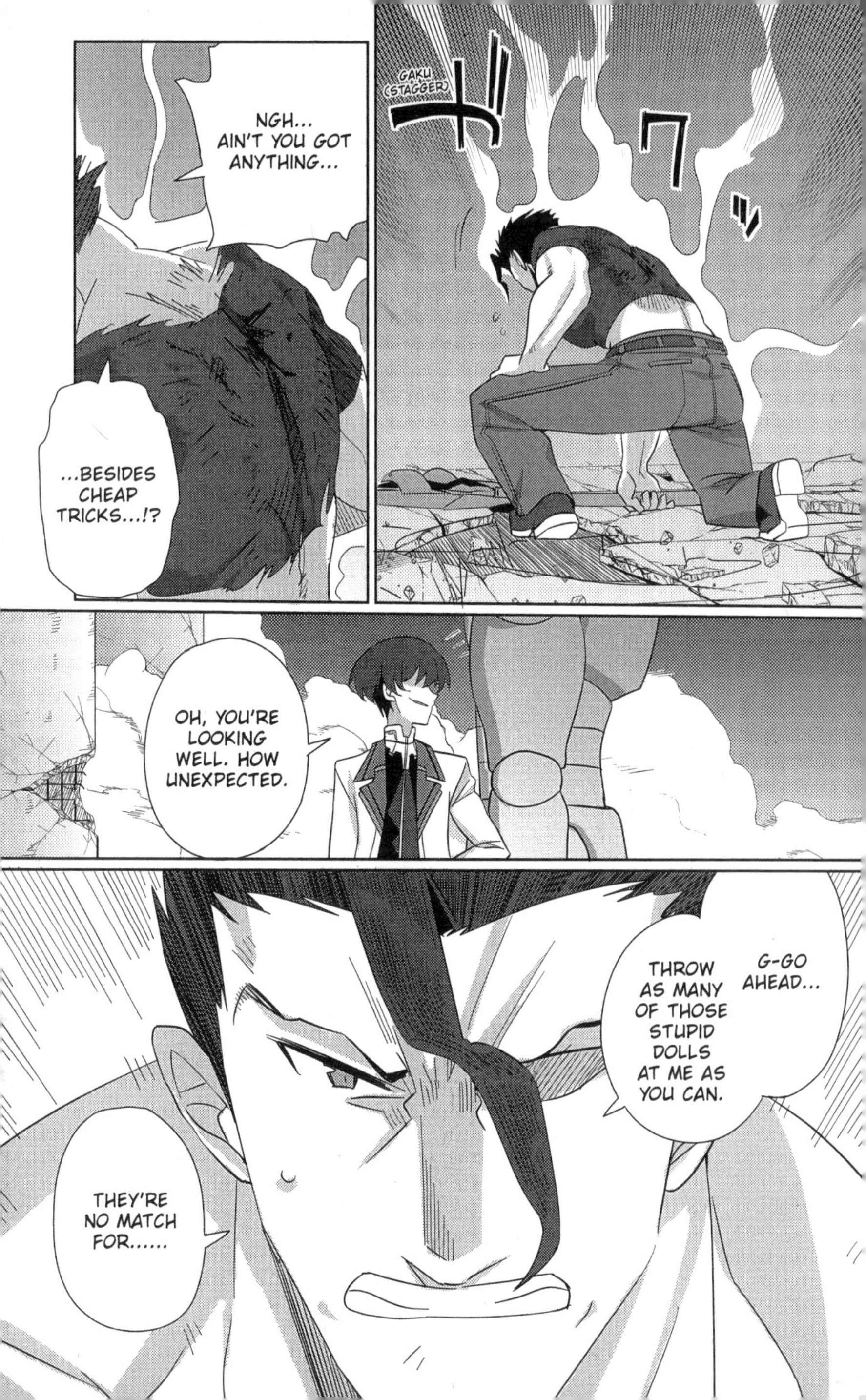
GAKU (STAGGER)
NGH... AIN'T YOU GOT ANYTHING...
...BESIDES CHEAP TRICKS...!?
OH, YOU'RE LOOKING WELL. HOW UNEXPECTED.
G-GO AHEAD...
THROW AS MANY OF THOSE STUPID DOLLS AT ME AS YOU CAN.
THEY'RE NO MATCH FOR......

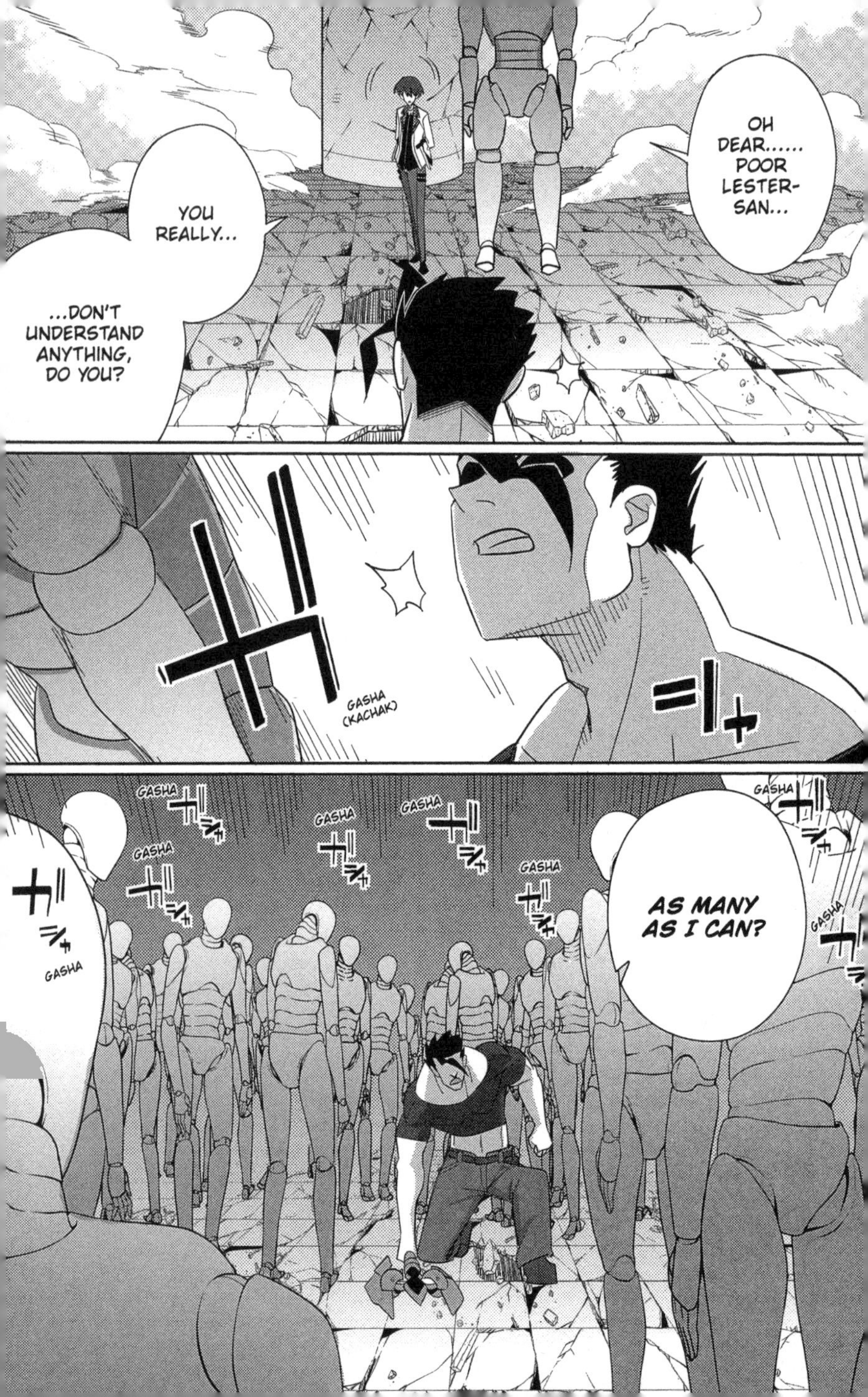
OH DEAR...... POOR LESTER-SAN...
YOU REALLY...
...DON'T UNDERSTAND ANYTHING, DO YOU?
GASHA (KACHAK)
GASHA
GASHA
GASHA
GASHA
AS MANY AS I CAN?
GASHA
GASHA
GASHA
GASHA

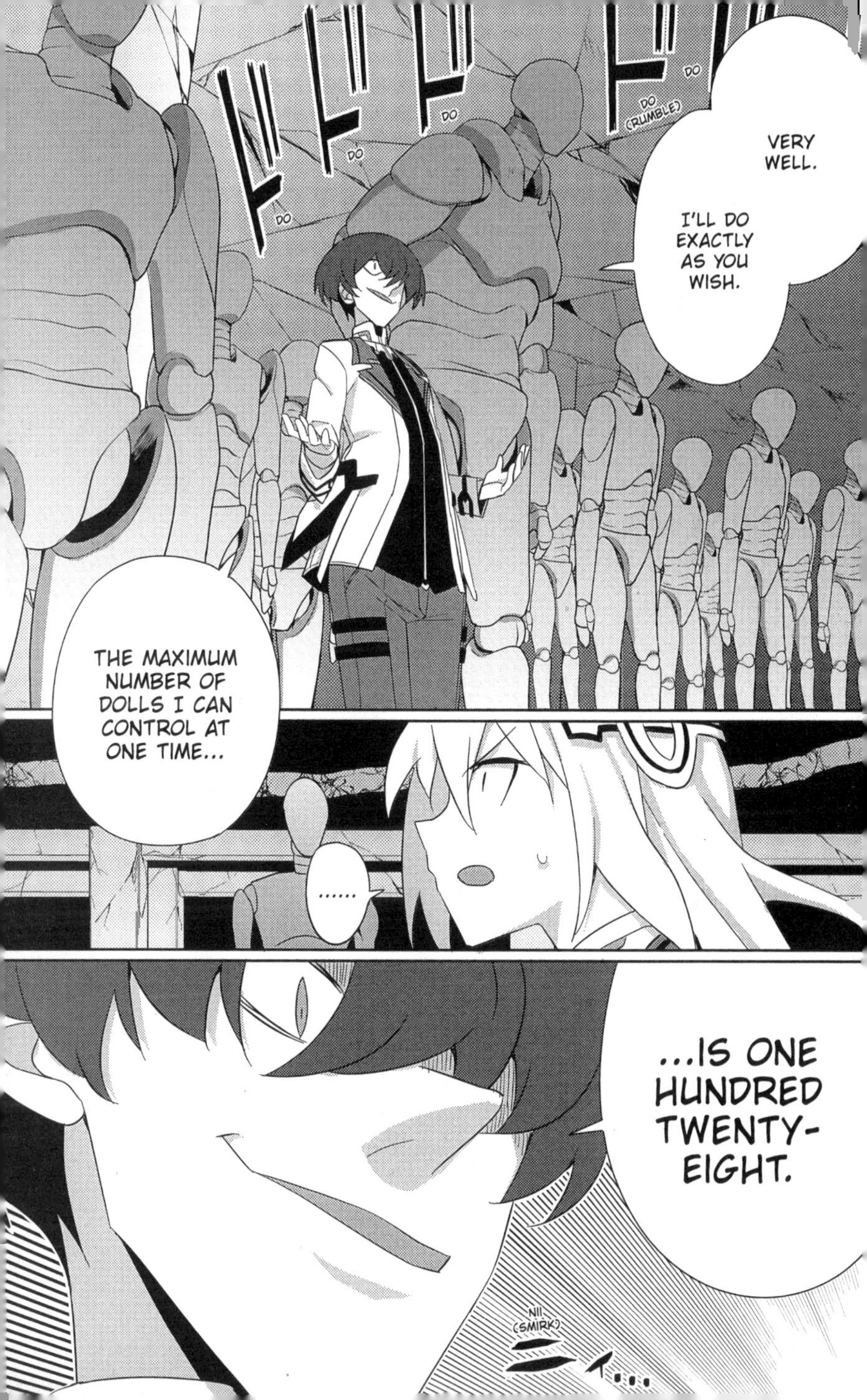
DO
DO (RUMBLE)
DO
DO
DO
VERY WELL.
I'LL DO EXACTLY AS YOU WISH.
THE MAXIMUM NUMBER OF DOLLS I CAN CONTROL AT ONE TIME...
......
...IS ONE HUNDRED TWENTY-EIGHT.
NII (SMIRK)

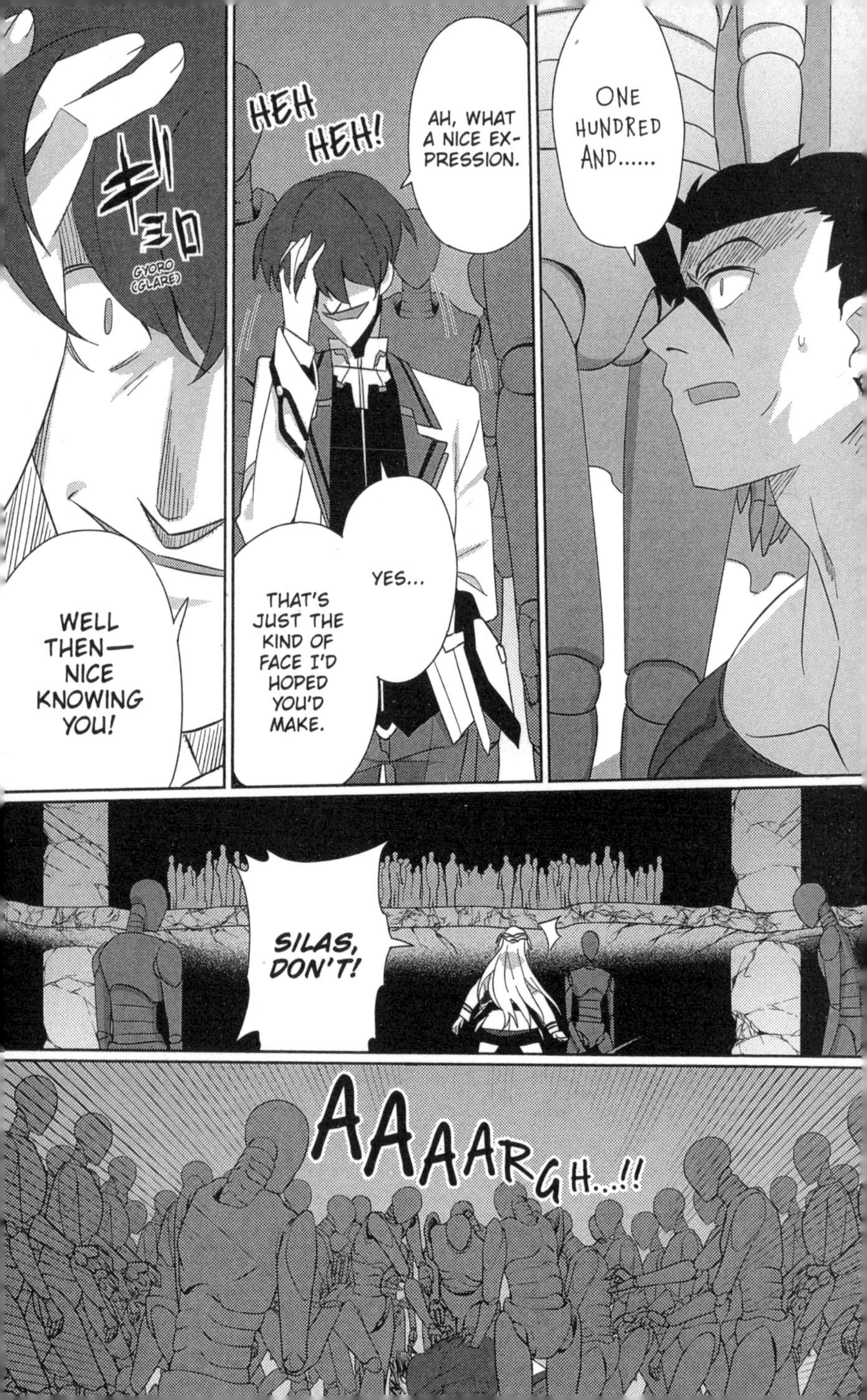
ONE HUNDRED AND......
AH, WHAT A NICE EX-PRESSION.
HEH HEH!
YES...
THAT'S JUST THE KIND OF FACE I'D HOPED YOU'D MAKE.
GYORO (GLARE)
WELL THEN—NICE KNOWING YOU!
SILAS, DON'T!
AAAAARGH...!!

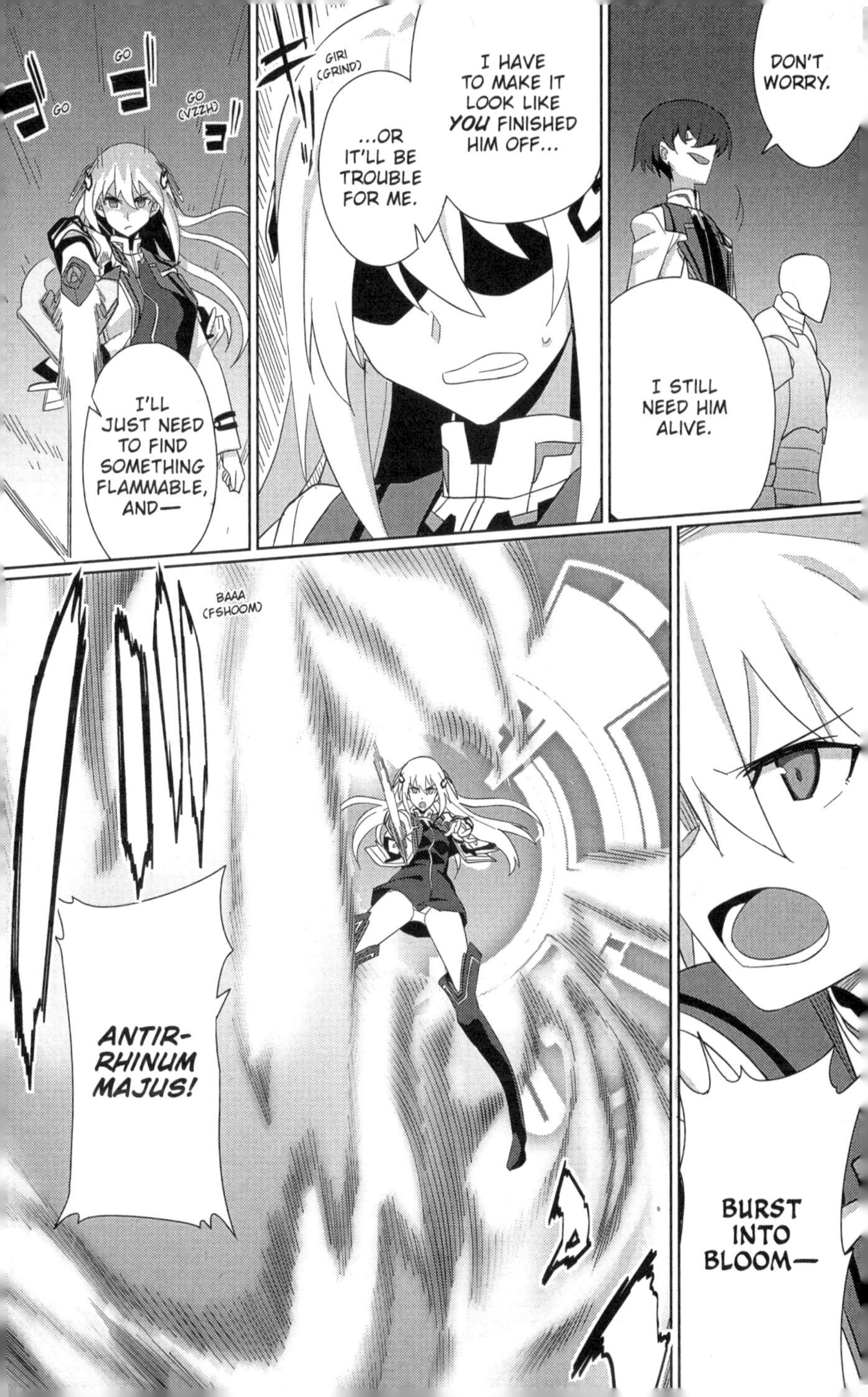
DON'T WORRY.
I STILL NEED HIM ALIVE.
GIRI (GRIND)
I HAVE TO MAKE IT LOOK LIKE *YOU* FINISHED HIM OFF...
...OR IT'LL BE TROUBLE FOR ME.
GO
GO
GO (VZZH)
I'LL JUST NEED TO FIND SOMETHING FLAMMABLE, AND—
BURST INTO BLOOM—
BAAA (FSHOOM)
ANTIR-RHINUM MAJUS!

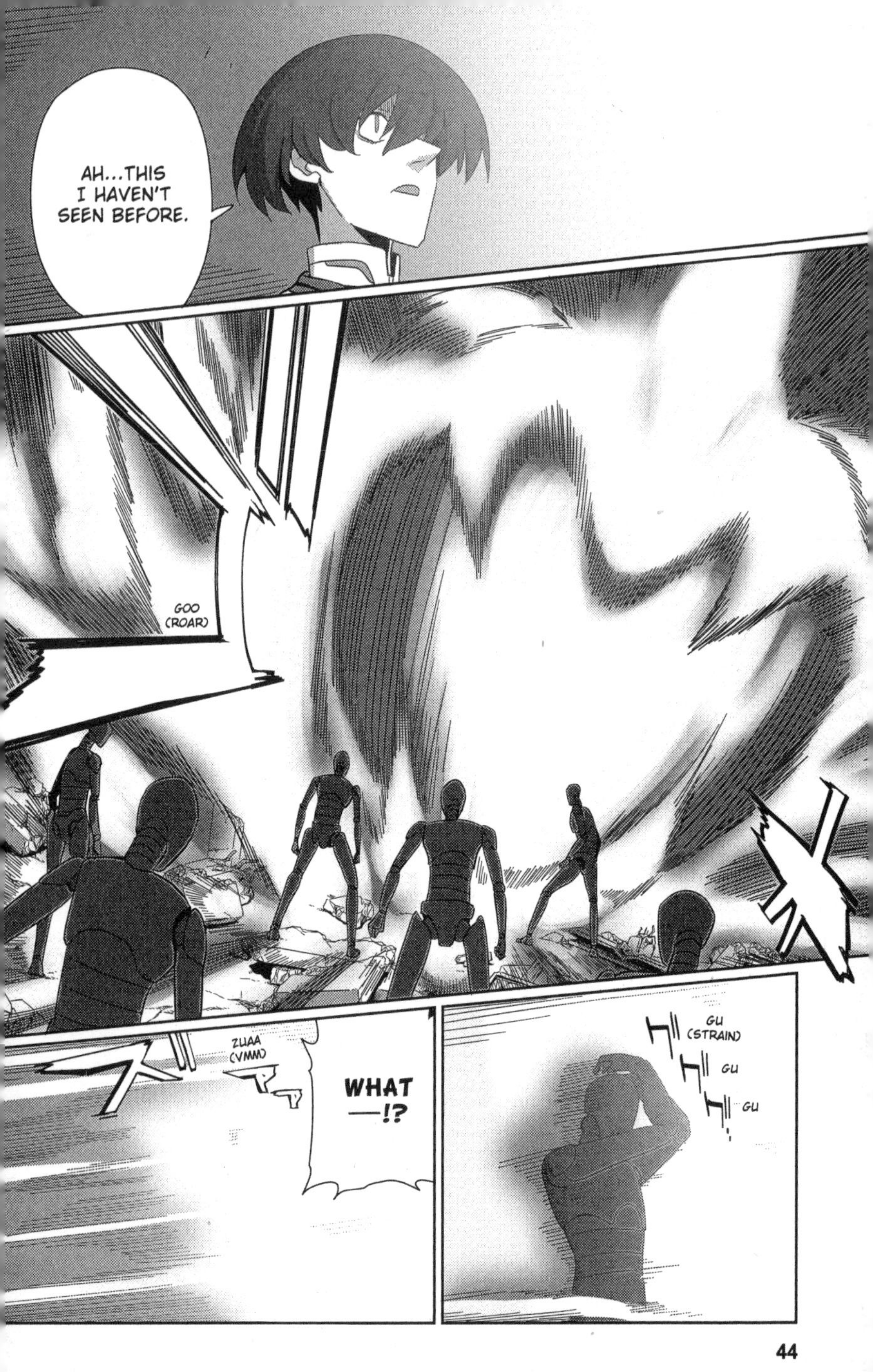
AH...THIS I HAVEN'T SEEN BEFORE.
GOO (ROAR)
GU (STRAIN)
GU
GU
ZUAA (VMM)
WHAT—!?

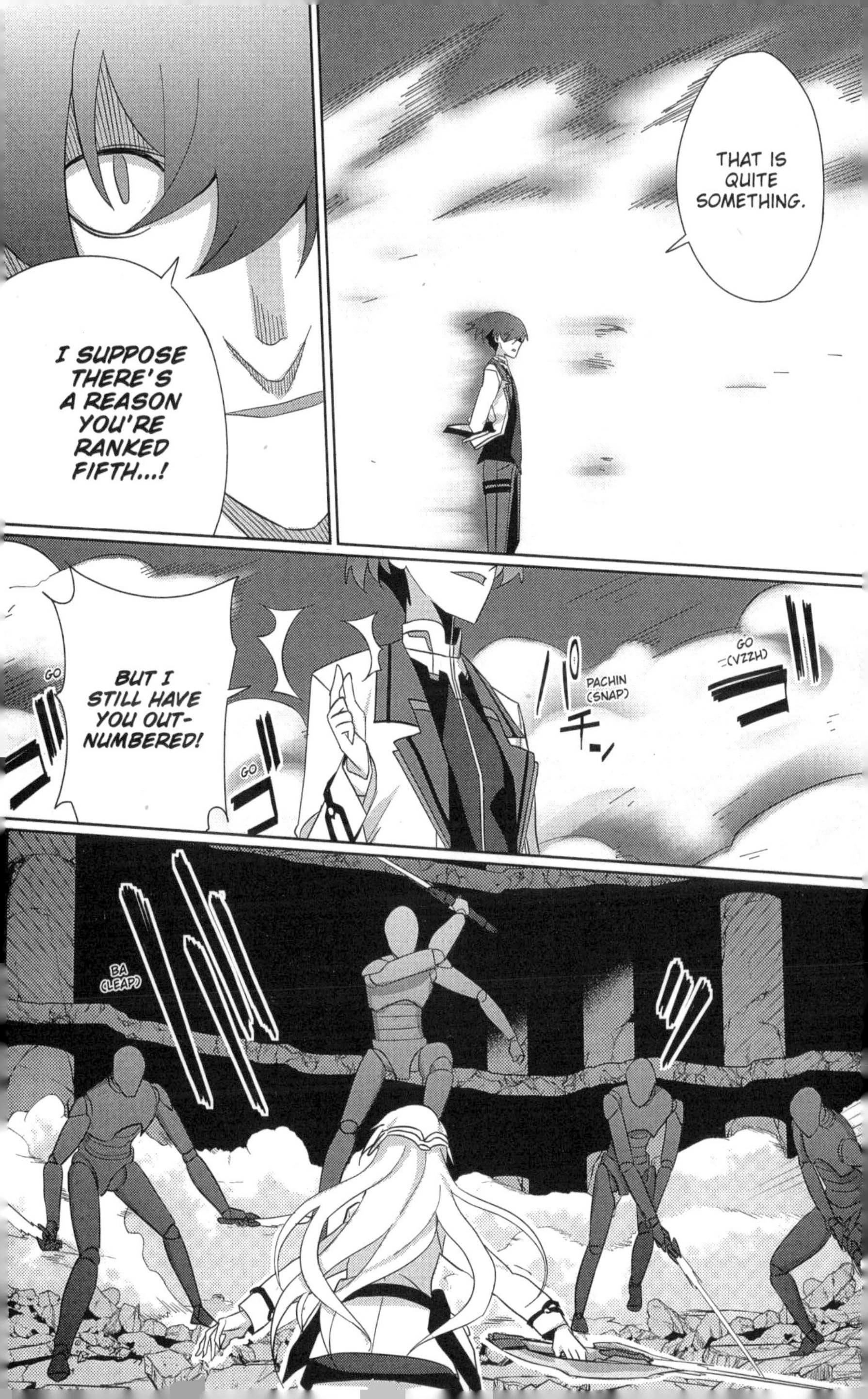
THAT IS QUITE SOMETHING.
I SUPPOSE THERE'S A REASON YOU'RE RANKED FIFTH...!
GO (VZZH)
PACHIN (SNAP)
BUT I STILL HAVE YOU OUT-NUMBERED!
GO
GO
BA (LEAP)

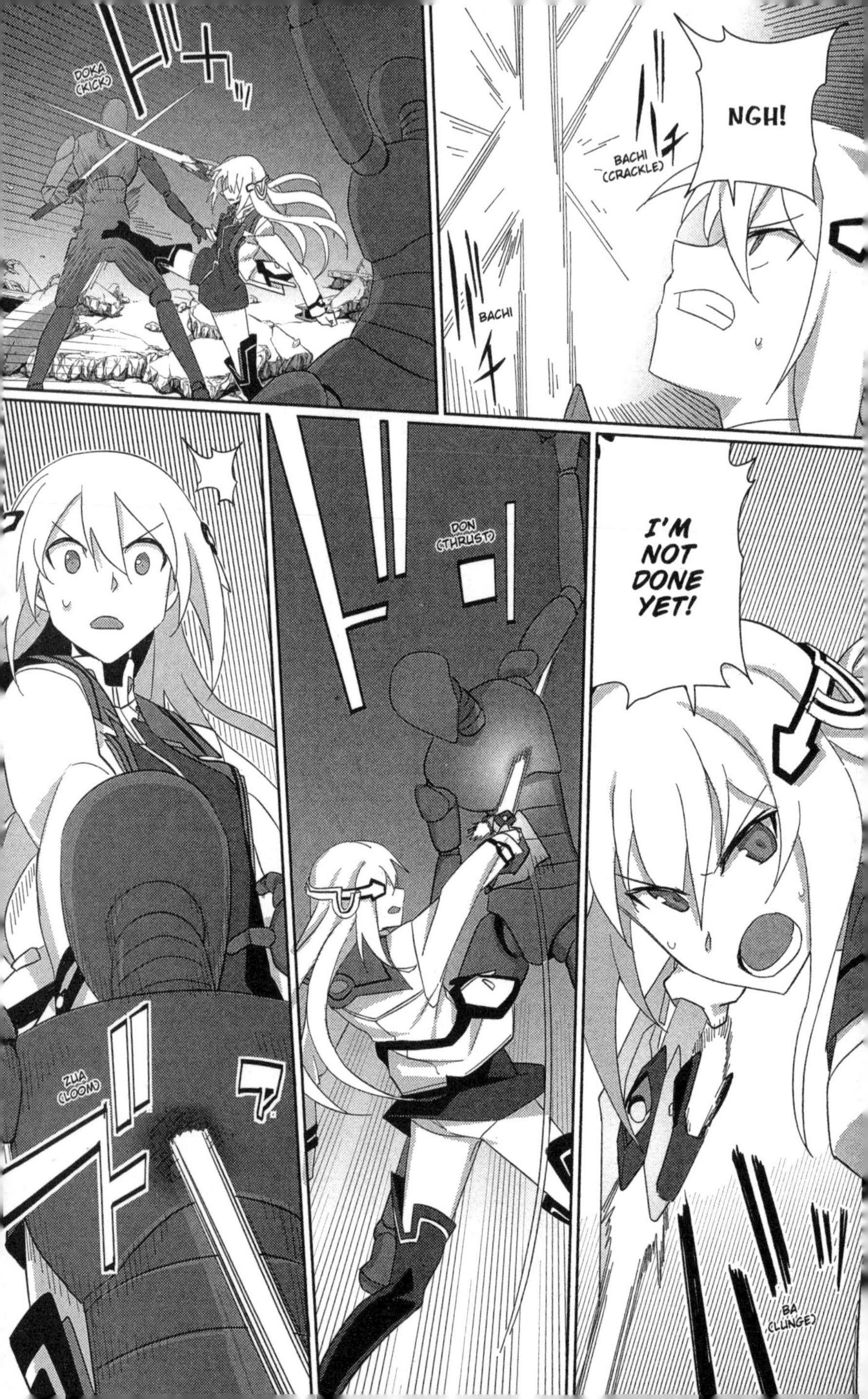
NGH!
BACHI (CRACKLE)
BACHI
DOKA (KICK)
I'M NOT DONE YET!
BA (LUNGE)
DON (THRUST)
ZUA (LOOM)

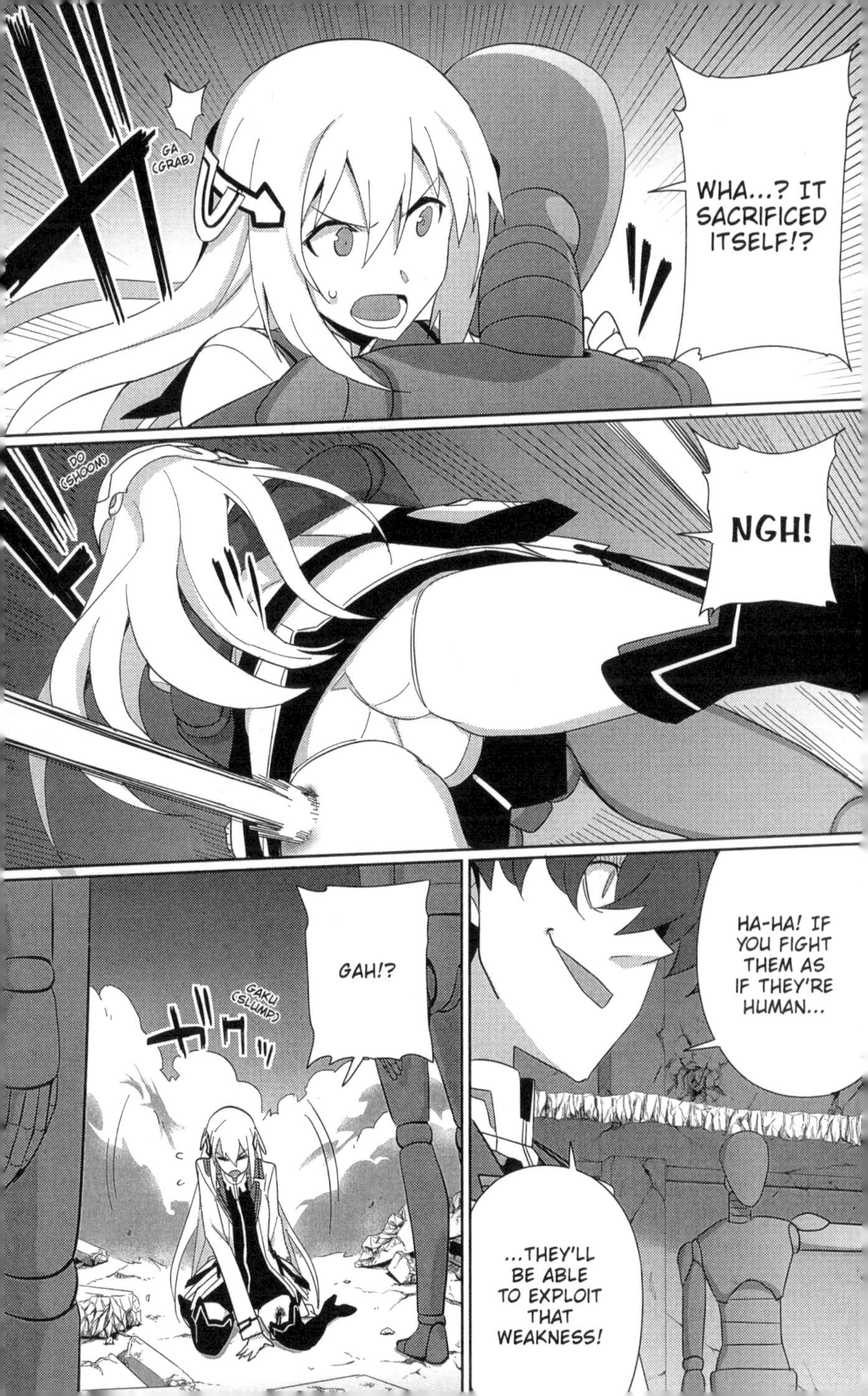
WHA...? IT SACRIFICED ITSELF!?
GA (GRAB)
NGH!
DO (SHOOM)
HA-HA! IF YOU FIGHT THEM AS IF THEY'RE HUMAN...
...THEY'LL BE ABLE TO EXPLOIT THAT WEAKNESS!
GAH!?
GAKU (SLUMP)

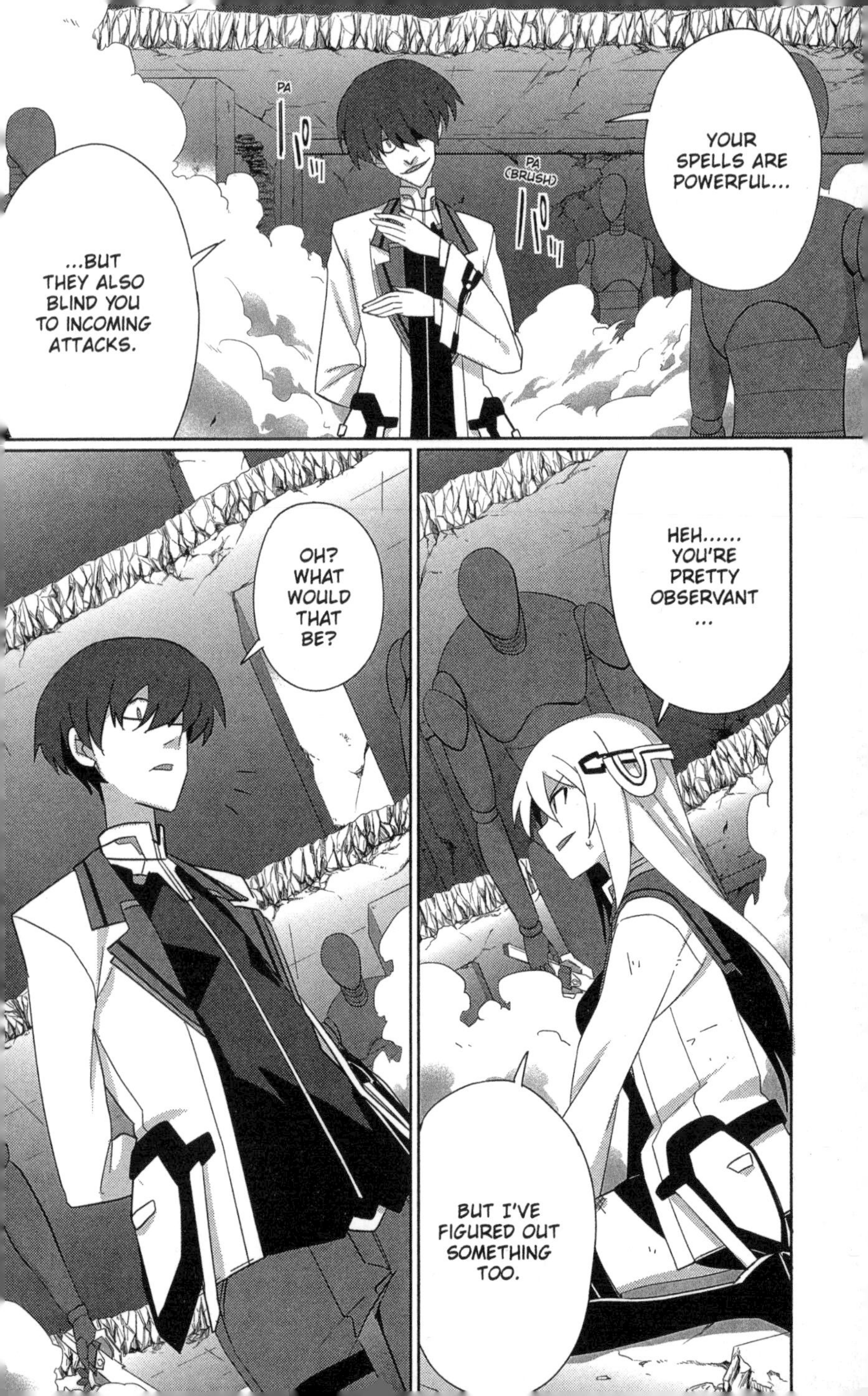
YOUR SPELLS ARE POWERFUL...
PA (BRUSH)
PA
...BUT THEY ALSO BLIND YOU TO INCOMING ATTACKS.
HEH...... YOU'RE PRETTY OBSERVANT ...
BUT I'VE FIGURED OUT SOMETHING TOO.
OH? WHAT WOULD THAT BE?

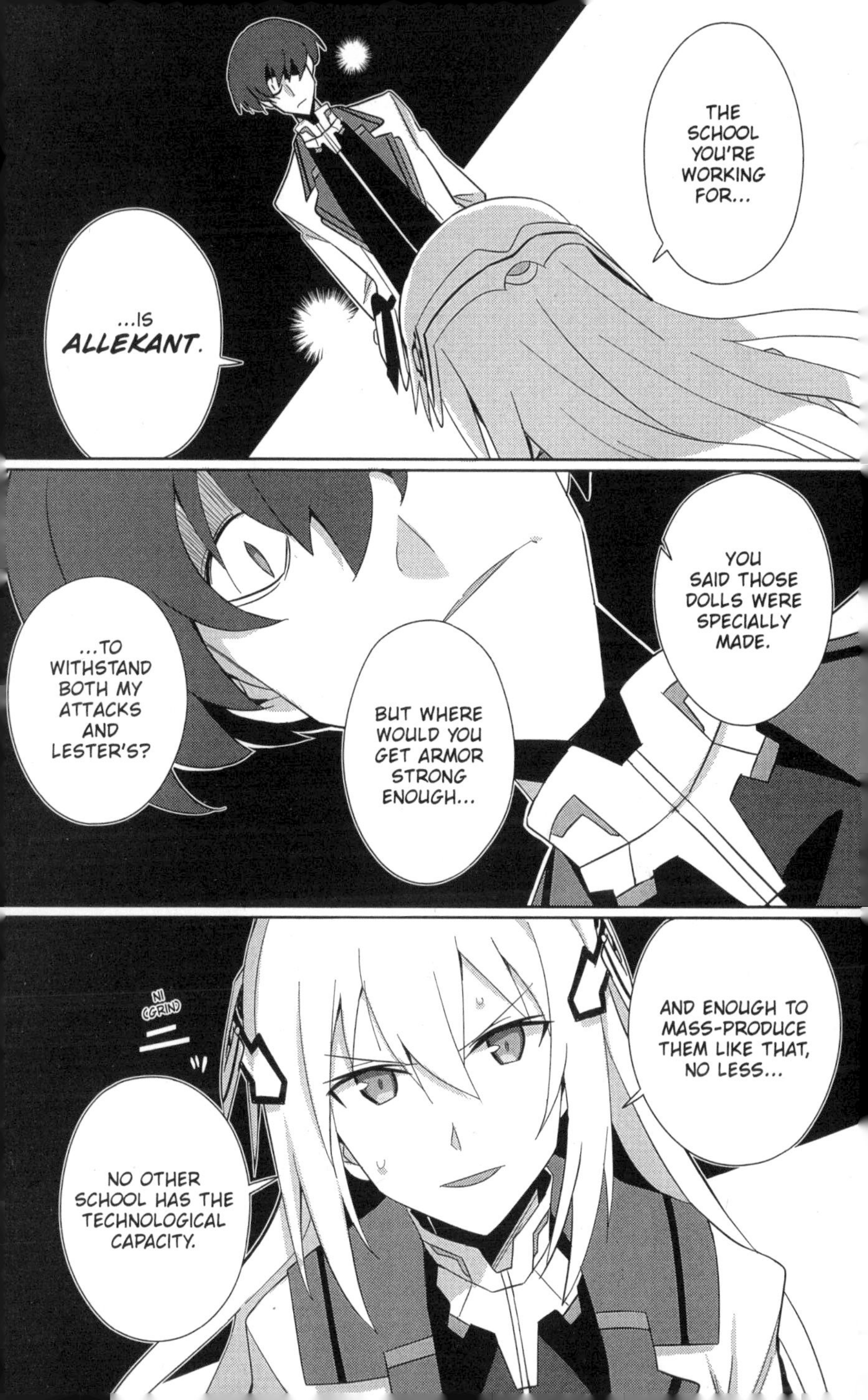
THE SCHOOL YOU'RE WORKING FOR...
...IS ALLEKANT.
YOU SAID THOSE DOLLS WERE SPECIALLY MADE.
BUT WHERE WOULD YOU GET ARMOR STRONG ENOUGH...
...TO WITHSTAND BOTH MY ATTACKS AND LESTER'S?
AND ENOUGH TO MASS-PRODUCE THEM LIKE THAT, NO LESS...
NI (GRIN)
NO OTHER SCHOOL HAS THE TECHNOLOGICAL CAPACITY.

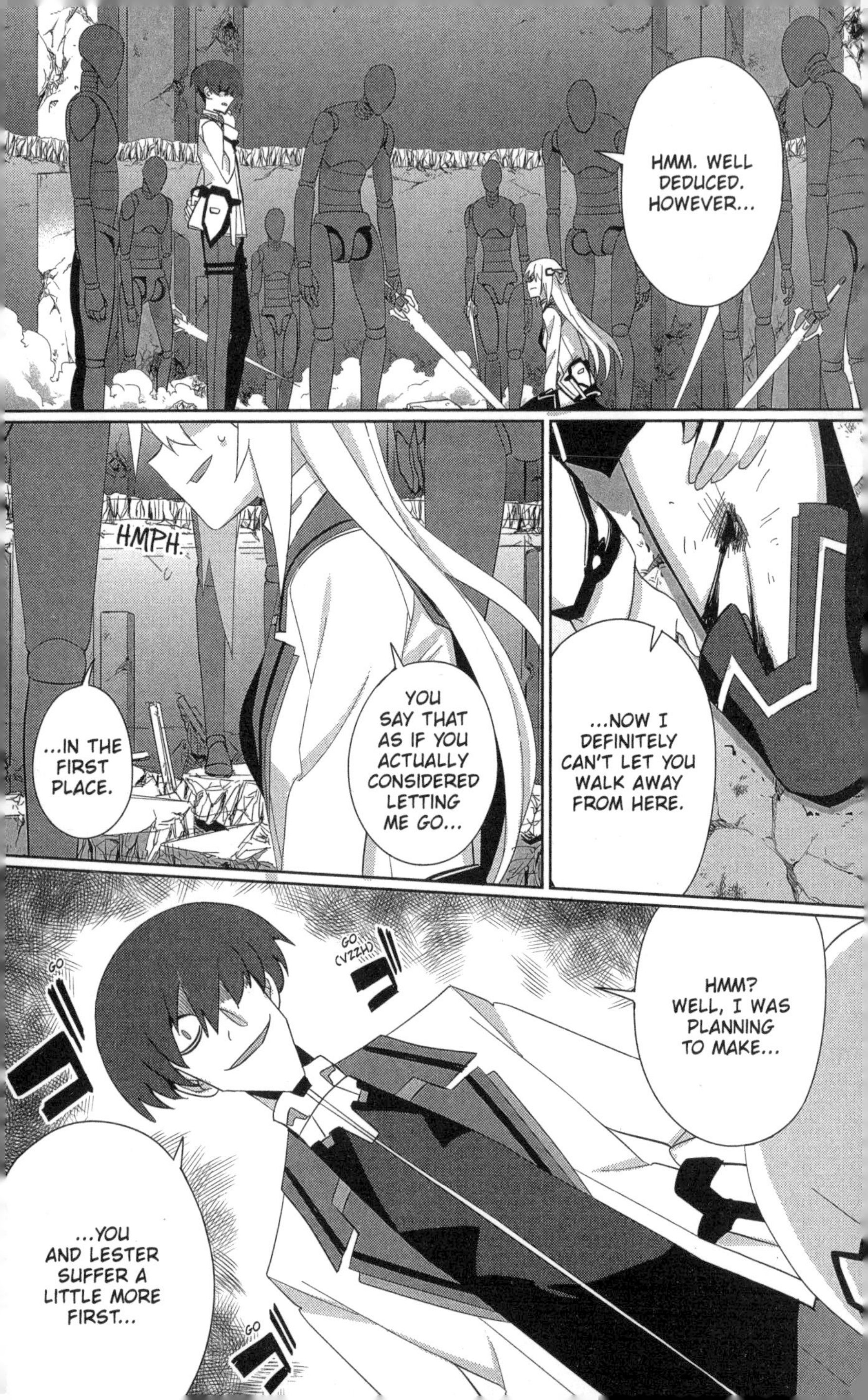
HMM. WELL DEDUCED. HOWEVER...
...NOW I DEFINITELY CAN'T LET YOU WALK AWAY FROM HERE.
HMPH.
YOU SAY THAT AS IF YOU ACTUALLY CONSIDERED LETTING ME GO...
...IN THE FIRST PLACE.
HMM? WELL, I WAS PLANNING TO MAKE...
GO (VZZH)
GO
...YOU AND LESTER SUFFER A LITTLE MORE FIRST...
GO

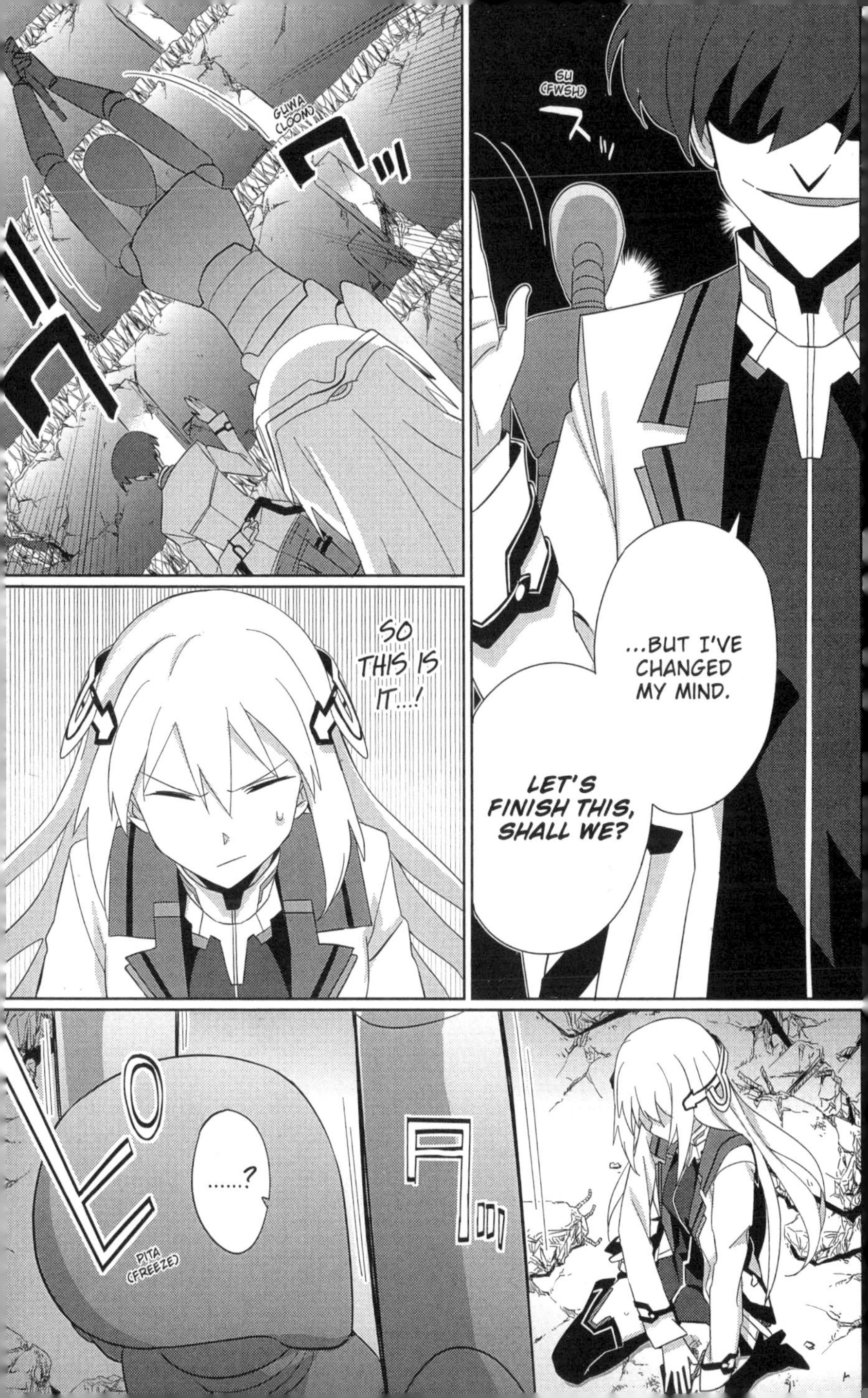
SU (FWSH)
GUWA (LOOM)
...BUT I'VE CHANGED MY MIND.
LET'S FINISH THIS, SHALL WE?
SO THIS IS IT...!
......?
PITA (FREEZE)

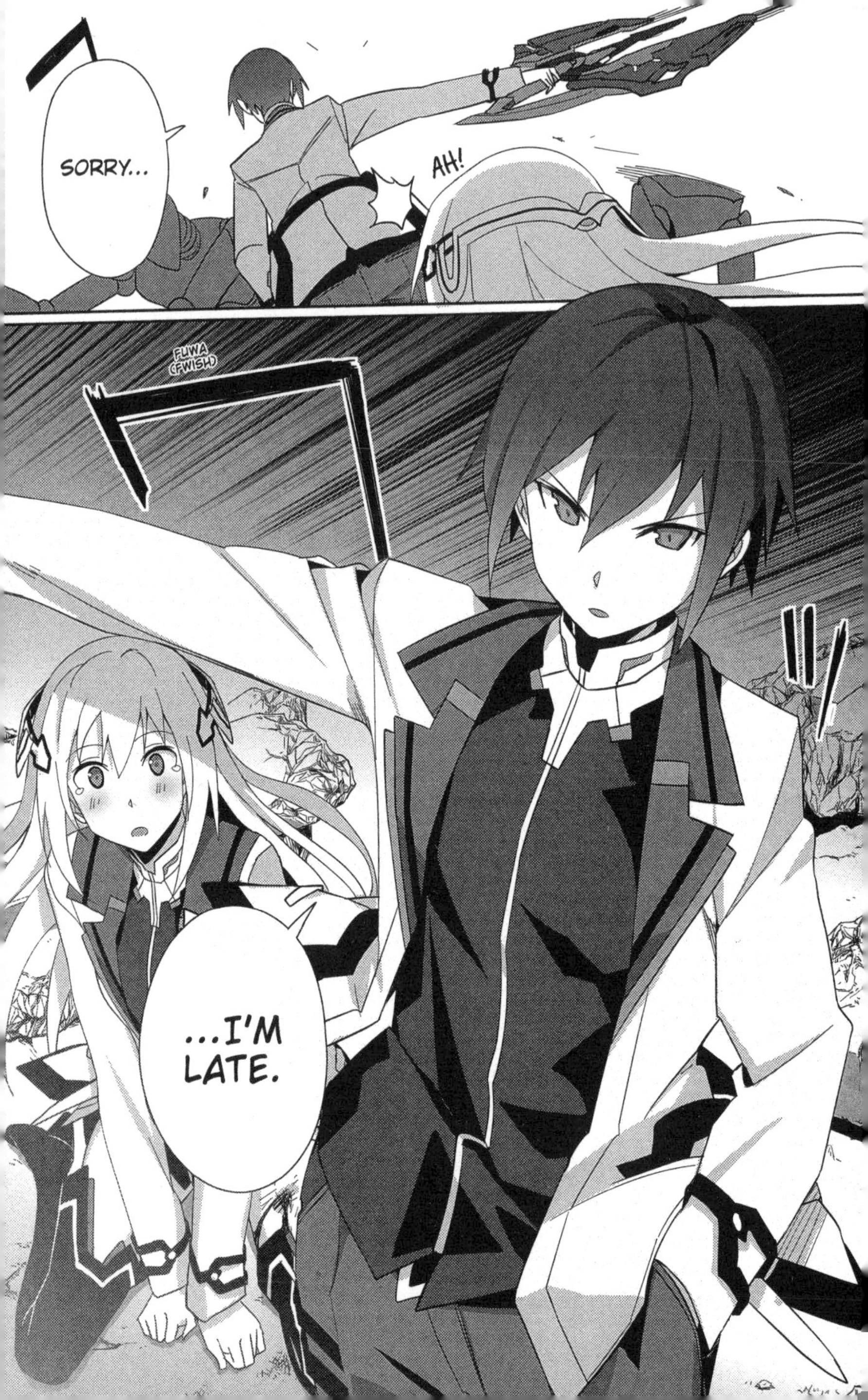
AH!
SORRY...
FUWA (FWISH)
...I'M LATE.

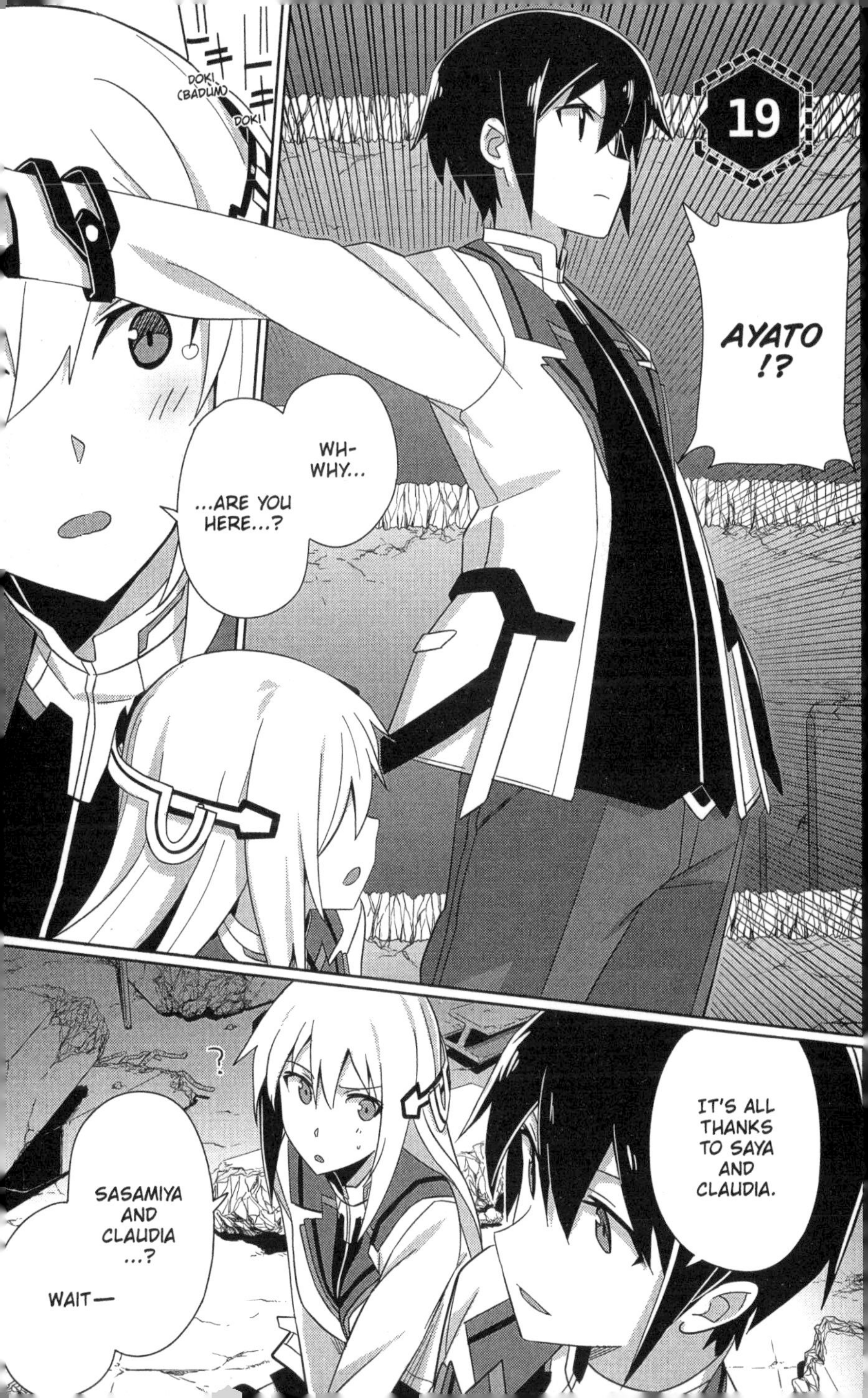
19
AYATO!?
WH-WHY...
...ARE YOU HERE...?
DOKI (BADUM) DOKI
IT'S ALL THANKS TO SAYA AND CLAUDIA.
?
SASAMIYA AND CLAUDIA ...?
WAIT—

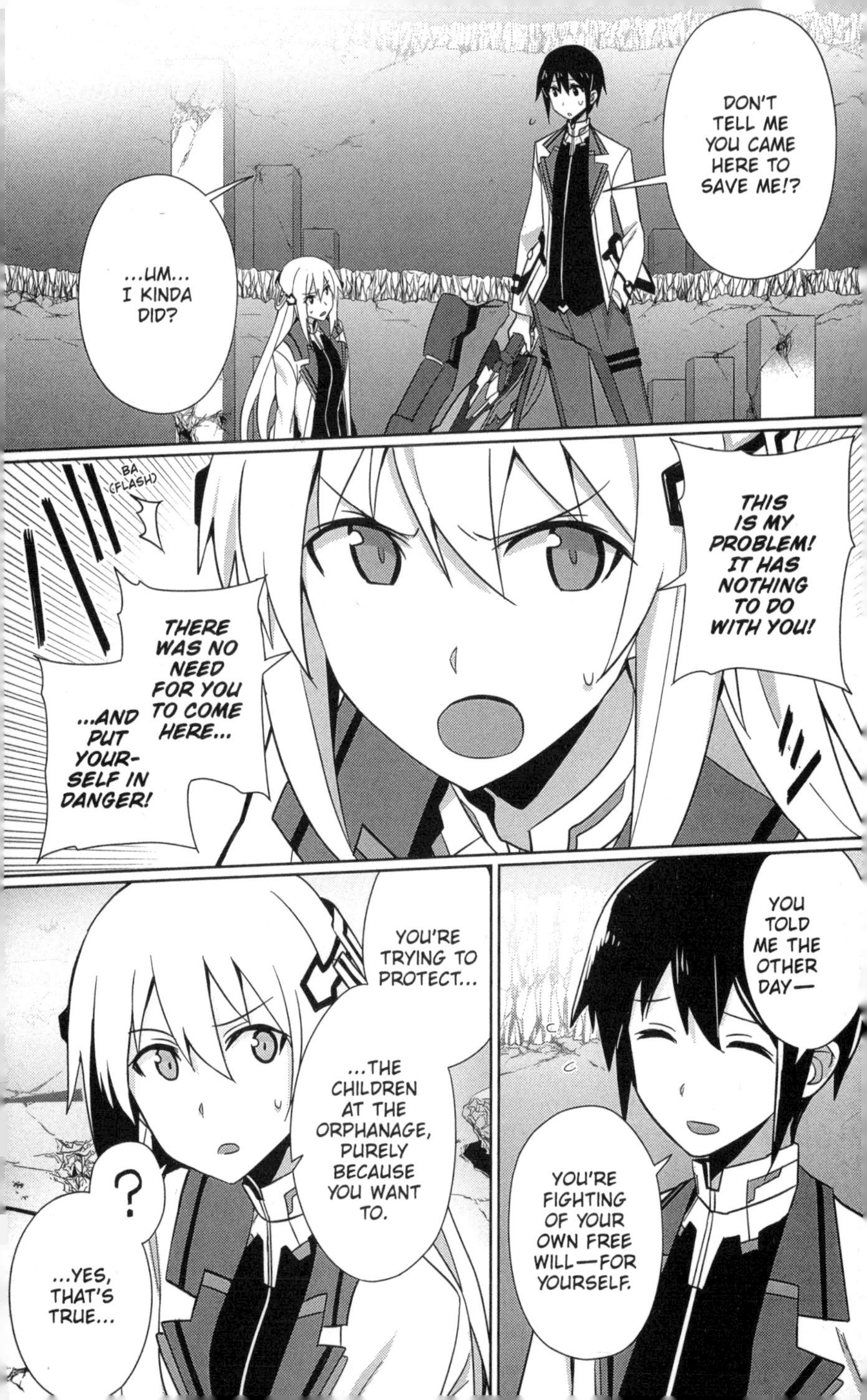
DON'T TELL ME YOU CAME HERE TO SAVE ME!?
...UM... I KINDA DID?
THIS IS MY PROBLEM! IT HAS NOTHING TO DO WITH YOU!
BA (FLASH)
THERE WAS NO NEED FOR YOU TO COME HERE...
...AND PUT YOURSELF IN DANGER!
YOU TOLD ME THE OTHER DAY—
YOU'RE FIGHTING OF YOUR OWN FREE WILL—FOR YOURSELF.
YOU'RE TRYING TO PROTECT...
...THE CHILDREN AT THE ORPHANAGE, PURELY BECAUSE YOU WANT TO.
?
...YES, THAT'S TRUE...

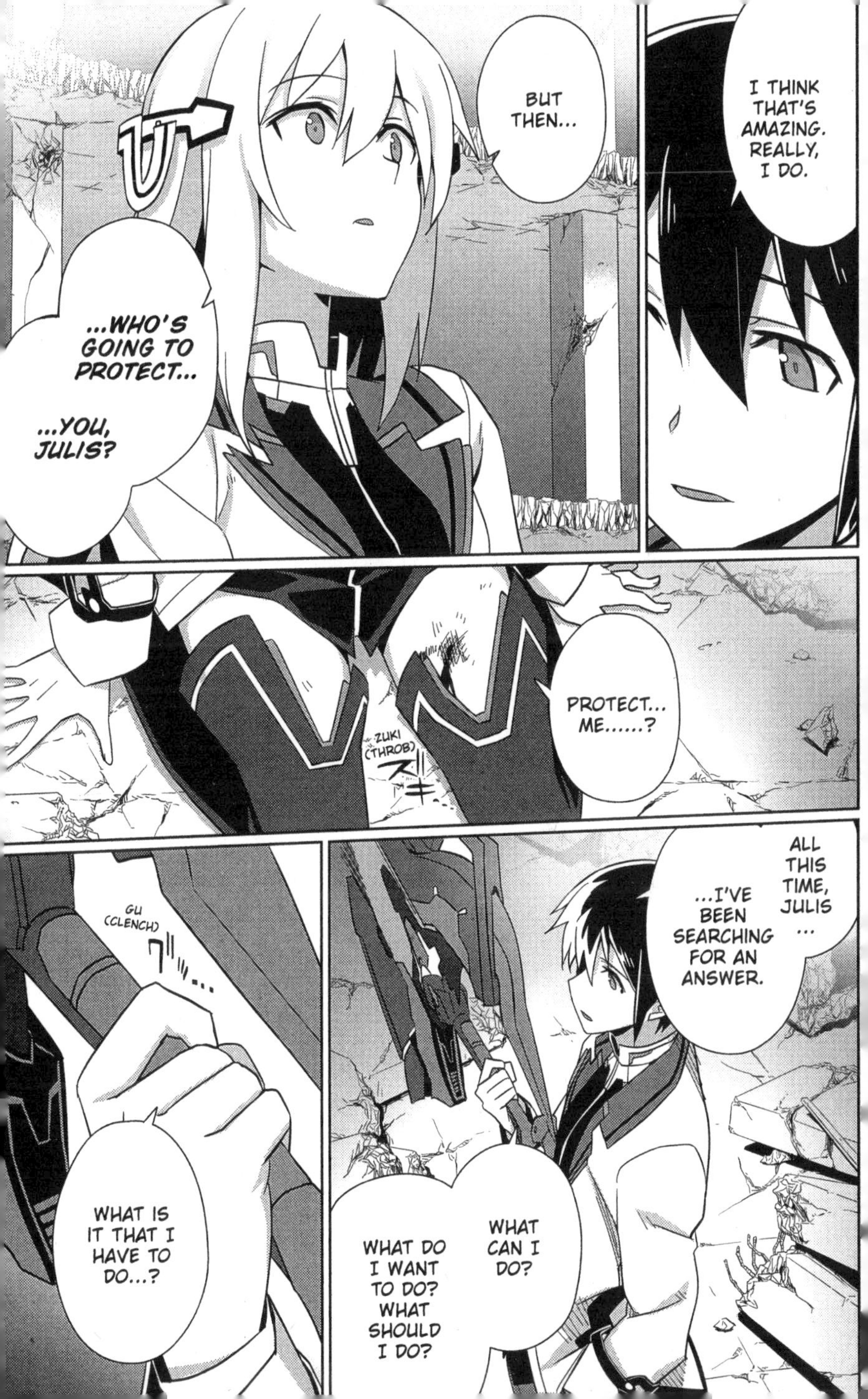
I THINK THAT'S AMAZING. REALLY, I DO.
BUT THEN...
...WHO'S GOING TO PROTECT...
...YOU, JULIS?
PROTECT... ME......?
ZUKI (THROB)
ALL THIS TIME, JULIS...
...I'VE BEEN SEARCHING FOR AN ANSWER.
WHAT CAN I DO?
WHAT DO I WANT TO DO? WHAT SHOULD I DO?
GU (CLENCH)
WHAT IS IT THAT I HAVE TO DO...?

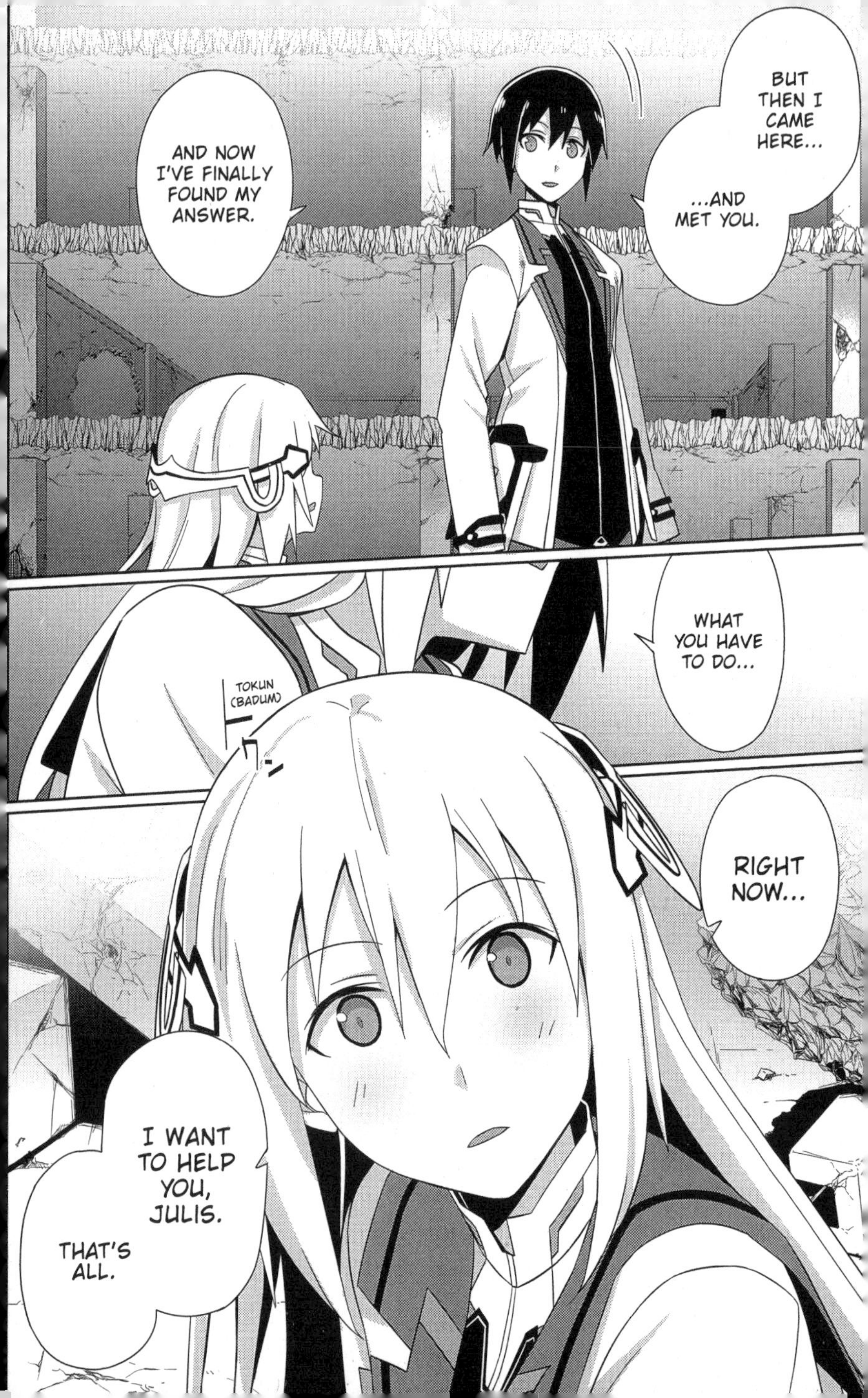
BUT THEN I CAME HERE...
...AND MET YOU.
AND NOW I'VE FINALLY FOUND MY ANSWER.
WHAT YOU HAVE TO DO...
TOKUN (BADUM)
RIGHT NOW...
I WANT TO HELP YOU, JULIS.
THAT'S ALL.

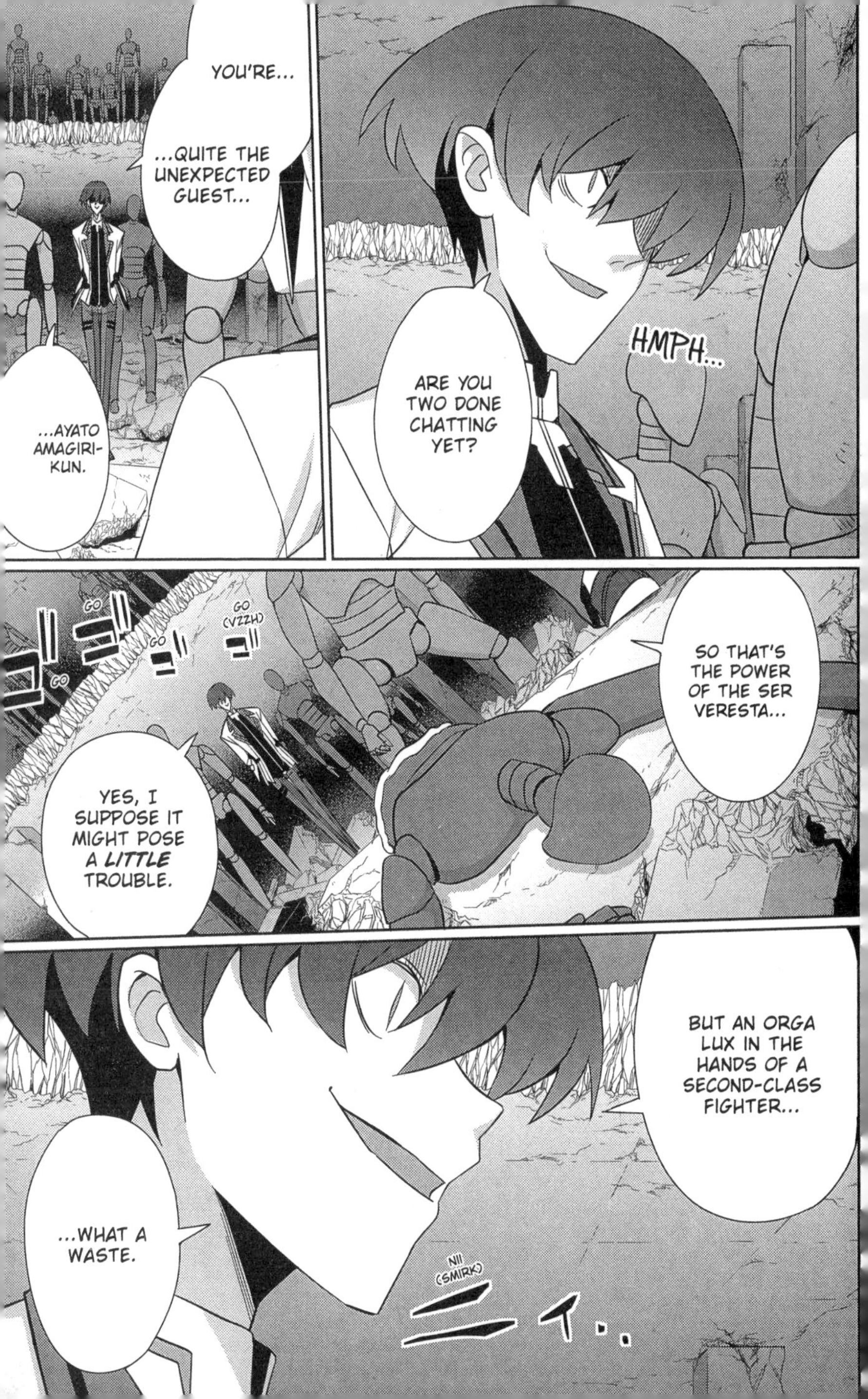
HMPH...
ARE YOU TWO DONE CHATTING YET?
YOU'RE...
...QUITE THE UNEXPECTED GUEST...
...AYATO AMAGIRI-KUN.
SO THAT'S THE POWER OF THE SER VERESTA...
GO (VZZH)
GO
GO
GO
YES, I SUPPOSE IT MIGHT POSE A *LITTLE* TROUBLE.
BUT AN ORGA LUX IN THE HANDS OF A SECOND-CLASS FIGHTER...
...WHAT A WASTE.
NII (SMIRK)

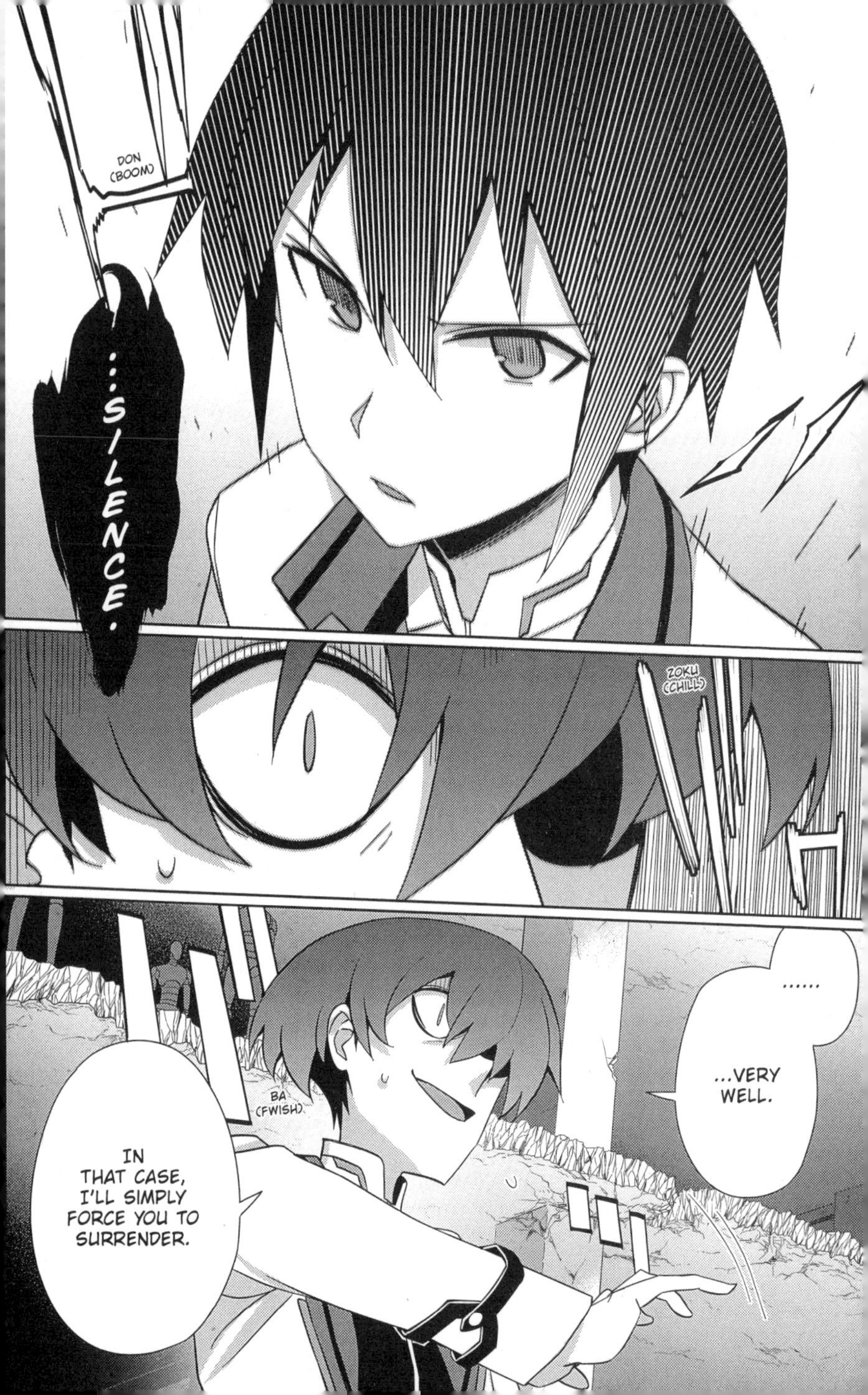
DON (BOOM)
...SILENCE.
ZOKU (CHILL)
......
...VERY WELL.
BA (FWISH)
IN THAT CASE, I'LL SIMPLY FORCE YOU TO SURRENDER.

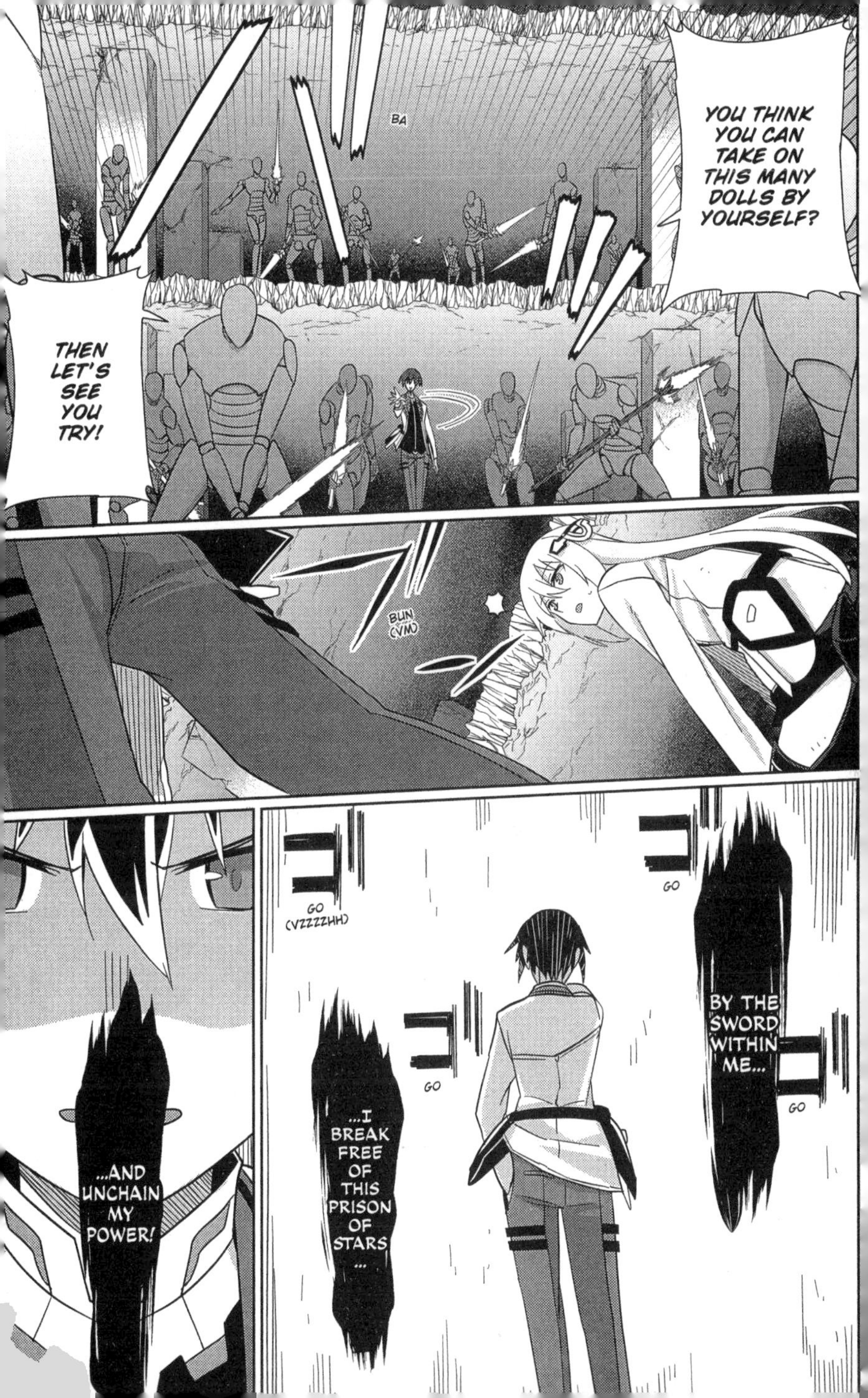
YOU THINK YOU CAN TAKE ON THIS MANY DOLLS BY YOURSELF?
BA
THEN LET'S SEE YOU TRY!
BUN (VM)
GO
GO (VZZZZHH)
BY THE SWORD WITHIN ME...
GO
GO
...I BREAK FREE OF THIS PRISON OF STARS...
...AND UNCHAIN MY POWER!

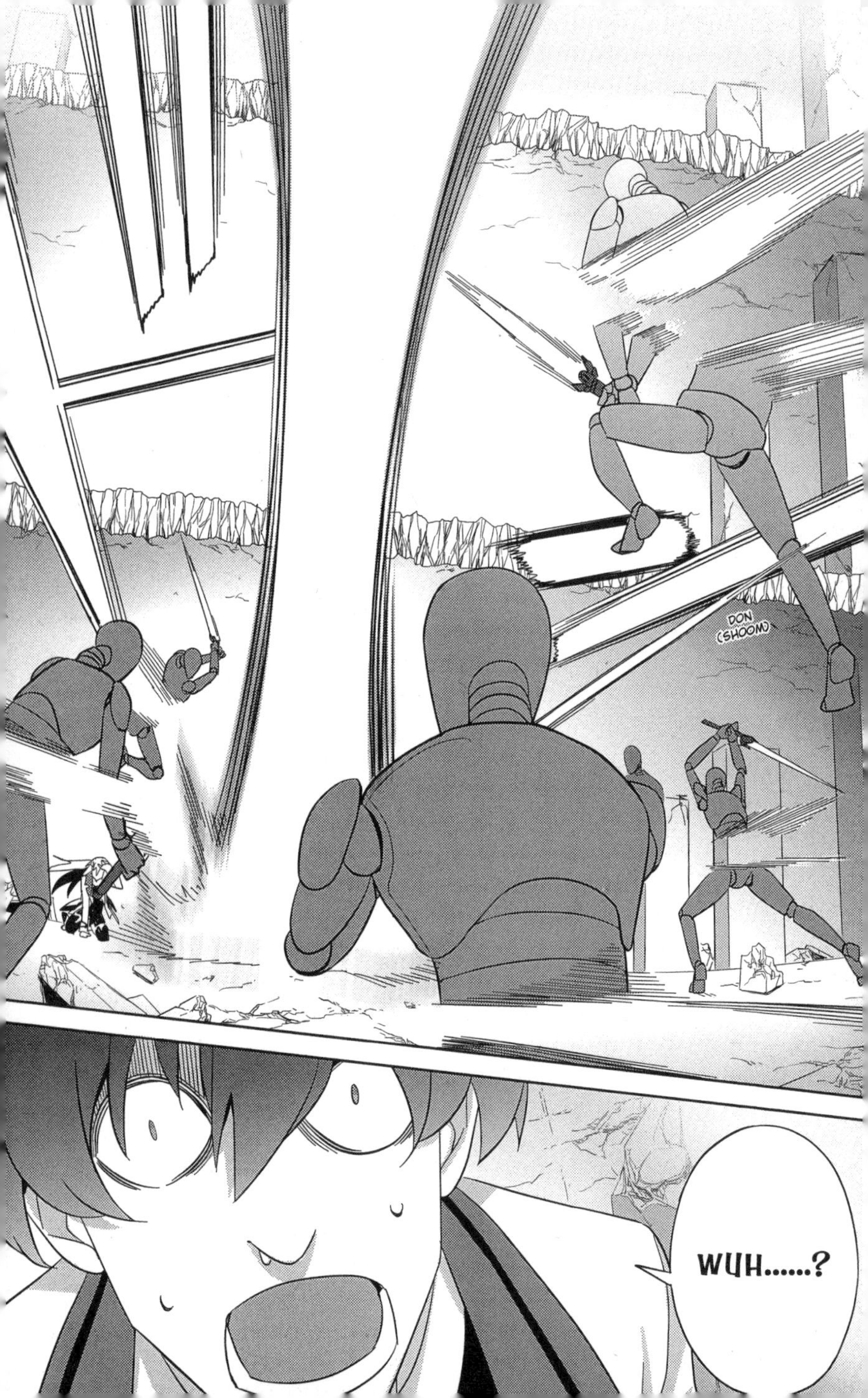
DON
(SHOOM)
WUH......?

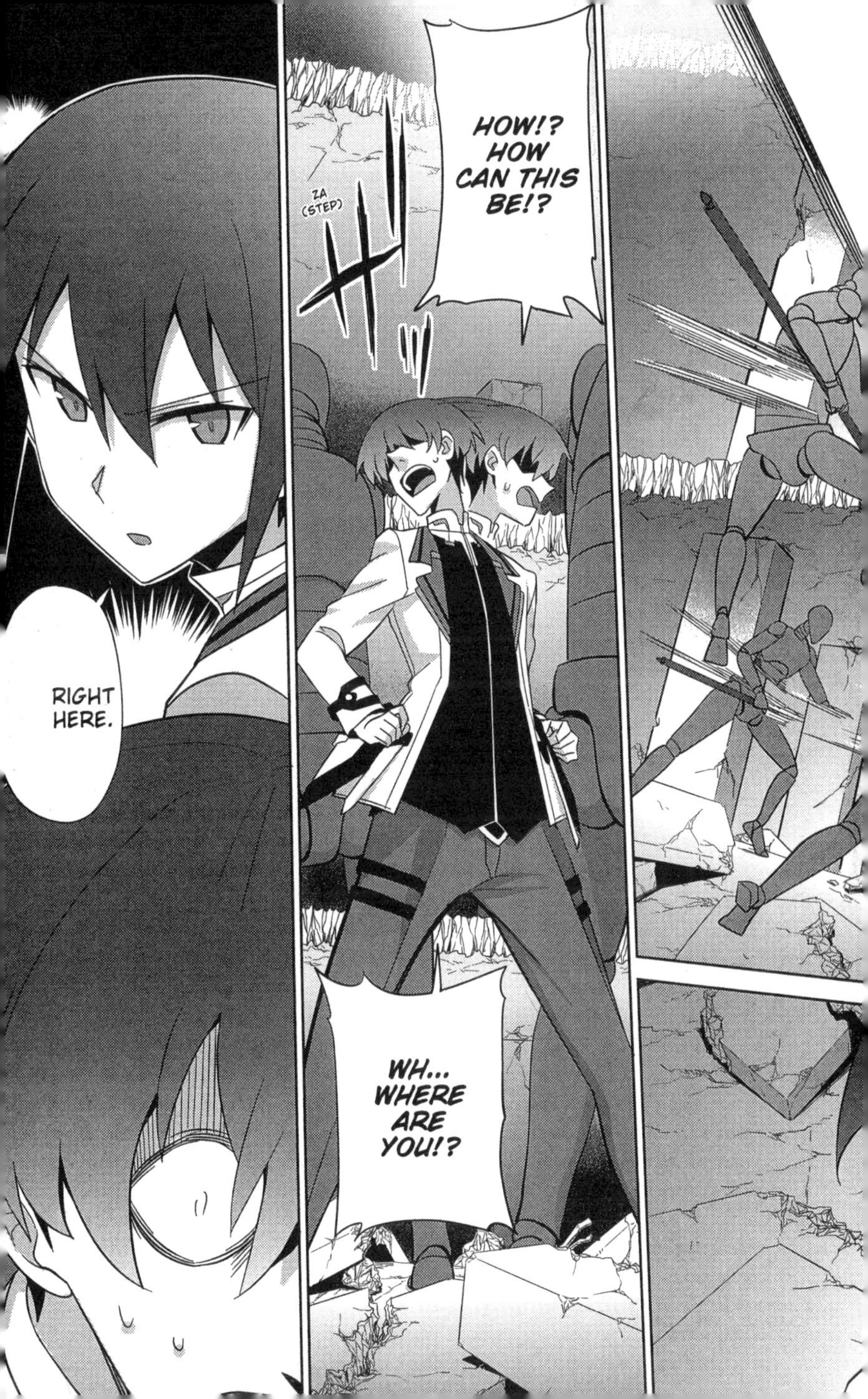
HOW!? HOW CAN THIS BE!?
ZA (STEP)
WH... WHERE ARE YOU!?
RIGHT HERE.

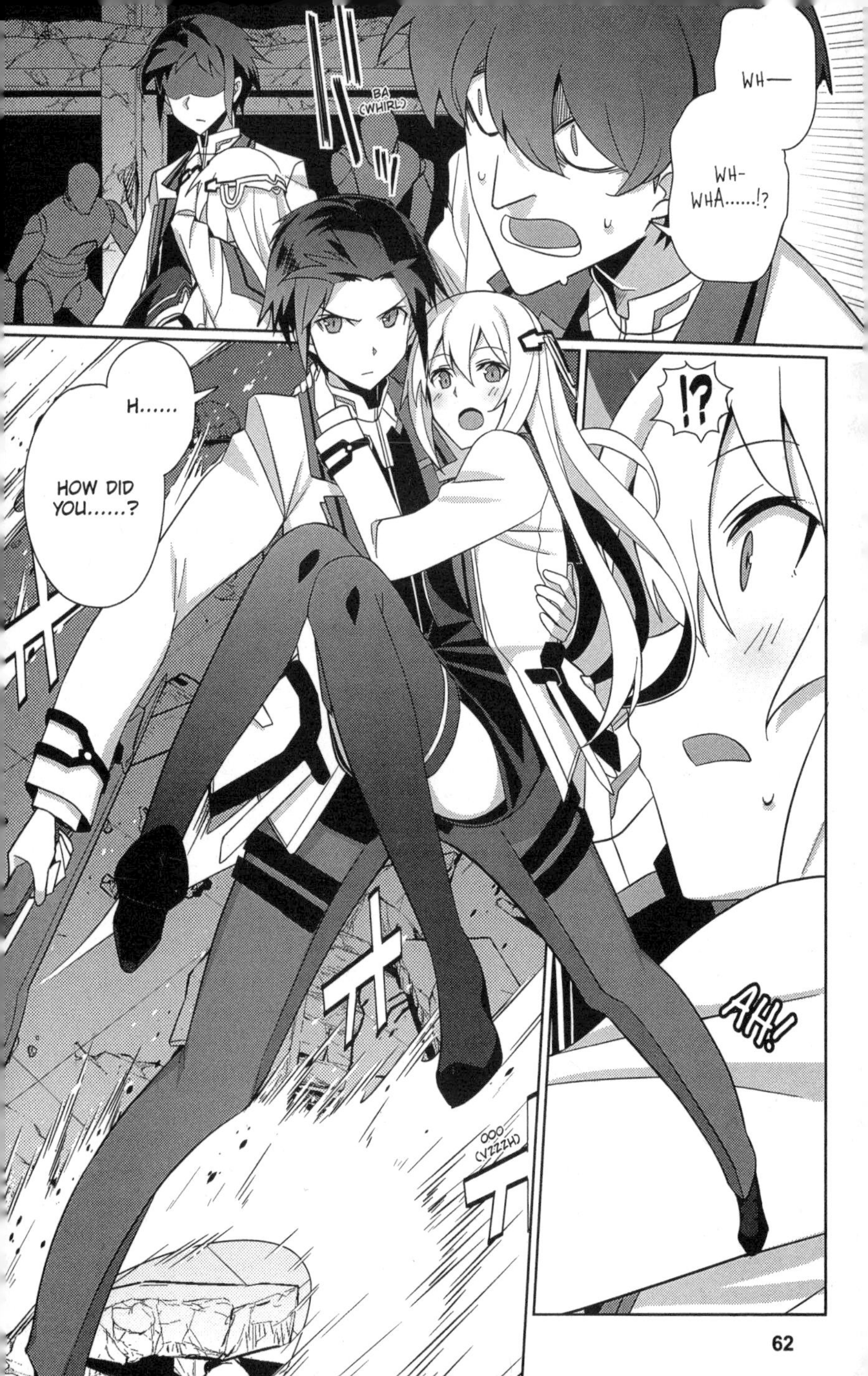
WH—
WH-
WHA......!?
BA
(WHIRL)
!?
H......
HOW DID
YOU......?
AH!
OOO
(VZZZH)

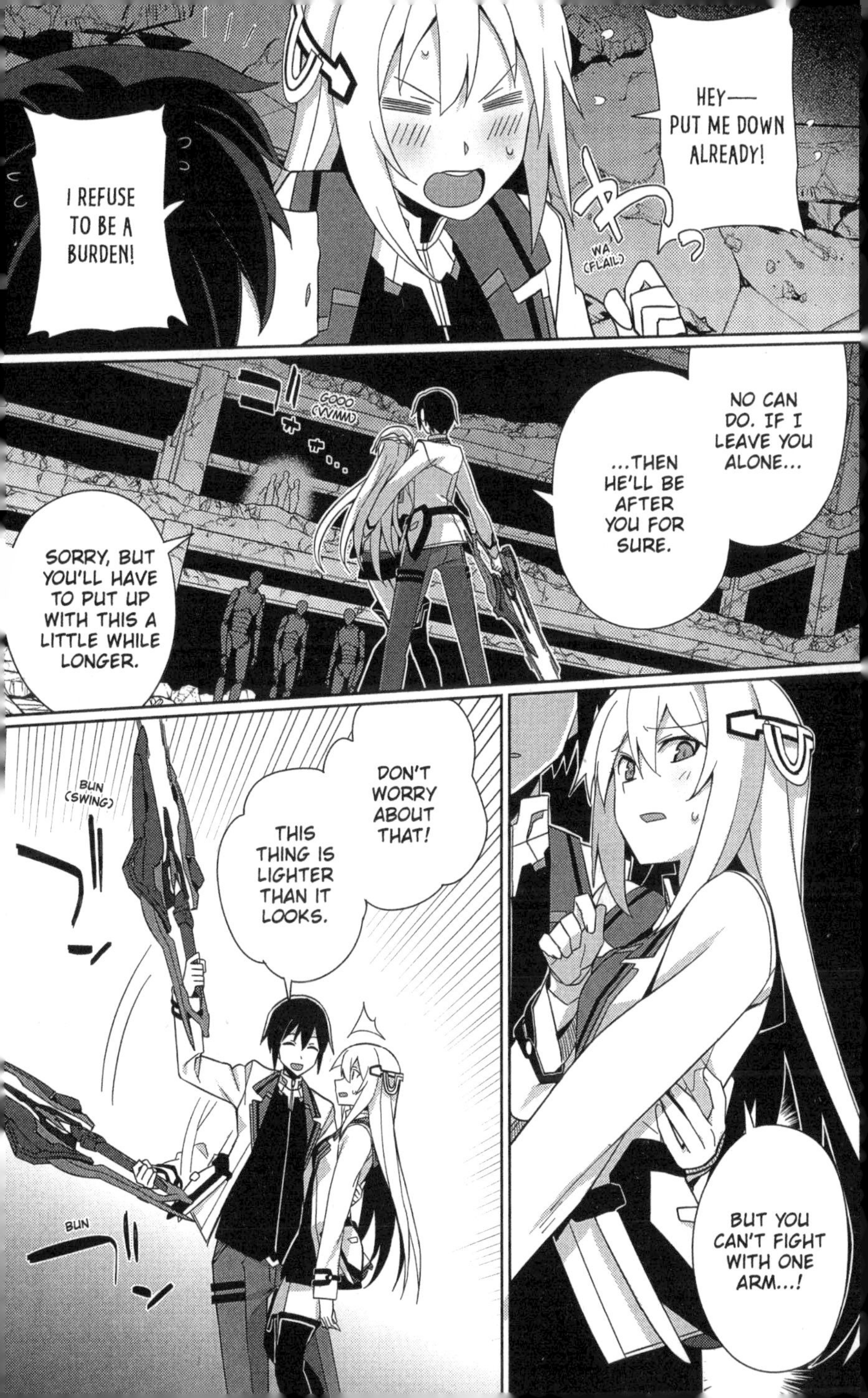
HEY— PUT ME DOWN ALREADY!
WA (FLAIL)
I REFUSE TO BE A BURDEN!
NO CAN DO. IF I LEAVE YOU ALONE...
...THEN HE'LL BE AFTER YOU FOR SURE.
GOOO (VVMM)
SORRY, BUT YOU'LL HAVE TO PUT UP WITH THIS A LITTLE WHILE LONGER.
BUT YOU CAN'T FIGHT WITH ONE ARM...!
DON'T WORRY ABOUT THAT!
THIS THING IS LIGHTER THAN IT LOOKS.
BUN (SWING)
BUN

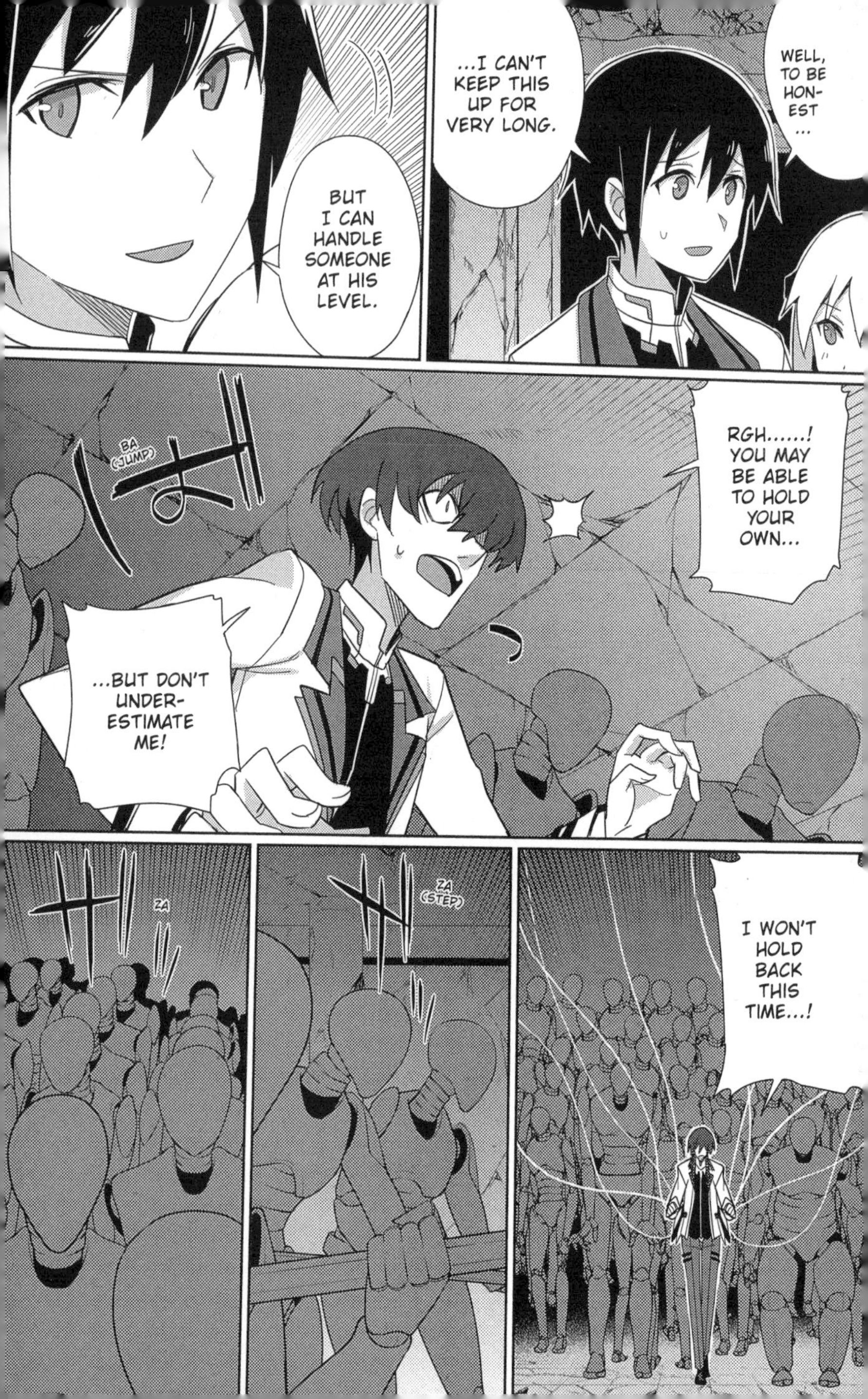
WELL, TO BE HON-EST...
...I CAN'T KEEP THIS UP FOR VERY LONG.
BUT I CAN HANDLE SOMEONE AT HIS LEVEL.
RGH......! YOU MAY BE ABLE TO HOLD YOUR OWN...
BA (JUMP)
...BUT DON'T UNDER-ESTIMATE ME!
I WON'T HOLD BACK THIS TIME...!
ZA (STEP)
ZA

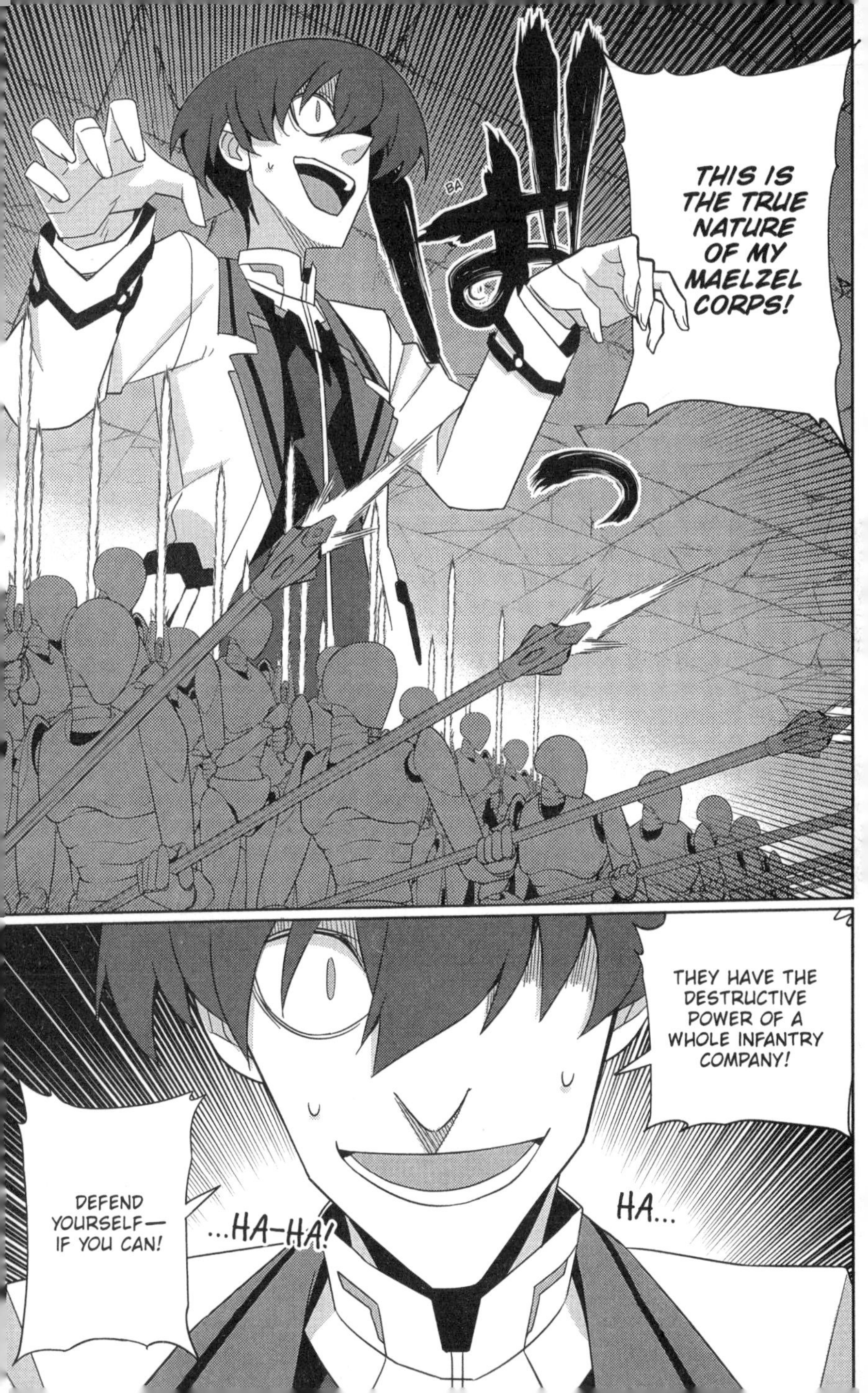

THIS IS THE TRUE NATURE OF MY MAELZEL CORPS!
BA
THEY HAVE THE DESTRUCTIVE POWER OF A WHOLE INFANTRY COMPANY!
HA...
...HA-HA!
DEFEND YOURSELF—IF YOU CAN!

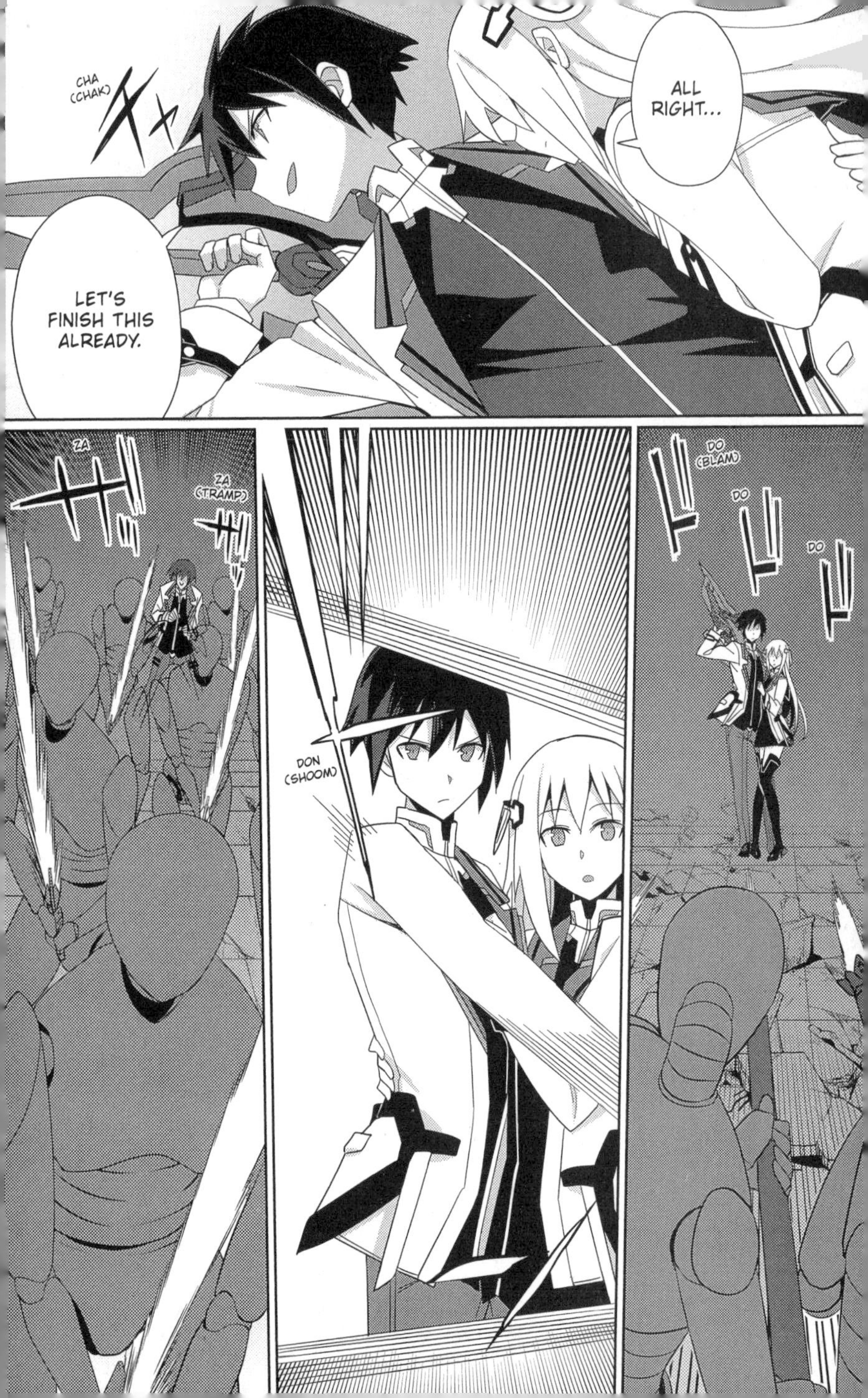
ALL RIGHT...
CHA (CHAK)
LET'S FINISH THIS ALREADY.
DO (BLAM)
DO
DO
DON (SHOOM)
ZA
ZA (TRAMP)

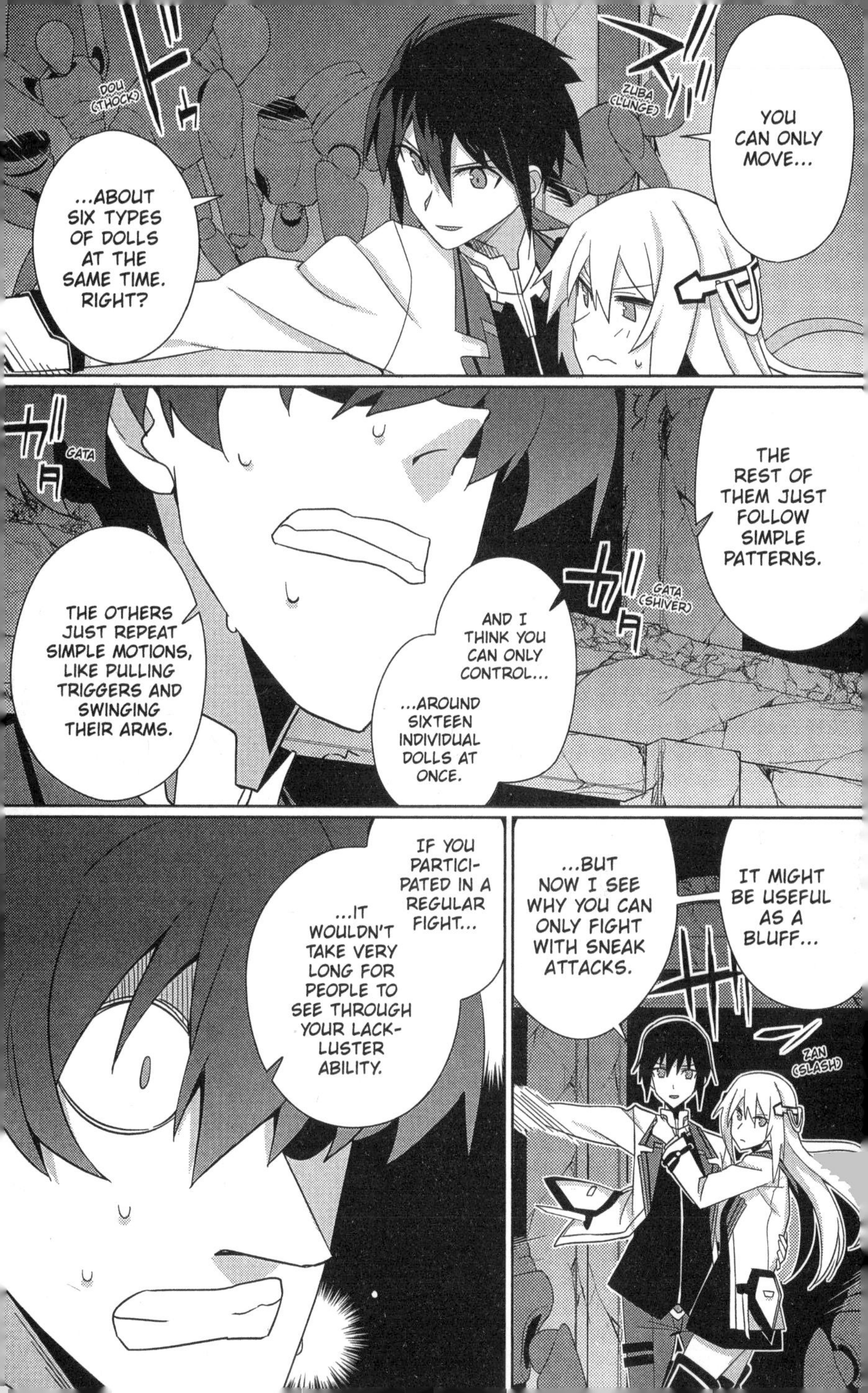
ZUBA (LUNGE)
YOU CAN ONLY MOVE...
DOU (THOCK)
...ABOUT SIX TYPES OF DOLLS AT THE SAME TIME. RIGHT?
THE REST OF THEM JUST FOLLOW SIMPLE PATTERNS.
GATA (SHIVER)
AND I THINK YOU CAN ONLY CONTROL...
...AROUND SIXTEEN INDIVIDUAL DOLLS AT ONCE.
GATA
THE OTHERS JUST REPEAT SIMPLE MOTIONS, LIKE PULLING TRIGGERS AND SWINGING THEIR ARMS.
IT MIGHT BE USEFUL AS A BLUFF...
...BUT NOW I SEE WHY YOU CAN ONLY FIGHT WITH SNEAK ATTACKS.
ZAN (SLASH)
IF YOU PARTICI-PATED IN A REGULAR FIGHT...
...IT WOULDN'T TAKE VERY LONG FOR PEOPLE TO SEE THROUGH YOUR LACK-LUSTER ABILITY.

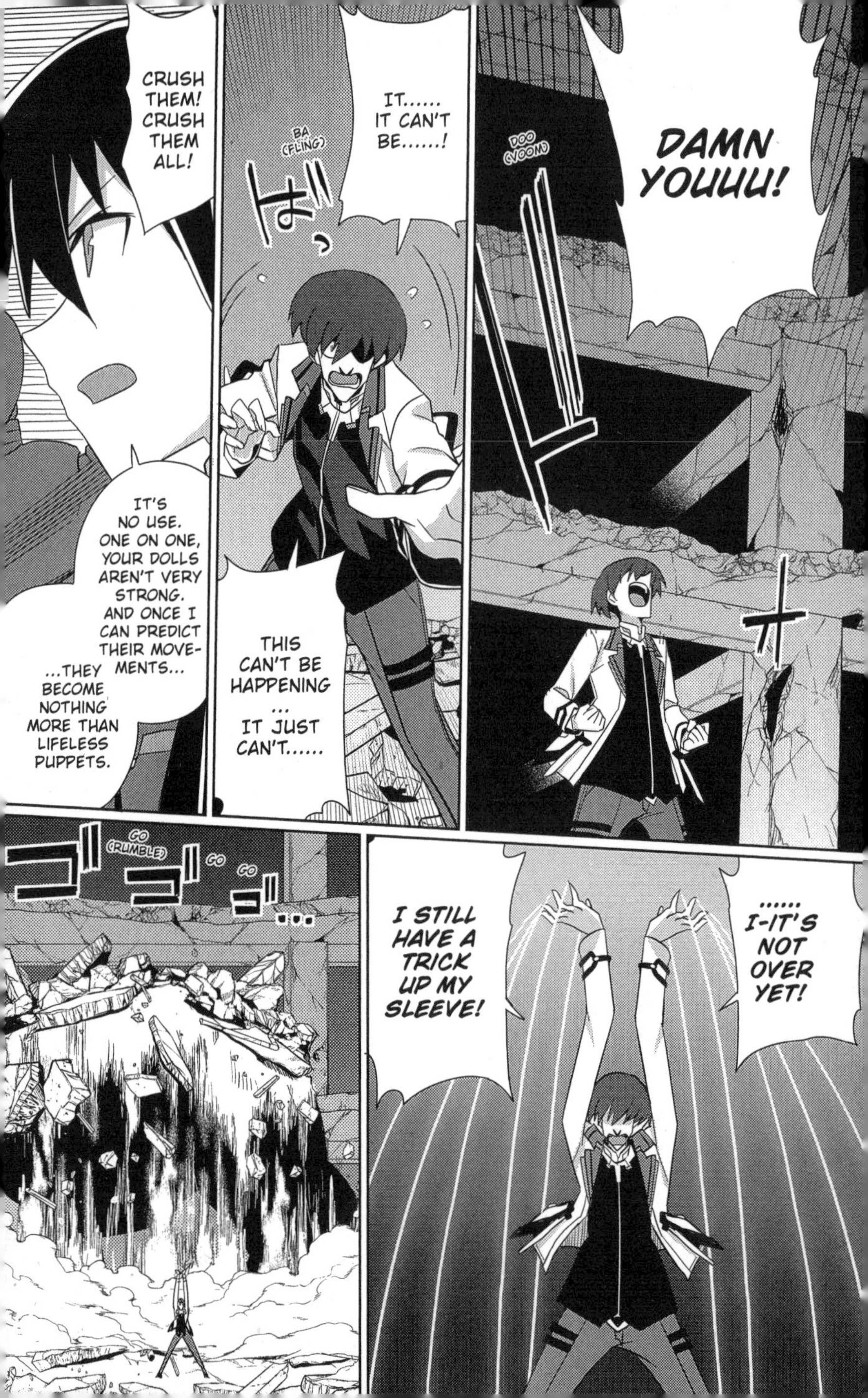
DAMN YOUUU!
DOO (VOOM)
IT...... IT CAN'T BE......!
BA (FLING)
THIS CAN'T BE HAPPENING ... IT JUST CAN'T......
CRUSH THEM! CRUSH THEM ALL!
IT'S NO USE. ONE ON ONE, YOUR DOLLS AREN'T VERY STRONG. AND ONCE I CAN PREDICT THEIR MOVEMENTS...
...THEY BECOME NOTHING MORE THAN LIFELESS PUPPETS.
...... I-IT'S NOT OVER YET!
I STILL HAVE A TRICK UP MY SLEEVE!
GO (RUMBLE) GO GO

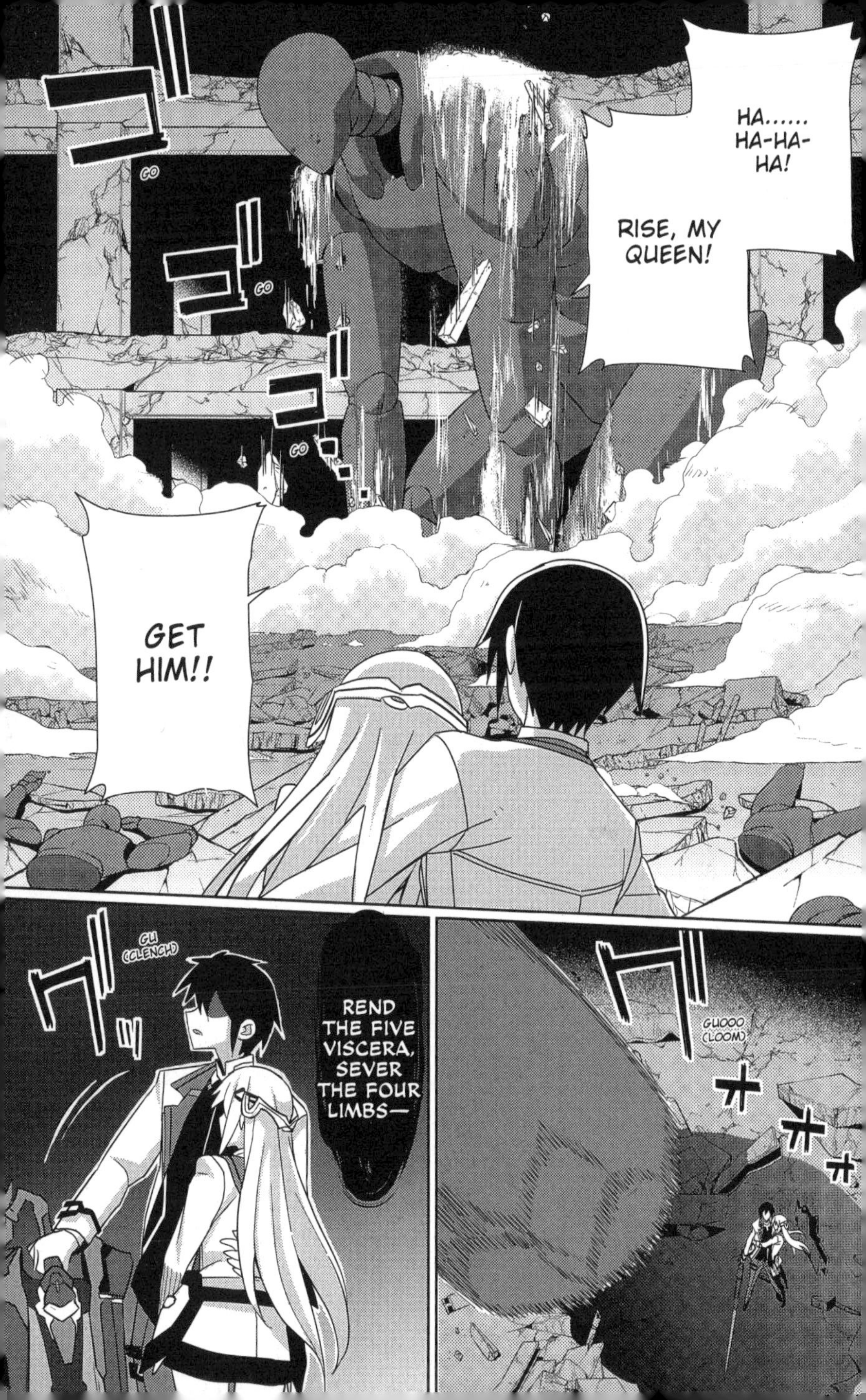
HA...... HA-HA-HA!
RISE, MY QUEEN!
GO
GO
GO
GET HIM!!
GUOOO (LOOM)
REND THE FIVE VISCERA, SEVER THE FOUR LIMBS—
GU (CLENCH)

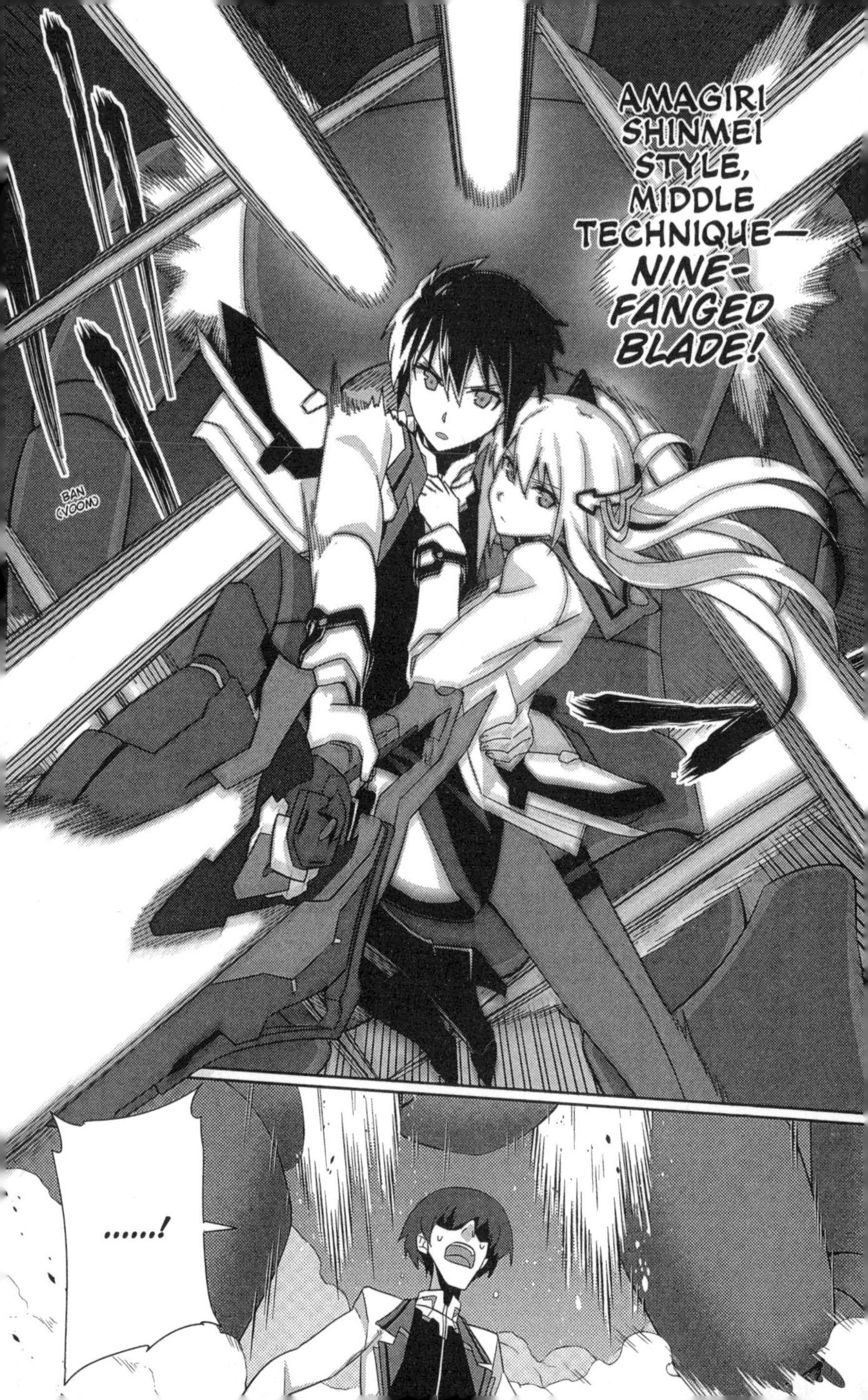
AMAGIRI SHINMEI STYLE, MIDDLE TECHNIQUE—NINE-FANGED BLADE!
BAN (VOOM)
......!

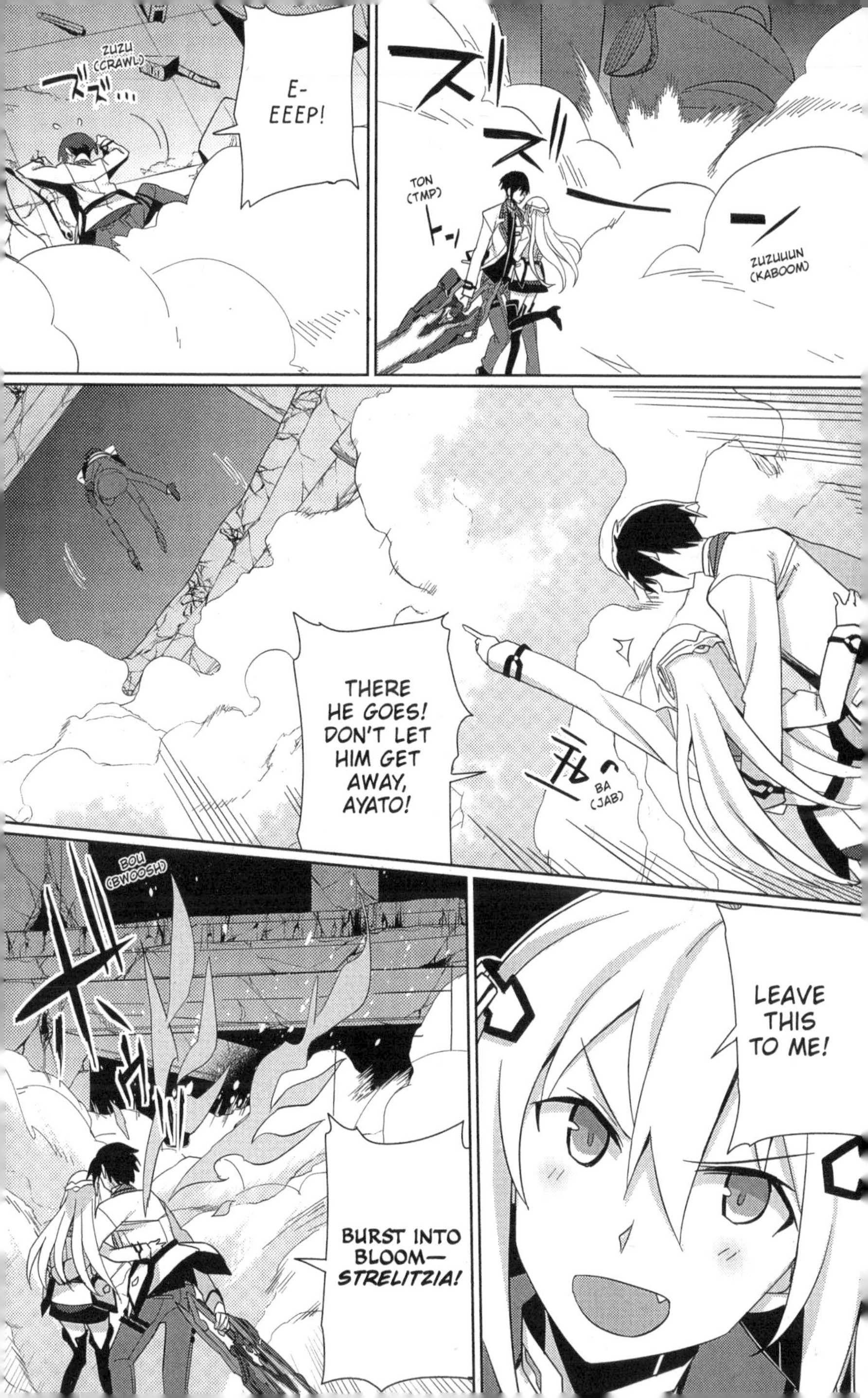

TON (TMP)
ZUZUUUN (KABOOM)
ZUZU (CRAWL)
E- EEEP!
THERE HE GOES! DON'T LET HIM GET AWAY, AYATO!
BA (JAB)
LEAVE THIS TO ME!
BOU (BWOOSH)
BURST INTO BLOOM—*STRELITZIA!*

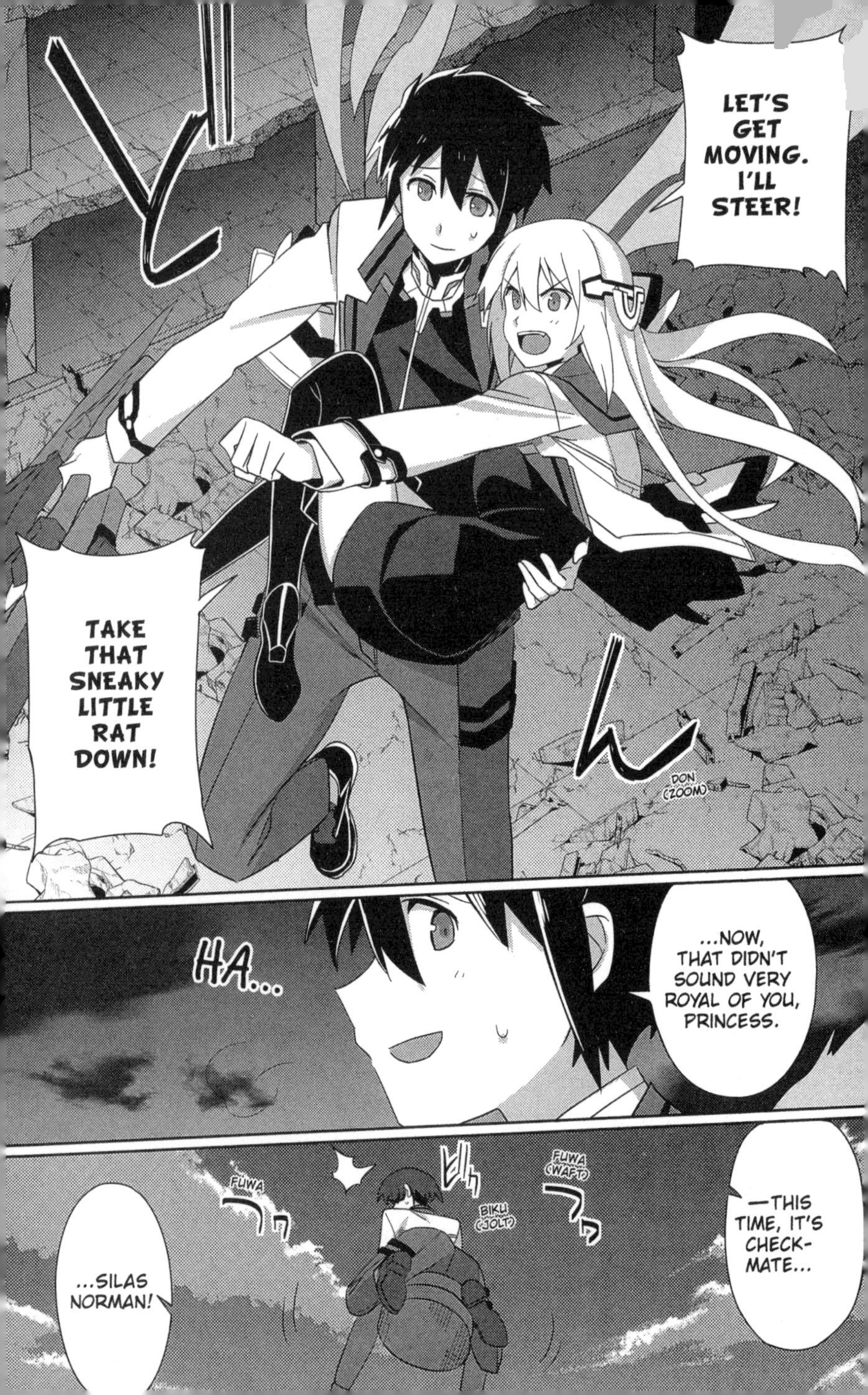
LET'S GET MOVING. I'LL STEER!
TAKE THAT SNEAKY LITTLE RAT DOWN!
DON (ZOOM)
...NOW, THAT DIDN'T SOUND VERY ROYAL OF YOU, PRINCESS.
HA...
—THIS TIME, IT'S CHECK-MATE...
FUWA (WAFT)
BIKU (JOLT)
FUWA
...SILAS NORMAN!

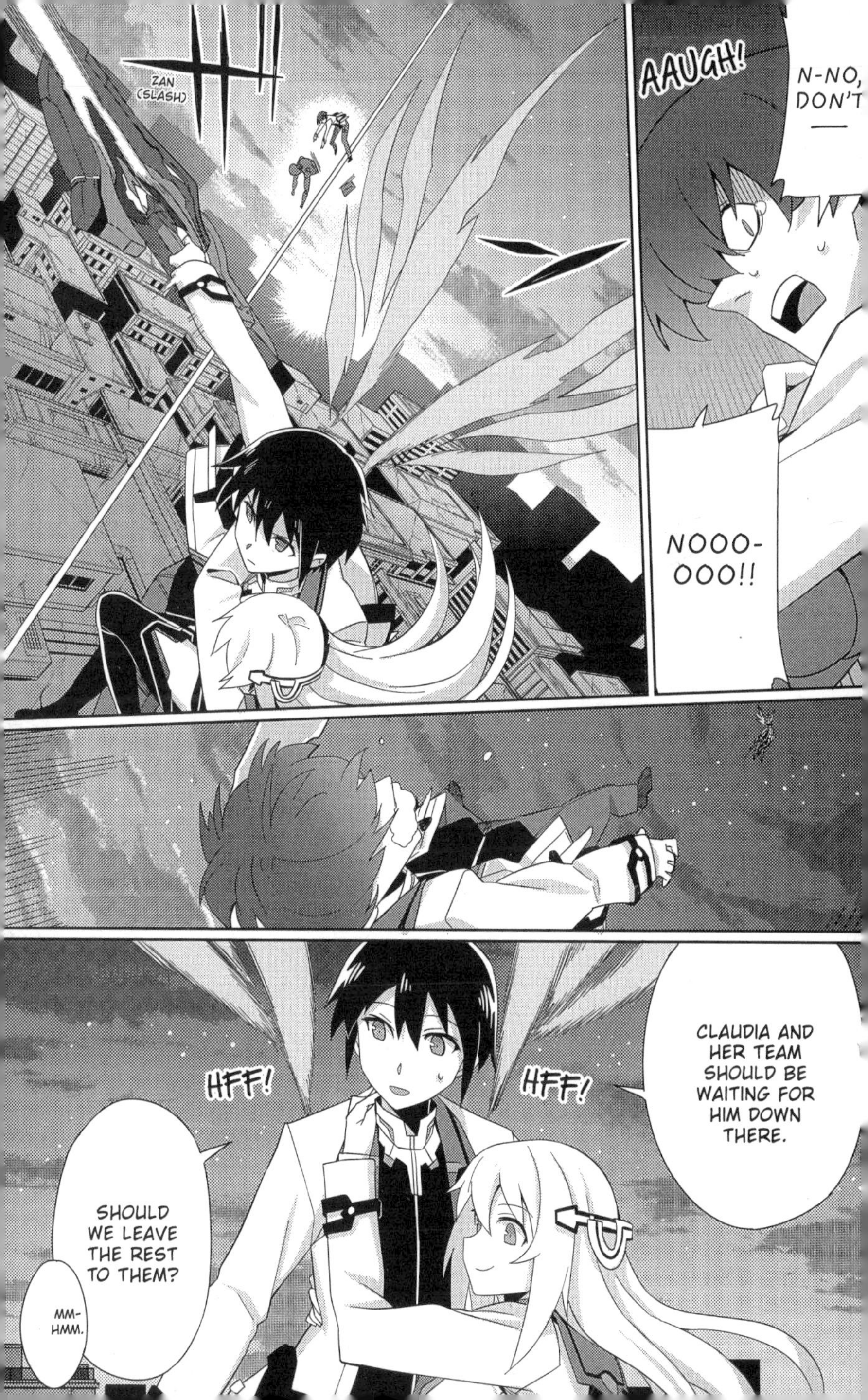
AAUGH!
N-NO, DON'T —
NOOO-OOO!!
ZAN (SLASH)
CLAUDIA AND HER TEAM SHOULD BE WAITING FOR HIM DOWN THERE.
HFF!
HFF!
SHOULD WE LEAVE THE REST TO THEM?
MM-HMM.

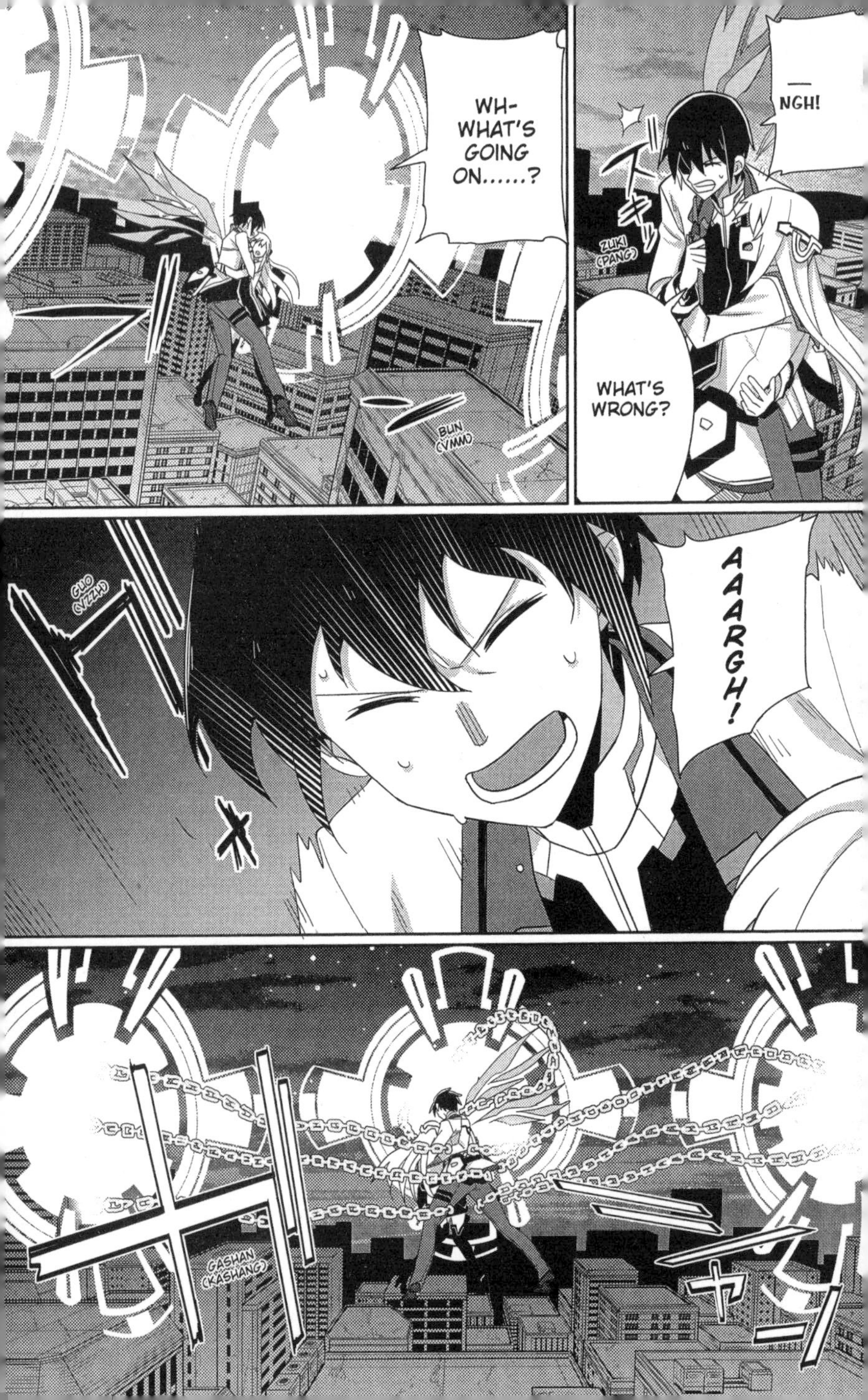
—NGH!
ZUKI (PANG)
WHAT'S WRONG?
WH- WHAT'S GOING ON......?
BUN (VMM)
AAARGH!
GUO (VZZH)
GASHAN (KASHANG)

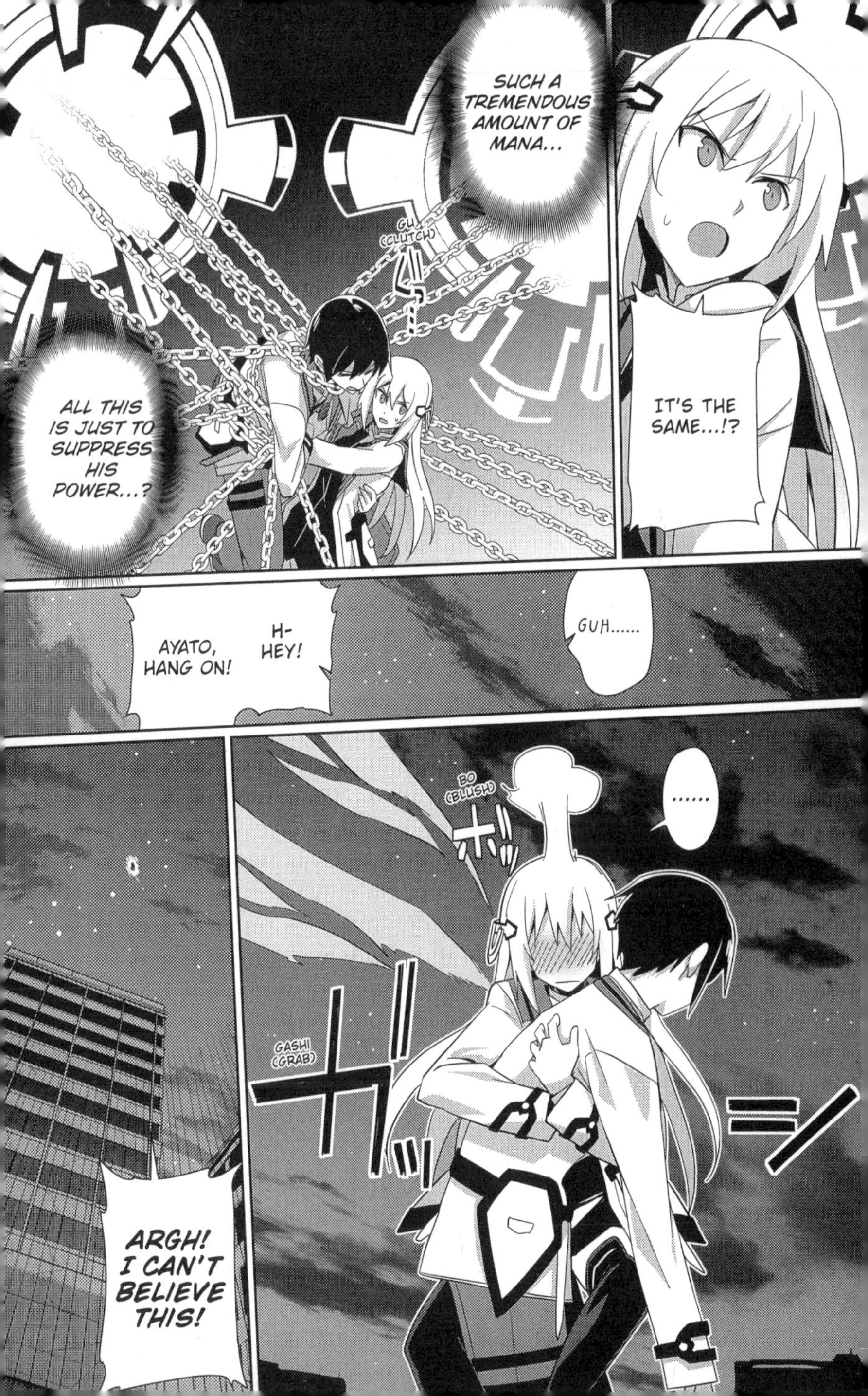
IT'S THE SAME...!?
SUCH A TREMENDOUS AMOUNT OF MANA...
GU (CLUTCH)
ALL THIS IS JUST TO SUPPRESS HIS POWER...?
GUH......
H- HEY!
AYATO, HANG ON!
......
BO (BLUSH)
GASHI (GRAB)
ARGH! I CAN'T BELIEVE THIS!

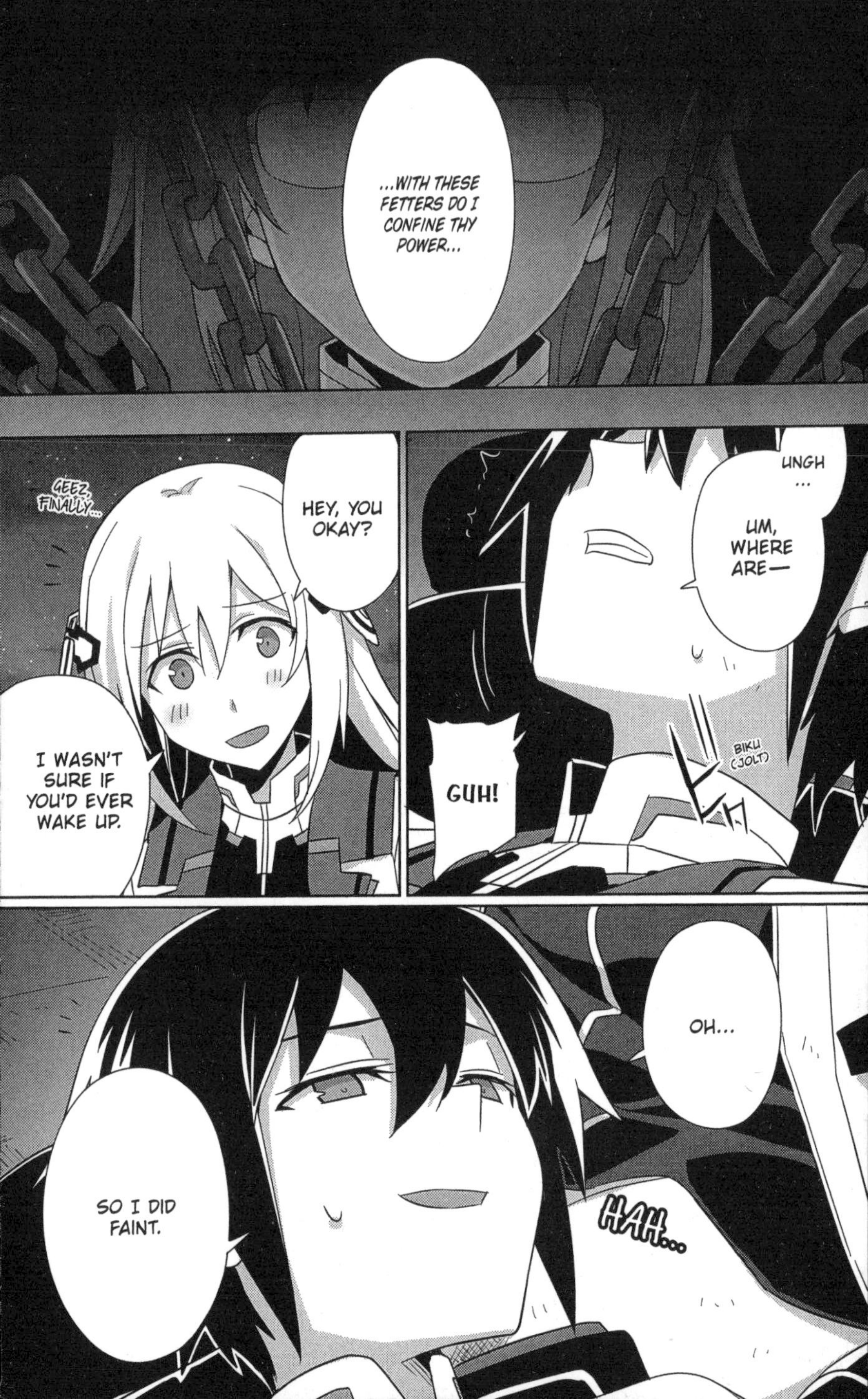
...WITH THESE FETTERS DO I CONFINE THY POWER...
UNGH ...
UM, WHERE ARE—
BIKU (JOLT)
GUH!
HEY, YOU OKAY?
GEEZ, FINALLY...
I WASN'T SURE IF YOU'D EVER WAKE UP.
OH...
HAH...
SO I DID FAINT.

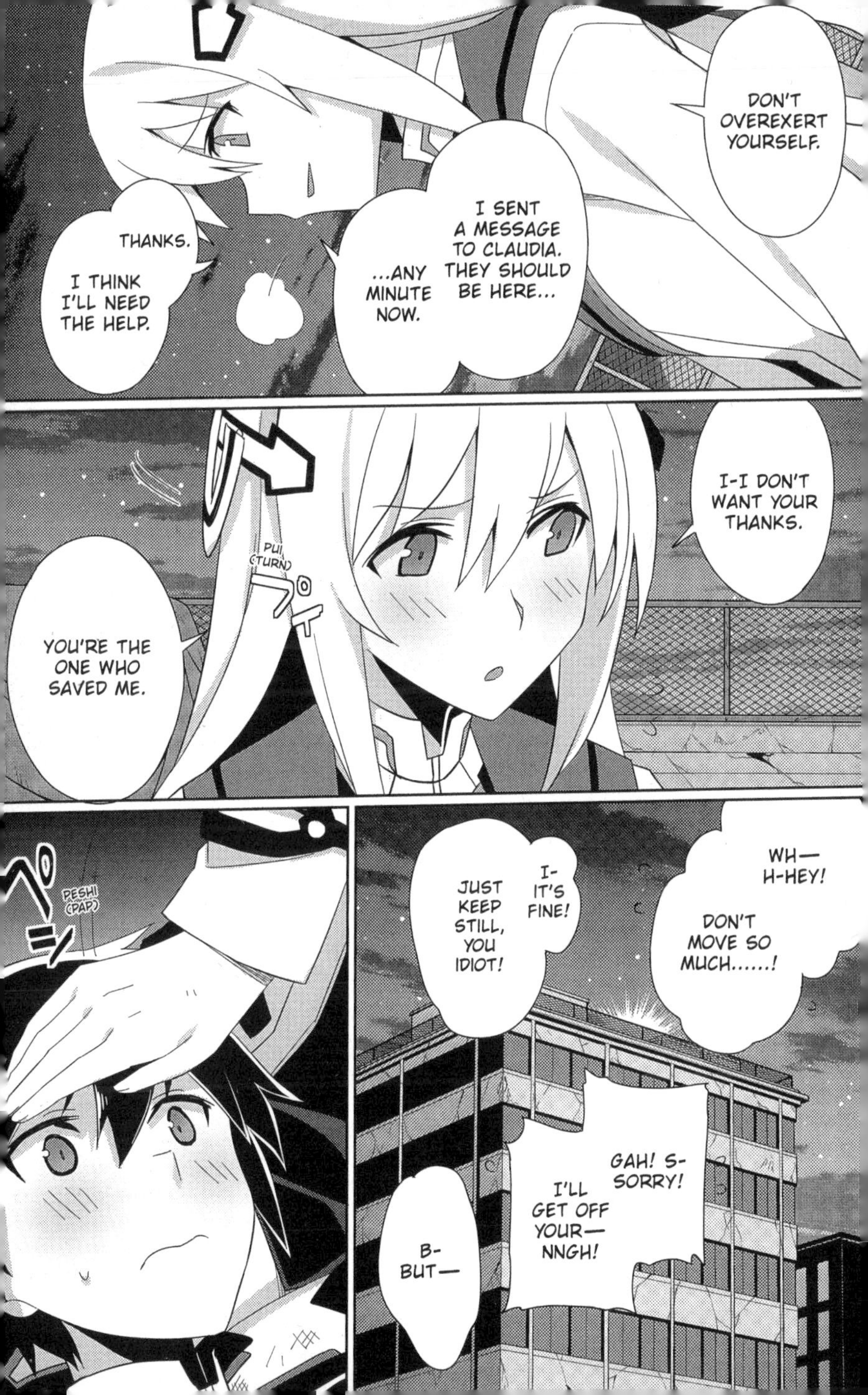
DON'T OVEREXERT YOURSELF.
I SENT A MESSAGE TO CLAUDIA. THEY SHOULD BE HERE...
...ANY MINUTE NOW.
THANKS.
I THINK I'LL NEED THE HELP.
I-I DON'T WANT YOUR THANKS.
PUI (TURN)
YOU'RE THE ONE WHO SAVED ME.
WH— H-HEY!
DON'T MOVE SO MUCH......!
I- IT'S FINE!
JUST KEEP STILL, YOU IDIOT!
GAH! S-SORRY!
I'LL GET OFF YOUR— NNGH!
B-BUT—
PESHI (PAP)

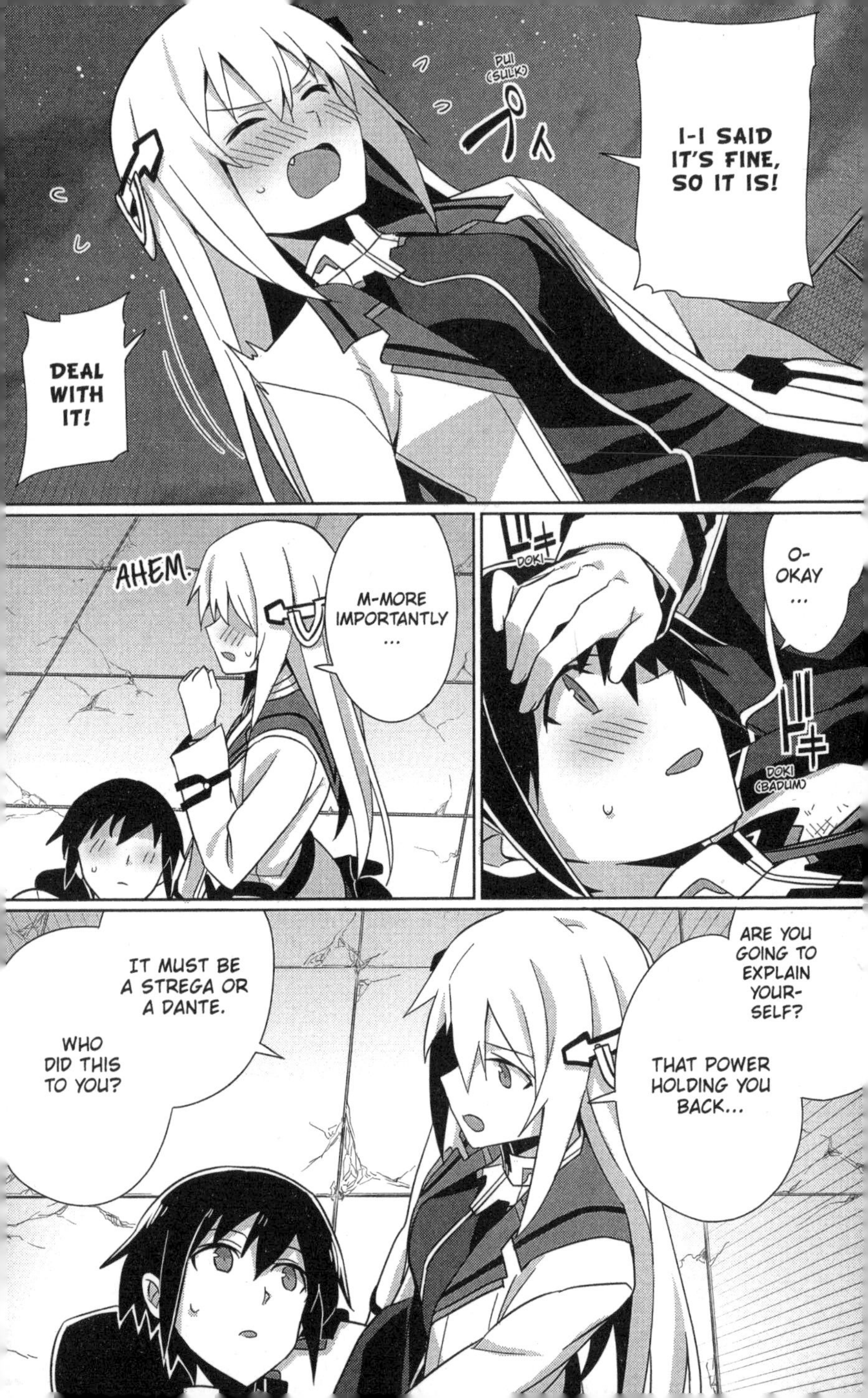
I-I SAID IT'S FINE, SO IT IS!
PUI (SULK)
DEAL WITH IT!
DOKI
O-OKAY...
DOKI (BADUM)
M-MORE IMPORTANTLY...
AHEM.
ARE YOU GOING TO EXPLAIN YOURSELF?
THAT POWER HOLDING YOU BACK...
IT MUST BE A STREGA OR A DANTE.
WHO DID THIS TO YOU?

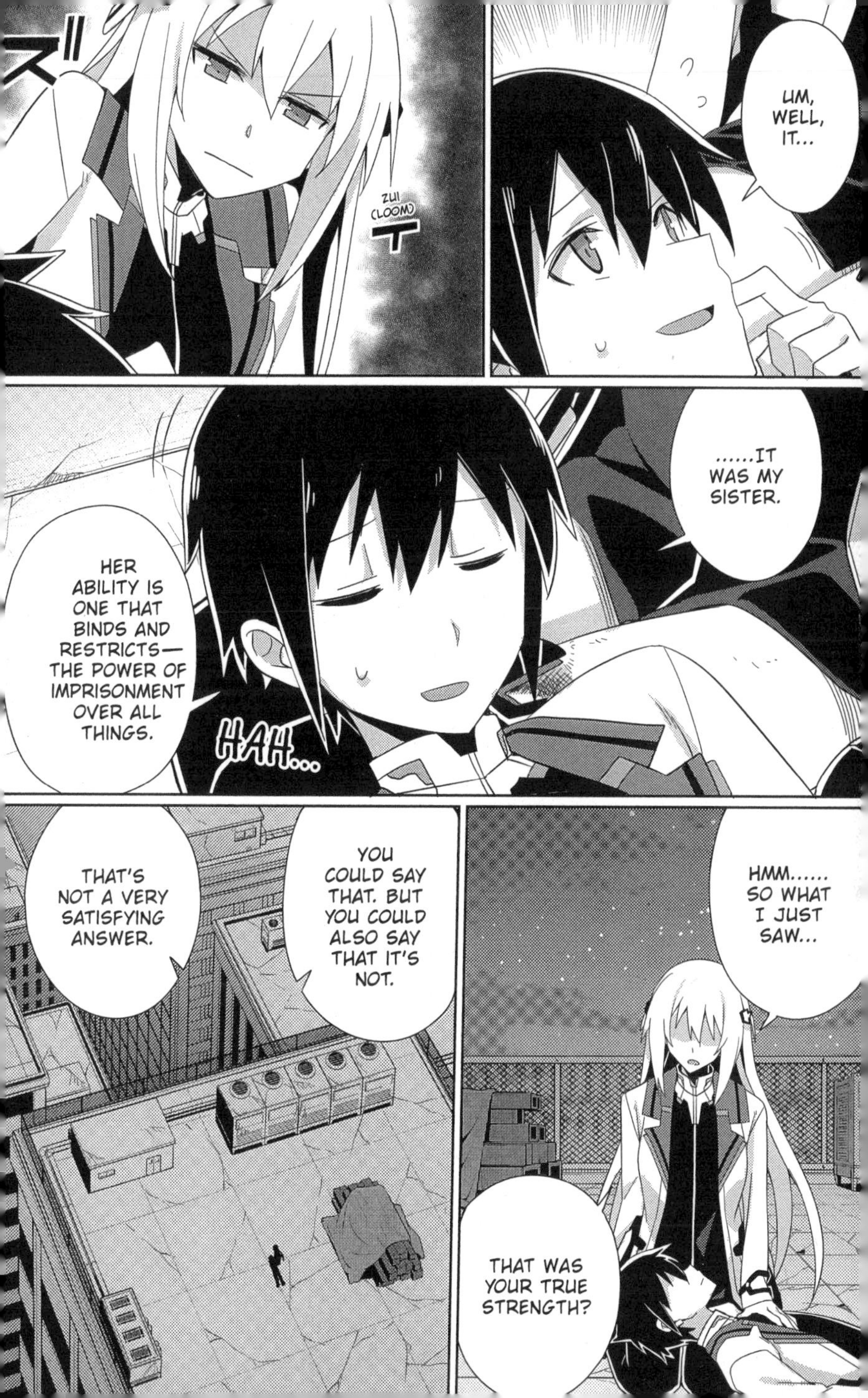
UM, WELL, IT...
ZUI (LOOM)
......IT WAS MY SISTER.
HER ABILITY IS ONE THAT BINDS AND RESTRICTS— THE POWER OF IMPRISONMENT OVER ALL THINGS.
HAH...
HMM...... SO WHAT I JUST SAW...
THAT WAS YOUR TRUE STRENGTH?
YOU COULD SAY THAT. BUT YOU COULD ALSO SAY THAT IT'S NOT.
THAT'S NOT A VERY SATISFYING ANSWER.

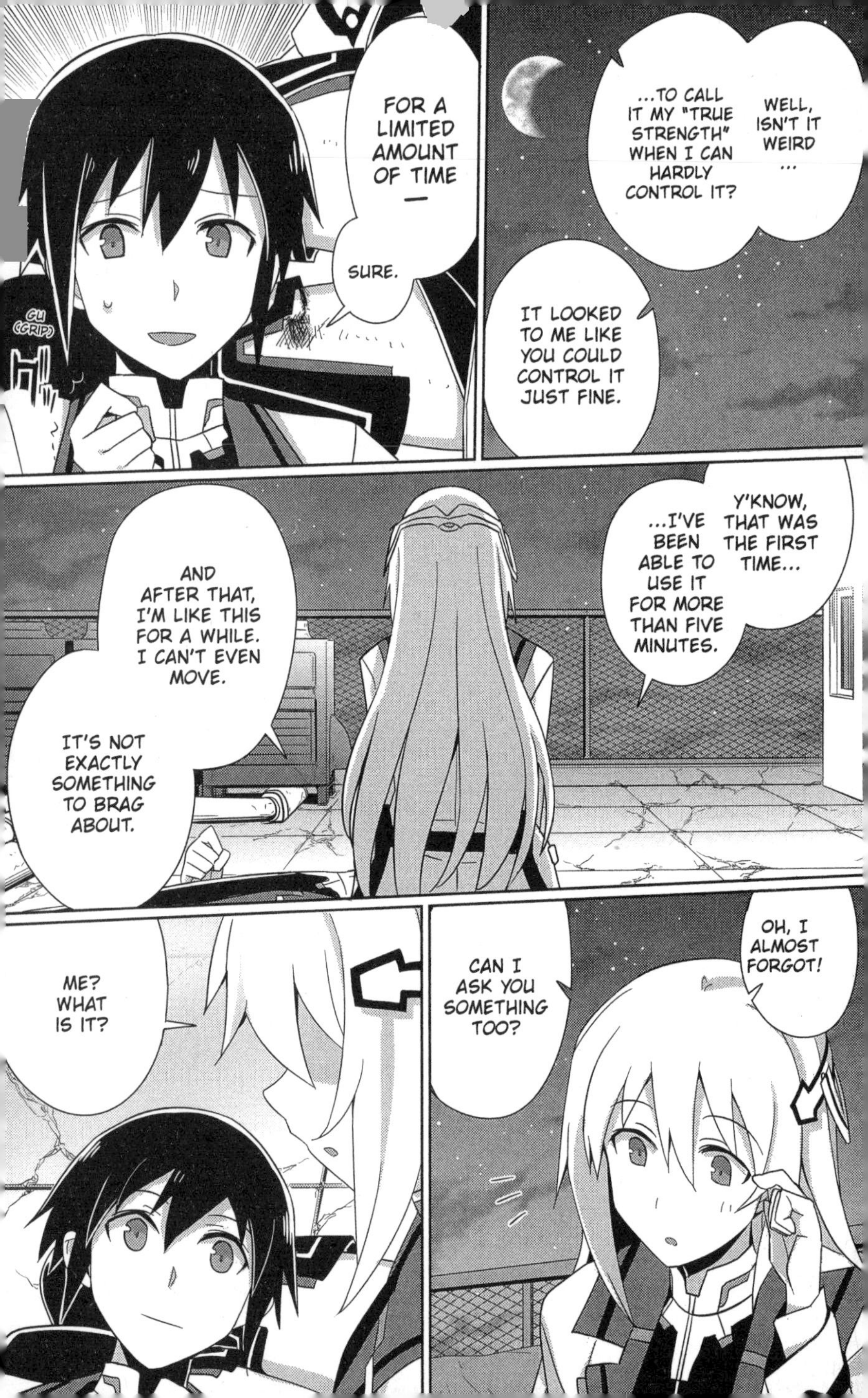
WELL, ISN'T IT WEIRD...
...TO CALL IT MY "TRUE STRENGTH" WHEN I CAN HARDLY CONTROL IT?
IT LOOKED TO ME LIKE YOU COULD CONTROL IT JUST FINE.
FOR A LIMITED AMOUNT OF TIME—
SURE.
GU (GRIP)
Y'KNOW, THAT WAS THE FIRST TIME...
...I'VE BEEN ABLE TO USE IT FOR MORE THAN FIVE MINUTES.
AND AFTER THAT, I'M LIKE THIS FOR A WHILE. I CAN'T EVEN MOVE.
IT'S NOT EXACTLY SOMETHING TO BRAG ABOUT.
OH, I ALMOST FORGOT!
CAN I ASK YOU SOMETHING TOO?
ME? WHAT IS IT?

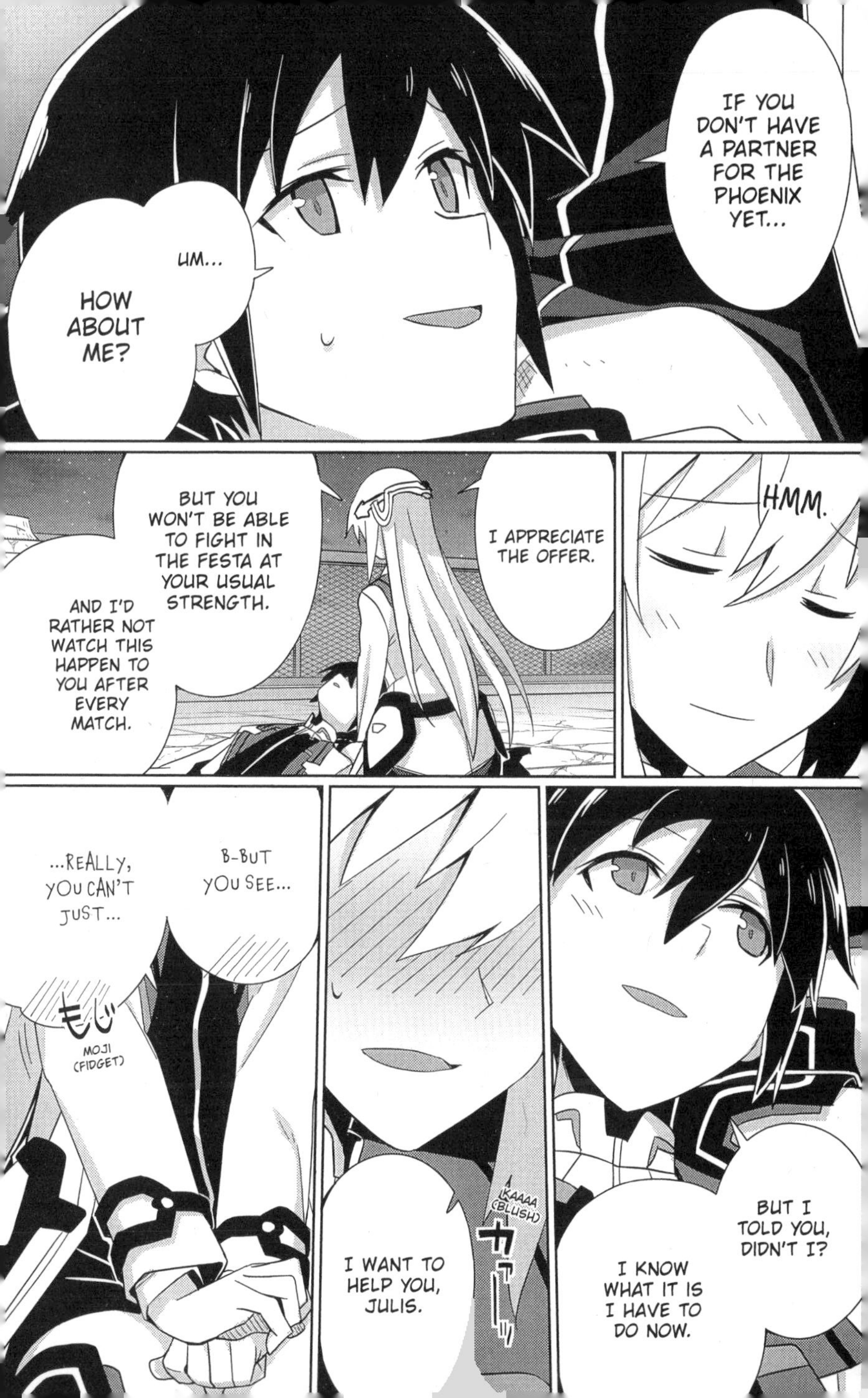
IF YOU DON'T HAVE A PARTNER FOR THE PHOENIX YET...
UM...
HOW ABOUT ME?
HMM.
I APPRECIATE THE OFFER.
BUT YOU WON'T BE ABLE TO FIGHT IN THE FESTA AT YOUR USUAL STRENGTH.
AND I'D RATHER NOT WATCH THIS HAPPEN TO YOU AFTER EVERY MATCH.
BUT I TOLD YOU, DIDN'T I?
I KNOW WHAT IT IS I HAVE TO DO NOW.
I WANT TO HELP YOU, JULIS.
カァーッ
KAAAA (BLUSH)
B-BUT YOU SEE...
...REALLY, YOU CAN'T JUST...
もじ
MOJI (FIDGET)

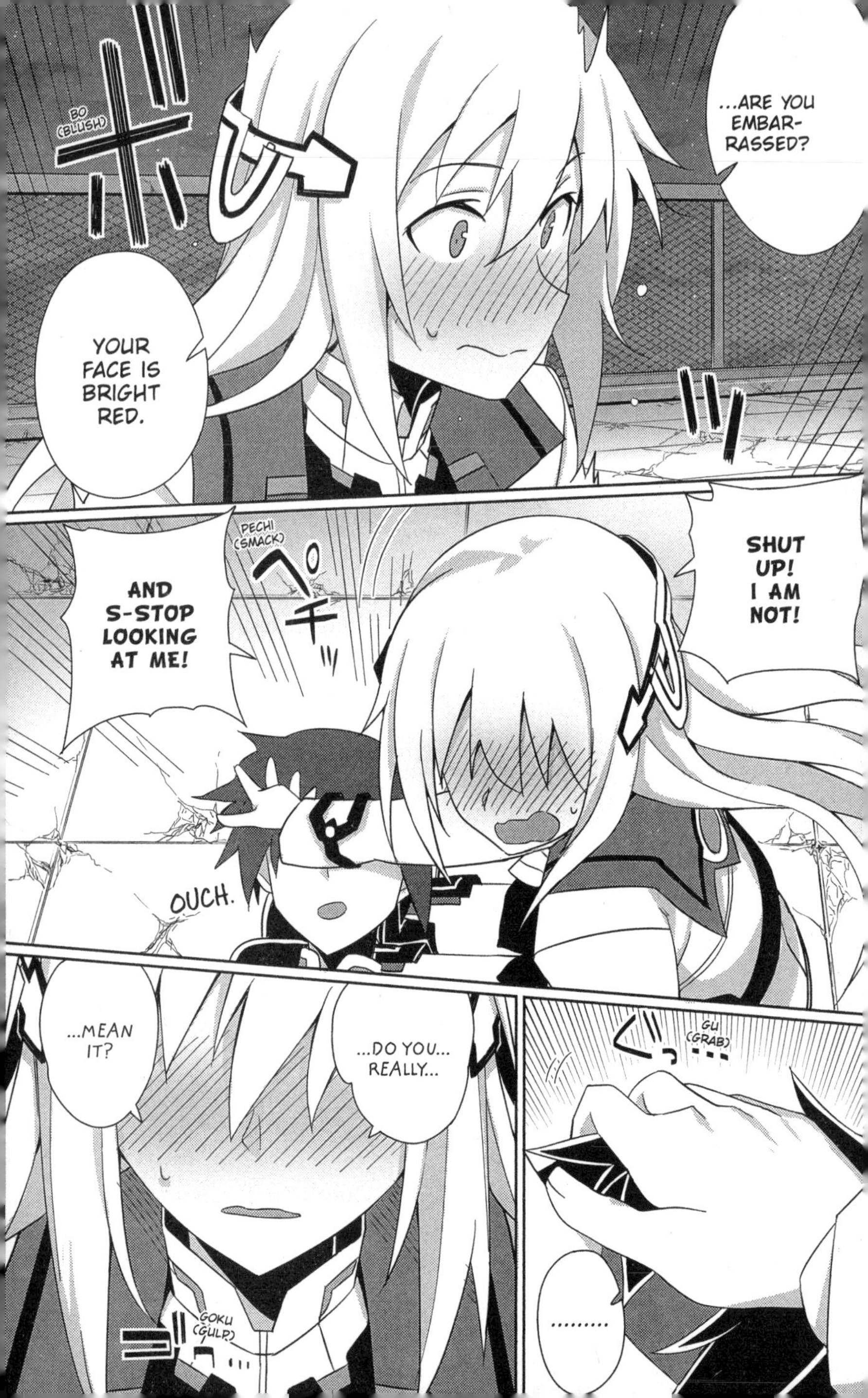
...ARE YOU EMBAR-RASSED?
BO (BLUSH)
YOUR FACE IS BRIGHT RED.
SHUT UP! I AM NOT!
PECHI (SMACK)
AND S-STOP LOOKING AT ME!
OUCH.
GU (GRAB)
....
...DO YOU... REALLY...
...MEAN IT?
GOKU (GULP)

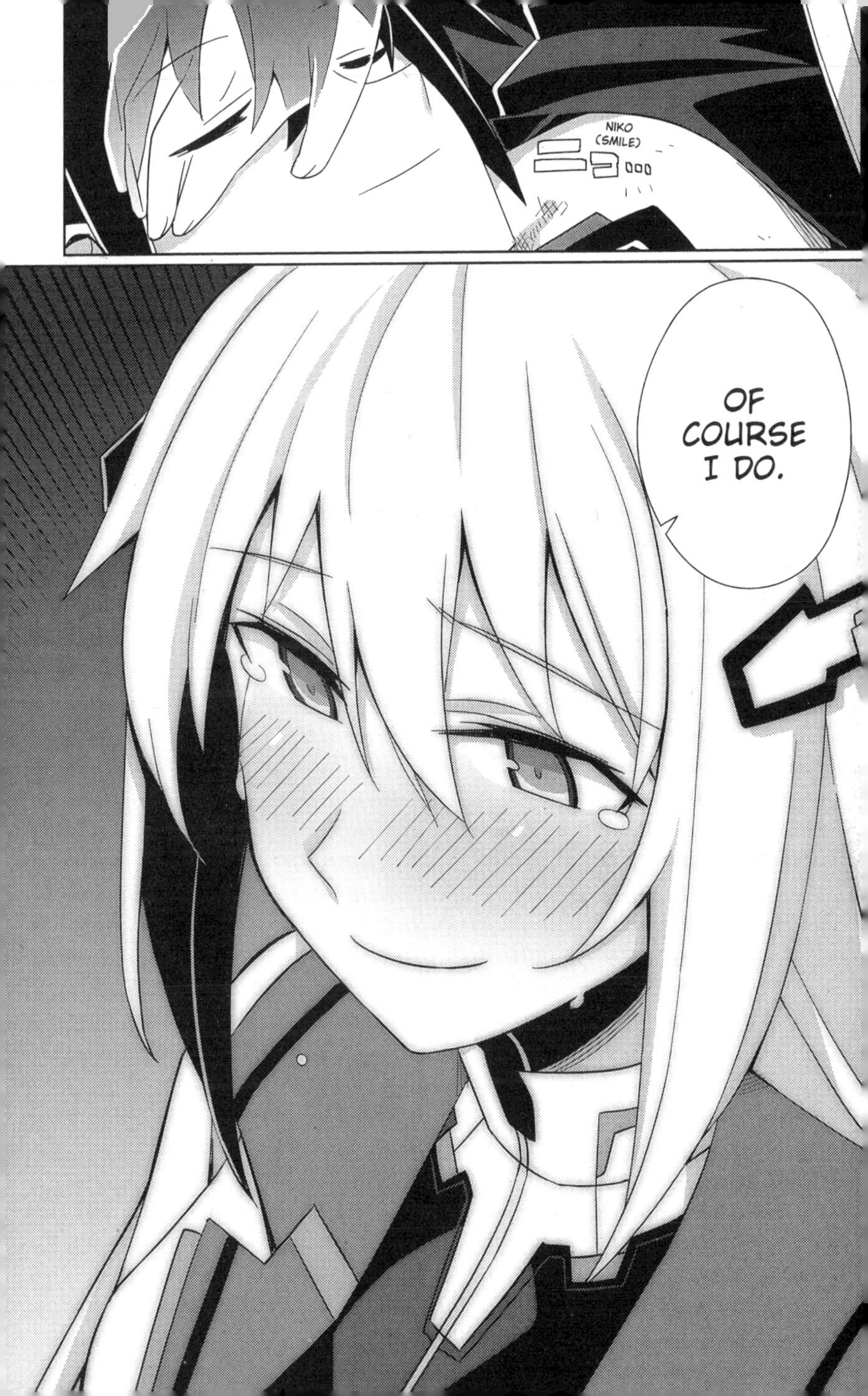
NIKO (SMILE)
OF COURSE I DO.

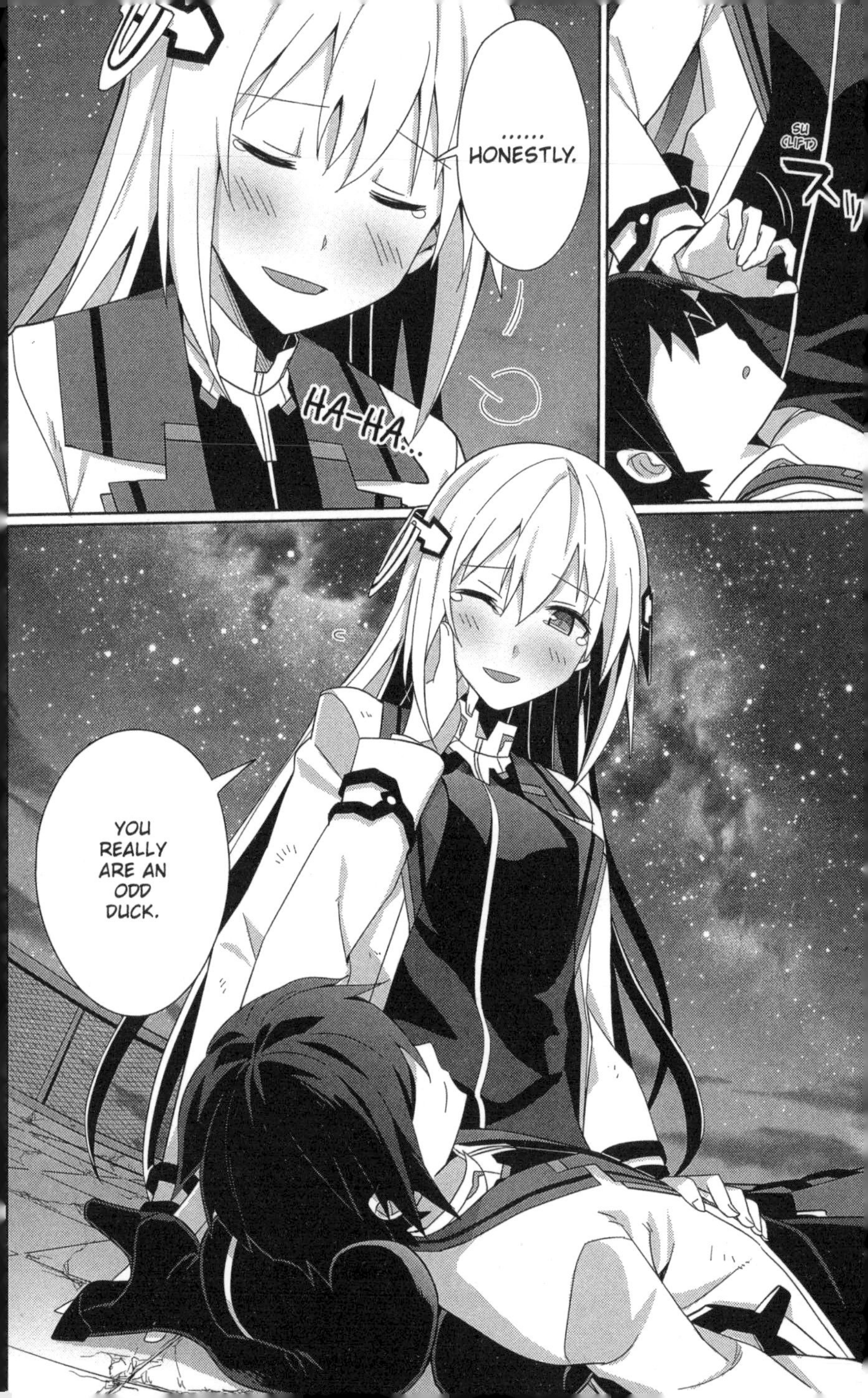
SU (LIFT)
スッ
......
HONESTLY.
HA-HA...
YOU REALLY ARE AN ODD DUCK.

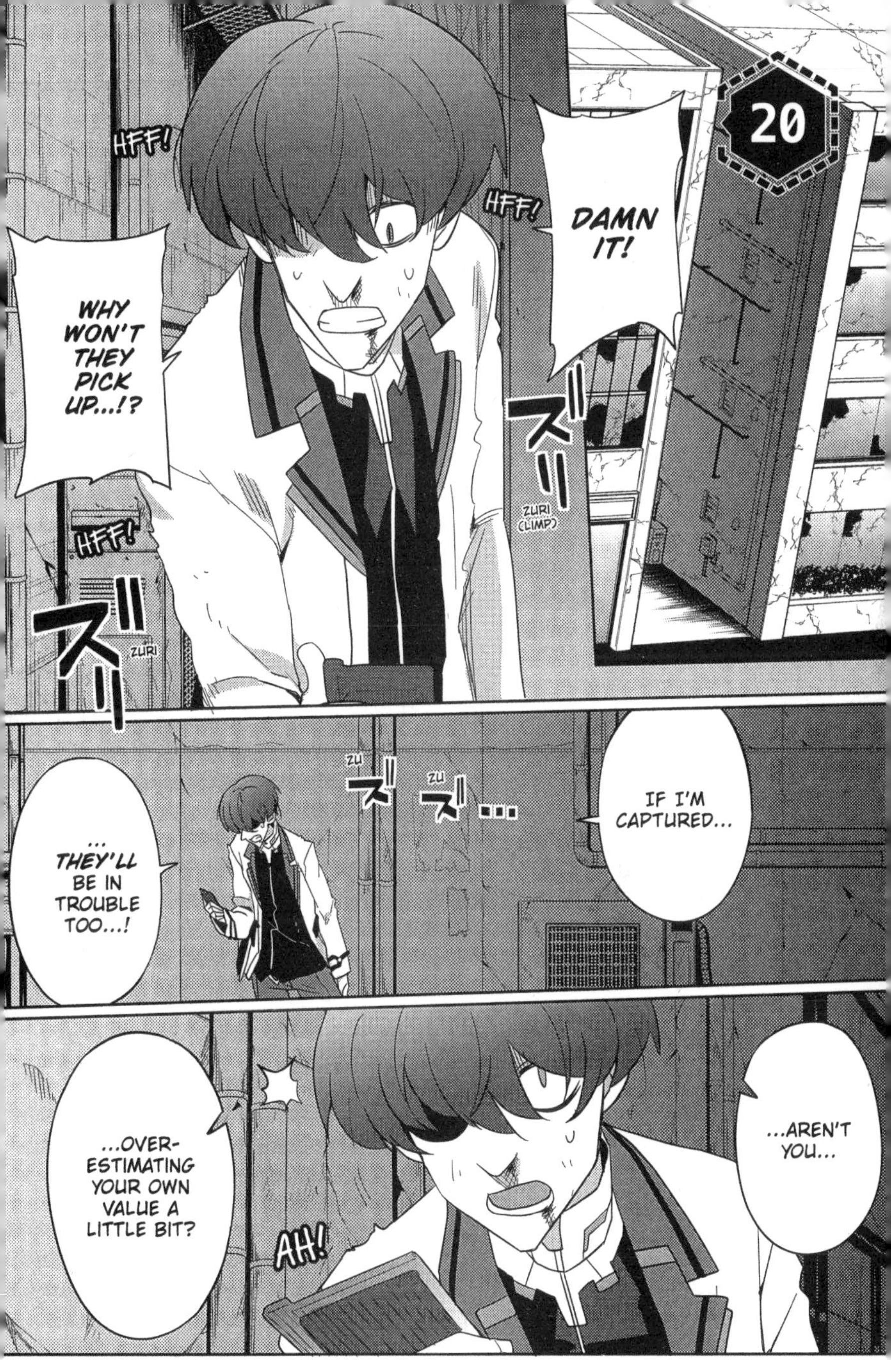

20
DAMN IT!
HFF!
HFF!
WHY WON'T THEY PICK UP...!?
ズリ
ZURI (LIMP)
HFF!
ズリ
ZURI
IF I'M CAPTURED...
ズ
ZU
ズ...
ZU
...THEY'LL BE IN TROUBLE TOO...!
...AREN'T YOU...
...OVER-ESTIMATING YOUR OWN VALUE A LITTLE BIT?
AH!

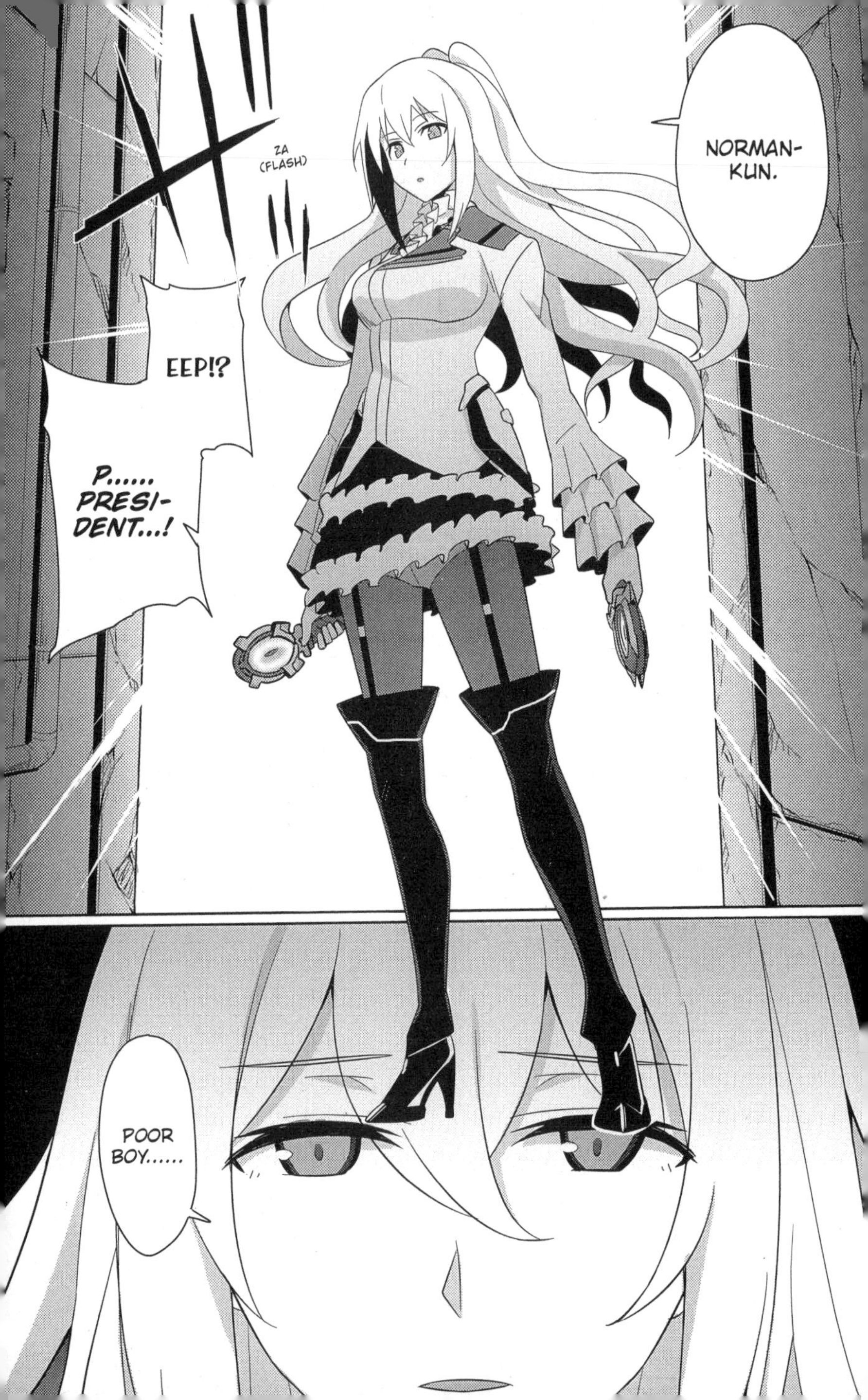
NORMAN-KUN.
ZA (FLASH)
EEP!?
P...... PRESI-DENT...!
POOR BOY......

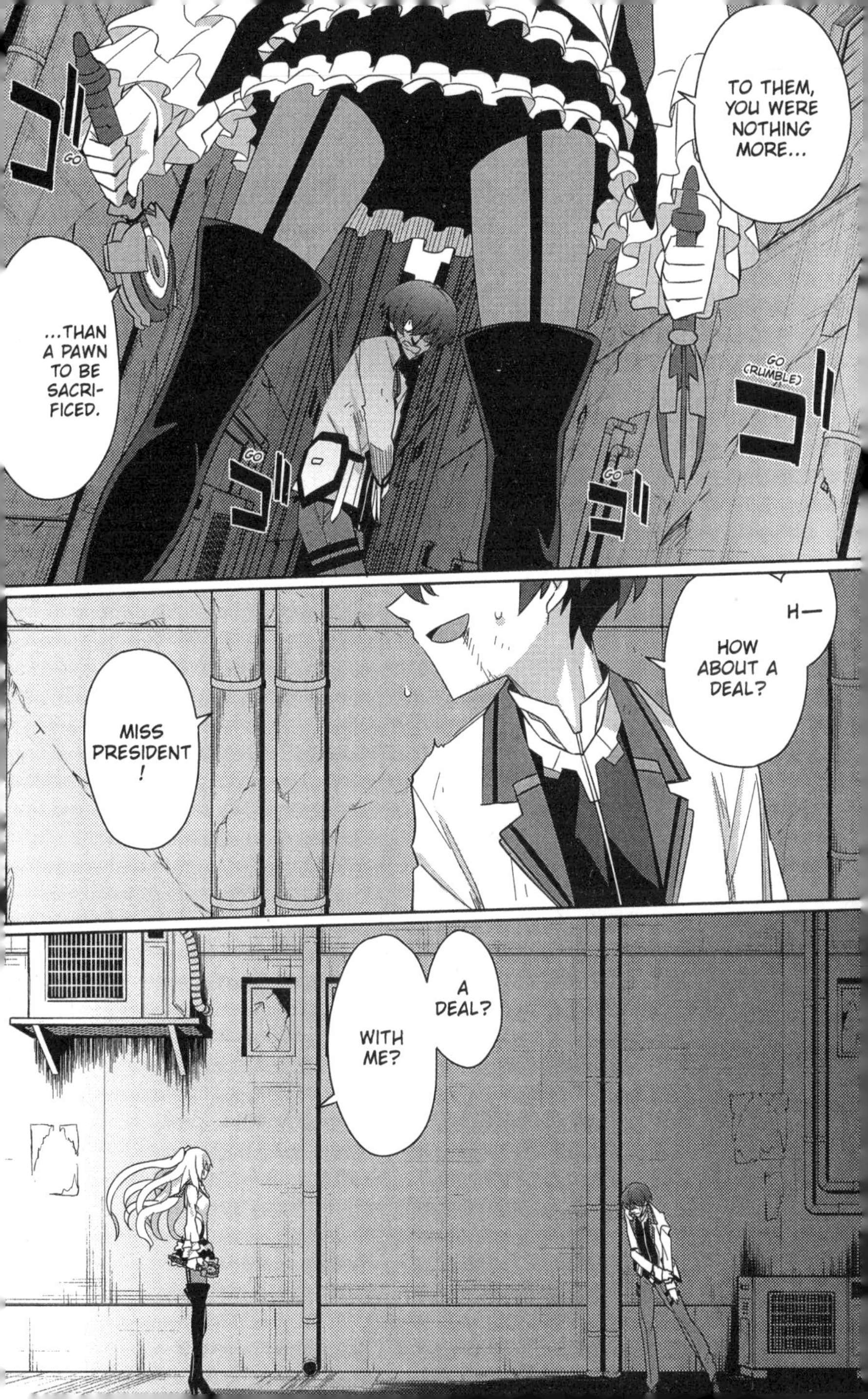
TO THEM, YOU WERE NOTHING MORE...
GO (RUMBLE)
GO
GO
...THAN A PAWN TO BE SACRIFICED.
GO
H—
HOW ABOUT A DEAL?
MISS PRESIDENT!
A DEAL?
WITH ME?

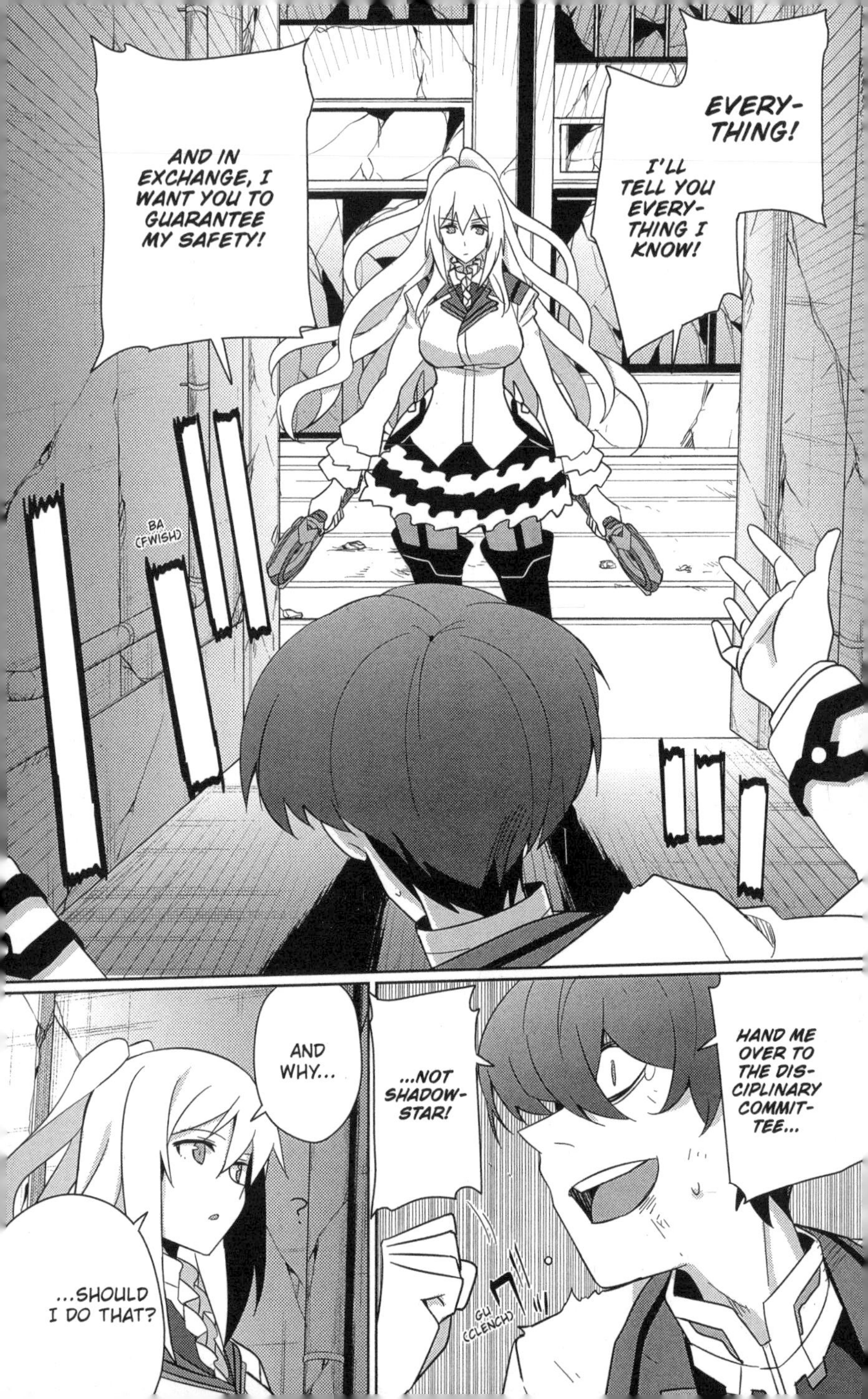
EVERYTHING!
I'LL TELL YOU EVERYTHING I KNOW!
AND IN EXCHANGE, I WANT YOU TO GUARANTEE MY SAFETY!
BA (FWISH)
HAND ME OVER TO THE DISCIPLINARY COMMITTEE...
...NOT SHADOWSTAR!
GU (CLENCH)
AND WHY...
...SHOULD I DO THAT?

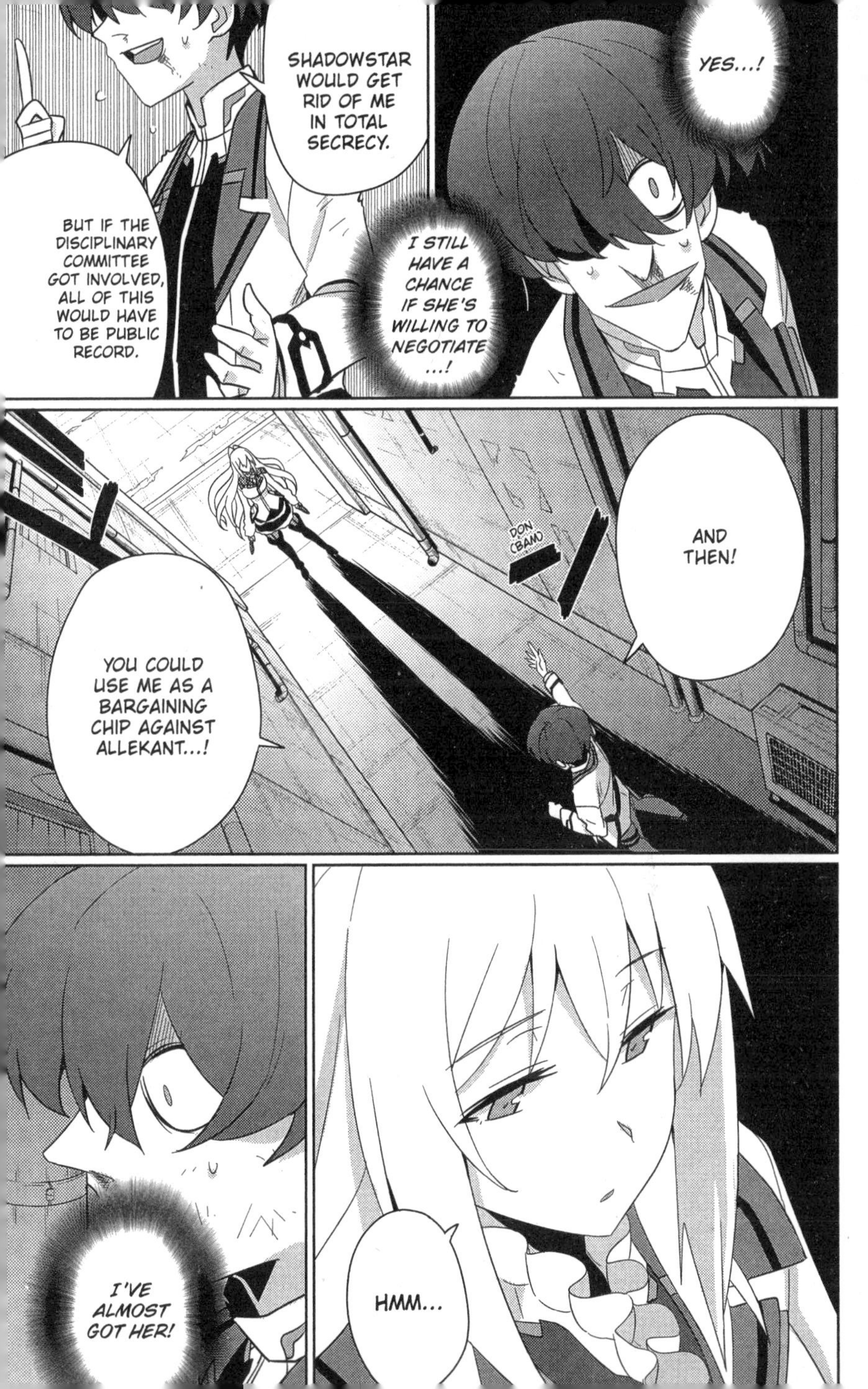
YES...!
I STILL HAVE A CHANCE IF SHE'S WILLING TO NEGOTIATE...!
SHADOWSTAR WOULD GET RID OF ME IN TOTAL SECRECY.
BUT IF THE DISCIPLINARY COMMITTEE GOT INVOLVED, ALL OF THIS WOULD HAVE TO BE PUBLIC RECORD.
AND THEN!
DON (BAM)
YOU COULD USE ME AS A BARGAINING CHIP AGAINST ALLEKANT...!
HMM...
I'VE ALMOST GOT HER!

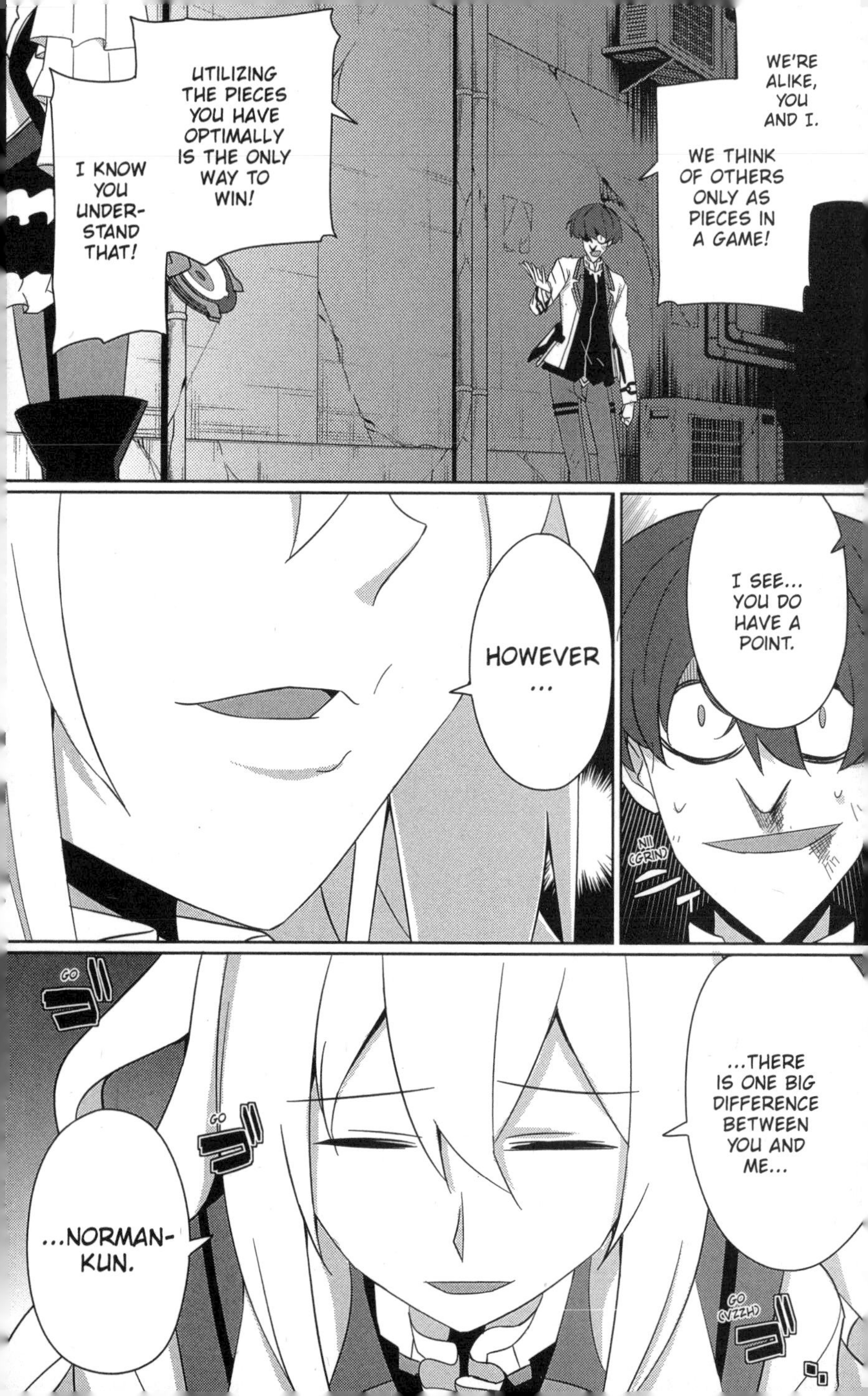
WE'RE ALIKE, YOU AND I.
WE THINK OF OTHERS ONLY AS PIECES IN A GAME!
UTILIZING THE PIECES YOU HAVE OPTIMALLY IS THE ONLY WAY TO WIN!
I KNOW YOU UNDER-STAND THAT!
I SEE... YOU DO HAVE A POINT.
NII (GRIN)
HOWEVER ...
GO (VZZH)
...THERE IS ONE BIG DIFFERENCE BETWEEN YOU AND ME...
GO
...NORMAN-KUN.
GO

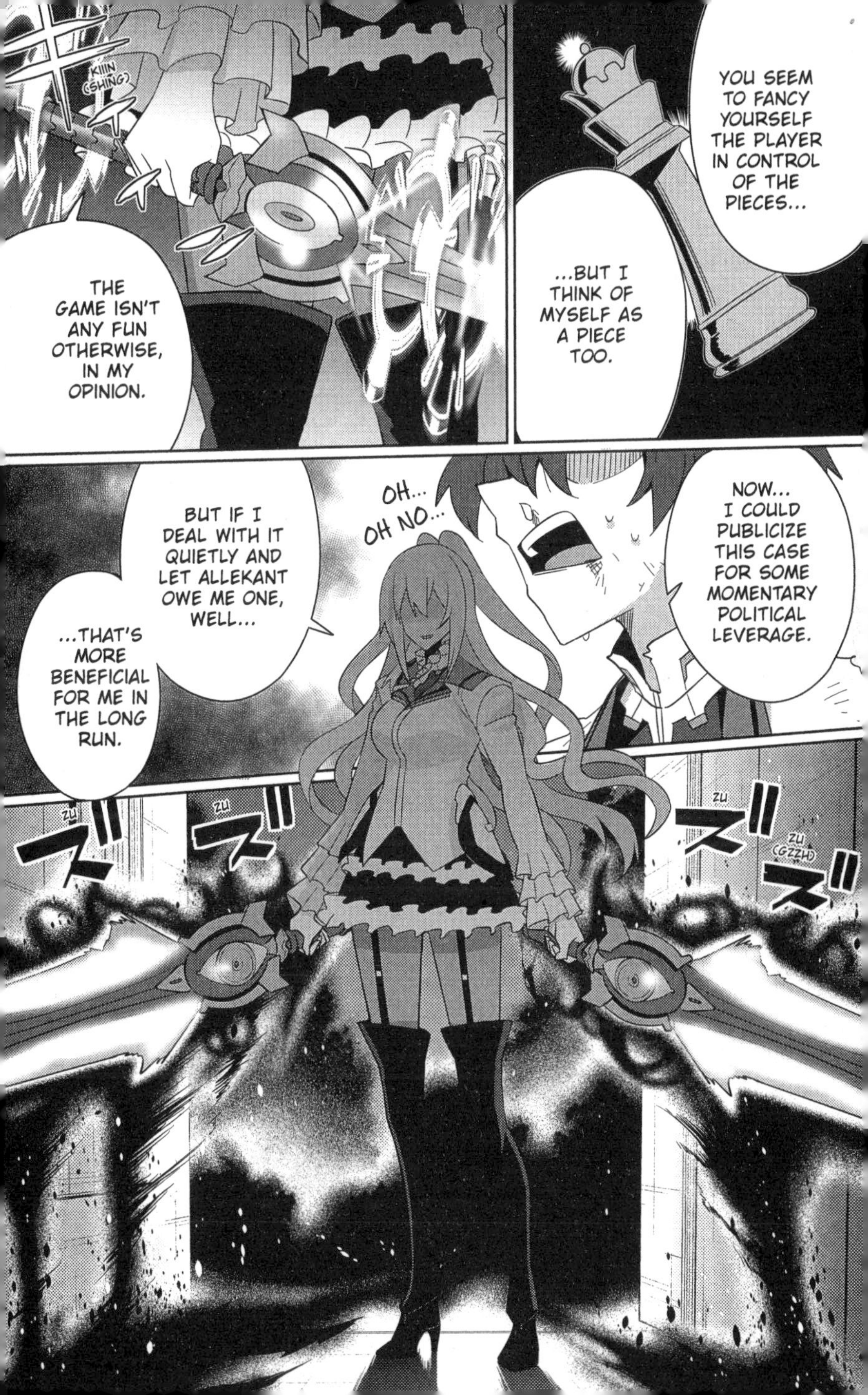

YOU SEEM TO FANCY YOURSELF THE PLAYER IN CONTROL OF THE PIECES...
...BUT I THINK OF MYSELF AS A PIECE TOO.
KIIN (SHING)
THE GAME ISN'T ANY FUN OTHERWISE, IN MY OPINION.
NOW... I COULD PUBLICIZE THIS CASE FOR SOME MOMENTARY POLITICAL LEVERAGE.
OH... OH NO...
BUT IF I DEAL WITH IT QUIETLY AND LET ALLEKANT OWE ME ONE, WELL...
...THAT'S MORE BENEFICIAL FOR ME IN THE LONG RUN.
ZU
ZU (GZZH)
ZU
ZU

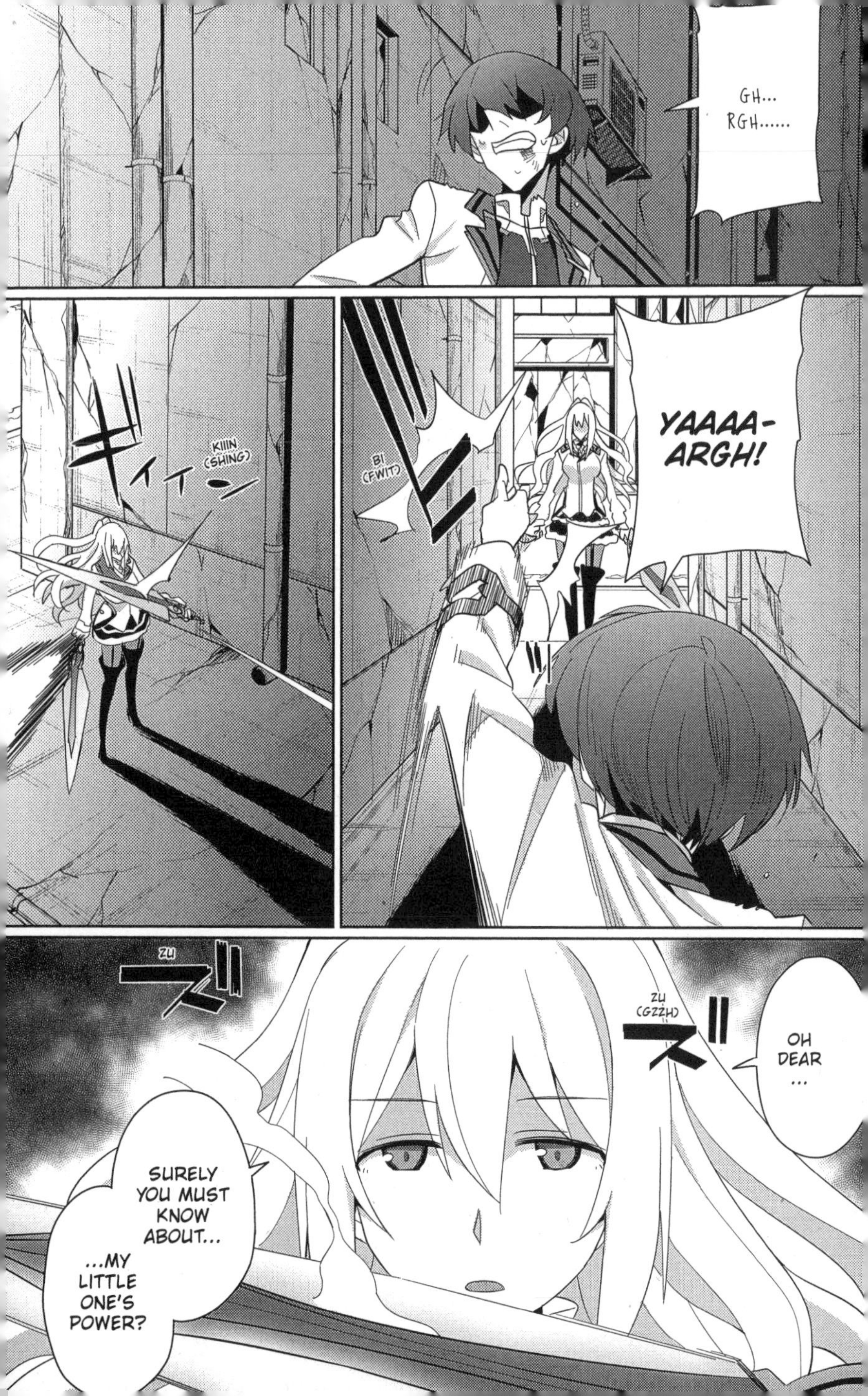
GH... RGH......
YAAAA-ARGH!
BI (FWIT)
KIIN (SHING)
OH DEAR ...
ZU (GZZH)
ZU
SURELY YOU MUST KNOW ABOUT...
...MY LITTLE ONE'S POWER?

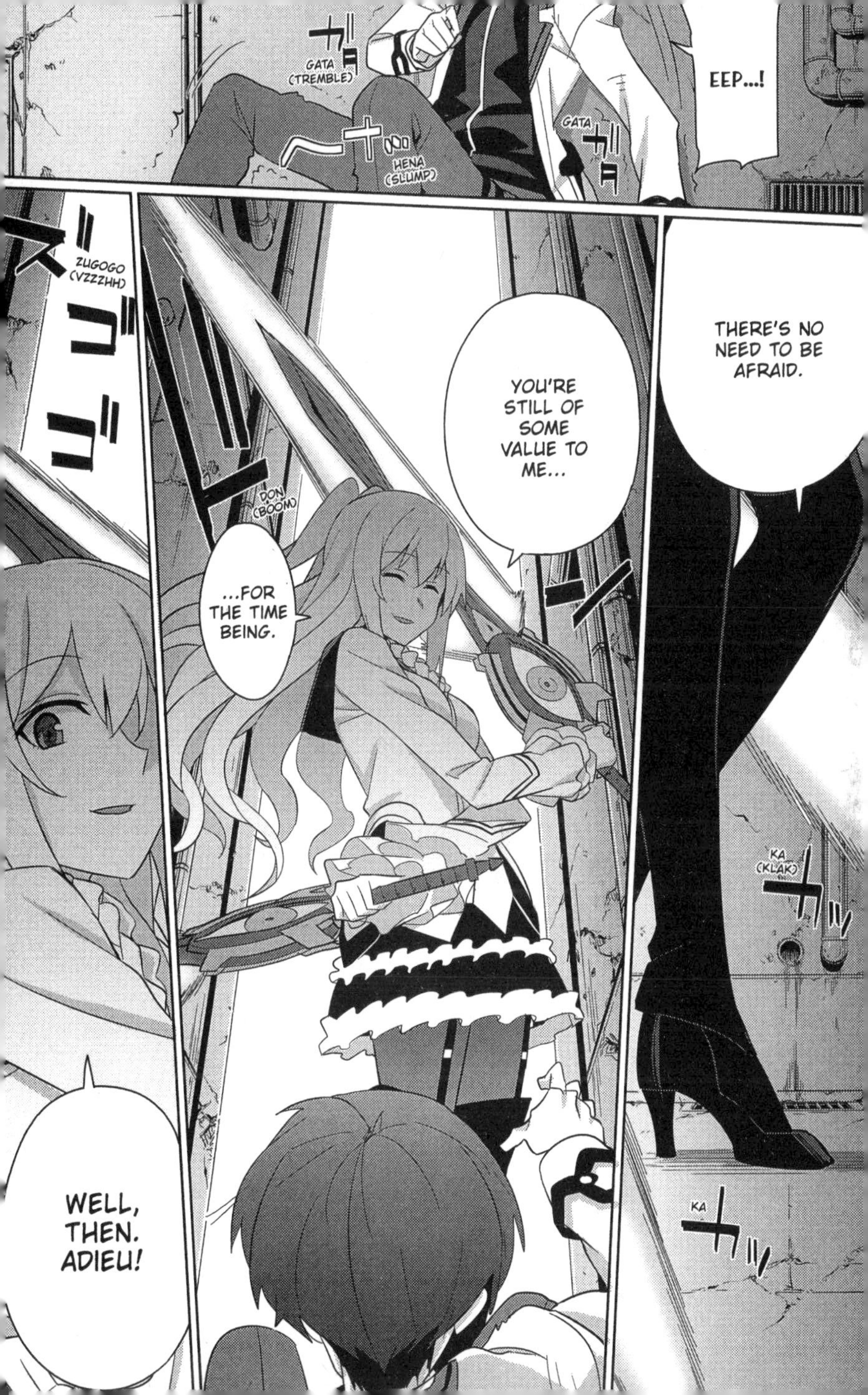
EEP...!
GATA
HENA (SLUMP)
GATA (TREMBLE)
THERE'S NO NEED TO BE AFRAID.
KA (KLAK)
KA
YOU'RE STILL OF SOME VALUE TO ME...
DON (BOOM)
...FOR THE TIME BEING.
ZUGOGO (VZZZHH)
WELL, THEN. ADIEU!

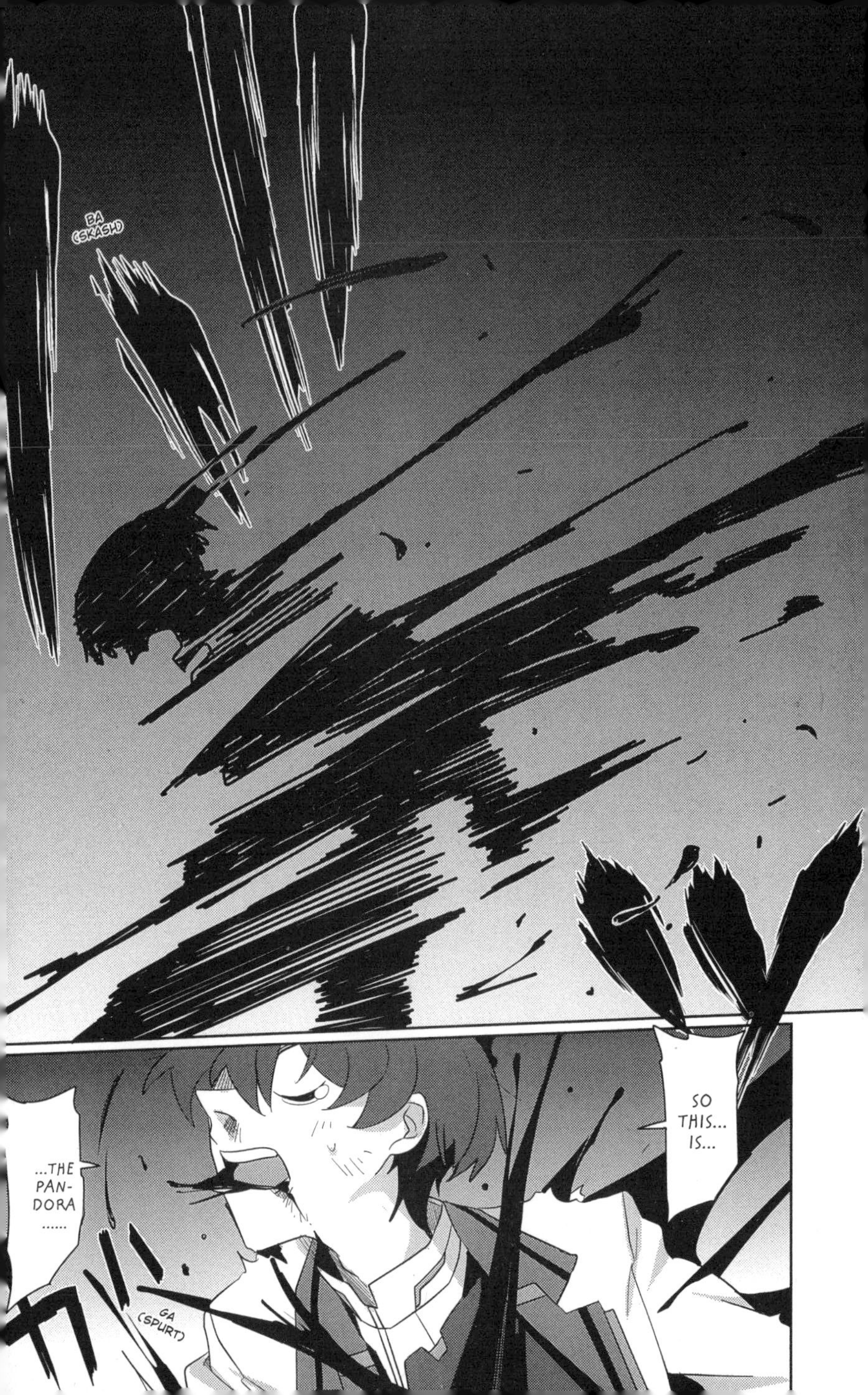
BA (SKASH)
SO THIS... IS...
...THE PANDORA......
GA (SPURT)

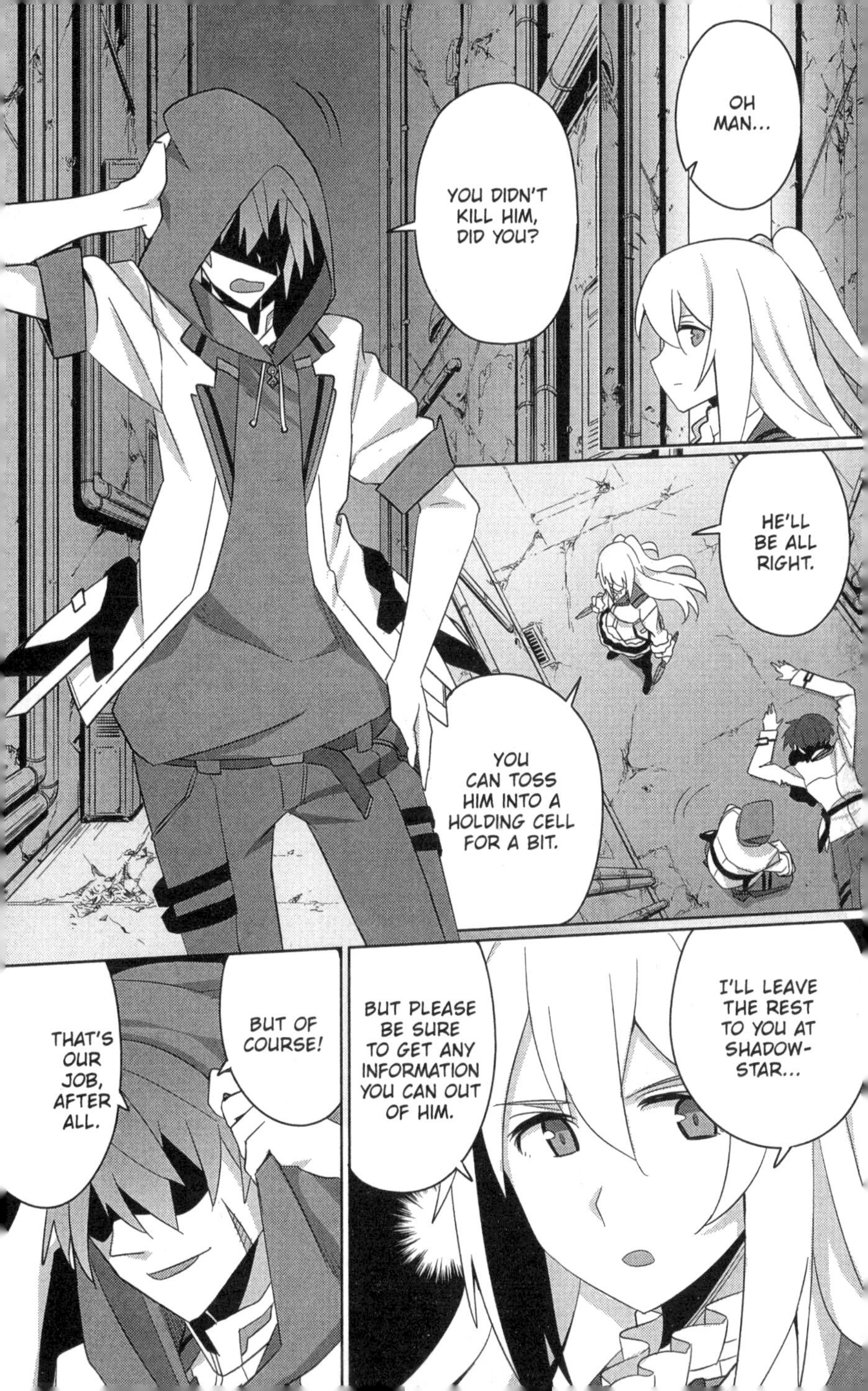
OH MAN...
YOU DIDN'T KILL HIM, DID YOU?
HE'LL BE ALL RIGHT.
YOU CAN TOSS HIM INTO A HOLDING CELL FOR A BIT.
I'LL LEAVE THE REST TO YOU AT SHADOW-STAR...
BUT PLEASE BE SURE TO GET ANY INFORMATION YOU CAN OUT OF HIM.
BUT OF COURSE!
THAT'S OUR JOB, AFTER ALL.

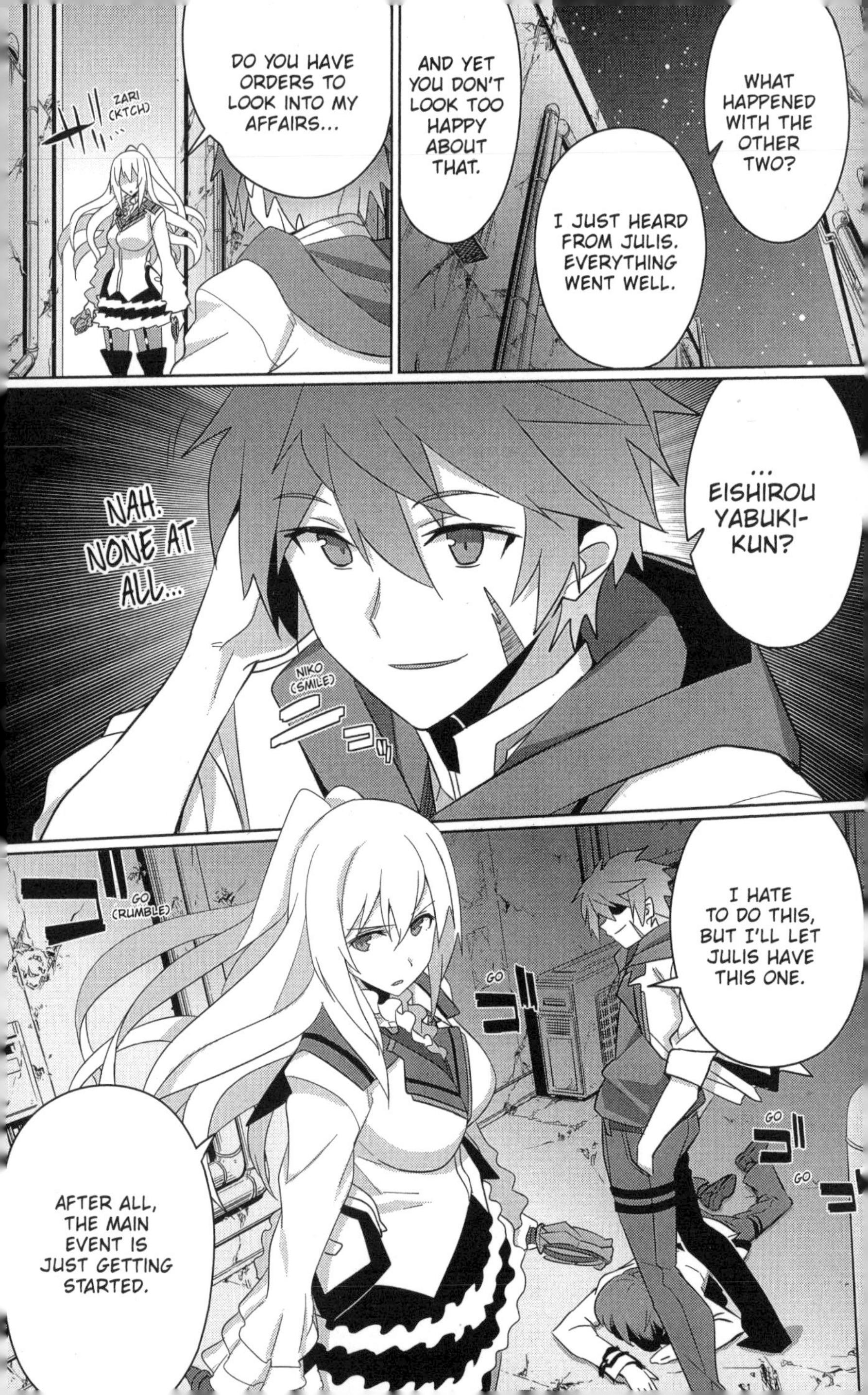
WHAT HAPPENED WITH THE OTHER TWO?
I JUST HEARD FROM JULIS. EVERYTHING WENT WELL.
AND YET YOU DON'T LOOK TOO HAPPY ABOUT THAT.
DO YOU HAVE ORDERS TO LOOK INTO MY AFFAIRS...
ZARI (KTCH)
... EISHIROU YABUKI-KUN?
NAH. NONE AT ALL...
NIKO (SMILE)
I HATE TO DO THIS, BUT I'LL LET JULIS HAVE THIS ONE.
GO (RUMBLE)
GO
GO
GO
AFTER ALL, THE MAIN EVENT IS JUST GETTING STARTED.

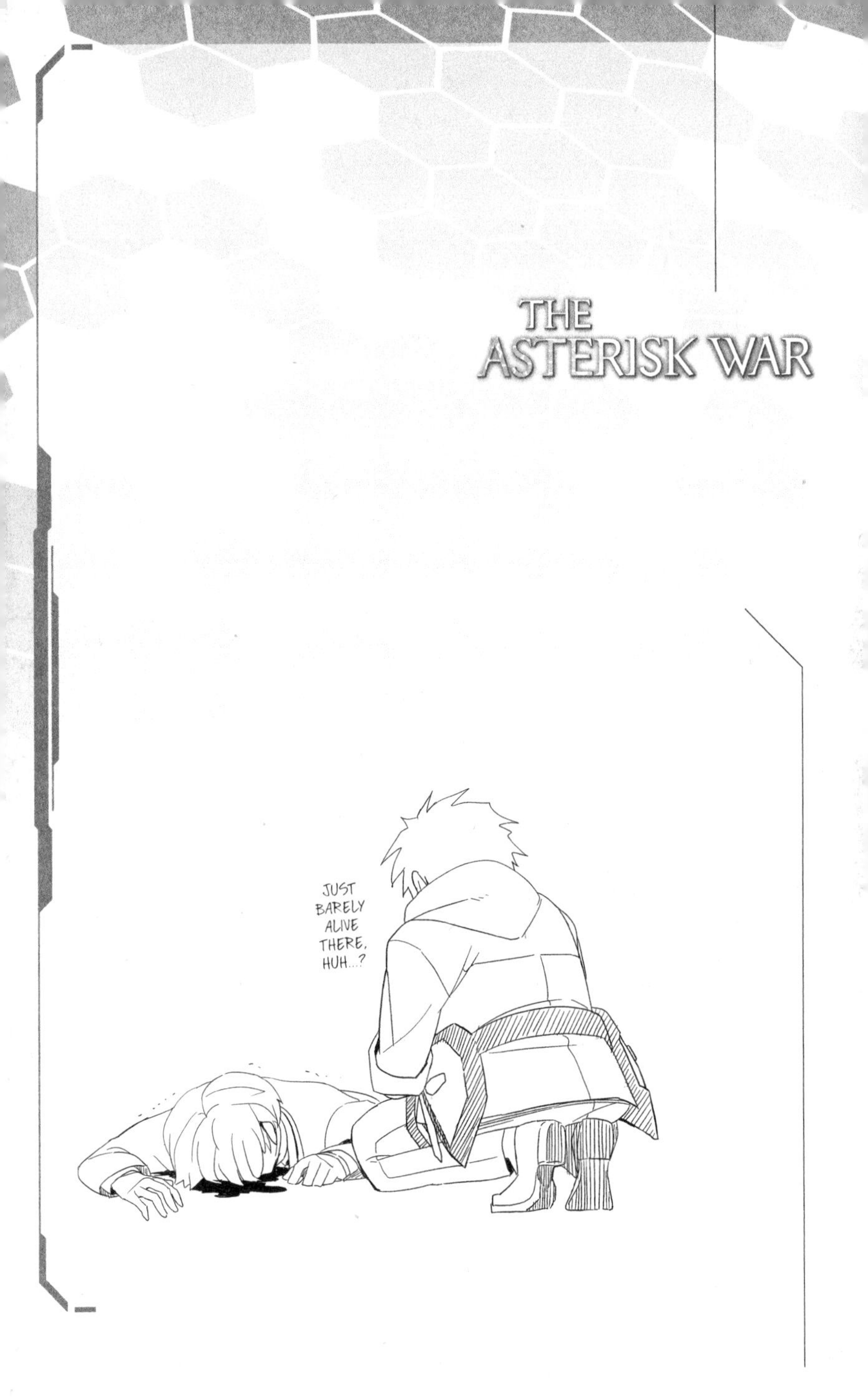
THE ASTERISK WAR
JUST BARELY ALIVE THERE, HUH...?

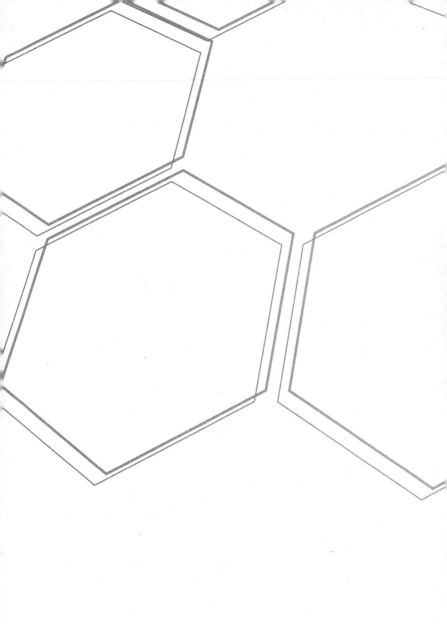

THE
ASTERISK WAR

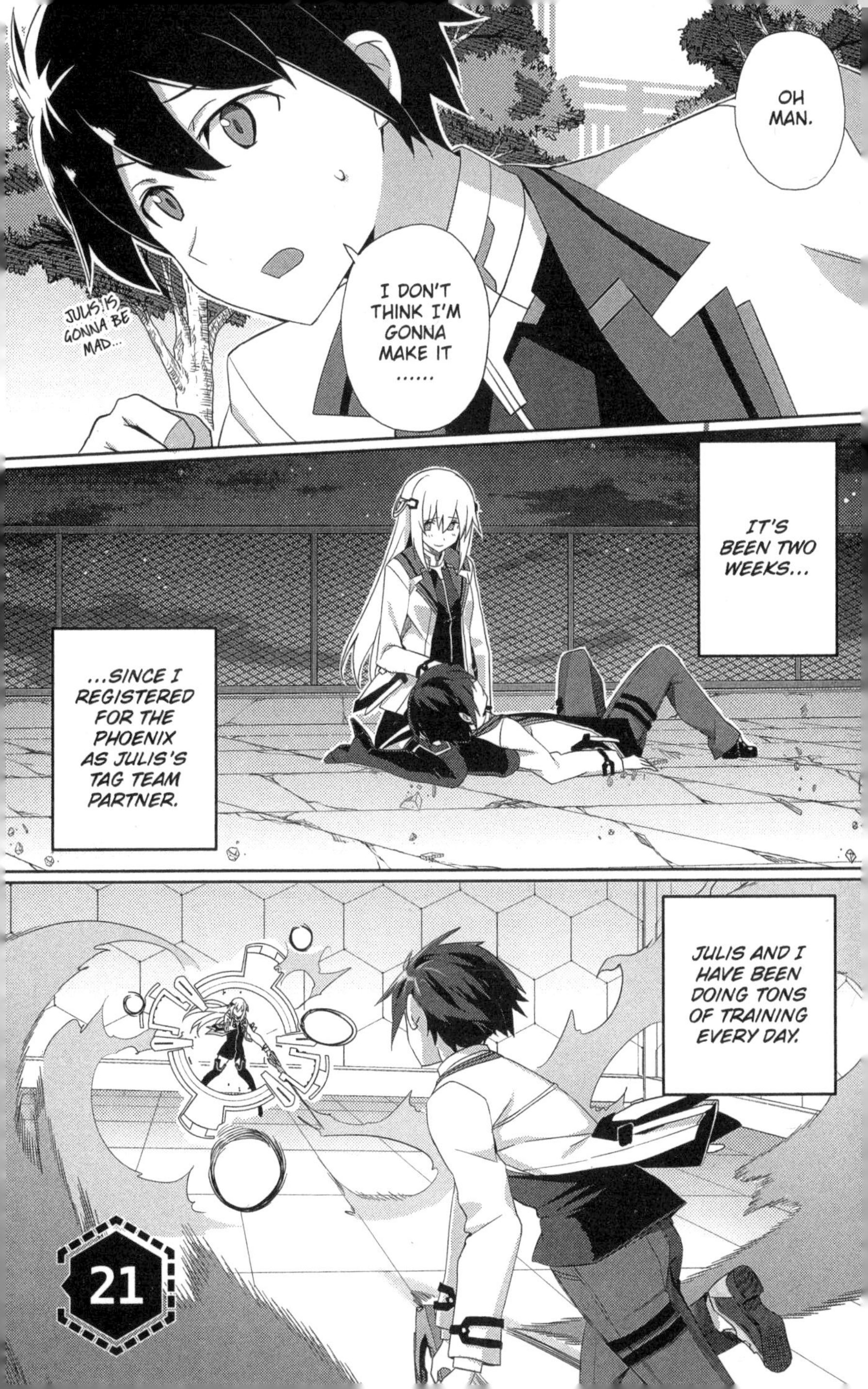
OH MAN.
I DON'T THINK I'M GONNA MAKE IT ......
JULIS IS GONNA BE MAD...
IT'S BEEN TWO WEEKS...
...SINCE I REGISTERED FOR THE PHOENIX AS JULIS'S TAG TEAM PARTNER.
JULIS AND I HAVE BEEN DOING TONS OF TRAINING EVERY DAY.

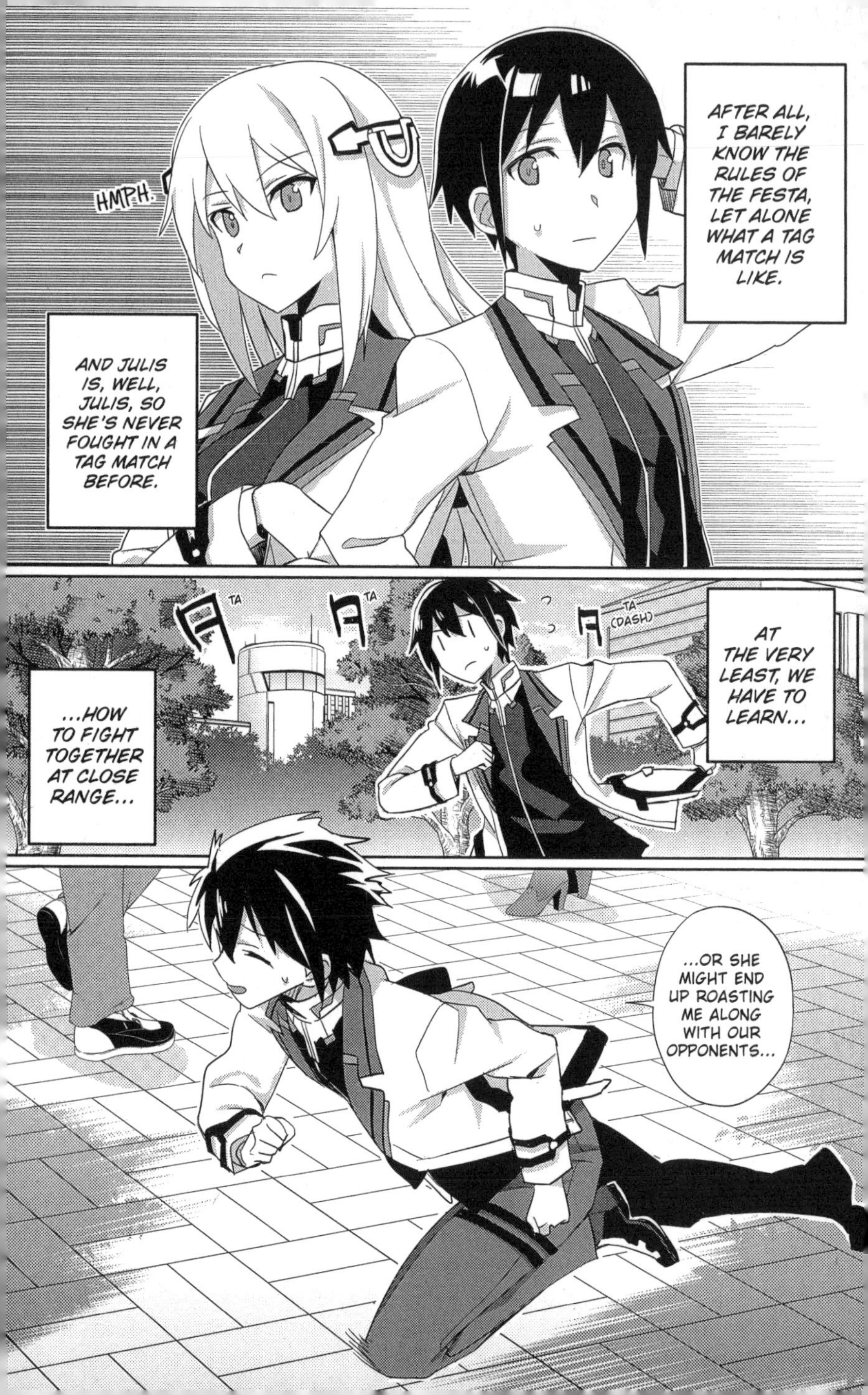
AFTER ALL, I BARELY KNOW THE RULES OF THE FESTA, LET ALONE WHAT A TAG MATCH IS LIKE.
HMPH.
AND JULIS IS, WELL, JULIS, SO SHE'S NEVER FOUGHT IN A TAG MATCH BEFORE.
TA (DASH)
TA
TA
AT THE VERY LEAST, WE HAVE TO LEARN...
...HOW TO FIGHT TOGETHER AT CLOSE RANGE...
...OR SHE MIGHT END UP ROASTING ME ALONG WITH OUR OPPONENTS...

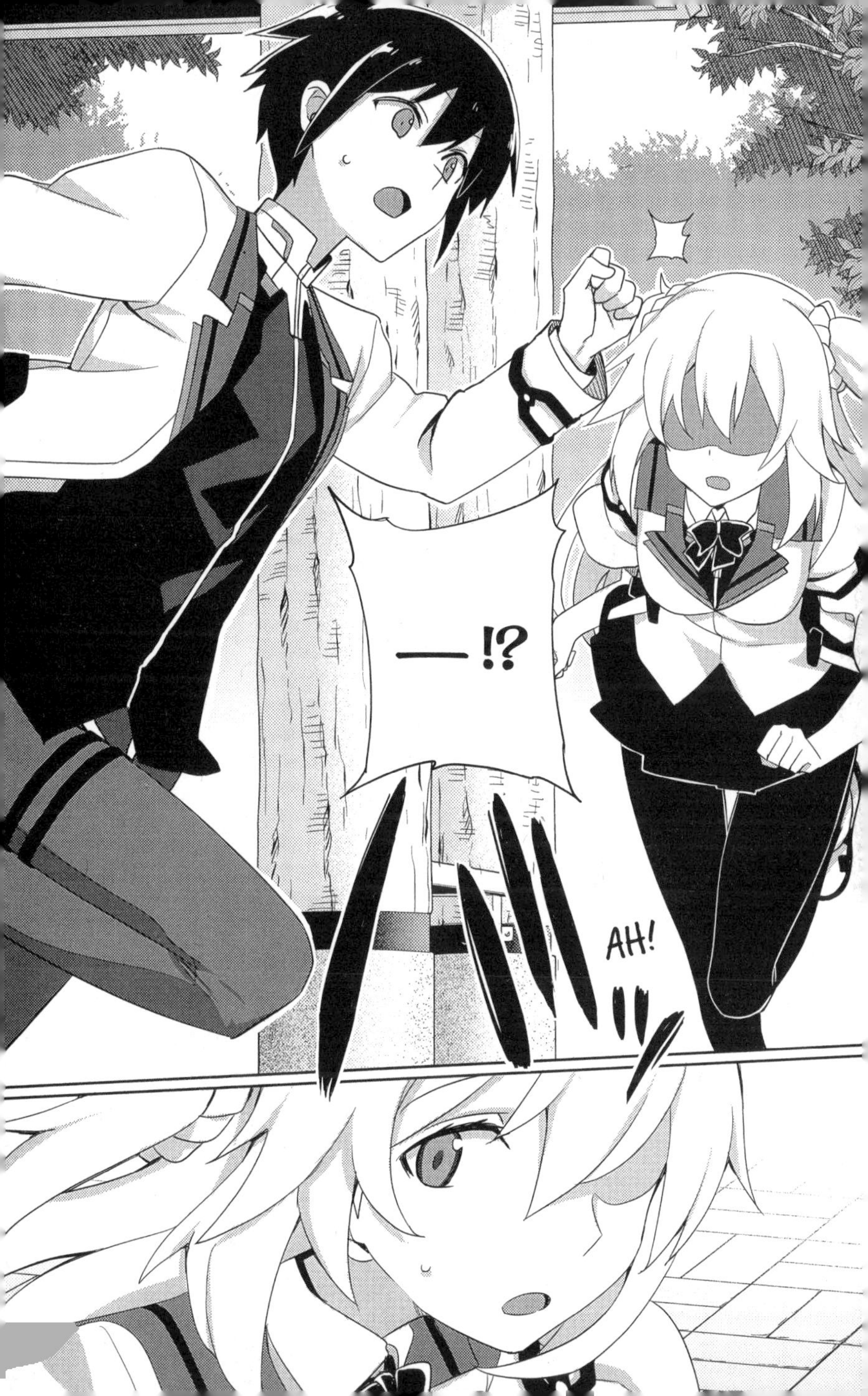

——!?
AH!

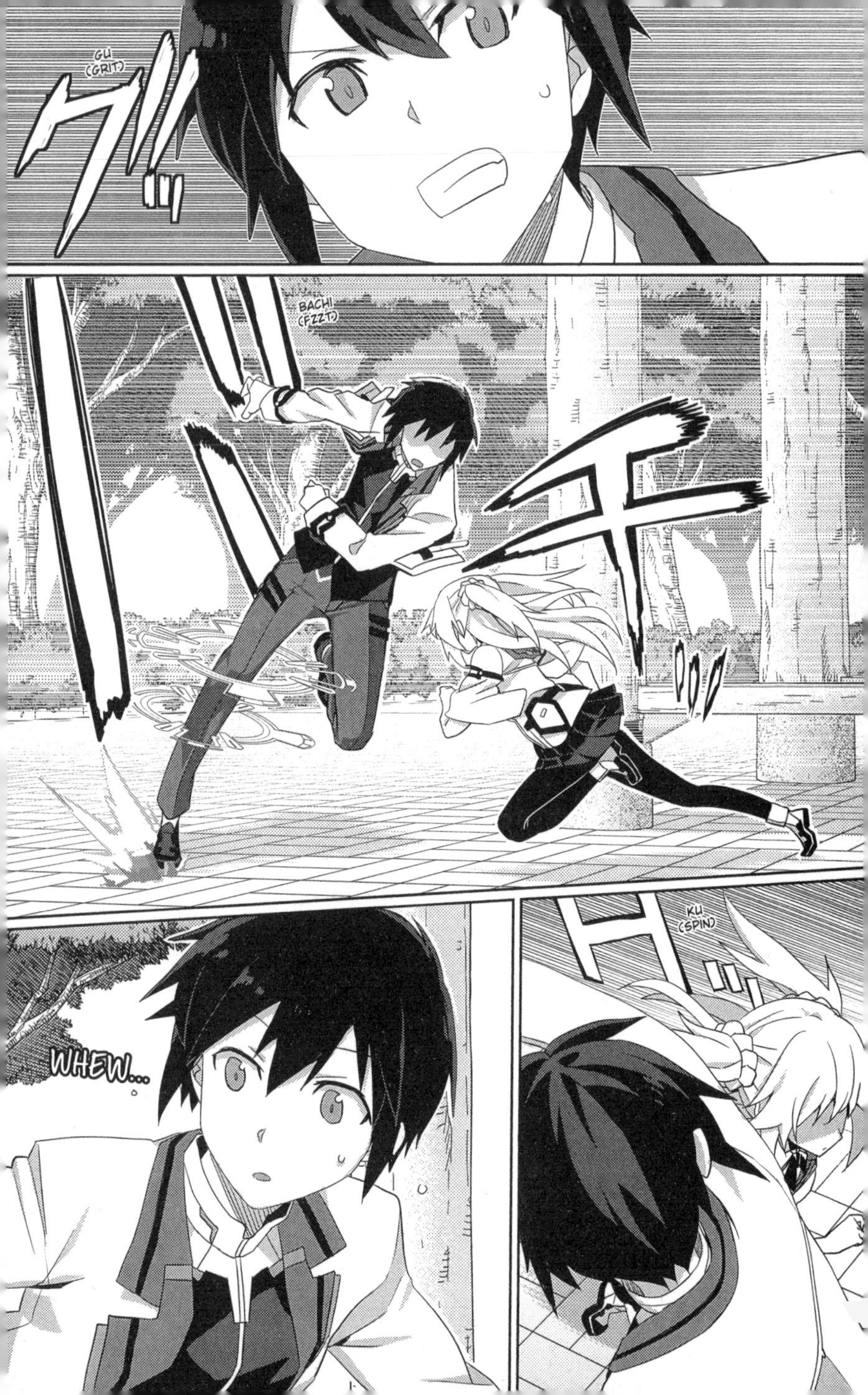
GU
(GRIT)
BACHI
(FZZT)
KU
(SPIN)
WHEW...

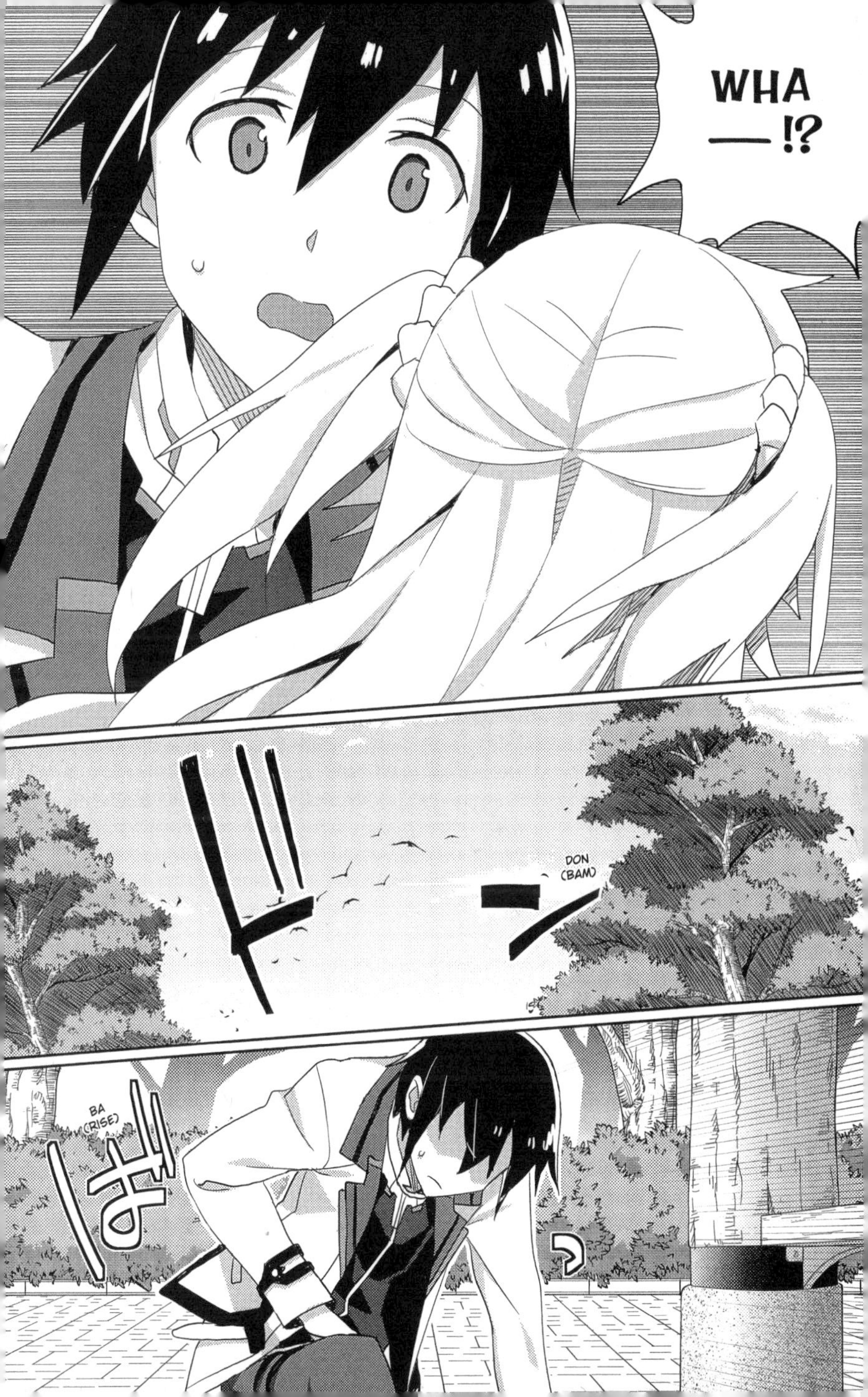
WHA —!?
ド ー ン
DON (BAM)
ばっ
BA (RISE)

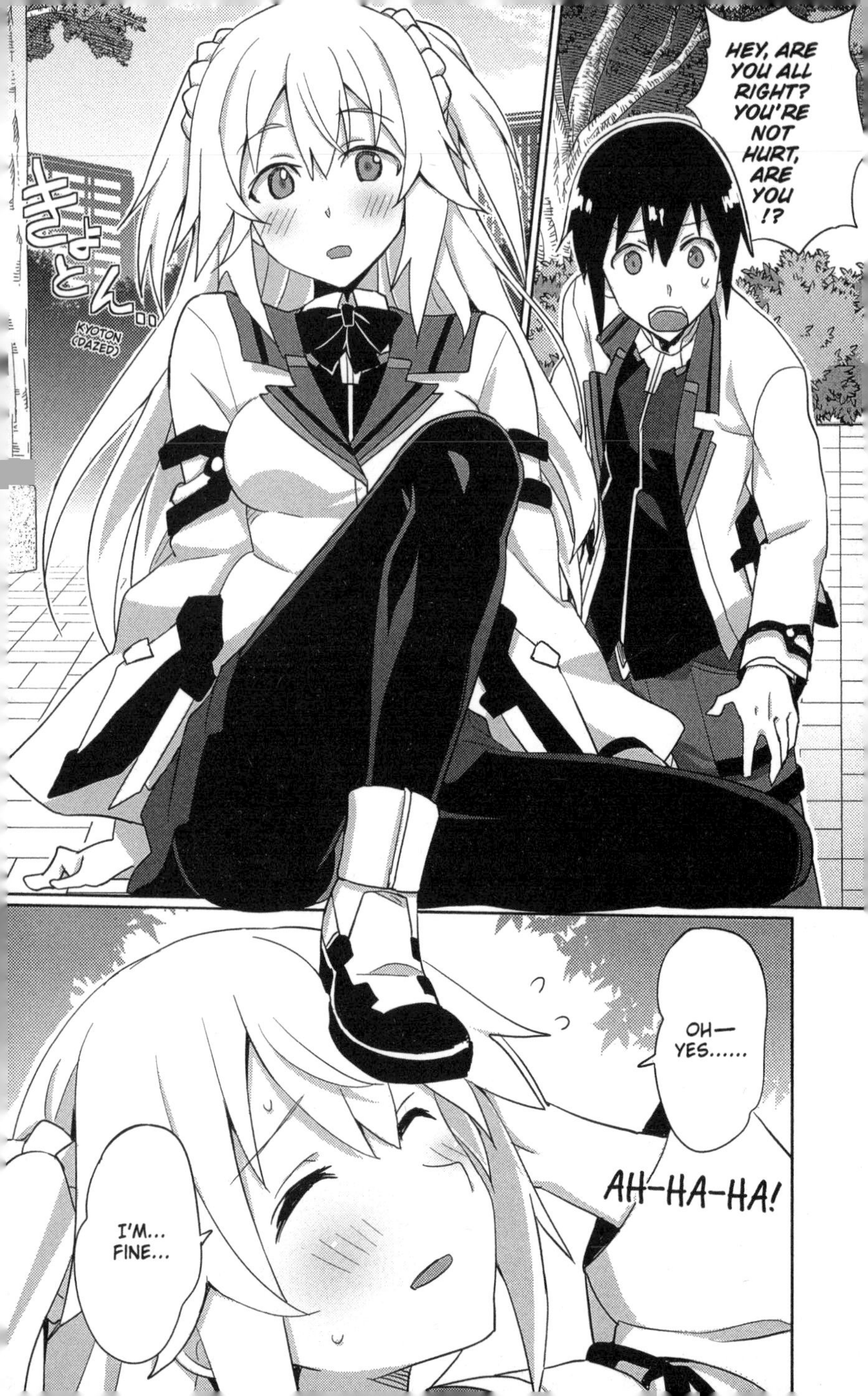
HEY, ARE YOU ALL RIGHT? YOU'RE NOT HURT, ARE YOU!?
きょとん。。
KYOTON (DAZED)
OH— YES......
AH-HA-HA!
I'M... FINE...

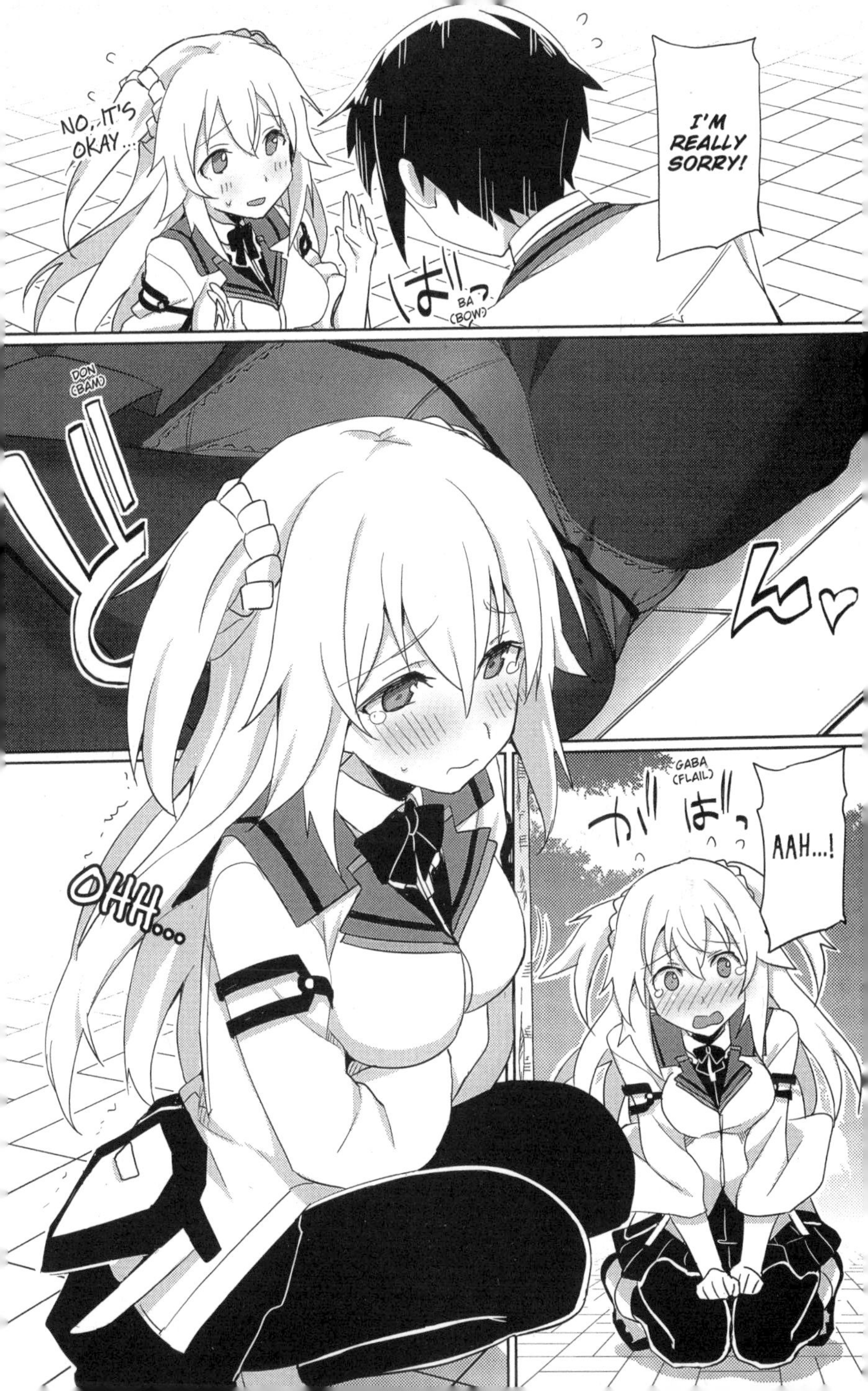
I'M REALLY SORRY!
はっ
BA (BOW)
NO, IT'S OKAY...
ん♡
DON (BAM)
AAH...!
がばっ
GABA (FLAIL)
OHH...

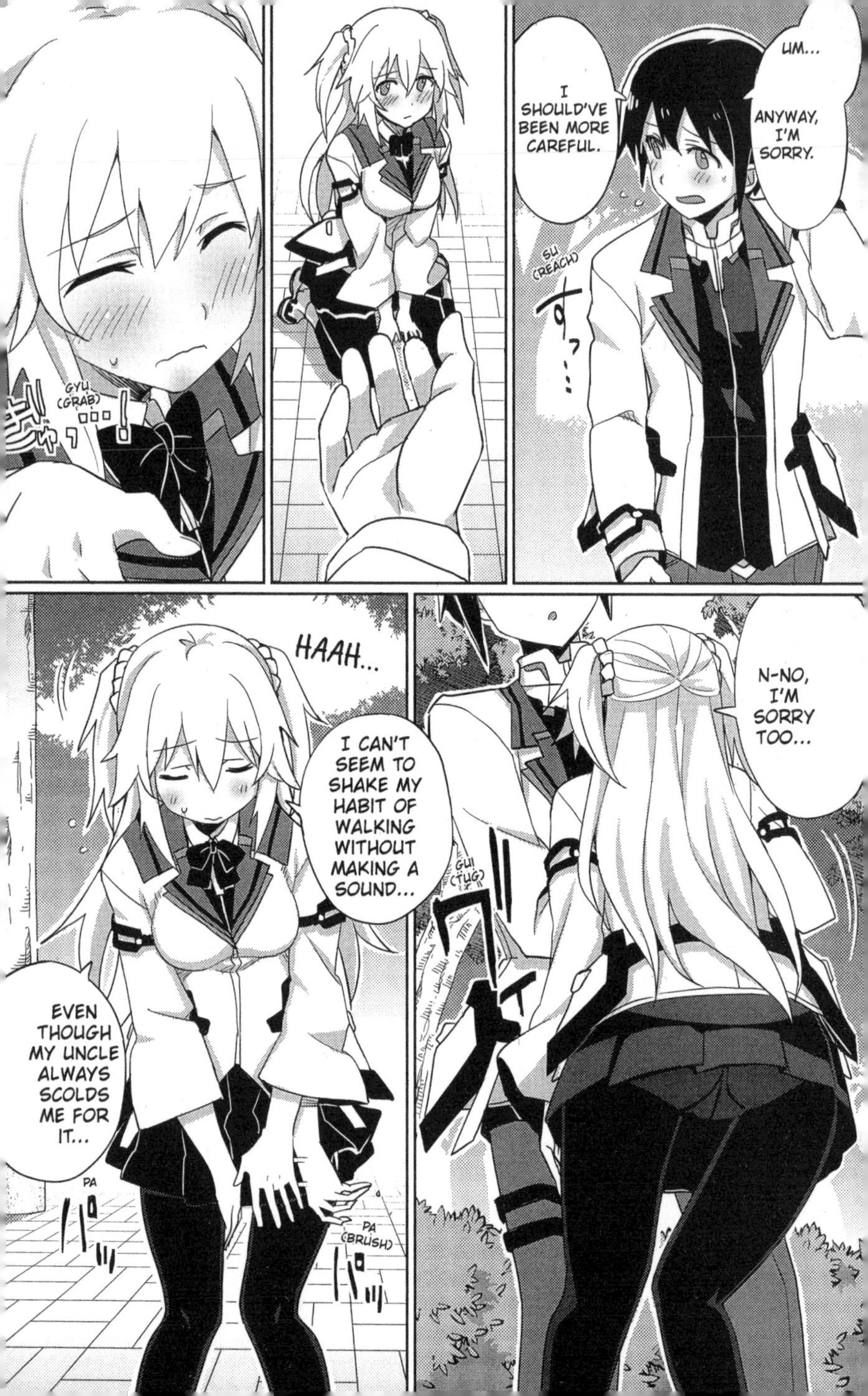
UM...
ANYWAY, I'M SORRY.
I SHOULD'VE BEEN MORE CAREFUL.
SU (REACH)
すっ…
GYU (GRAB)
ぎゅっ
N-NO, I'M SORRY TOO...
GUI (TUG)
HAAH...
I CAN'T SEEM TO SHAKE MY HABIT OF WALKING WITHOUT MAKING A SOUND...
EVEN THOUGH MY UNCLE ALWAYS SCOLDS ME FOR IT...
PA
PA (BRUSH)

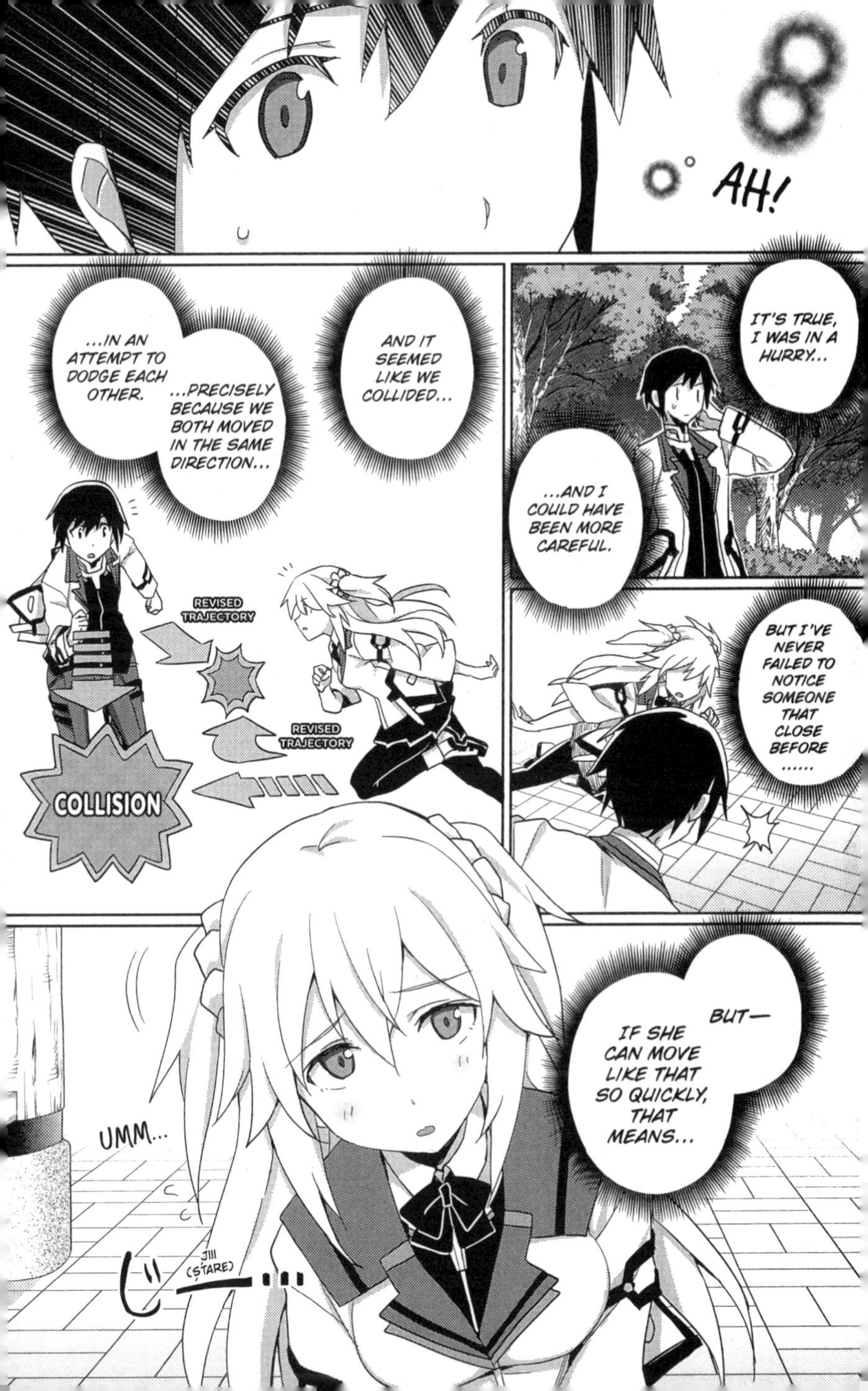
AH!
IT'S TRUE, I WAS IN A HURRY...
...AND I COULD HAVE BEEN MORE CAREFUL.
BUT I'VE NEVER FAILED TO NOTICE SOMEONE THAT CLOSE BEFORE ......
AND IT SEEMED LIKE WE COLLIDED...
...PRECISELY BECAUSE WE BOTH MOVED IN THE SAME DIRECTION...
...IN AN ATTEMPT TO DODGE EACH OTHER.
REVISED TRAJECTORY
REVISED TRAJECTORY
COLLISION
BUT—
IF SHE CAN MOVE LIKE THAT SO QUICKLY, THAT MEANS...
UMM...
JIII (STARE)

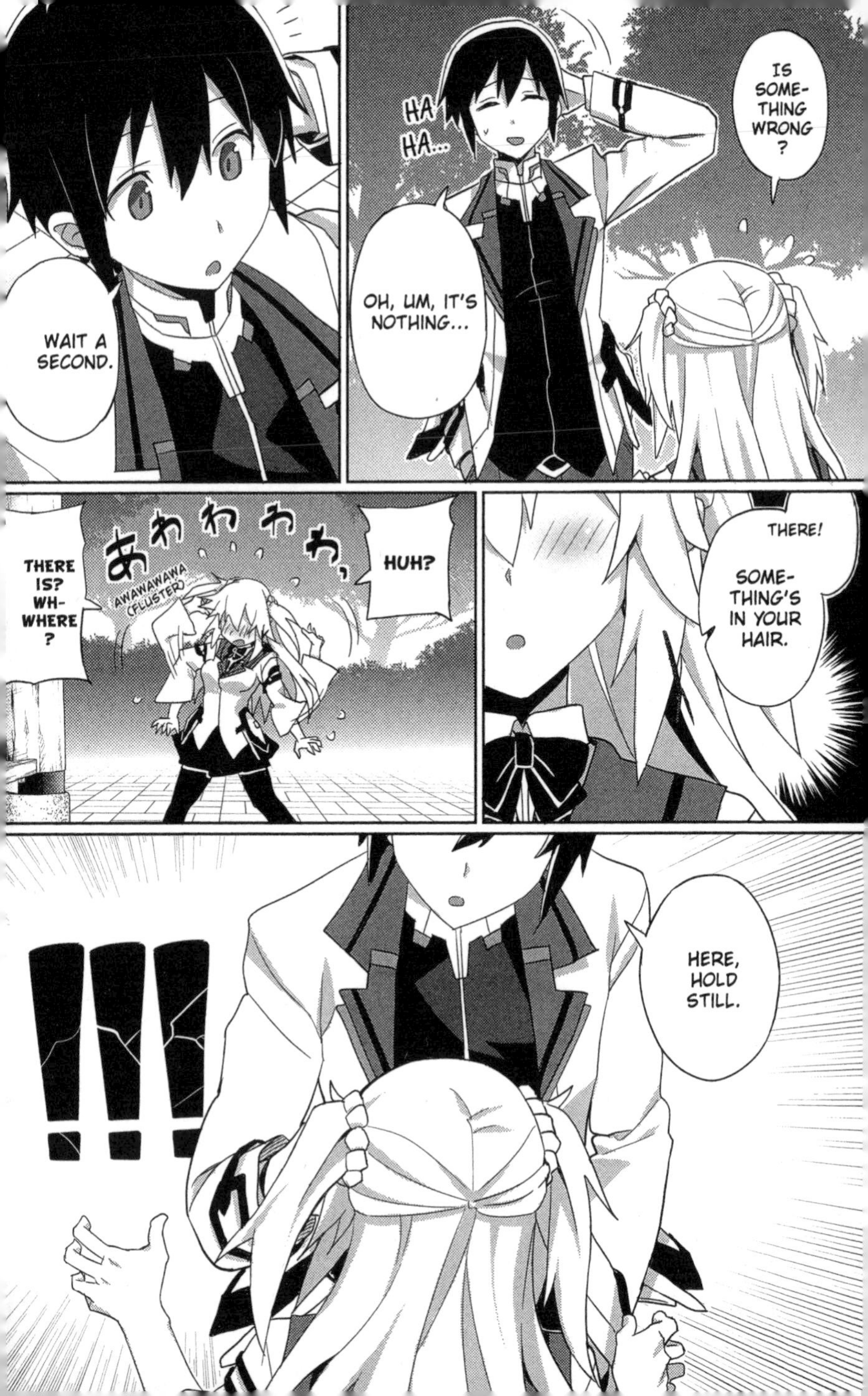
IS SOMETHING WRONG?
HA HA...
OH, UM, IT'S NOTHING...
WAIT A SECOND.
THERE!
SOMETHING'S IN YOUR HAIR.
HUH?
あわわわわ、
AWAWAWAWA (FLUSTER)
THERE IS? WH-WHERE?
HERE, HOLD STILL.
!!!

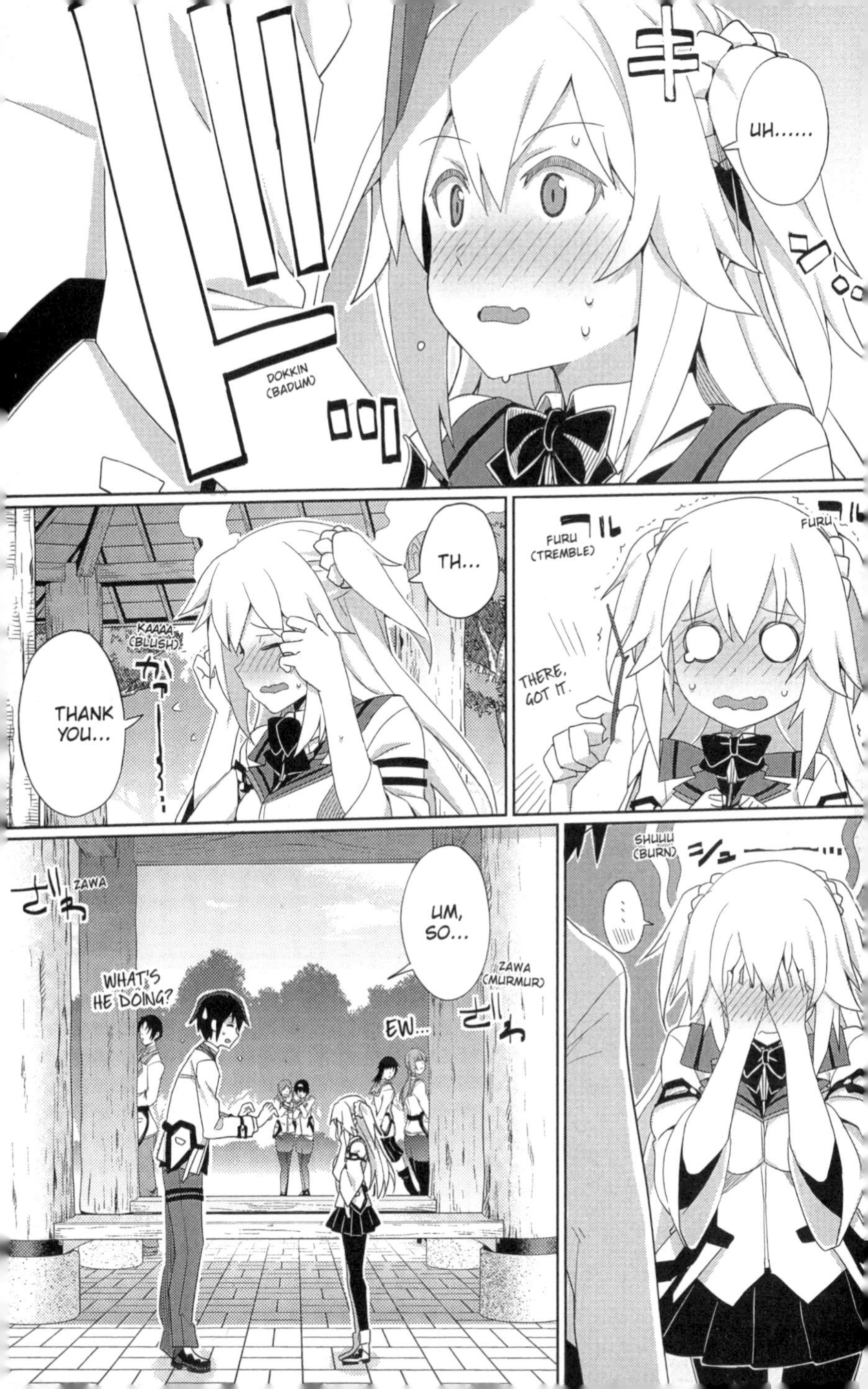
UH......
DOKKIN (BADUM)
FURU (TREMBLE)
FURU
THERE, GOT IT.
TH...
KAAAA (BLUSH)
THANK YOU...
SHUUU (BURN)
...
UM, SO...
ZAWA (MURMUR)
EW...
WHAT'S HE DOING?
ZAWA

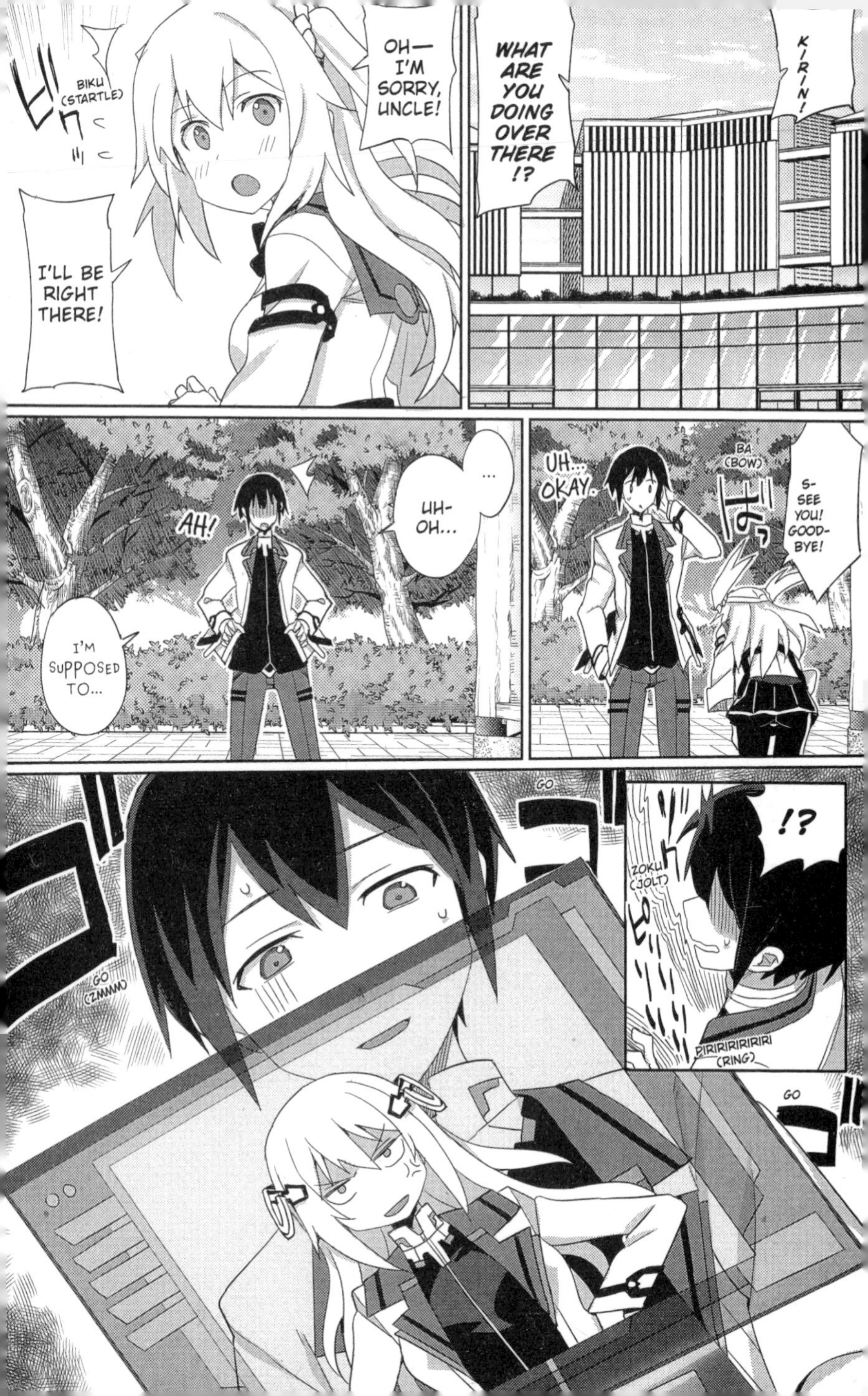
KIRIN!
WHAT ARE YOU DOING OVER THERE!?
OH— I'M SORRY, UNCLE!
BIKU (STARTLE)
I'LL BE RIGHT THERE!
S-SEE YOU! GOOD-BYE!
BA (BOW)
UH... OKAY.
...
UH-OH...
AH!
I'M SUPPOSED TO...
!?
ZOKU (JOLT)
PIRIRIRIRIRIRI (RING)
GO
GO (ZMMMM)
GO

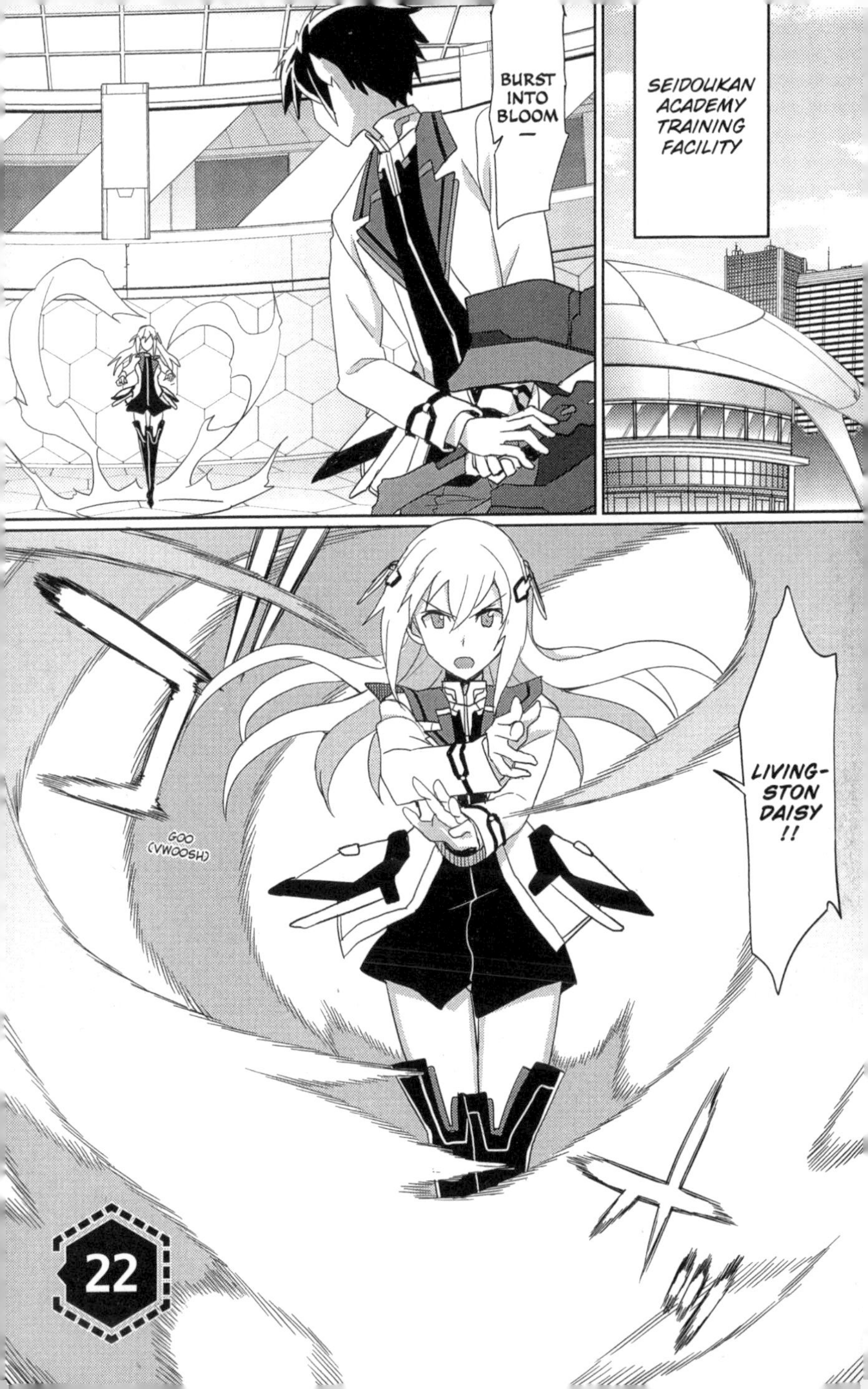
SEIDOUKAN ACADEMY TRAINING FACILITY
BURST INTO BLOOM —
GOO (VWOOSH)
LIVING-STON DAISY !!

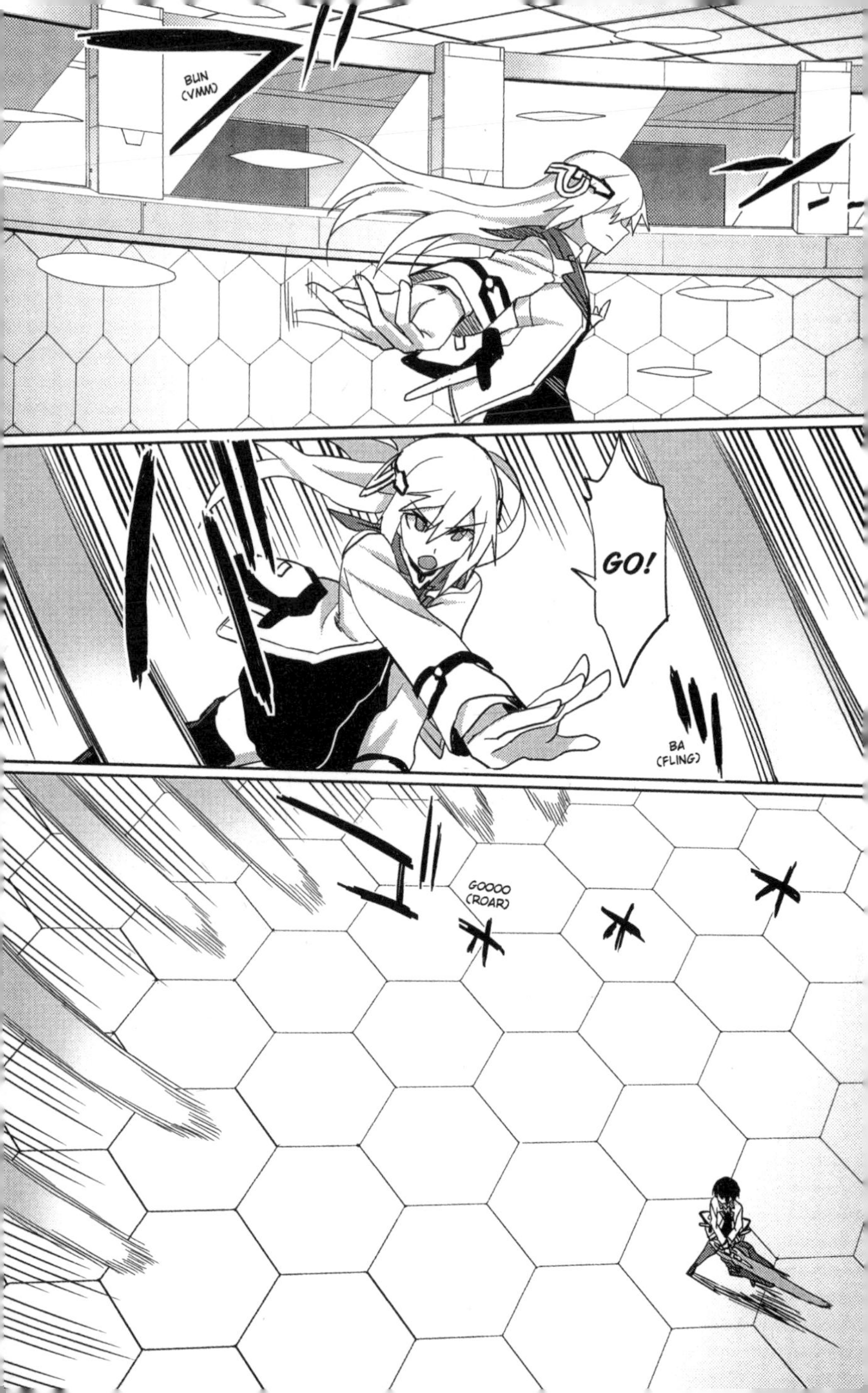
BUN
(VMM)
GO!
BA
(FLING)
GOOOO
(ROAR)

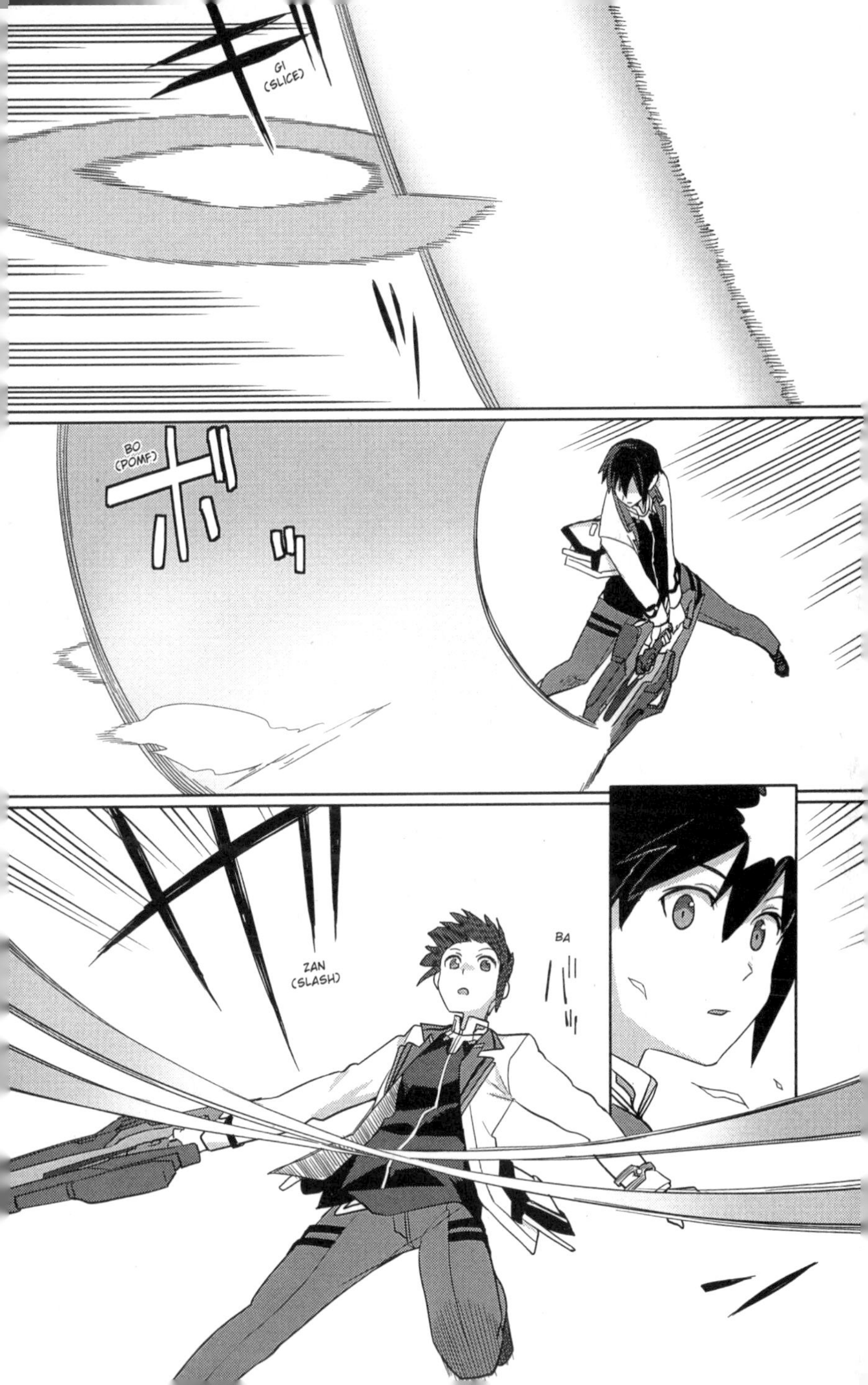
GI (SLICE)
BO (POMF)
BA
ZAN (SLASH)

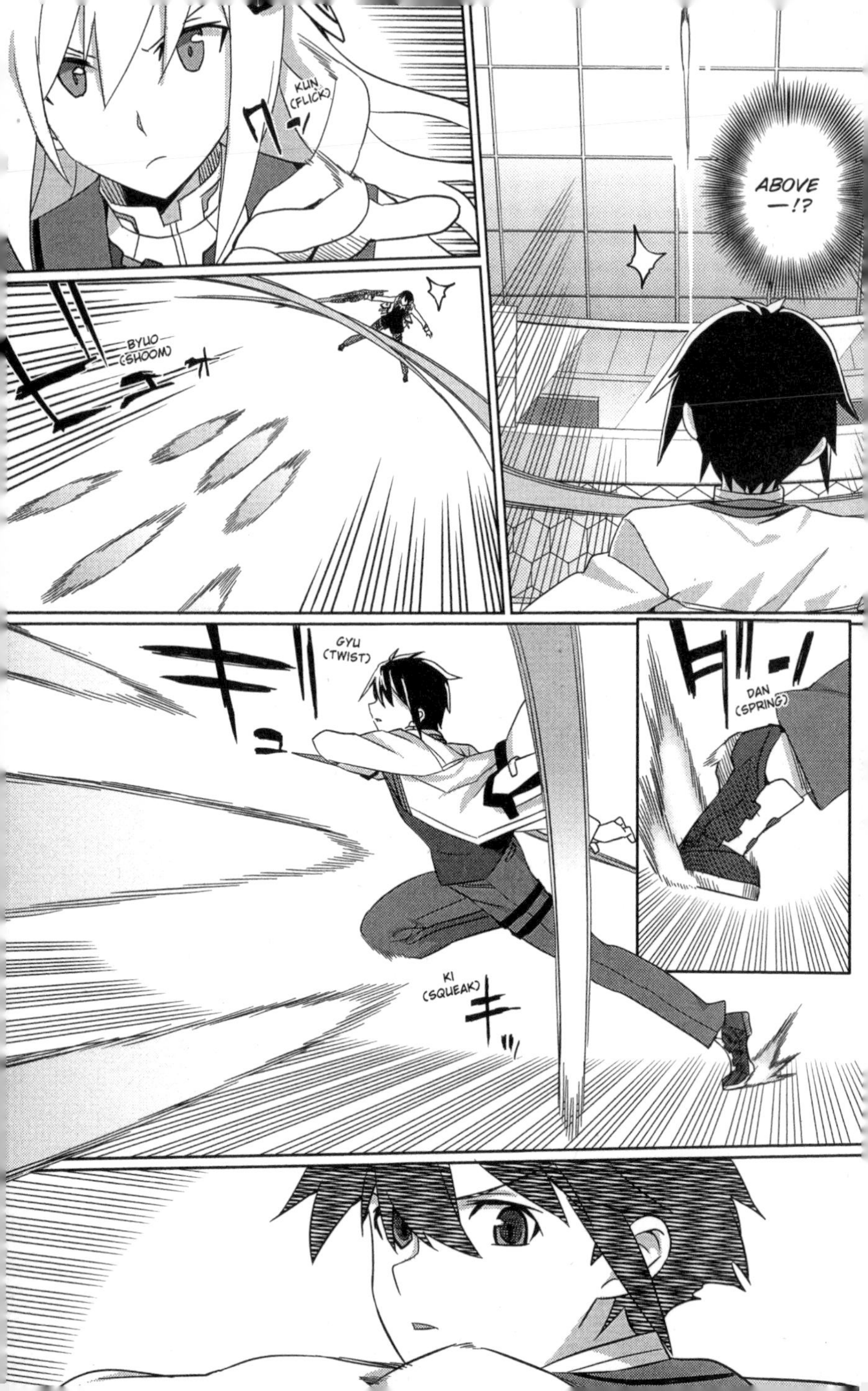
ABOVE —!?
KUN (FLICK)
BYUO (SHOOM)
DAN (SPRING)
GYU (TWIST)
KI (SQUEAK)

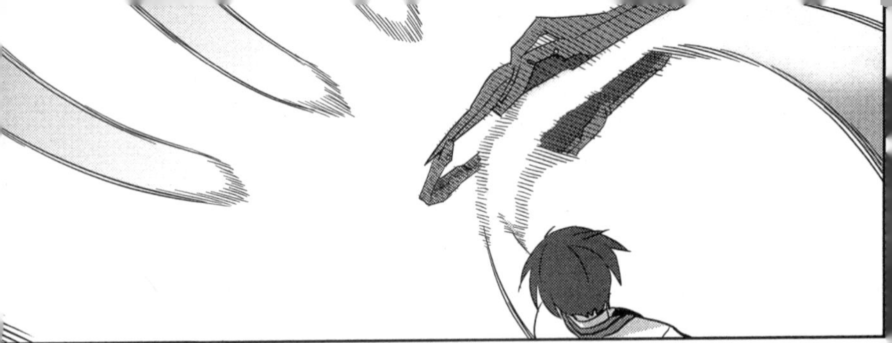

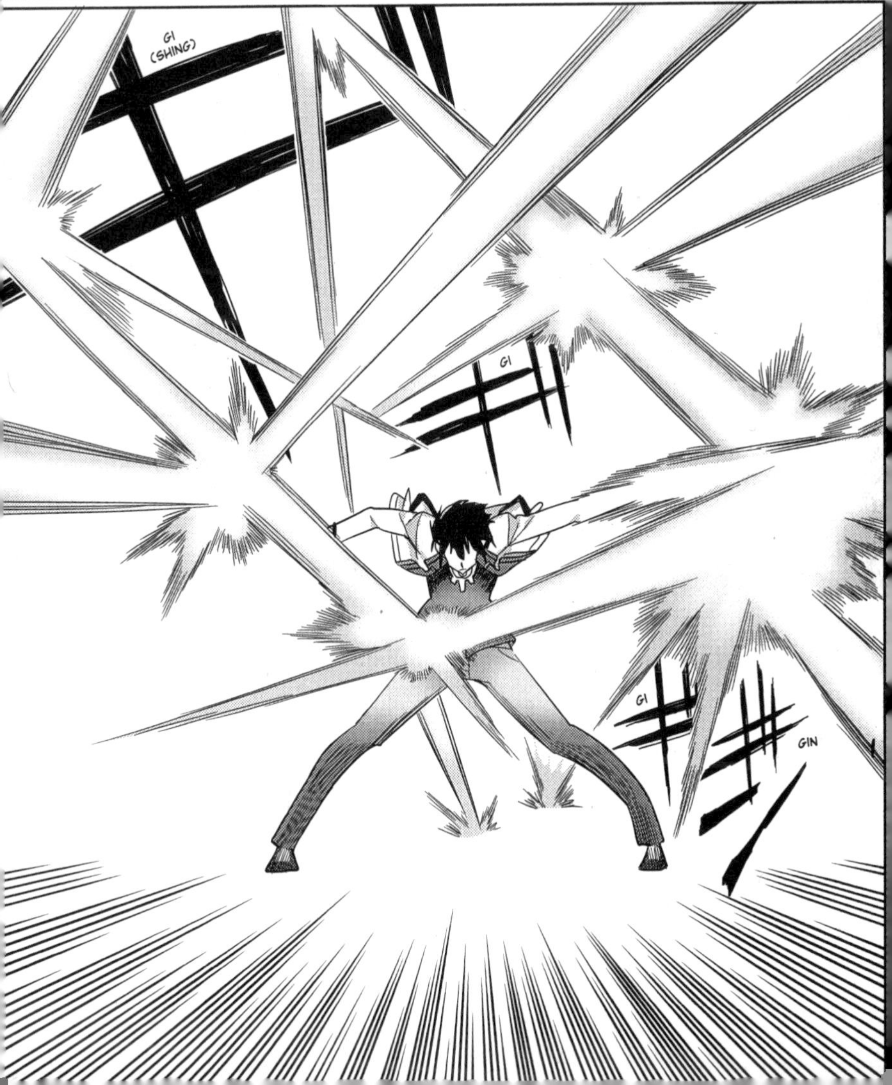
GI
(SHING)
GI
GI
GI
GIN

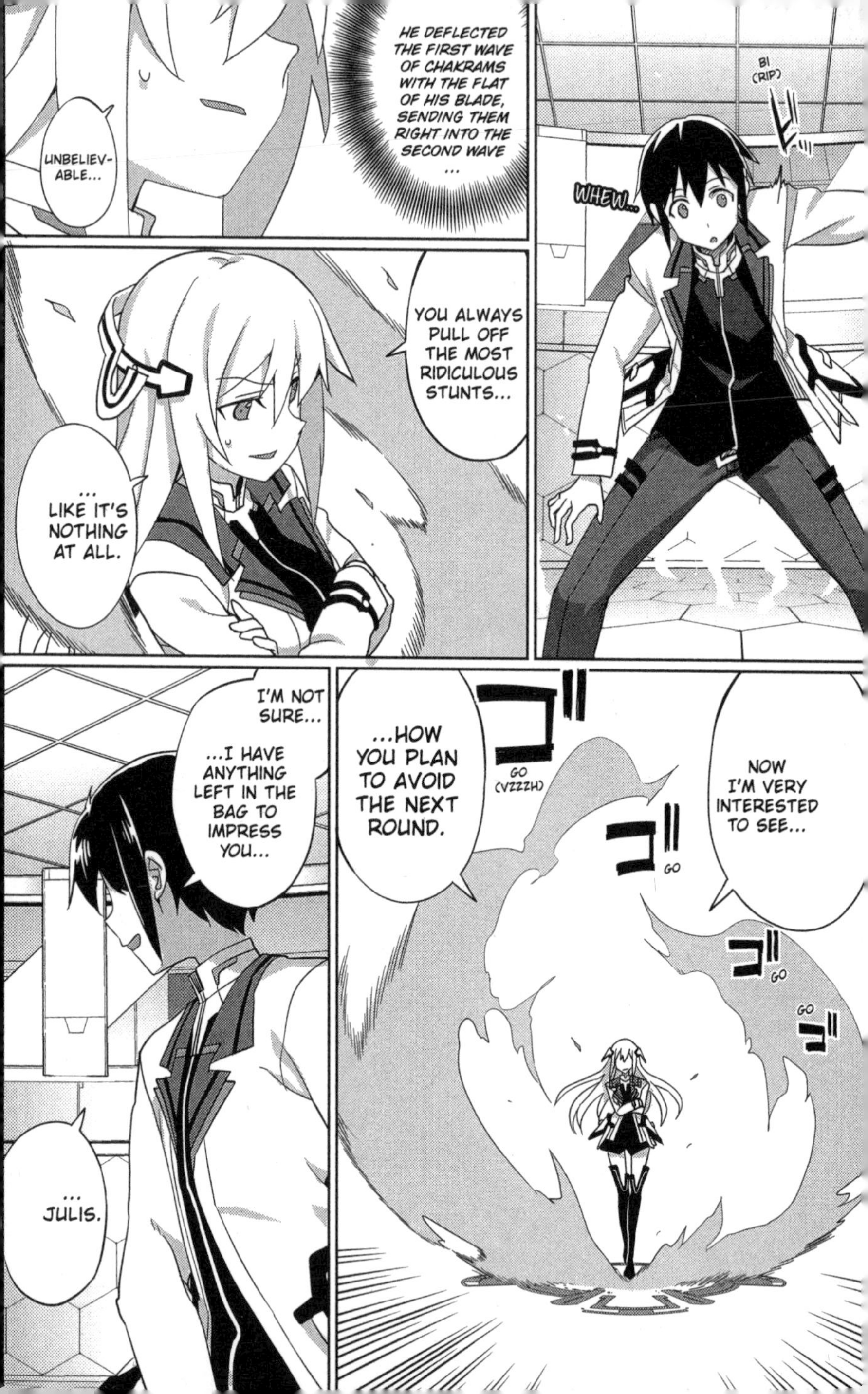
BI (RIP)
WHEW...
HE DEFLECTED THE FIRST WAVE OF CHAKRAMS WITH THE FLAT OF HIS BLADE, SENDING THEM RIGHT INTO THE SECOND WAVE ...
UNBELIEV-ABLE...
YOU ALWAYS PULL OFF THE MOST RIDICULOUS STUNTS...
... LIKE IT'S NOTHING AT ALL.
NOW I'M VERY INTERESTED TO SEE...
...HOW YOU PLAN TO AVOID THE NEXT ROUND.
GO (VZZZH)
GO
GO
GO
I'M NOT SURE...
...I HAVE ANYTHING LEFT IN THE BAG TO IMPRESS YOU...
... JULIS.

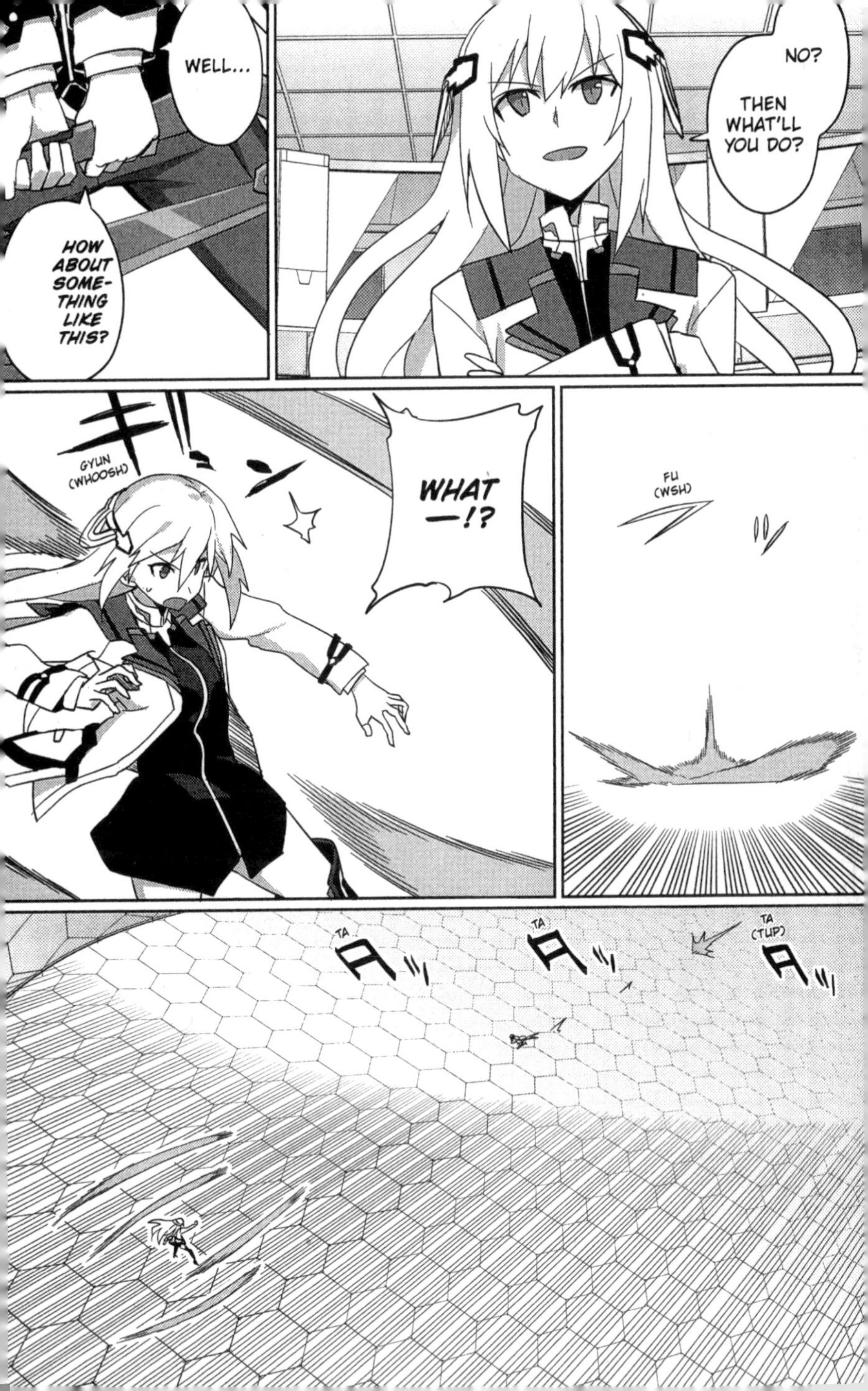
NO?
THEN WHAT'LL YOU DO?
WELL...
HOW ABOUT SOME-THING LIKE THIS?
FU (WSH)
GYUN (WHOOSH)
WHAT—!?
TA (TUP)
TA
TA

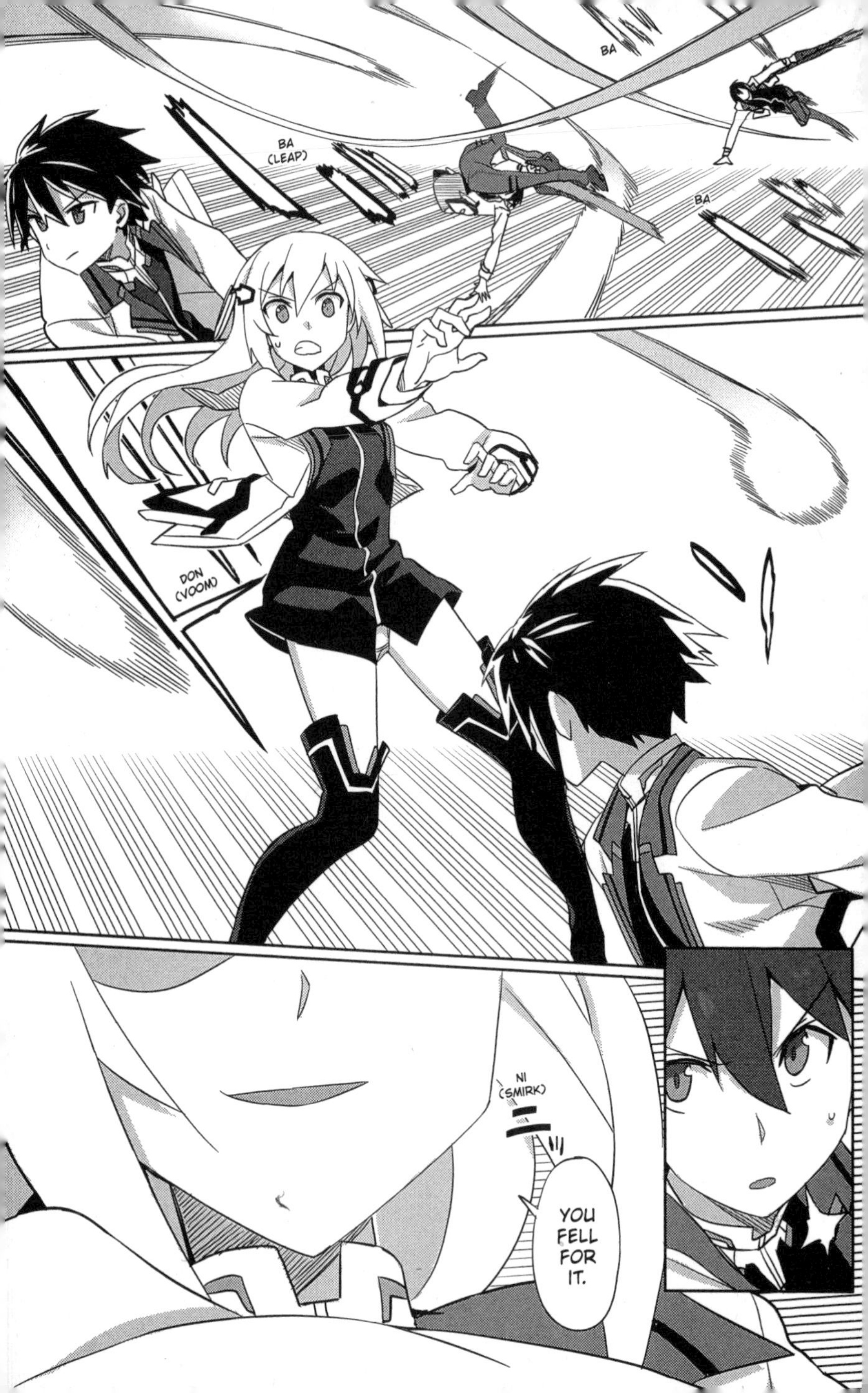
BA
BA
(LEAP)
BA
DON
(VOOM)
NI
(SMIRK)
YOU FELL FOR IT.

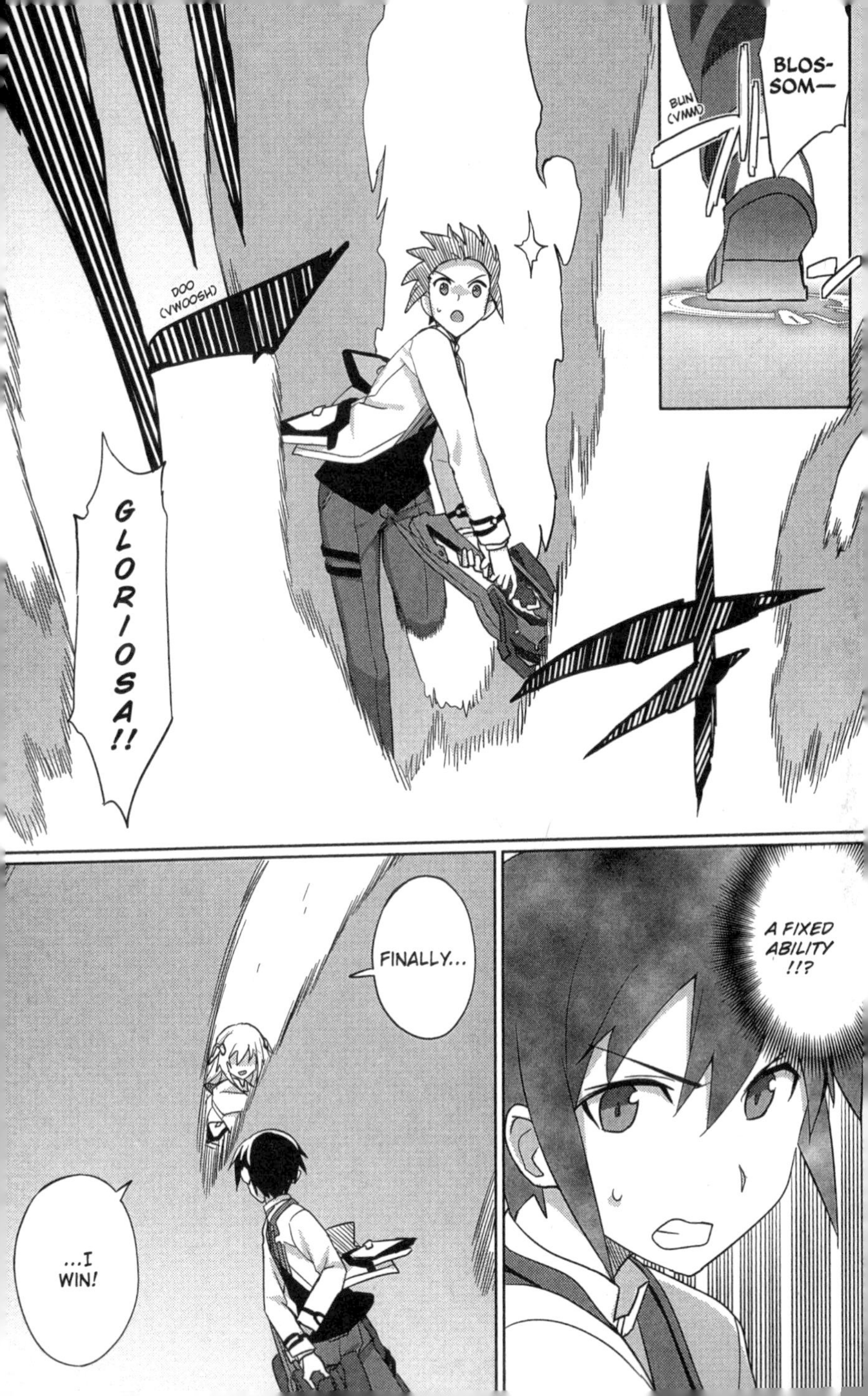
BLOS-SOM—
BUN (VMMM)
DOO (VWOOSH)
GLORIOSA!!
A FIXED ABILITY!!?
FINALLY...
...I WIN!

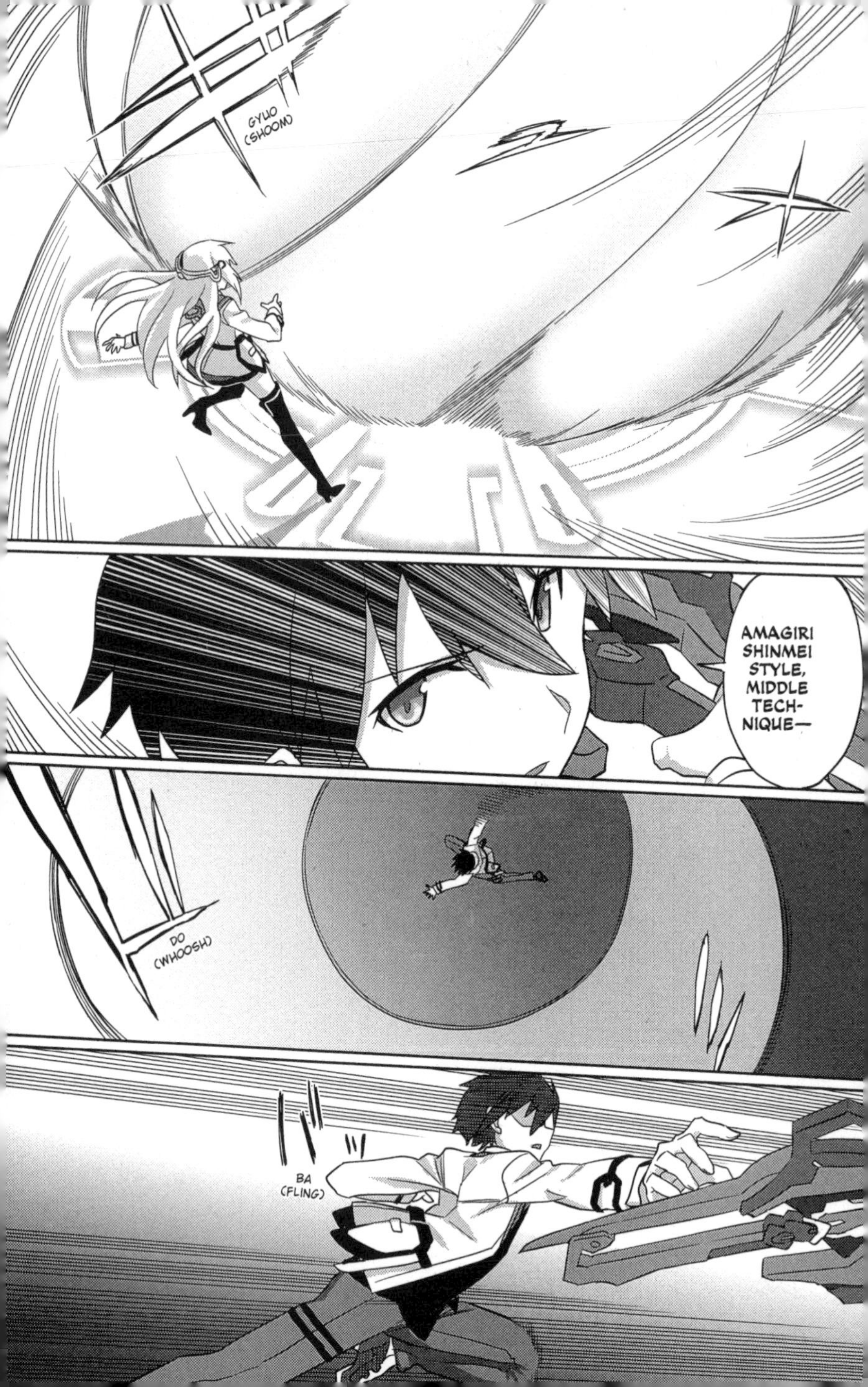
GYUO (SHOOM)
AMAGIRI SHINMEI STYLE, MIDDLE TECHNIQUE—
DO (WHOOSH)
BA (FLING)

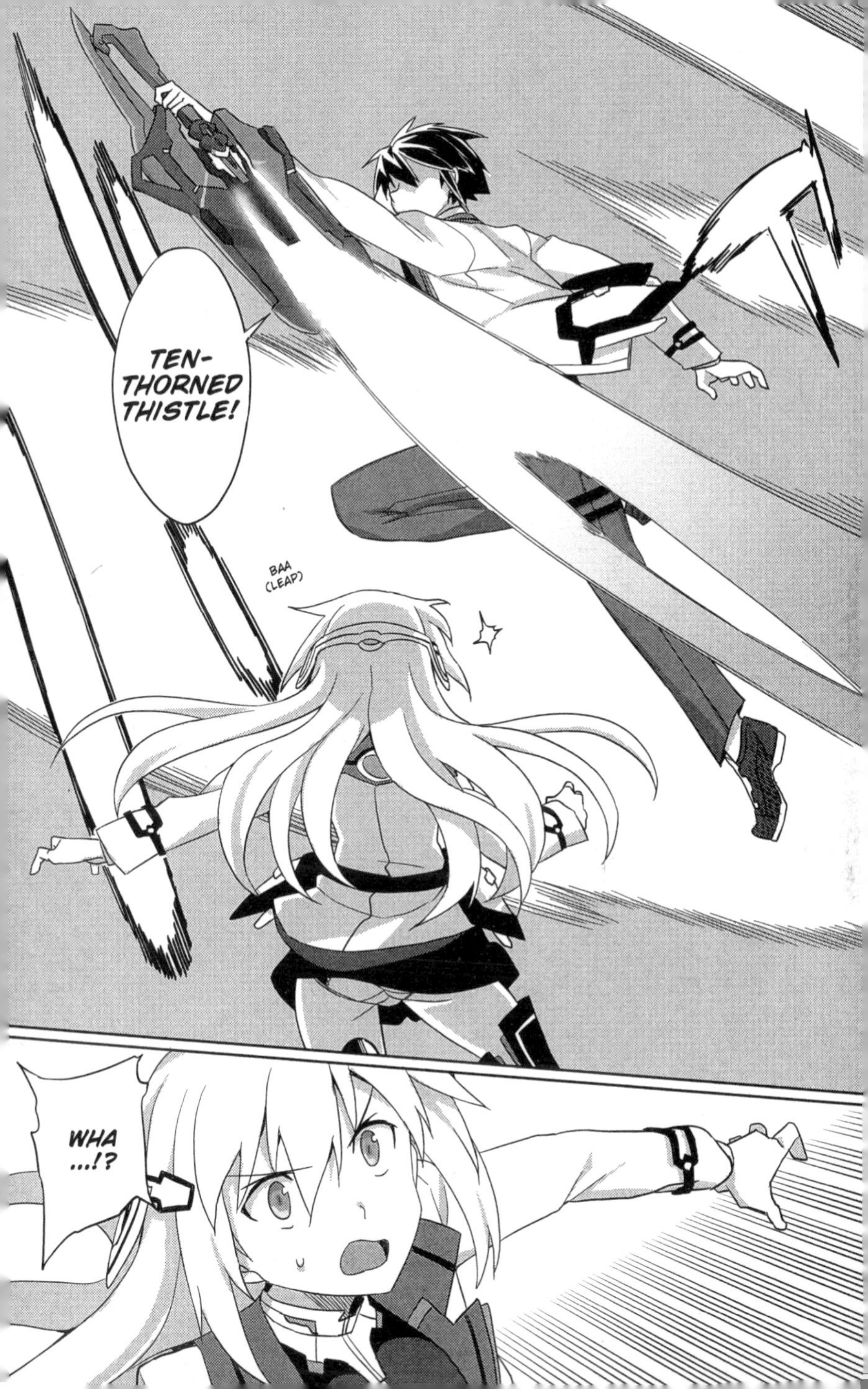
TEN-THORNED THISTLE!
BAA (LEAP)
WHA ...!?

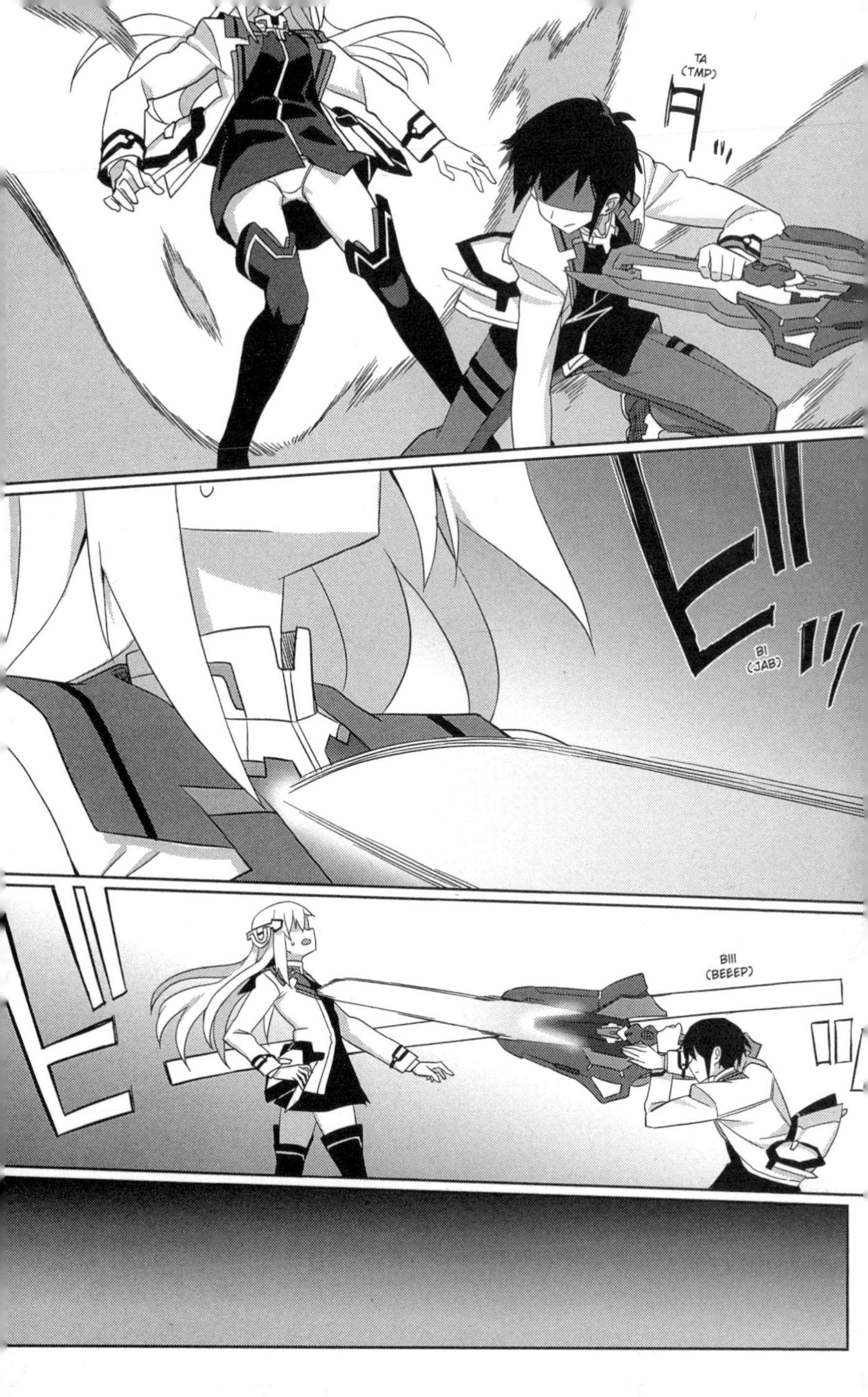
TA
(TMP)
BI
(JAB)
BIII
(BEEEP)

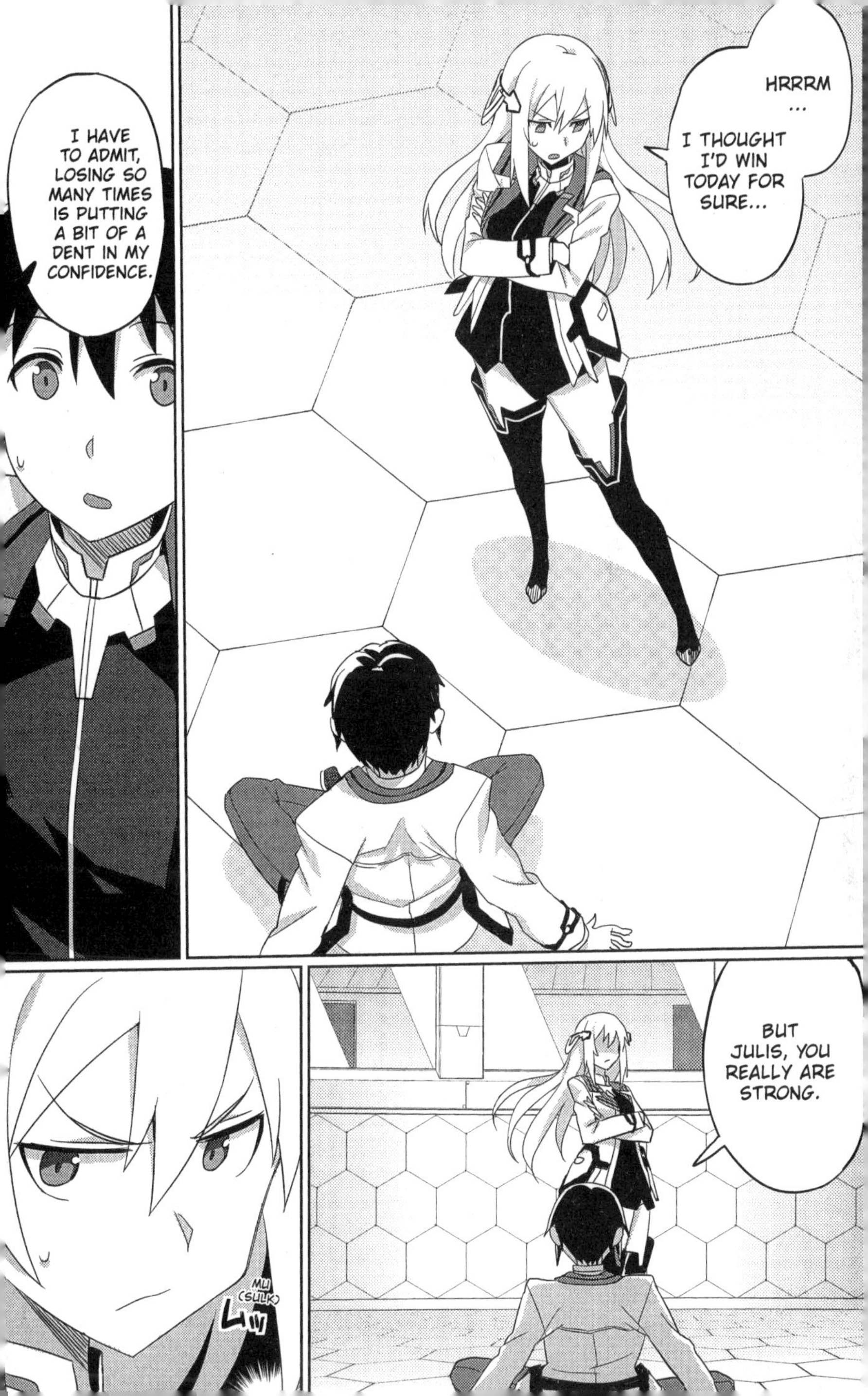
HRRRM ... I THOUGHT I'D WIN TODAY FOR SURE...
I HAVE TO ADMIT, LOSING SO MANY TIMES IS PUTTING A BIT OF A DENT IN MY CONFIDENCE.
BUT JULIS, YOU REALLY ARE STRONG.
MU (SULK)

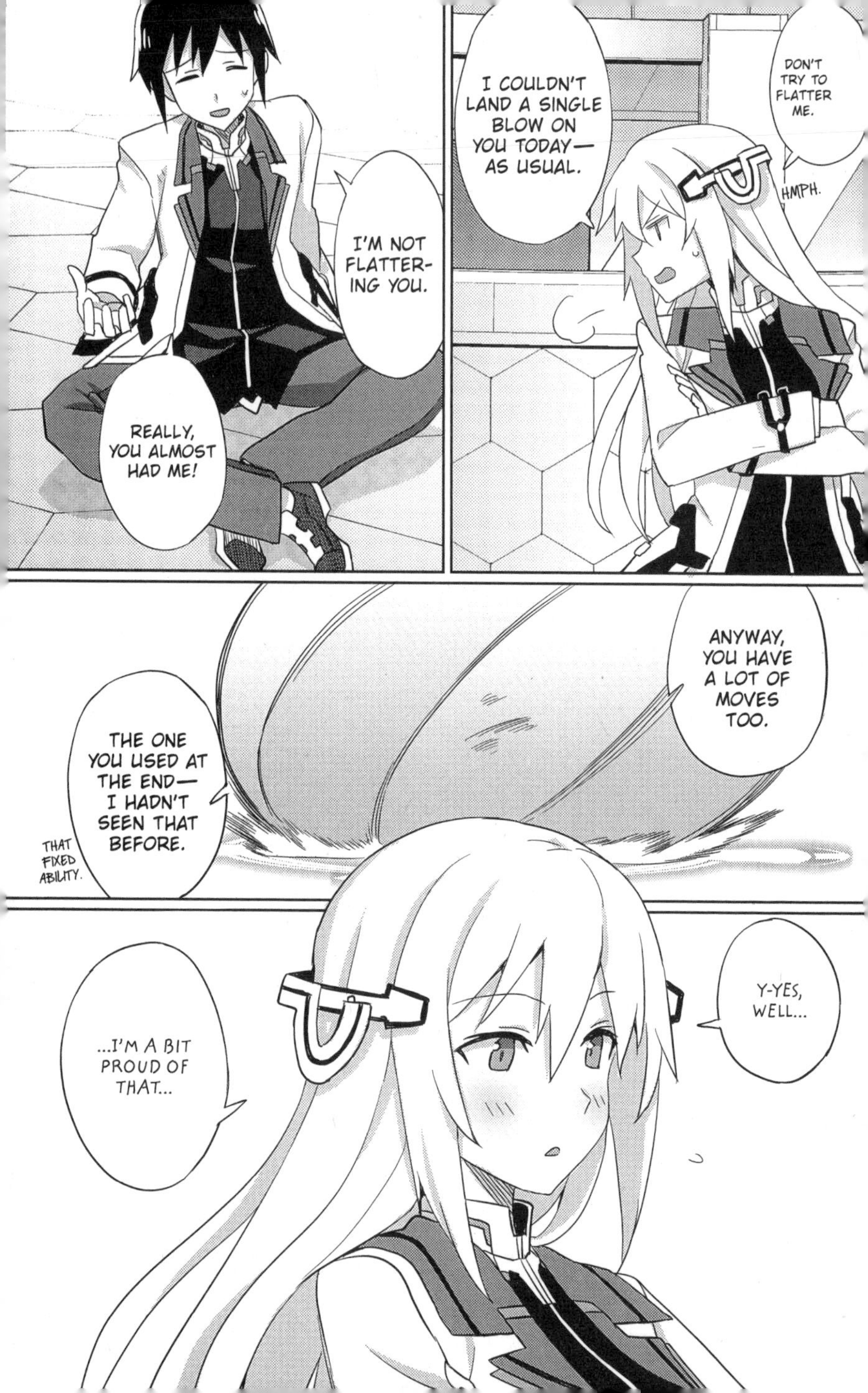
I COULDN'T LAND A SINGLE BLOW ON YOU TODAY—AS USUAL.
DON'T TRY TO FLATTER ME.
HMPH.
I'M NOT FLATTER-ING YOU.
REALLY, YOU ALMOST HAD ME!
ANYWAY, YOU HAVE A LOT OF MOVES TOO.
THE ONE YOU USED AT THE END—I HADN'T SEEN THAT BEFORE.
THAT FIXED ABILITY.
Y-YES, WELL...
...I'M A BIT PROUD OF THAT...

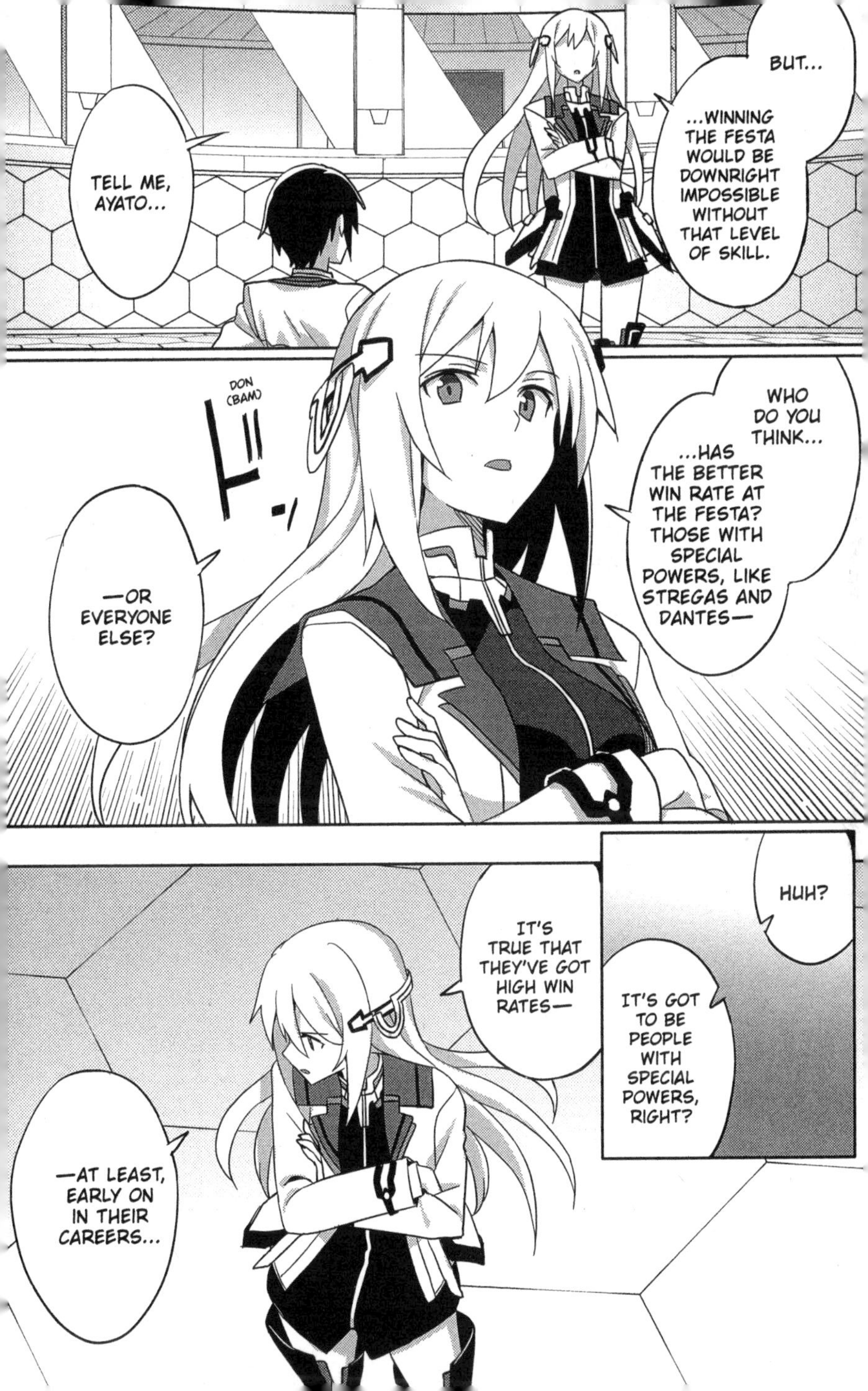
BUT...
...WINNING THE FESTA WOULD BE DOWNRIGHT IMPOSSIBLE WITHOUT THAT LEVEL OF SKILL.
TELL ME, AYATO...
WHO DO YOU THINK...
...HAS THE BETTER WIN RATE AT THE FESTA? THOSE WITH SPECIAL POWERS, LIKE STREGAS AND DANTES—
DON (BAM)
—OR EVERYONE ELSE?
HUH?
IT'S GOT TO BE PEOPLE WITH SPECIAL POWERS, RIGHT?
IT'S TRUE THAT THEY'VE GOT HIGH WIN RATES—
—AT LEAST, EARLY ON IN THEIR CAREERS...

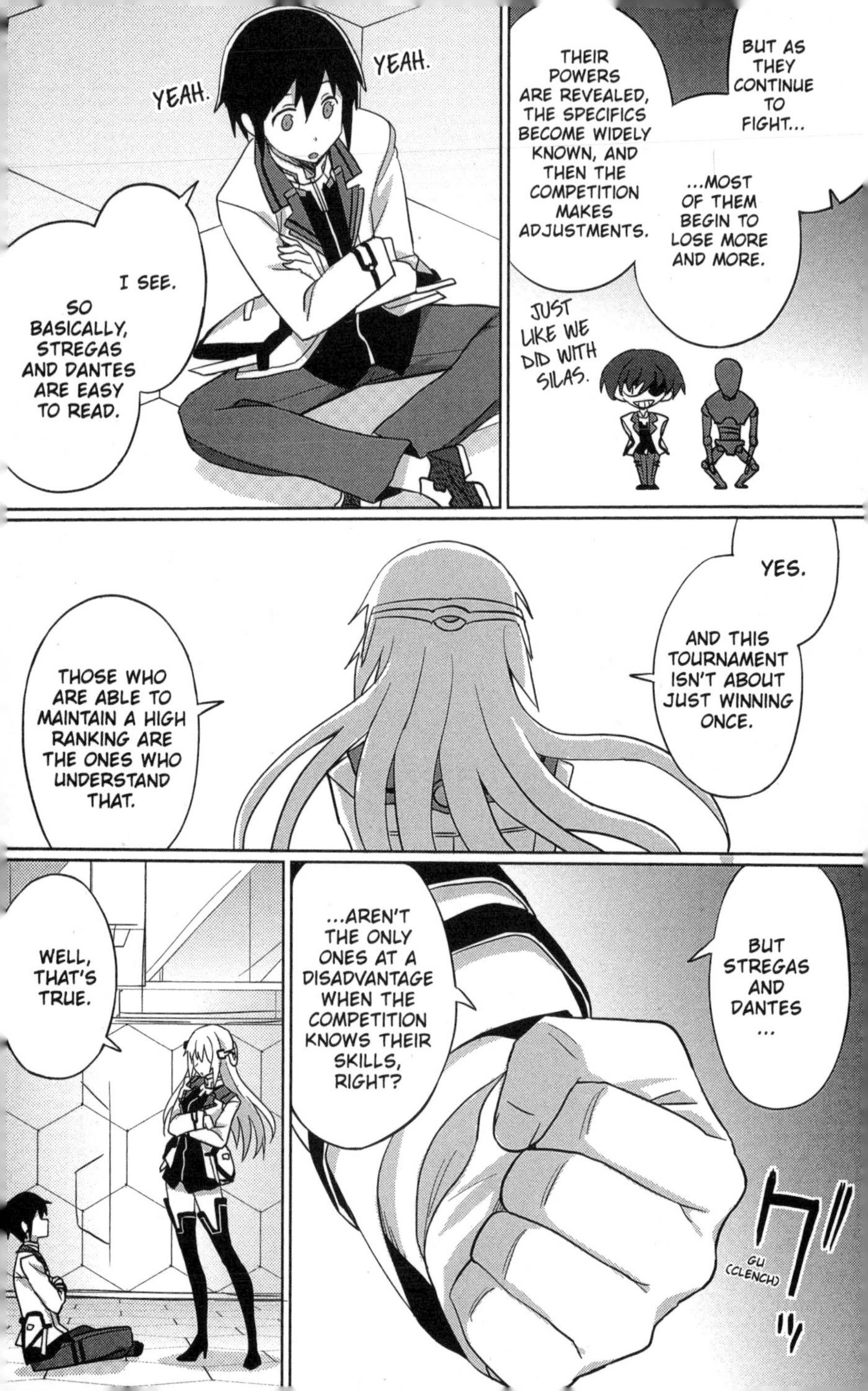
BUT AS THEY CONTINUE TO FIGHT...
THEIR POWERS ARE REVEALED, THE SPECIFICS BECOME WIDELY KNOWN, AND THEN THE COMPETITION MAKES ADJUSTMENTS.
...MOST OF THEM BEGIN TO LOSE MORE AND MORE.
JUST LIKE WE DID WITH SILAS.
YEAH.
YEAH.
I SEE.
SO BASICALLY, STREGAS AND DANTES ARE EASY TO READ.
YES.
AND THIS TOURNAMENT ISN'T ABOUT JUST WINNING ONCE.
THOSE WHO ARE ABLE TO MAINTAIN A HIGH RANKING ARE THE ONES WHO UNDERSTAND THAT.
BUT STREGAS AND DANTES ...
...AREN'T THE ONLY ONES AT A DISADVANTAGE WHEN THE COMPETITION KNOWS THEIR SKILLS, RIGHT?
GU (CLENCH)
WELL, THAT'S TRUE.

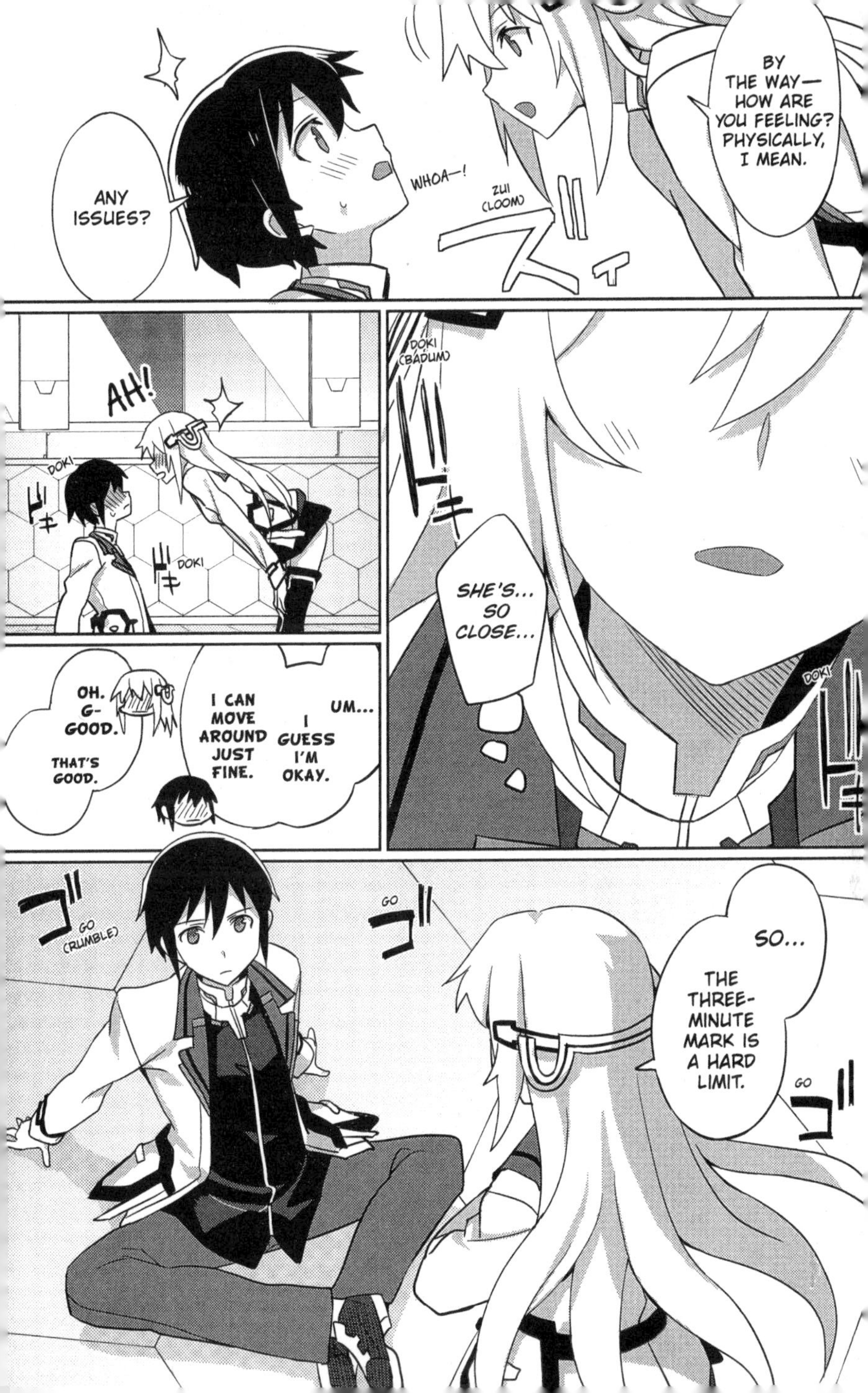
BY THE WAY— HOW ARE YOU FEELING? PHYSICALLY, I MEAN.
ZUI (LOOM)
WHOA—!
ANY ISSUES?
DOKI (BADUM)
SHE'S... SO CLOSE...
DOKI
AH!
DOKI
DOKI
UM...
I GUESS I'M OKAY.
I CAN MOVE AROUND JUST FINE.
OH. G-GOOD.
THAT'S GOOD.
SO...
THE THREE-MINUTE MARK IS A HARD LIMIT.
GO
GO
GO (RUMBLE)

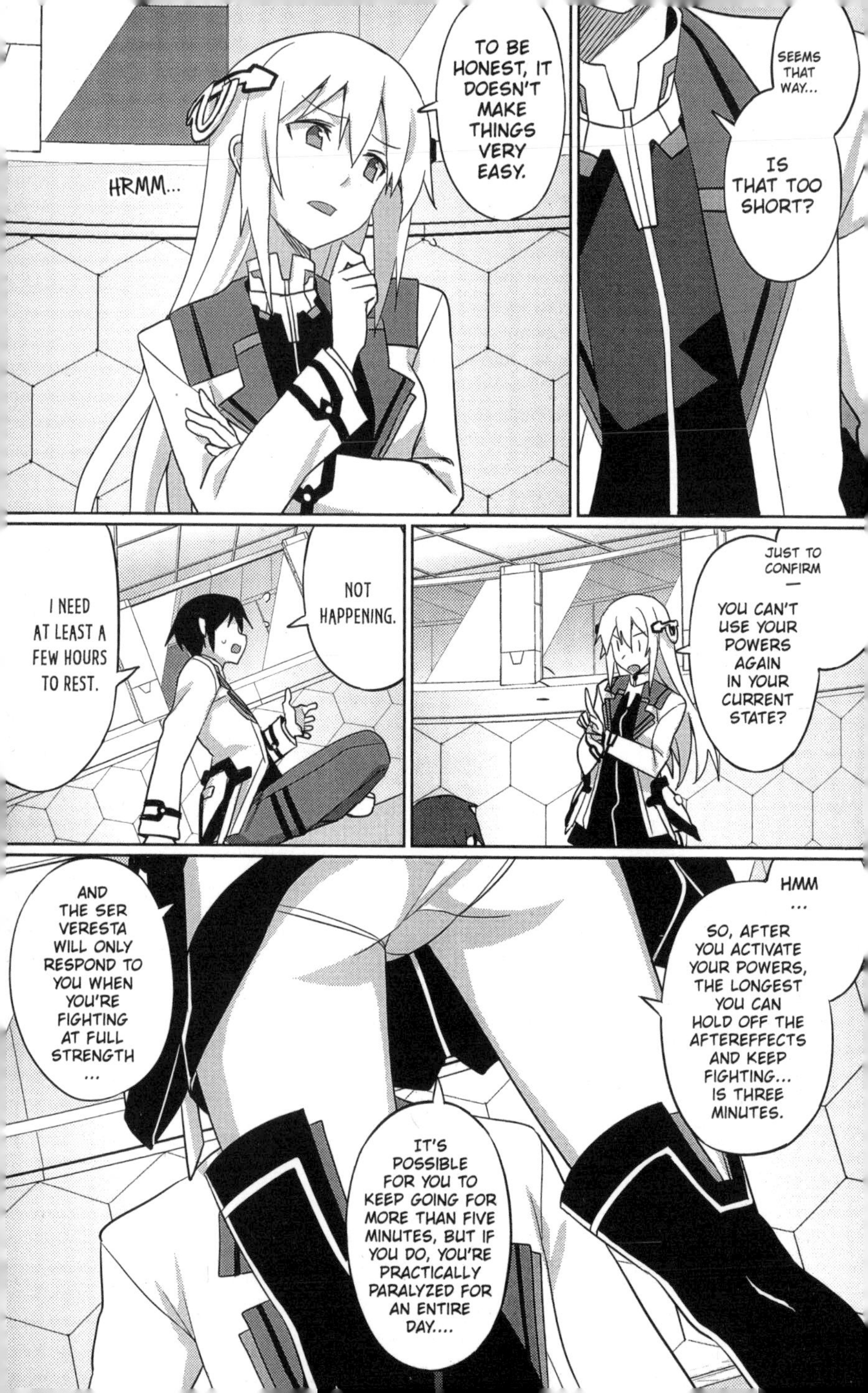
SEEMS THAT WAY...
IS THAT TOO SHORT?
TO BE HONEST, IT DOESN'T MAKE THINGS VERY EASY.
HRMM...
JUST TO CONFIRM —
YOU CAN'T USE YOUR POWERS AGAIN IN YOUR CURRENT STATE?
NOT HAPPENING.
I NEED AT LEAST A FEW HOURS TO REST.
HMM...
SO, AFTER YOU ACTIVATE YOUR POWERS, THE LONGEST YOU CAN HOLD OFF THE AFTEREFFECTS AND KEEP FIGHTING... IS THREE MINUTES.
IT'S POSSIBLE FOR YOU TO KEEP GOING FOR MORE THAN FIVE MINUTES, BUT IF YOU DO, YOU'RE PRACTICALLY PARALYZED FOR AN ENTIRE DAY....
AND THE SER VERESTA WILL ONLY RESPOND TO YOU WHEN YOU'RE FIGHTING AT FULL STRENGTH...

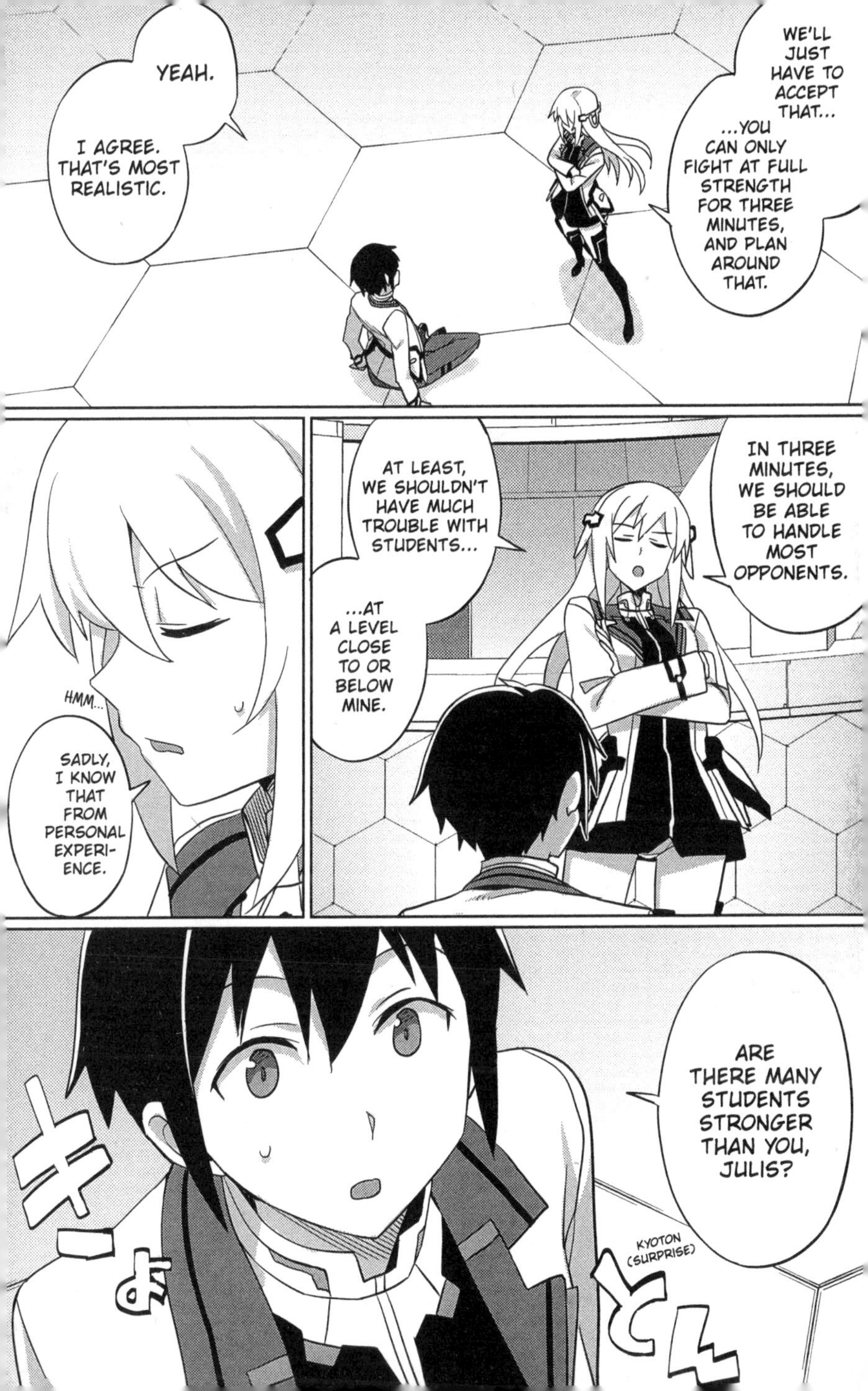
WE'LL JUST HAVE TO ACCEPT THAT... ...YOU CAN ONLY FIGHT AT FULL STRENGTH FOR THREE MINUTES, AND PLAN AROUND THAT.
YEAH.
I AGREE. THAT'S MOST REALISTIC.
IN THREE MINUTES, WE SHOULD BE ABLE TO HANDLE MOST OPPONENTS.
AT LEAST, WE SHOULDN'T HAVE MUCH TROUBLE WITH STUDENTS...
...AT A LEVEL CLOSE TO OR BELOW MINE.
HMM...
SADLY, I KNOW THAT FROM PERSONAL EXPERIENCE.
ARE THERE MANY STUDENTS STRONGER THAN YOU, JULIS?
KYOTON (SURPRISE)

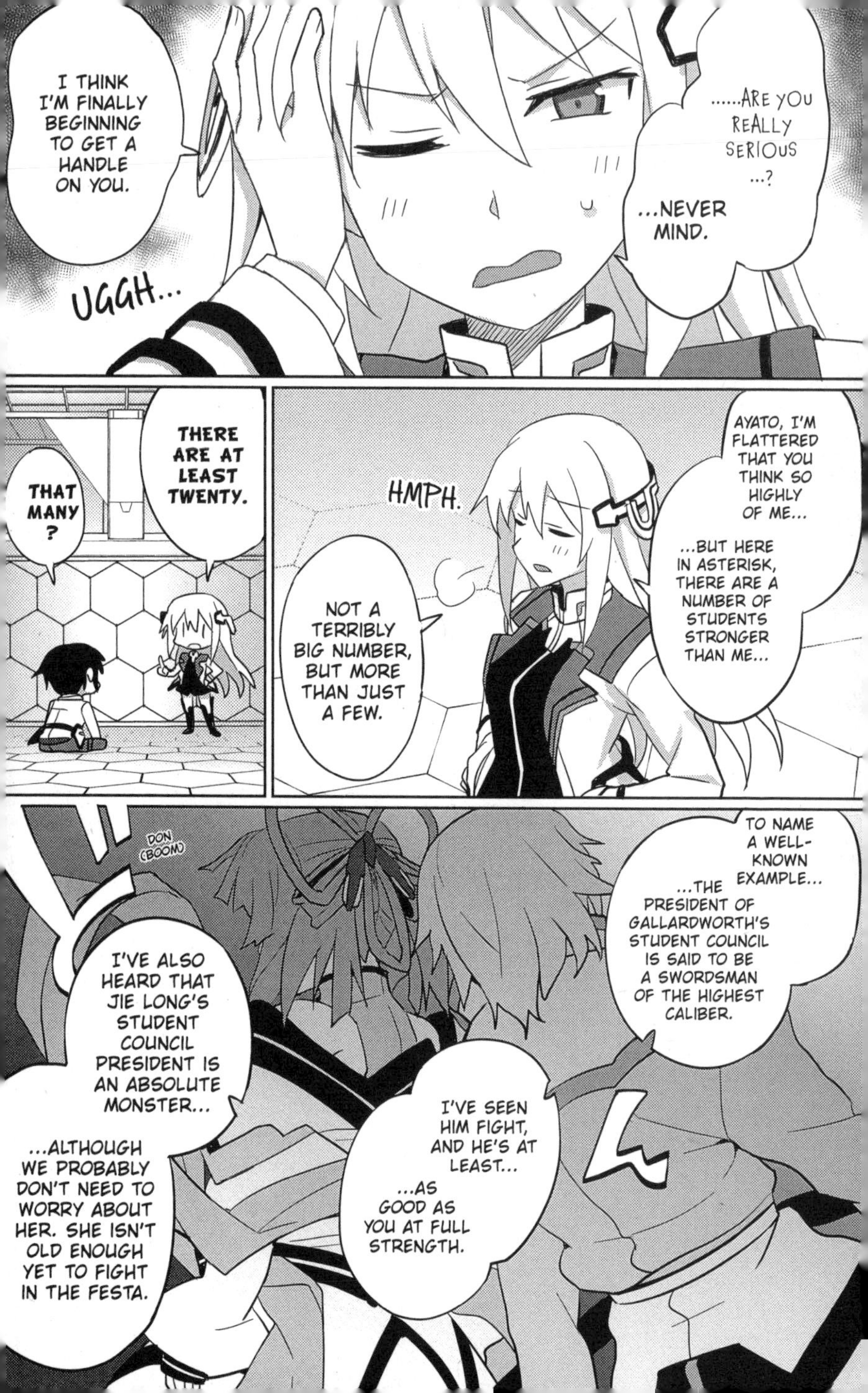
......ARE YOU REALLY SERIOUS ...?
...NEVER MIND.
I THINK I'M FINALLY BEGINNING TO GET A HANDLE ON YOU.
UGGH...
AYATO, I'M FLATTERED THAT YOU THINK SO HIGHLY OF ME...
...BUT HERE IN ASTERISK, THERE ARE A NUMBER OF STUDENTS STRONGER THAN ME...
HMPH.
NOT A TERRIBLY BIG NUMBER, BUT MORE THAN JUST A FEW.
THERE ARE AT LEAST TWENTY.
THAT MANY?
TO NAME A WELL-KNOWN EXAMPLE...
...THE PRESIDENT OF GALLARDWORTH'S STUDENT COUNCIL IS SAID TO BE A SWORDSMAN OF THE HIGHEST CALIBER.
DON (BOOM)
I'VE SEEN HIM FIGHT, AND HE'S AT LEAST...
...AS GOOD AS YOU AT FULL STRENGTH.
I'VE ALSO HEARD THAT JIE LONG'S STUDENT COUNCIL PRESIDENT IS AN ABSOLUTE MONSTER...
...ALTHOUGH WE PROBABLY DON'T NEED TO WORRY ABOUT HER. SHE ISN'T OLD ENOUGH YET TO FIGHT IN THE FESTA.

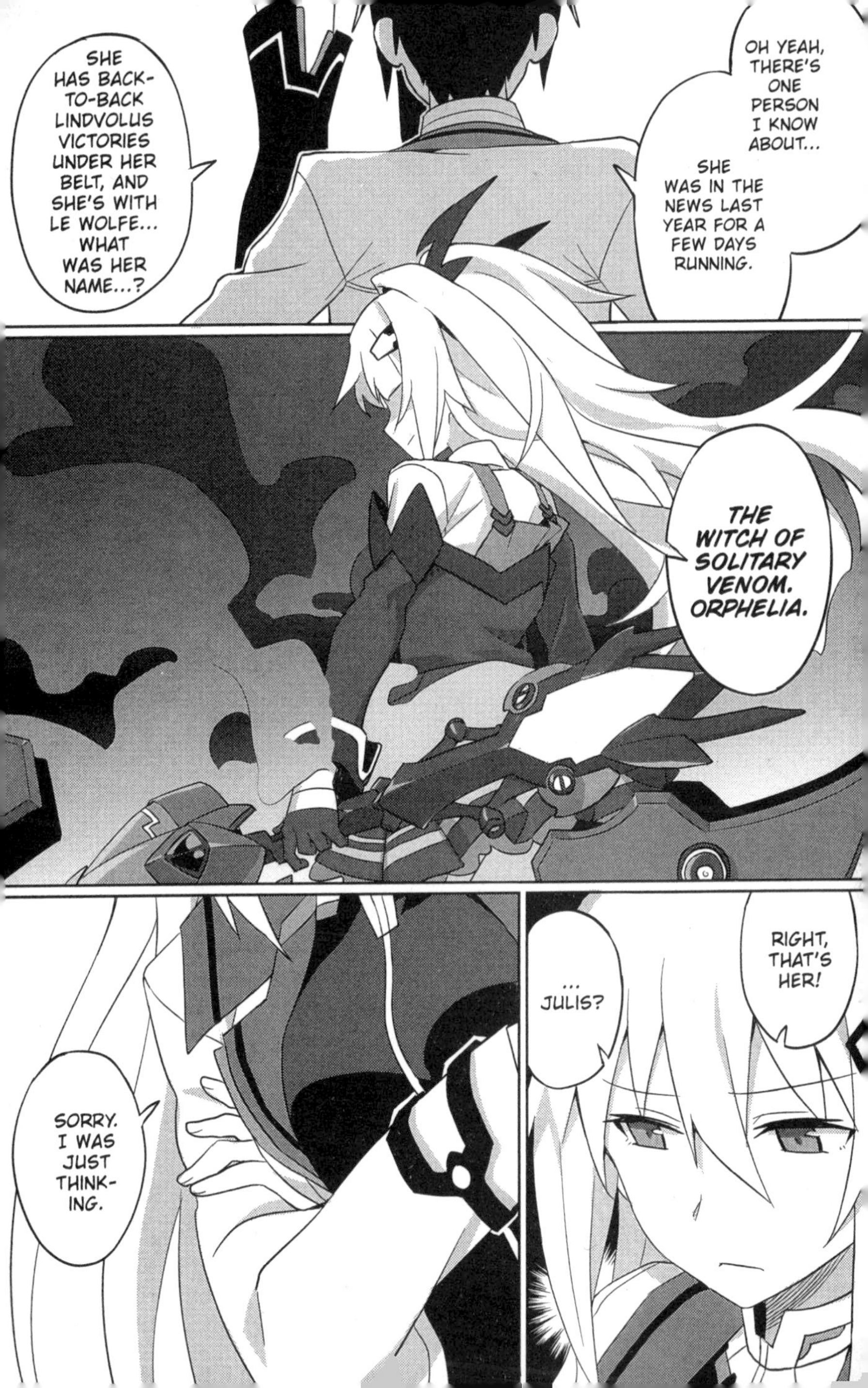
OH YEAH, THERE'S ONE PERSON I KNOW ABOUT...
SHE WAS IN THE NEWS LAST YEAR FOR A FEW DAYS RUNNING.
SHE HAS BACK-TO-BACK LINDVOLUS VICTORIES UNDER HER BELT, AND SHE'S WITH LE WOLFE... WHAT WAS HER NAME...?
THE WITCH OF SOLITARY VENOM. ORPHELIA.
RIGHT, THAT'S HER!
...JULIS?
SORRY. I WAS JUST THINKING.

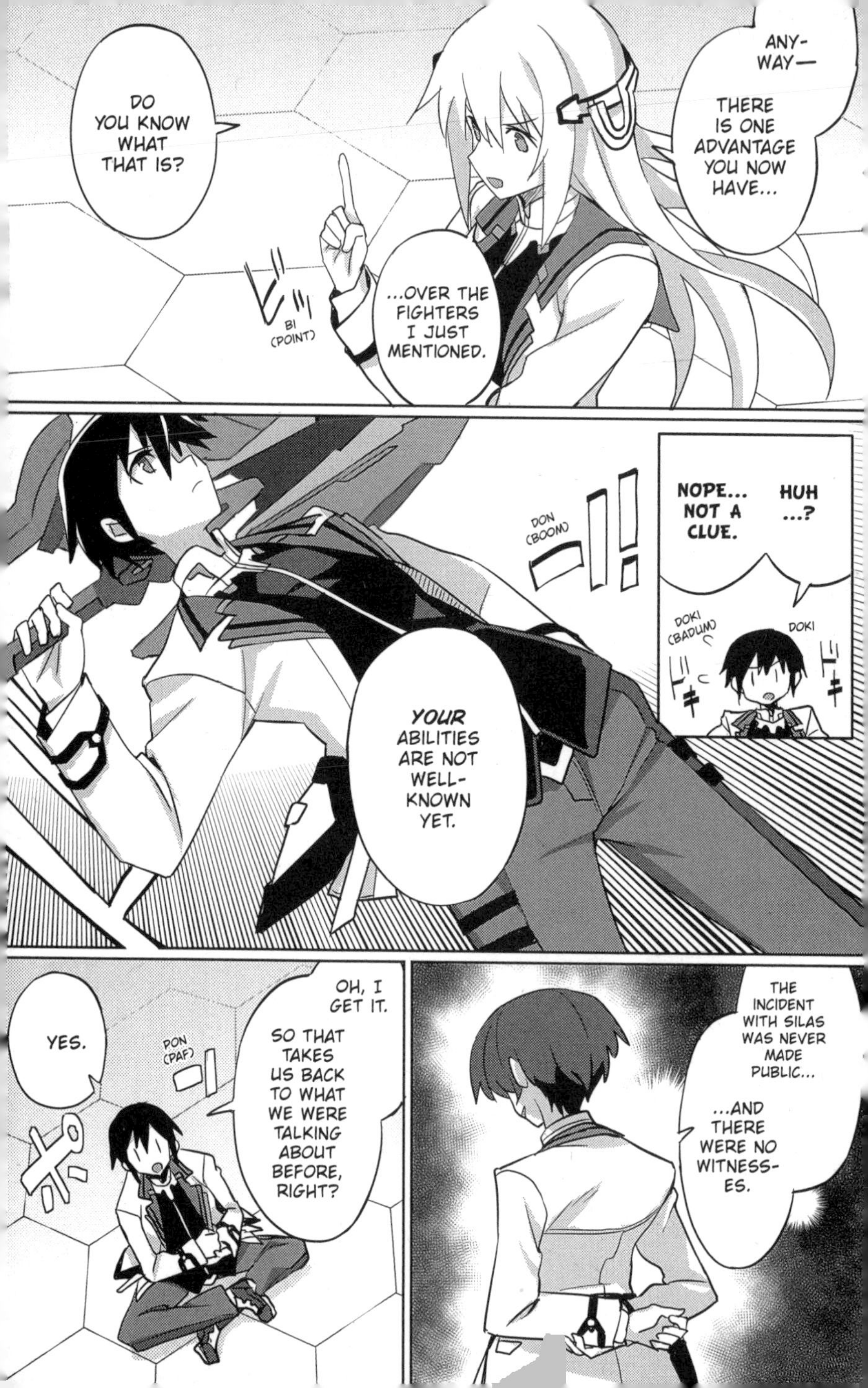
ANY-WAY— THERE IS ONE ADVANTAGE YOU NOW HAVE...
...OVER THE FIGHTERS I JUST MENTIONED.
BI (POINT)
DO YOU KNOW WHAT THAT IS?
HUH ...?
NOPE... NOT A CLUE.
DOKI
DOKI (BADUM)
DON (BOOM)
YOUR ABILITIES ARE NOT WELL-KNOWN YET.
THE INCIDENT WITH SILAS WAS NEVER MADE PUBLIC...
...AND THERE WERE NO WITNESS-ES.
OH, I GET IT.
SO THAT TAKES US BACK TO WHAT WE WERE TALKING ABOUT BEFORE, RIGHT?
PON (PAF)
YES.

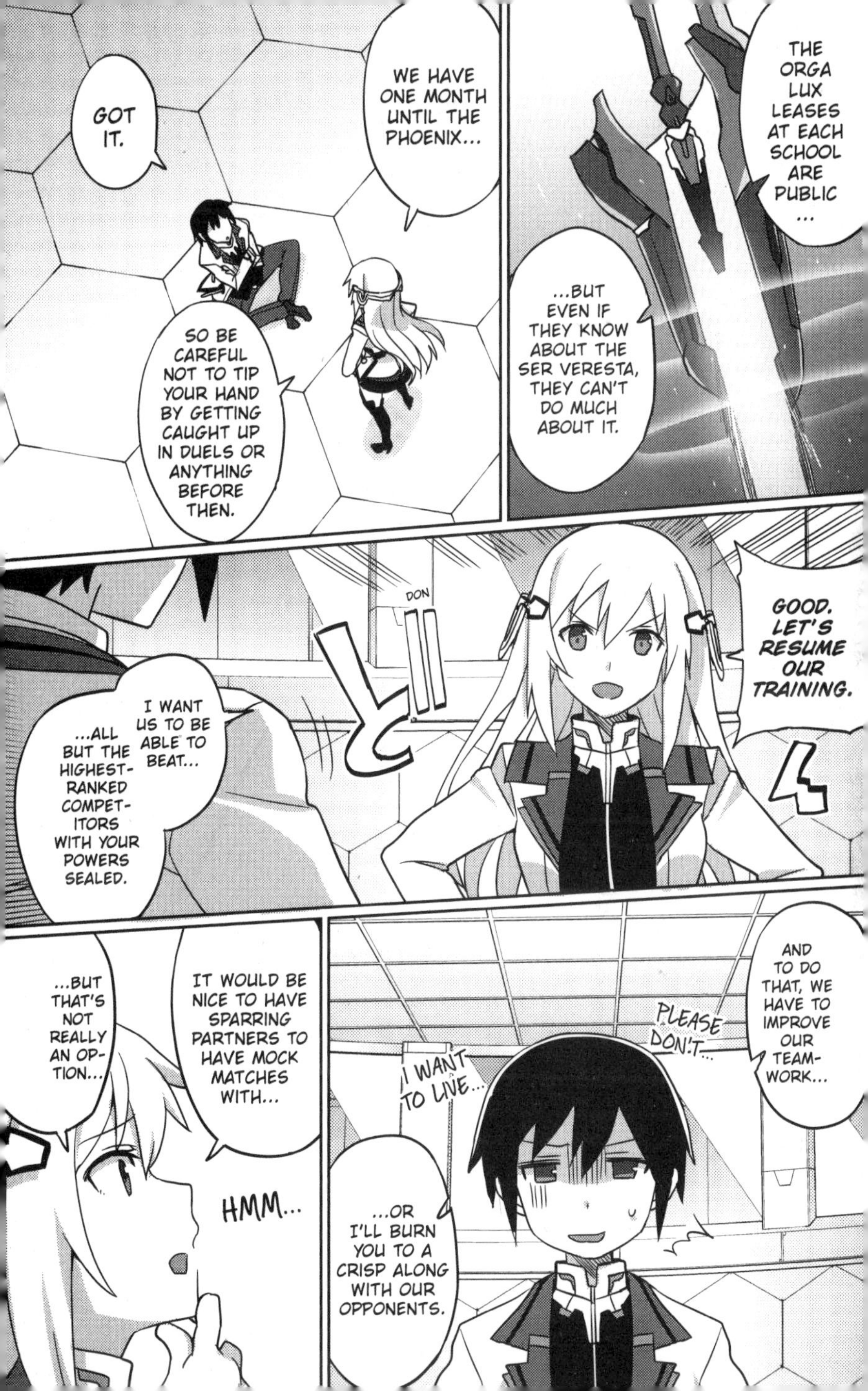
THE ORGA LUX LEASES AT EACH SCHOOL ARE PUBLIC...
...BUT EVEN IF THEY KNOW ABOUT THE SER VERESTA, THEY CAN'T DO MUCH ABOUT IT.
WE HAVE ONE MONTH UNTIL THE PHOENIX...
SO BE CAREFUL NOT TO TIP YOUR HAND BY GETTING CAUGHT UP IN DUELS OR ANYTHING BEFORE THEN.
GOT IT.
GOOD. LET'S RESUME OUR TRAINING.
DON
I WANT US TO BE ABLE TO BEAT...
...ALL BUT THE HIGHEST-RANKED COMPETITORS WITH YOUR POWERS SEALED.
AND TO DO THAT, WE HAVE TO IMPROVE OUR TEAMWORK...
...OR I'LL BURN YOU TO A CRISP ALONG WITH OUR OPPONENTS.
PLEASE DON'T...
I WANT TO LIVE...
IT WOULD BE NICE TO HAVE SPARRING PARTNERS TO HAVE MOCK MATCHES WITH...
...BUT THAT'S NOT REALLY AN OPTION...
HMM...

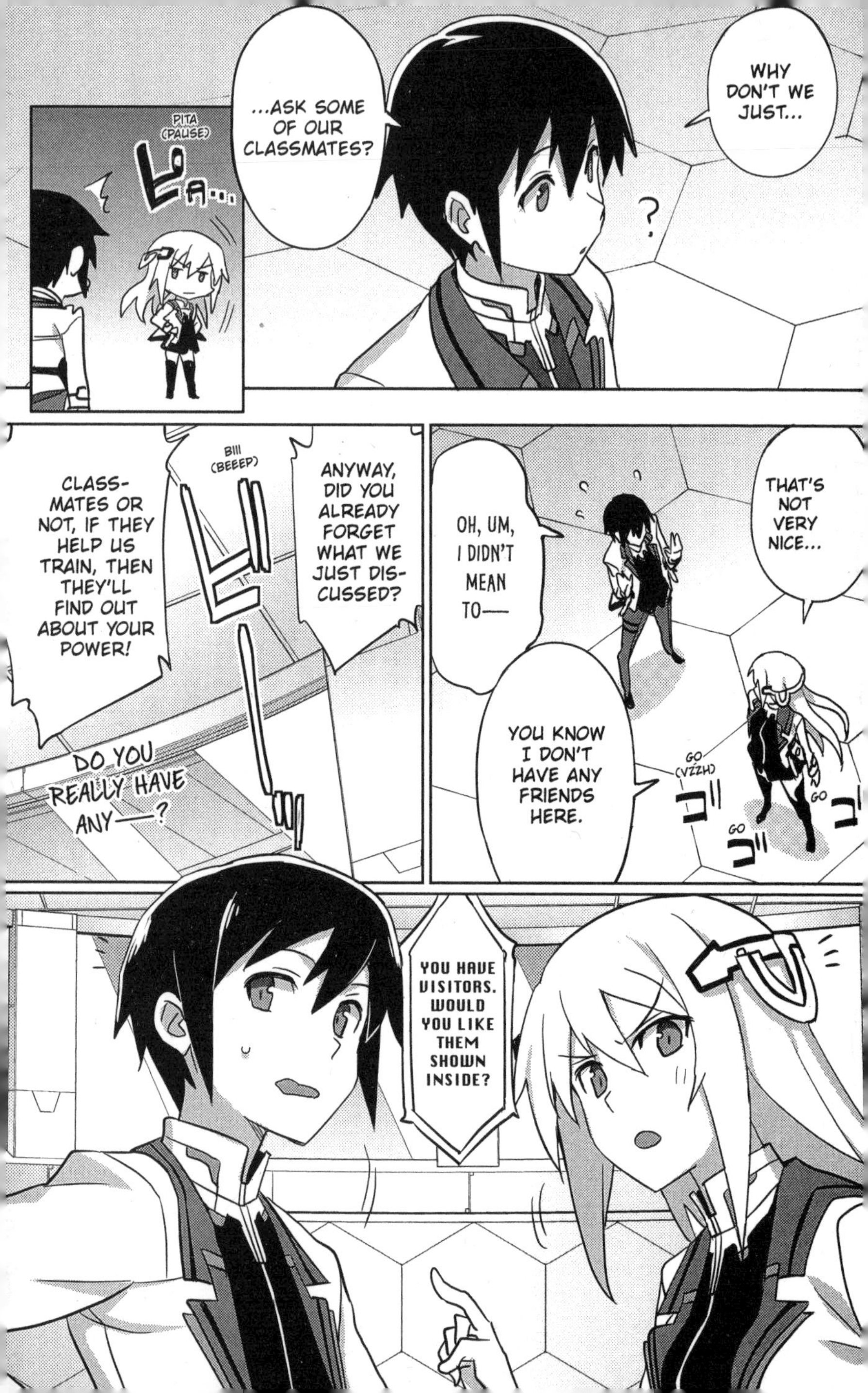
WHY DON'T WE JUST...
...ASK SOME OF OUR CLASSMATES?
PITA (PAUSE)
THAT'S NOT VERY NICE...
OH, UM, I DIDN'T MEAN TO—
YOU KNOW I DON'T HAVE ANY FRIENDS HERE.
GO (VZZH)
GO
GO
ANYWAY, DID YOU ALREADY FORGET WHAT WE JUST DISCUSSED?
BIII (BEEEP)
CLASS-MATES OR NOT, IF THEY HELP US TRAIN, THEN THEY'LL FIND OUT ABOUT YOUR POWER!
DO YOU REALLY HAVE ANY—?
YOU HAVE VISITORS. WOULD YOU LIKE THEM SHOWN INSIDE?

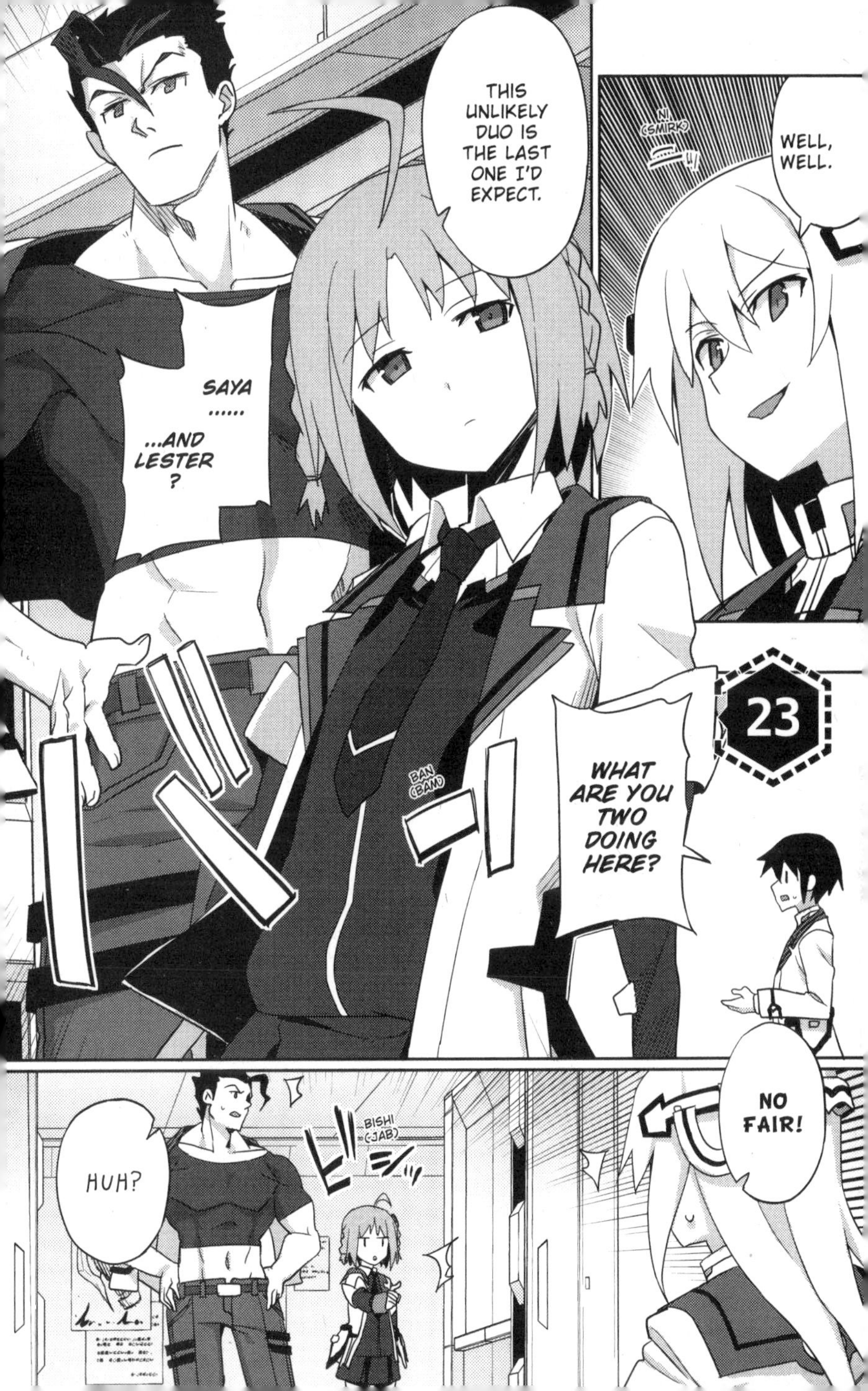

WELL, WELL.
NI (SMIRK)
23
WHAT ARE YOU TWO DOING HERE?
THIS UNLIKELY DUO IS THE LAST ONE I'D EXPECT.
SAYA ......
...AND LESTER ?
BAN (BAM)
NO FAIR!
BISHI (JAB)
HUH?

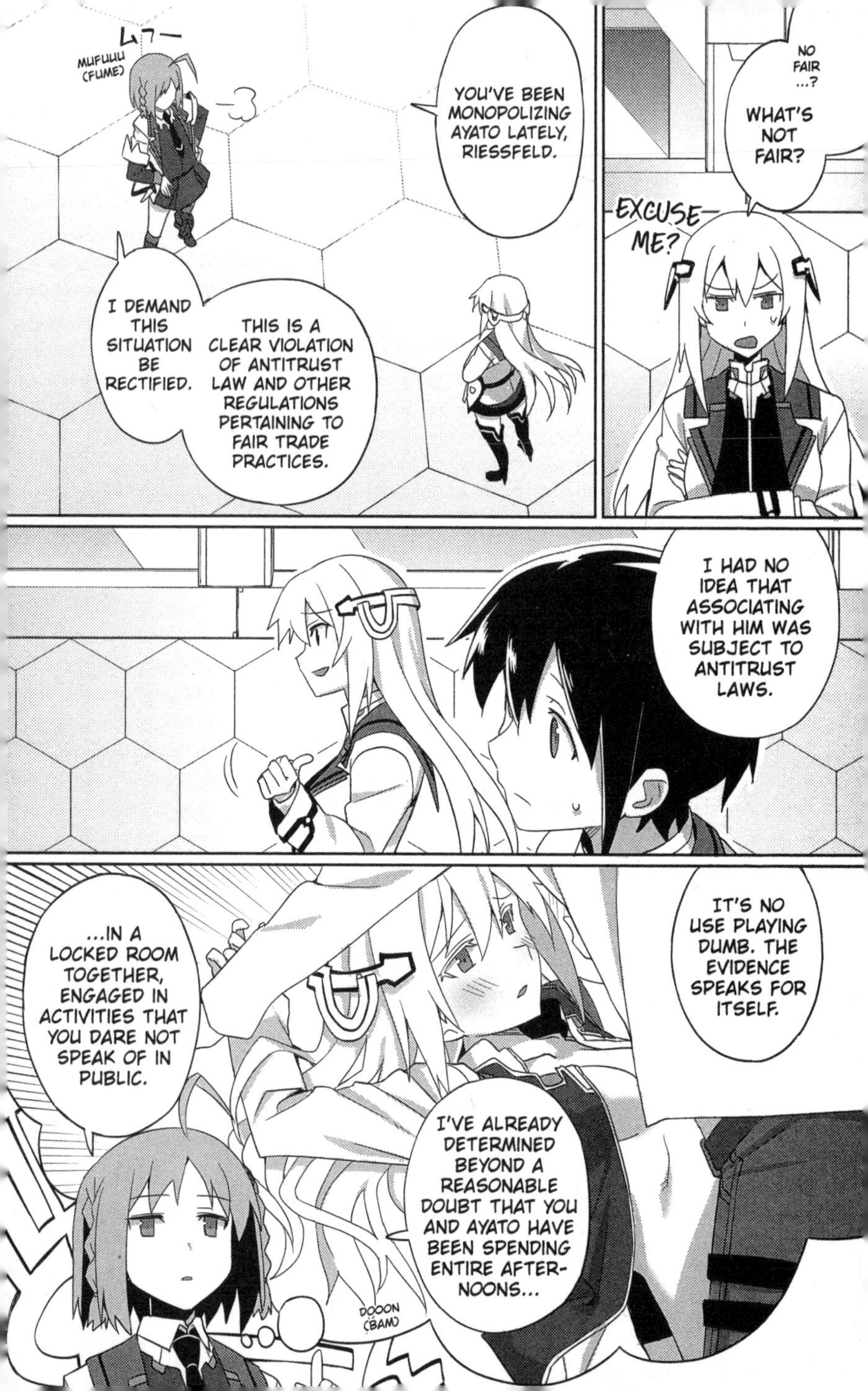
NO FAIR ...?
WHAT'S NOT FAIR?
EXCUSE ME?
YOU'VE BEEN MONOPOLIZING AYATO LATELY, RIESSFELD.
ムフー
MUFUUU (FUME)
THIS IS A CLEAR VIOLATION OF ANTITRUST LAW AND OTHER REGULATIONS PERTAINING TO FAIR TRADE PRACTICES.
I DEMAND THIS SITUATION BE RECTIFIED.
I HAD NO IDEA THAT ASSOCIATING WITH HIM WAS SUBJECT TO ANTITRUST LAWS.
IT'S NO USE PLAYING DUMB. THE EVIDENCE SPEAKS FOR ITSELF.
I'VE ALREADY DETERMINED BEYOND A REASONABLE DOUBT THAT YOU AND AYATO HAVE BEEN SPENDING ENTIRE AFTER-NOONS...
...IN A LOCKED ROOM TOGETHER, ENGAGED IN ACTIVITIES THAT YOU DARE NOT SPEAK OF IN PUBLIC.
DOOON (BAM)

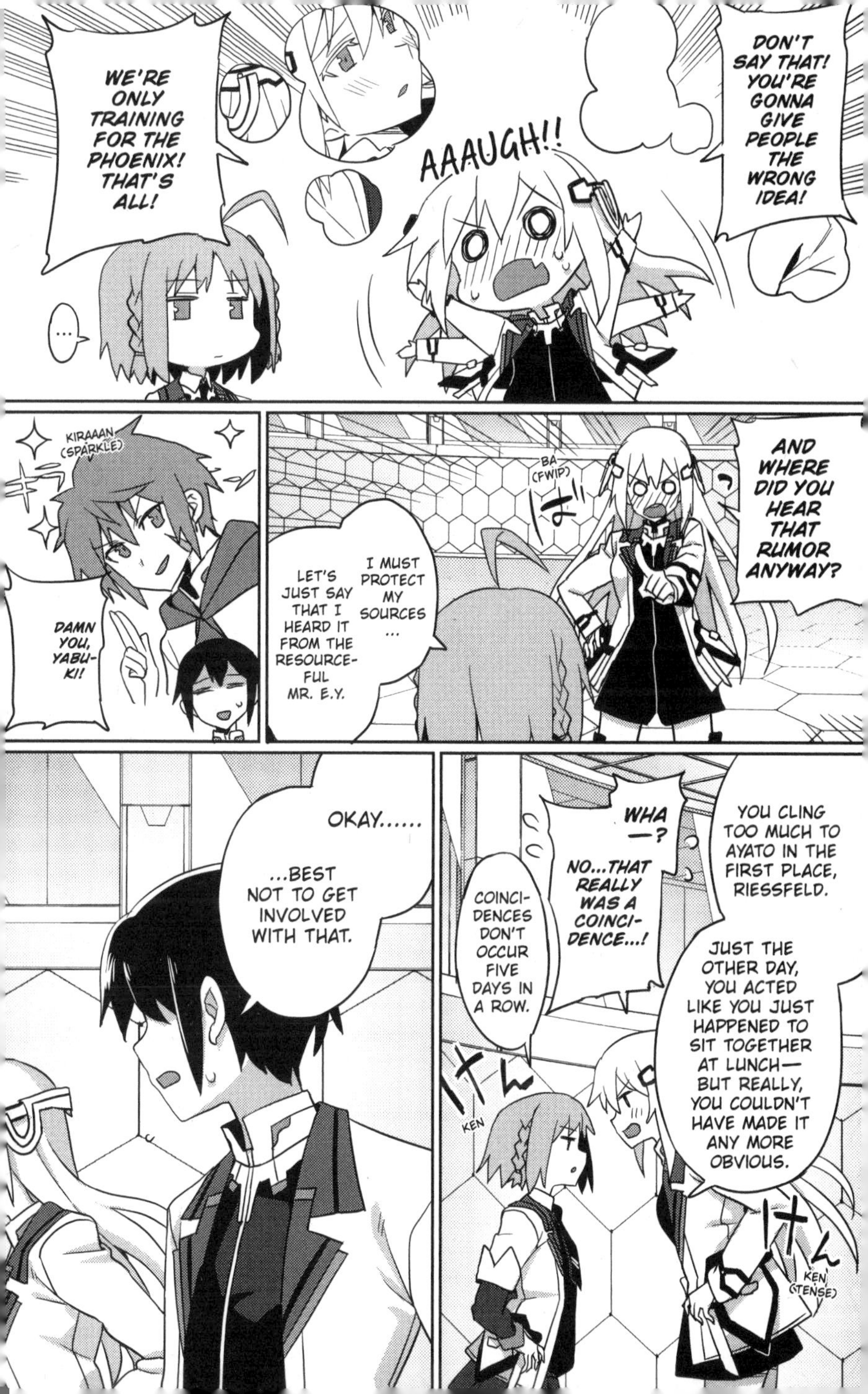
DON'T SAY THAT! YOU'RE GONNA GIVE PEOPLE THE WRONG IDEA!
AAAUGH!!
WE'RE ONLY TRAINING FOR THE PHOENIX! THAT'S ALL!
...
AND WHERE DID YOU HEAR THAT RUMOR ANYWAY?
BA (FWIP)
I MUST PROTECT MY SOURCES...
LET'S JUST SAY THAT I HEARD IT FROM THE RESOURCEFUL MR. E.Y.
KIRAAAN (SPARKLE)
DAMN YOU, YABUKI!
YOU CLING TOO MUCH TO AYATO IN THE FIRST PLACE, RIESSFELD.
JUST THE OTHER DAY, YOU ACTED LIKE YOU JUST HAPPENED TO SIT TOGETHER AT LUNCH—BUT REALLY, YOU COULDN'T HAVE MADE IT ANY MORE OBVIOUS.
WHA—?
NO...THAT REALLY WAS A COINCIDENCE...!
COINCIDENCES DON'T OCCUR FIVE DAYS IN A ROW.
KEN (TENSE)
KEN
OKAY......
...BEST NOT TO GET INVOLVED WITH THAT.

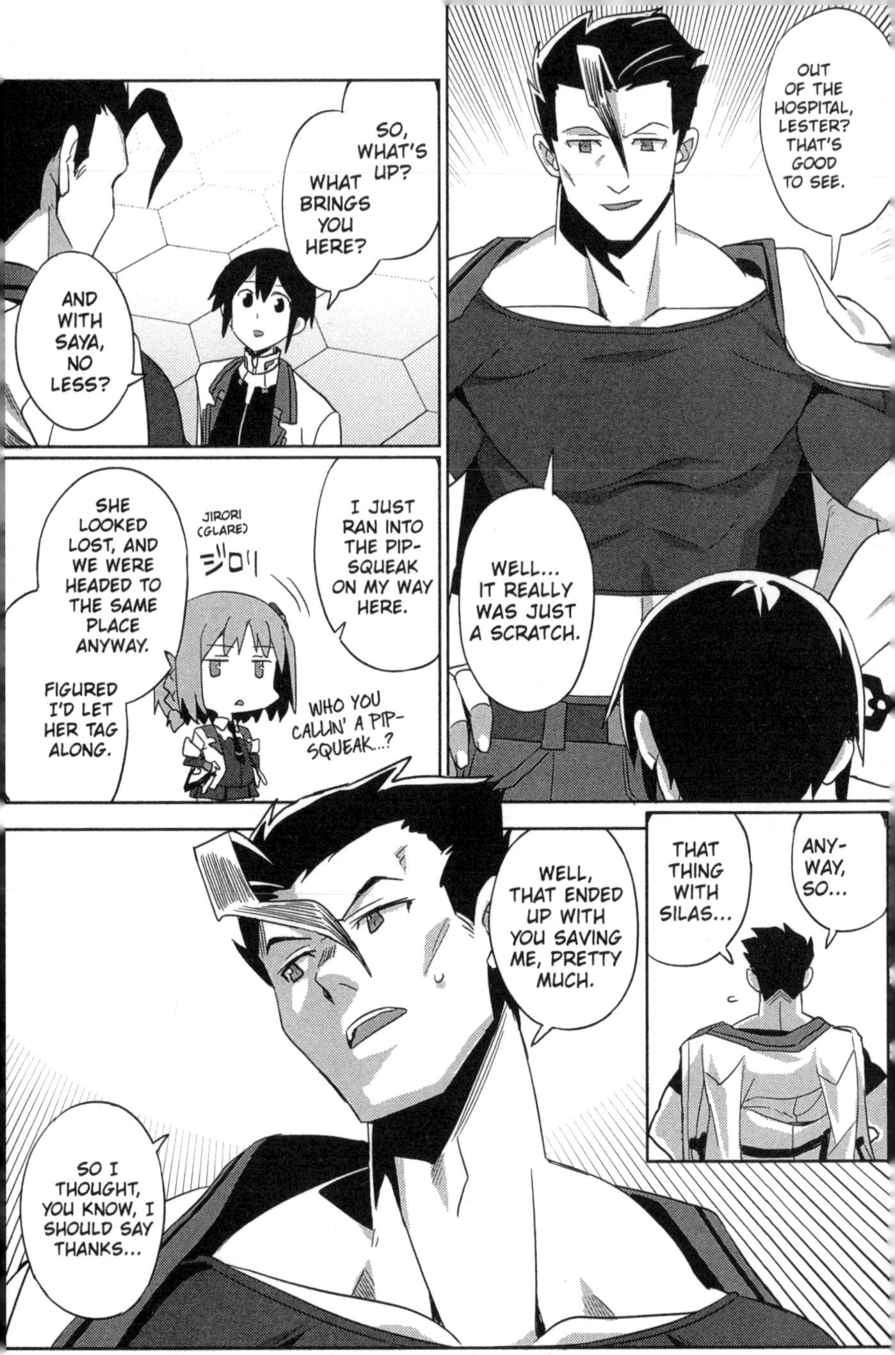
OUT OF THE HOSPITAL, LESTER? THAT'S GOOD TO SEE.
WELL... IT REALLY WAS JUST A SCRATCH.
SO, WHAT'S UP?
WHAT BRINGS YOU HERE?
AND WITH SAYA, NO LESS?
I JUST RAN INTO THE PIP-SQUEAK ON MY WAY HERE.
JIRORI (GLARE)
ジロリ
SHE LOOKED LOST, AND WE WERE HEADED TO THE SAME PLACE ANYWAY.
WHO YOU CALLIN' A PIP-SQUEAK...?
FIGURED I'D LET HER TAG ALONG.
ANY-WAY, SO...
THAT THING WITH SILAS...
WELL, THAT ENDED UP WITH YOU SAVING ME, PRETTY MUCH.
SO I THOUGHT, YOU KNOW, I SHOULD SAY THANKS...

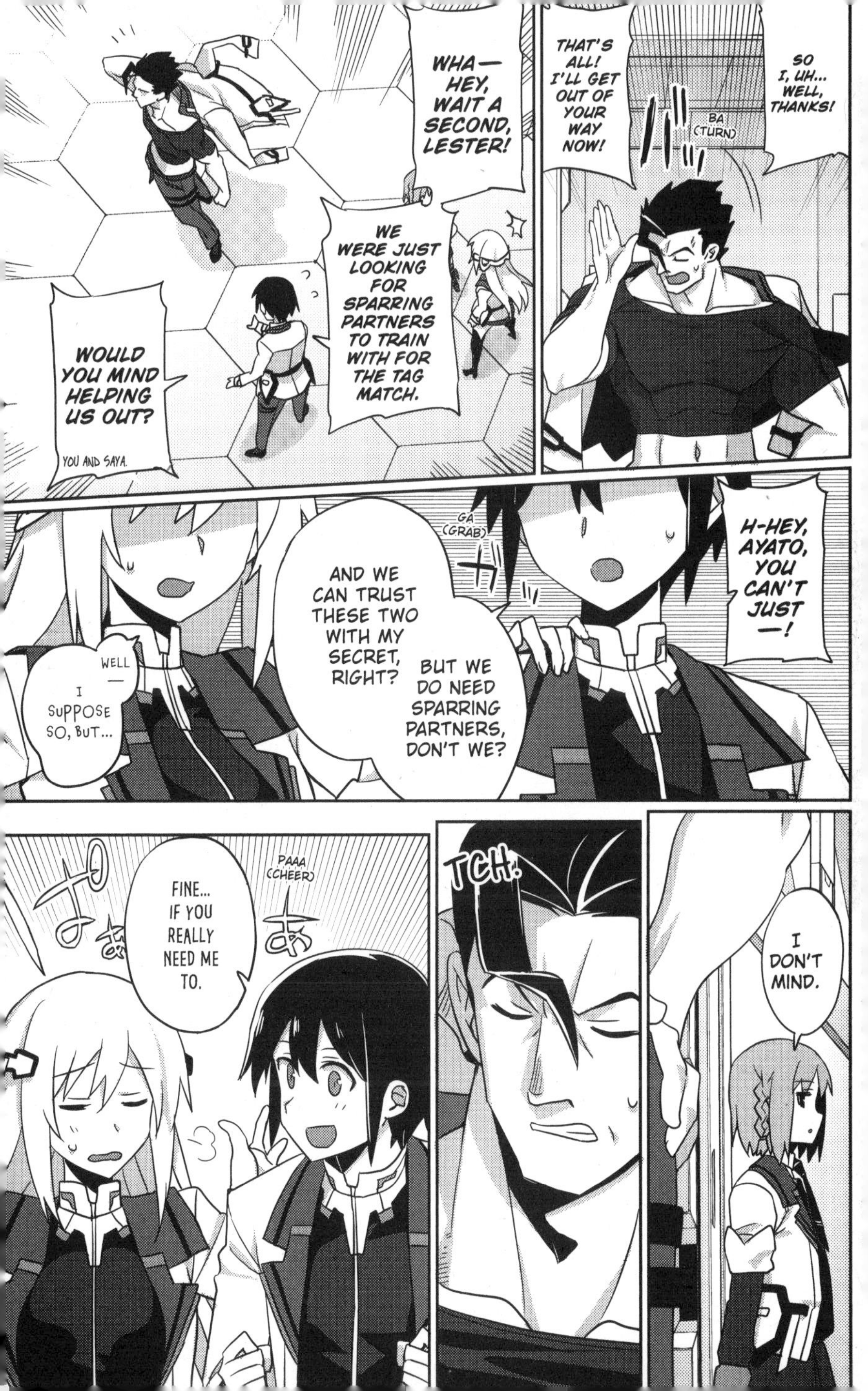
SO I, UH... WELL, THANKS!
BA (TURN)
THAT'S ALL! I'LL GET OUT OF YOUR WAY NOW!
WHA— HEY, WAIT A SECOND, LESTER!
WE WERE JUST LOOKING FOR SPARRING PARTNERS TO TRAIN WITH FOR THE TAG MATCH.
WOULD YOU MIND HELPING US OUT?
YOU AND SAYA.
H-HEY, AYATO, YOU CAN'T JUST—!
GA (GRAB)
BUT WE DO NEED SPARRING PARTNERS, DON'T WE?
AND WE CAN TRUST THESE TWO WITH MY SECRET, RIGHT?
WELL— I SUPPOSE SO, BUT...
I DON'T MIND.
TCH.
PAAA (CHEER)
FINE... IF YOU REALLY NEED ME TO.

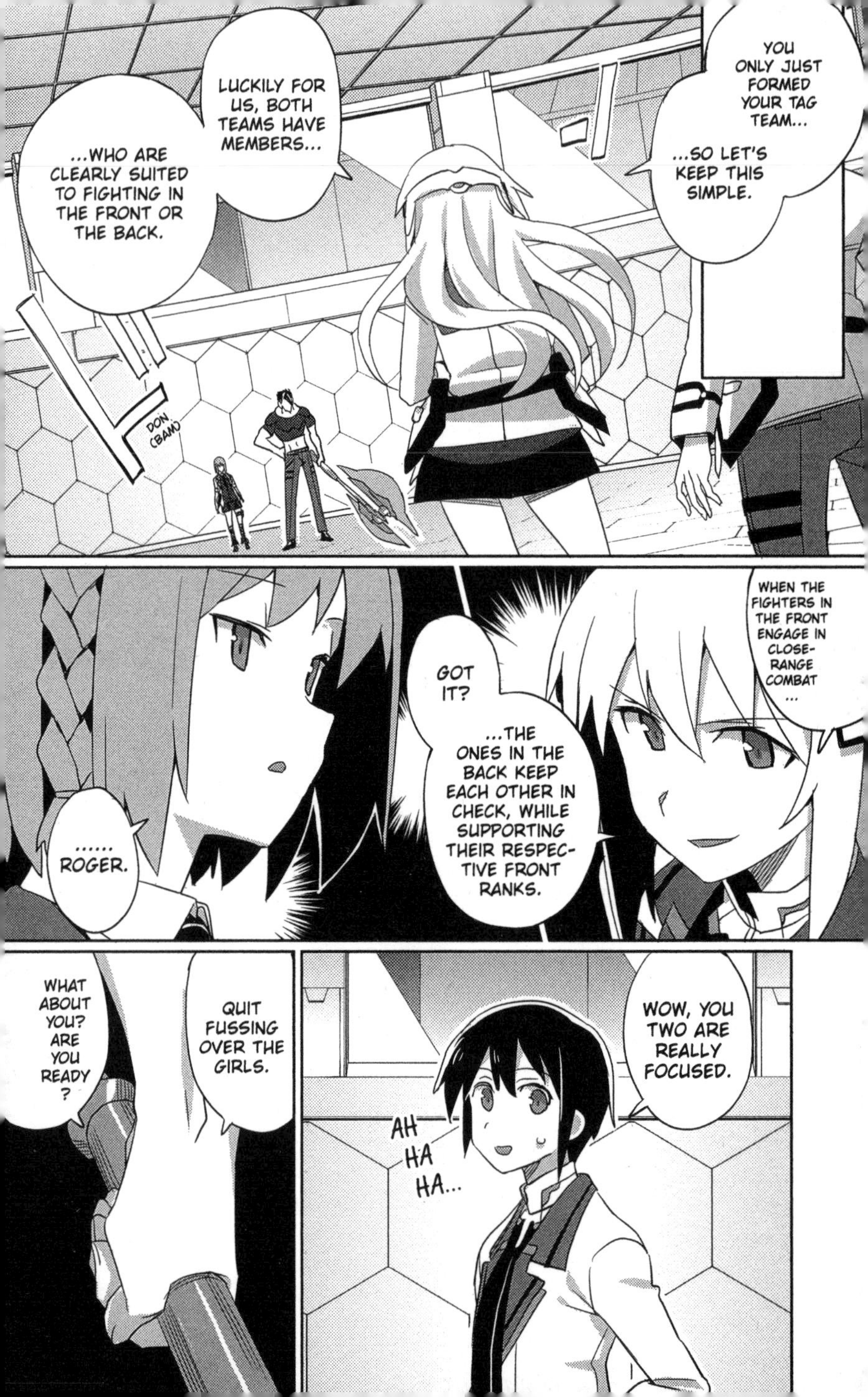
YOU ONLY JUST FORMED YOUR TAG TEAM...
...SO LET'S KEEP THIS SIMPLE.
LUCKILY FOR US, BOTH TEAMS HAVE MEMBERS...
...WHO ARE CLEARLY SUITED TO FIGHTING IN THE FRONT OR THE BACK.
DON (BAM)
WHEN THE FIGHTERS IN THE FRONT ENGAGE IN CLOSE-RANGE COMBAT...
...THE ONES IN THE BACK KEEP EACH OTHER IN CHECK, WHILE SUPPORTING THEIR RESPECTIVE FRONT RANKS.
GOT IT?
......ROGER.
WOW, YOU TWO ARE REALLY FOCUSED.
AH HA HA...
QUIT FUSSING OVER THE GIRLS.
WHAT ABOUT YOU? ARE YOU READY?

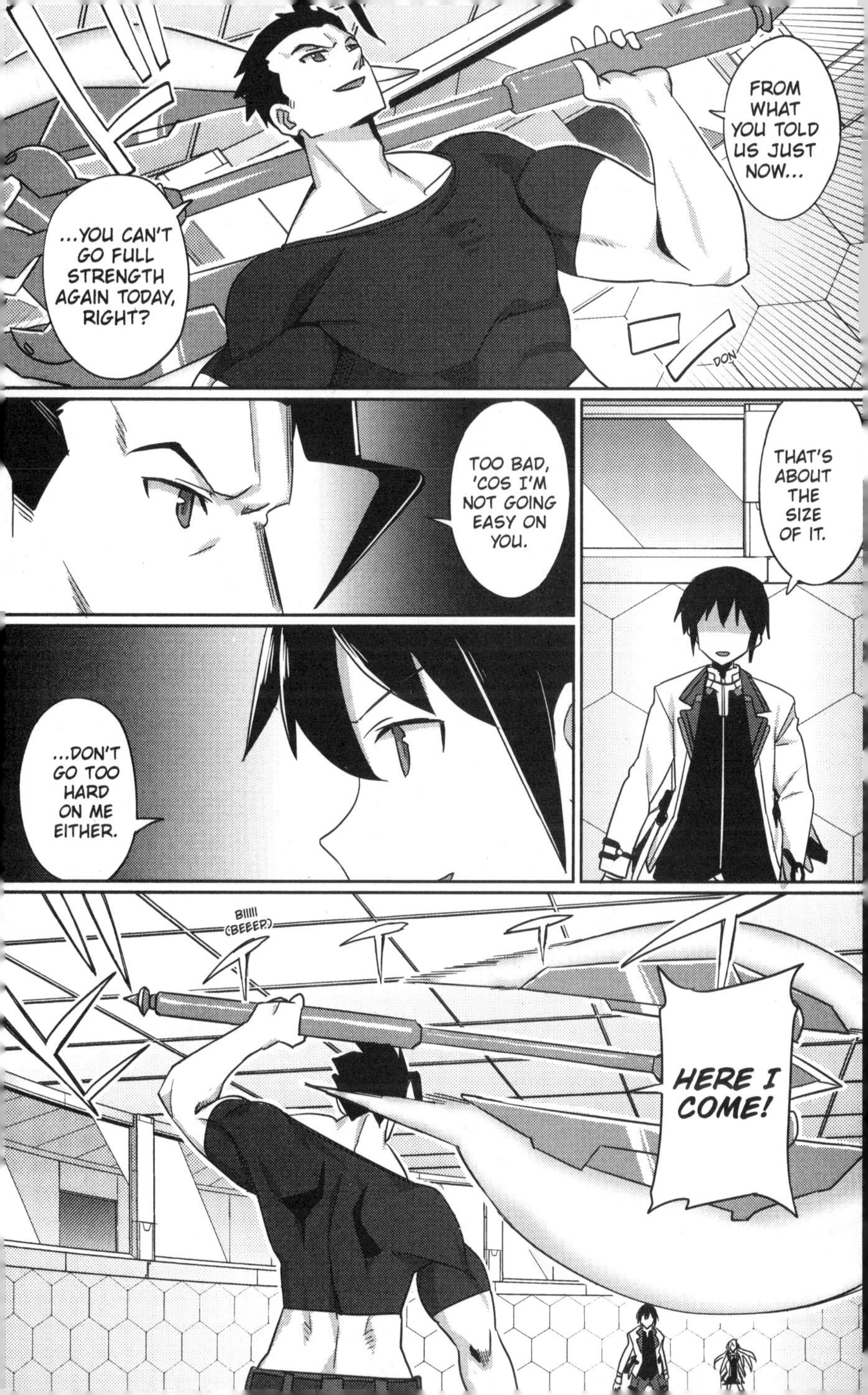
FROM WHAT YOU TOLD US JUST NOW...
...YOU CAN'T GO FULL STRENGTH AGAIN TODAY, RIGHT?
DON
THAT'S ABOUT THE SIZE OF IT.
TOO BAD, 'COS I'M NOT GOING EASY ON YOU.
...DON'T GO TOO HARD ON ME EITHER.
HERE I COME!
BIIIII (BEEEP.)

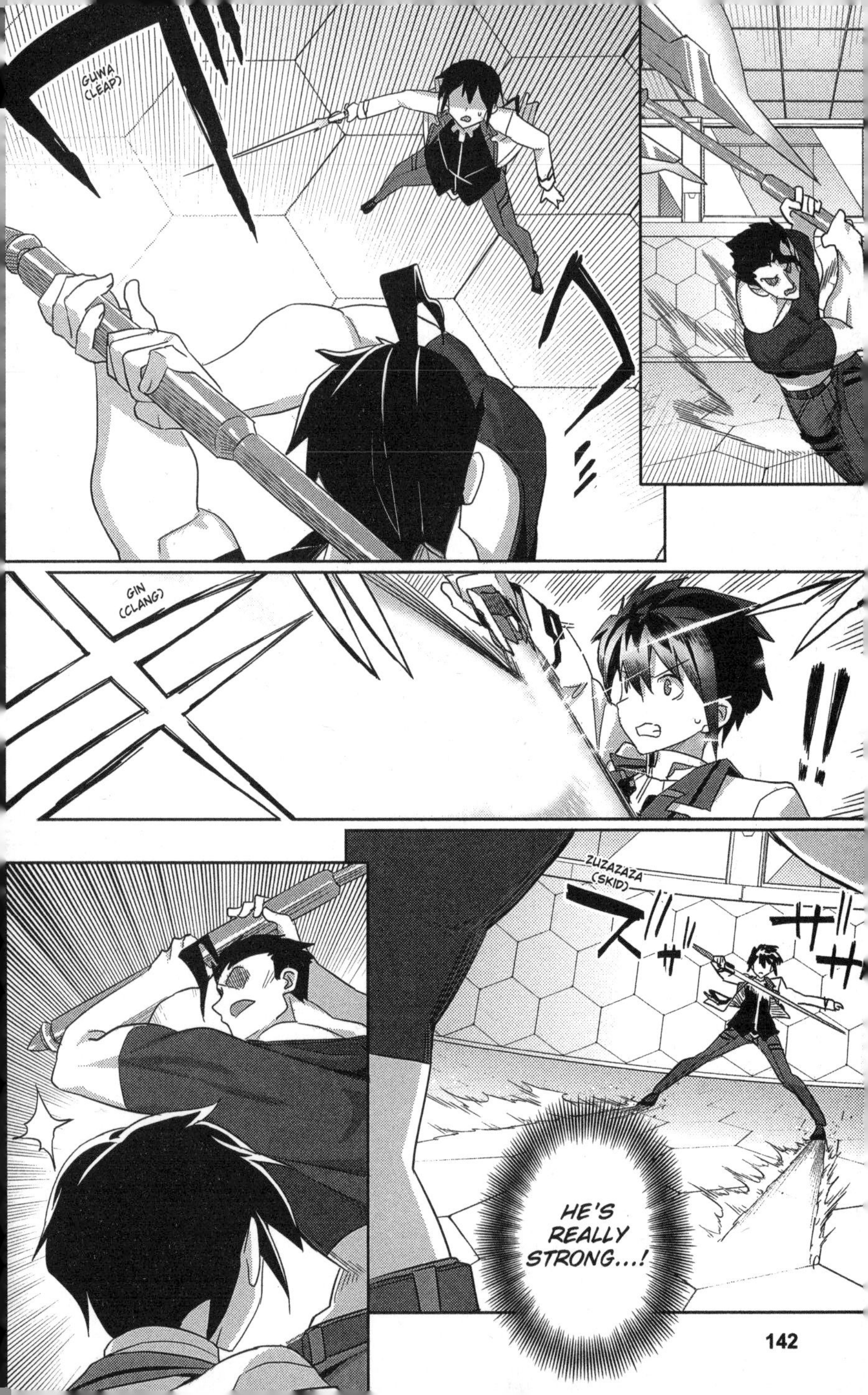
GUWA (LEAP)
GIN (CLANG)
ZUZAZAZA (SKID)
HE'S REALLY STRONG...!

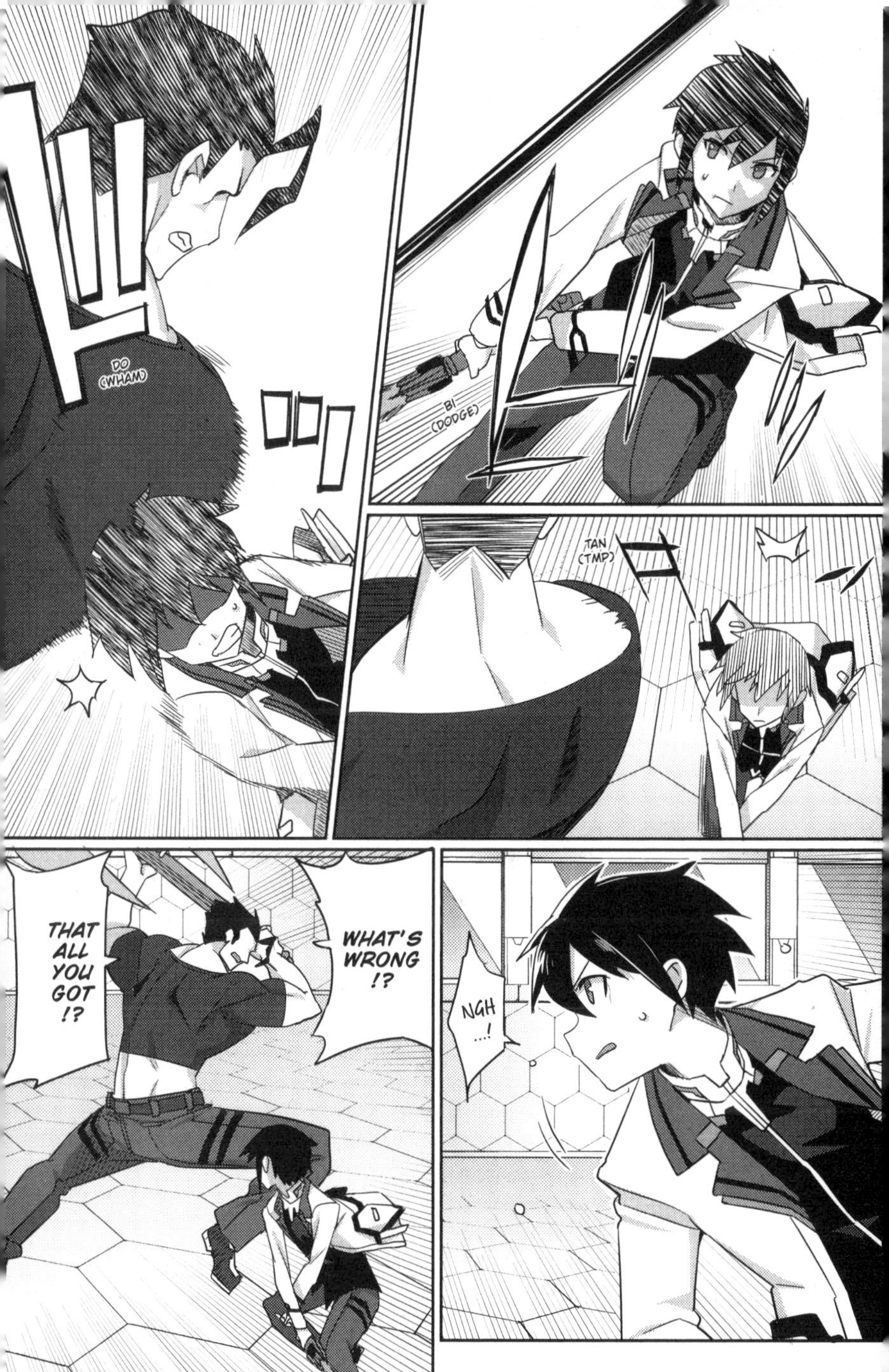
BI (DODGE)
TAN (TMP)
DO (WHAM)
NGH ...!
WHAT'S WRONG !?
THAT ALL YOU GOT !?

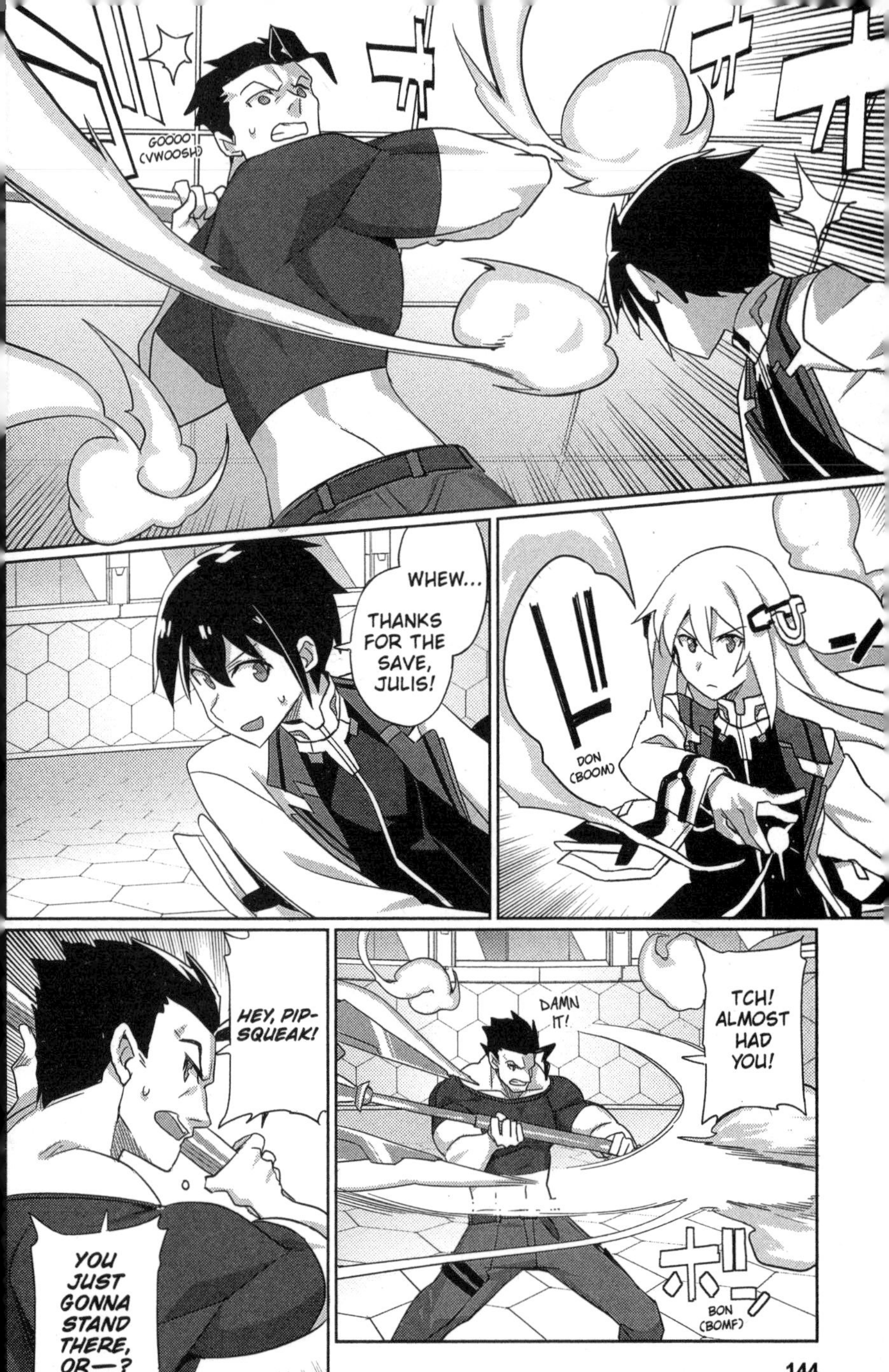
GOOOO (VWOOSH)
WHEW...
THANKS FOR THE SAVE, JULIS!
DON (BOOM)
TCH! ALMOST HAD YOU!
DAMN IT!
BON (BOMF)
HEY, PIP-SQUEAK!
YOU JUST GONNA STAND THERE, OR—?

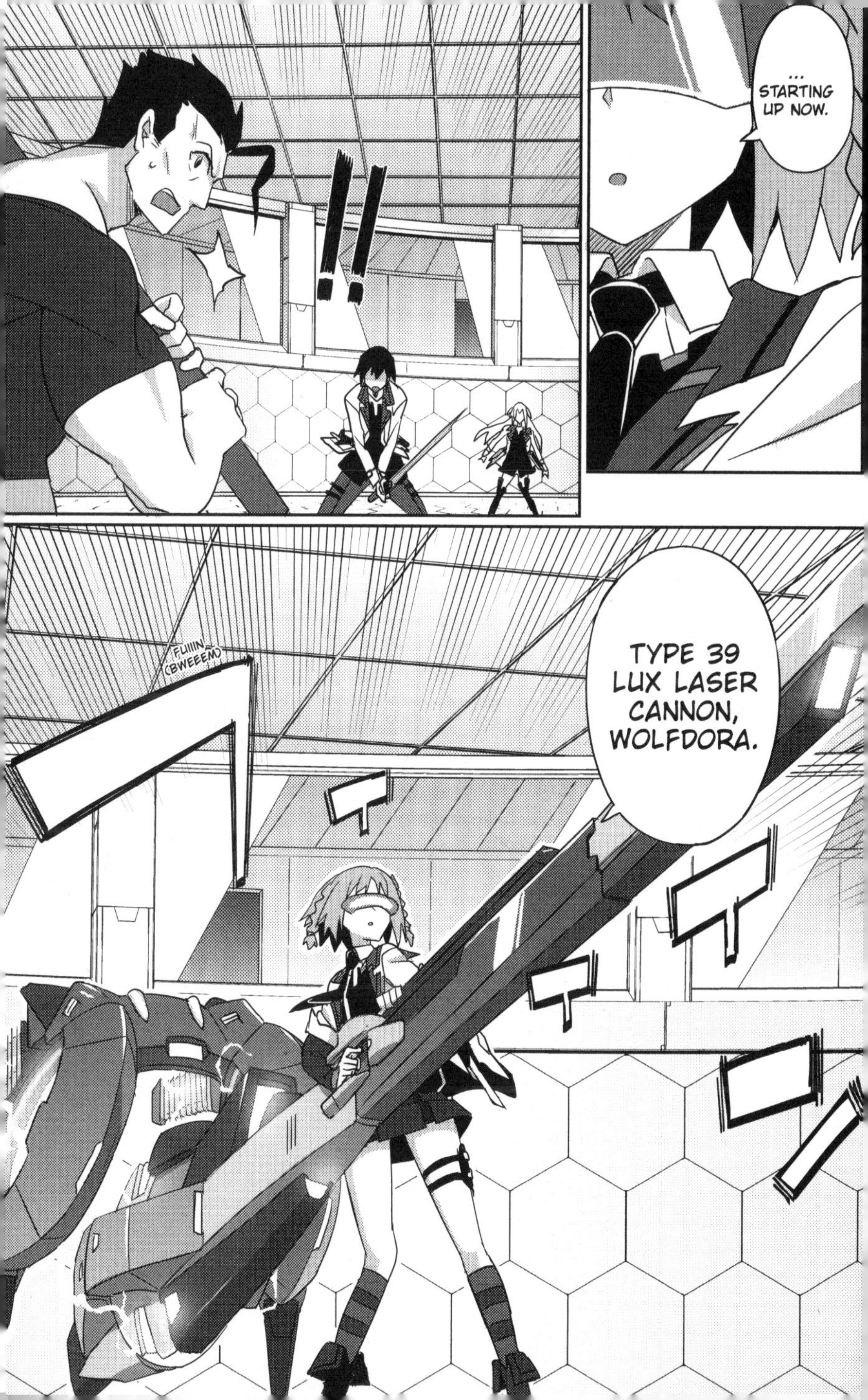
... STARTING UP NOW.
!!
TYPE 39 LUX LASER CANNON, WOLFDORA.
FUIIIN (BWEEEM)

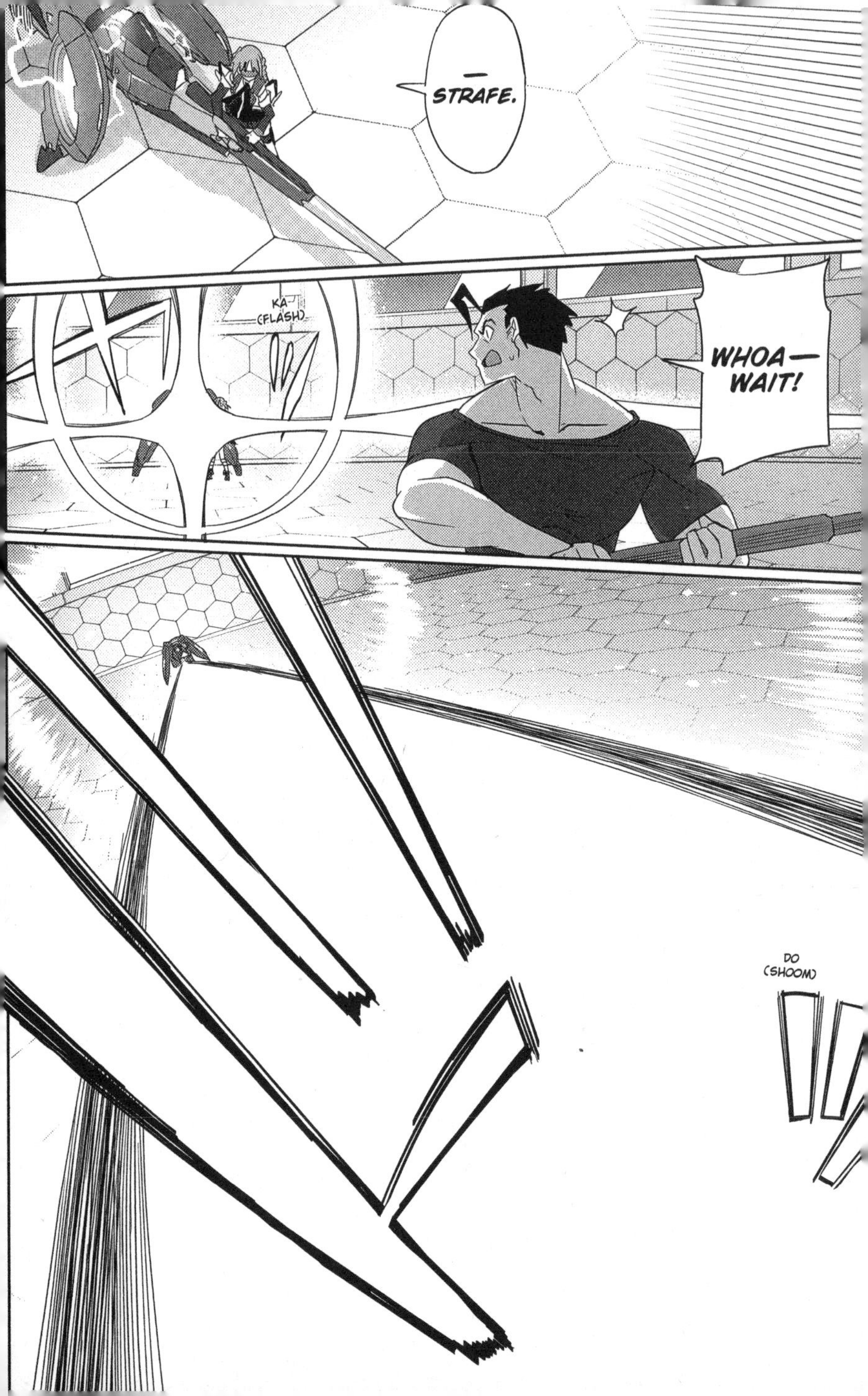
—STRAFE.
WHOA—WAIT!
KA (FLASH)
DO (SHOOM)

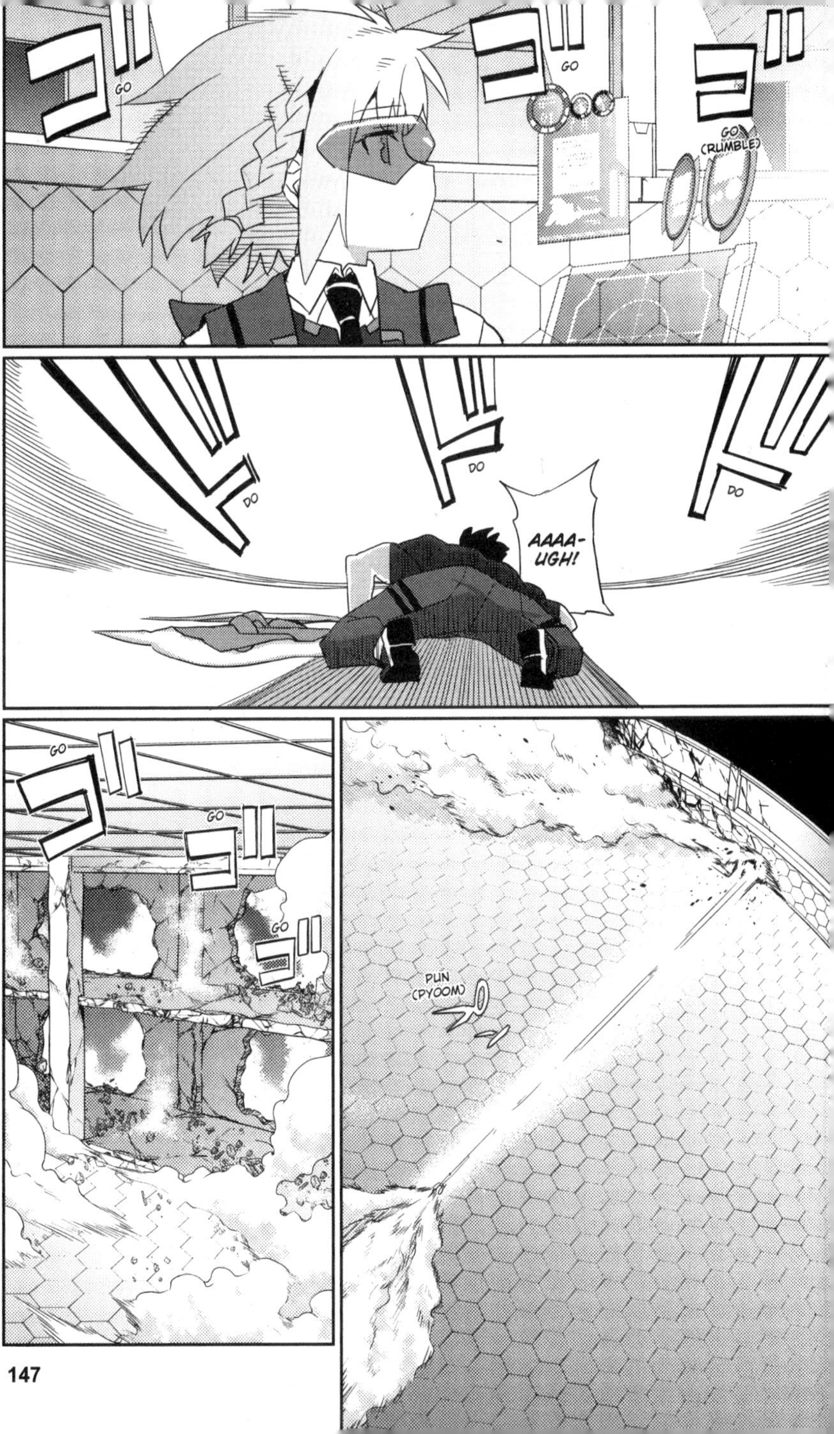
GO (RUMBLE)
GO
GO
DO
AAAA-UGH!
DO
DO
PUN (PYOOM)
GO
GO
GO

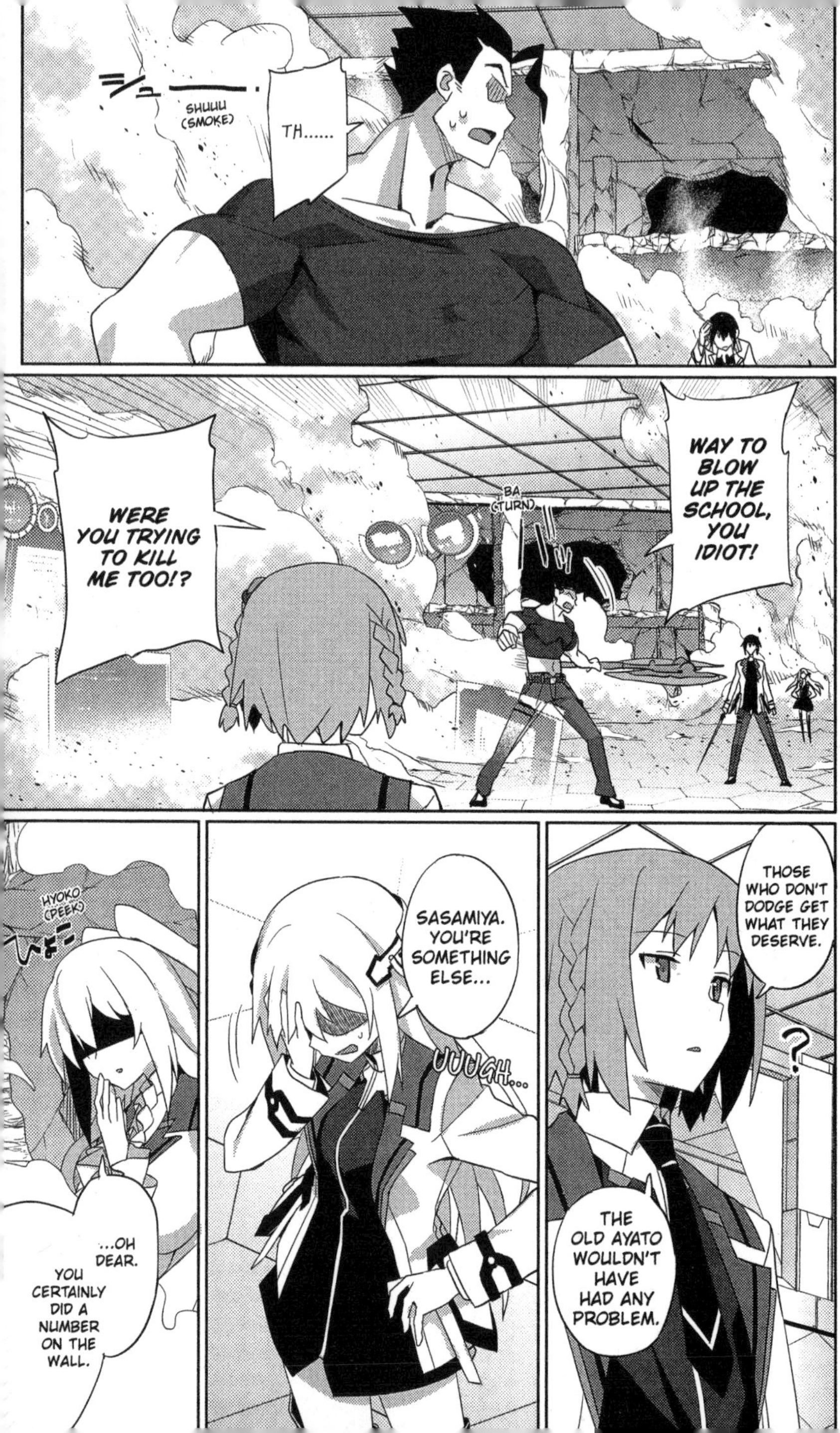

TH......
シュー
SHUUU (SMOKE)
WAY TO BLOW UP THE SCHOOL, YOU IDIOT!
BA (TURN)
WERE YOU TRYING TO KILL ME TOO!?
THOSE WHO DON'T DODGE GET WHAT THEY DESERVE.
THE OLD AYATO WOULDN'T HAVE HAD ANY PROBLEM.
SASAMIYA. YOU'RE SOMETHING ELSE...
UUUGH...
HYOKO (PEEK)
ひょこ
...OH DEAR. YOU CERTAINLY DID A NUMBER ON THE WALL.

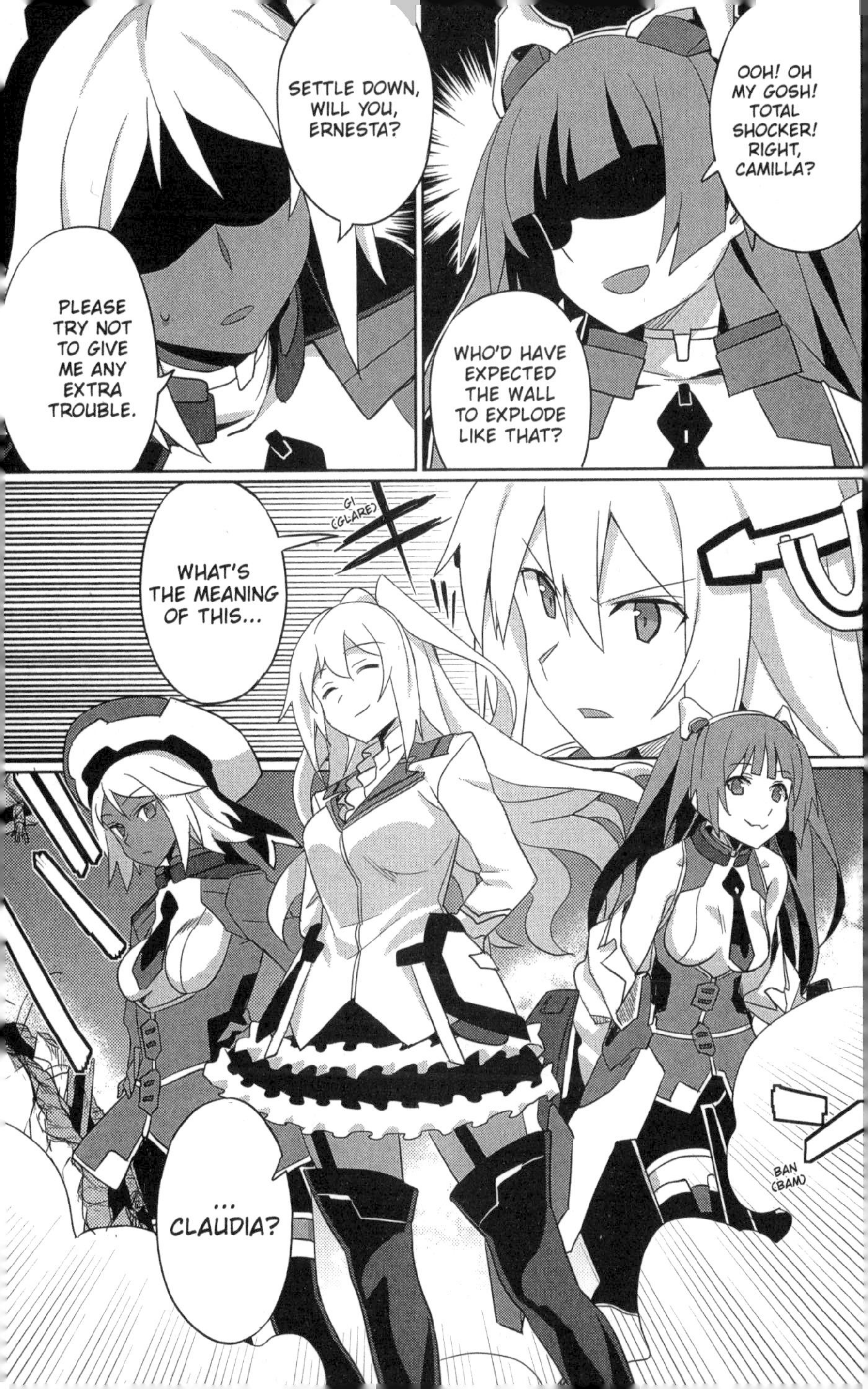
OOH! OH MY GOSH! TOTAL SHOCKER! RIGHT, CAMILLA?
WHO'D HAVE EXPECTED THE WALL TO EXPLODE LIKE THAT?
SETTLE DOWN, WILL YOU, ERNESTA?
PLEASE TRY NOT TO GIVE ME ANY EXTRA TROUBLE.
GI (GLARE)
WHAT'S THE MEANING OF THIS...
BAN (BAM)
... CLAUDIA?

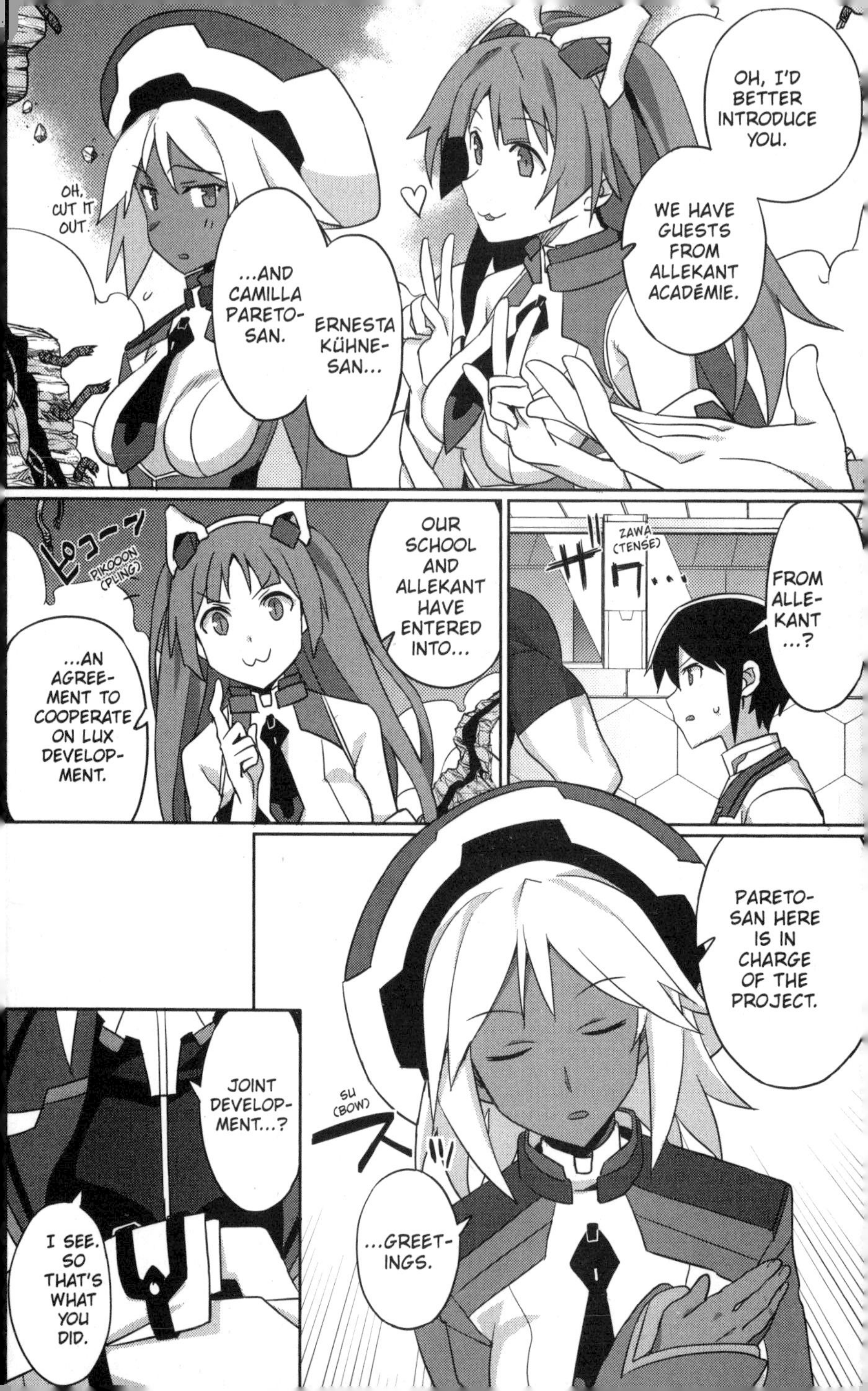

OH, I'D BETTER INTRODUCE YOU.
WE HAVE GUESTS FROM ALLEKANT ACADÉMIE.
ERNESTA KÜHNE-SAN...
...AND CAMILLA PARETO-SAN.
OH, CUT IT OUT.
ZAWA (TENSE)
FROM ALLEKANT...?
OUR SCHOOL AND ALLEKANT HAVE ENTERED INTO...
PIKOOON (PLING)
...AN AGREEMENT TO COOPERATE ON LUX DEVELOPMENT.
PARETO-SAN HERE IS IN CHARGE OF THE PROJECT.
SU (BOW)
...GREETINGS.
JOINT DEVELOPMENT...?
I SEE. SO THAT'S WHAT YOU DID.

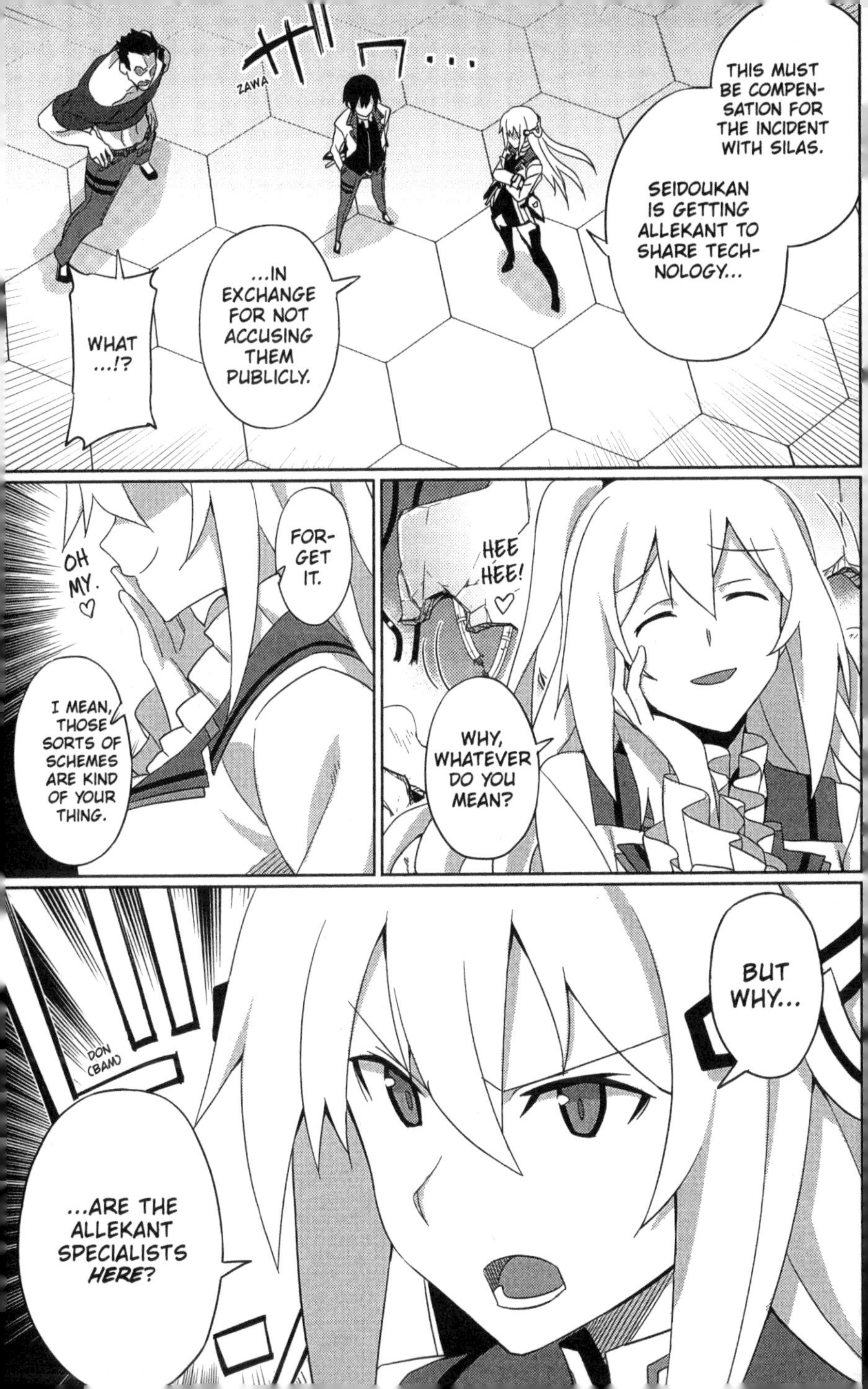
ZAWA
...
THIS MUST BE COMPENSATION FOR THE INCIDENT WITH SILAS.
SEIDOUKAN IS GETTING ALLEKANT TO SHARE TECHNOLOGY...
...IN EXCHANGE FOR NOT ACCUSING THEM PUBLICLY.
WHAT ...!?
HEE HEE! ♡
WHY, WHATEVER DO YOU MEAN?
FORGET IT.
OH MY. ♡
I MEAN, THOSE SORTS OF SCHEMES ARE KIND OF YOUR THING.
BUT WHY...
DON (BAM)
...ARE THE ALLEKANT SPECIALISTS *HERE*?

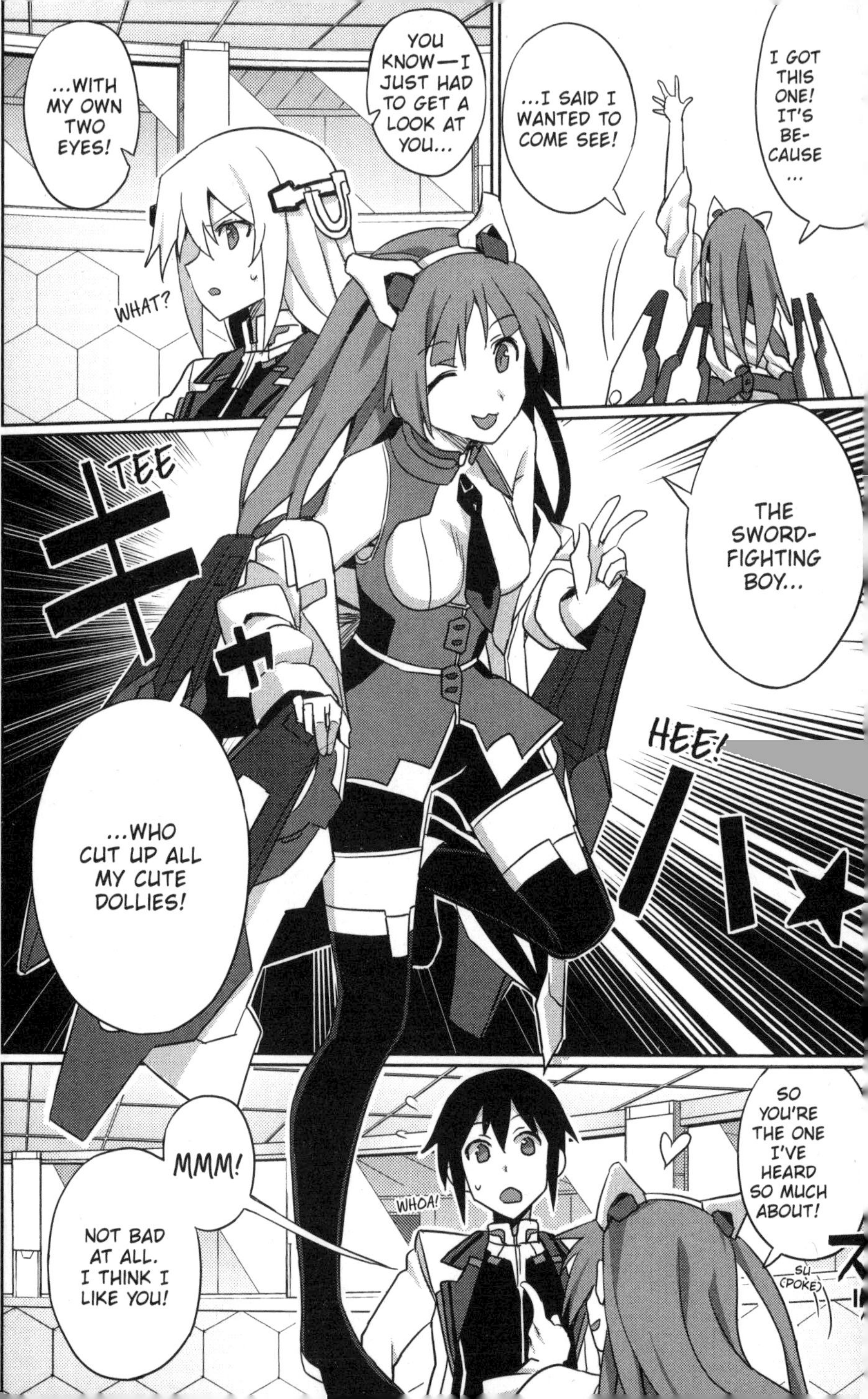
I GOT THIS ONE! IT'S BE-CAUSE...
...I SAID I WANTED TO COME SEE!
YOU KNOW—I JUST HAD TO GET A LOOK AT YOU...
...WITH MY OWN TWO EYES!
WHAT?
THE SWORD-FIGHTING BOY...
TEE
HEE!
...WHO CUT UP ALL MY CUTE DOLLIES!
SO YOU'RE THE ONE I'VE HEARD SO MUCH ABOUT!
SU (POKE)
WHOA!
MMM!
NOT BAD AT ALL. I THINK I LIKE YOU!

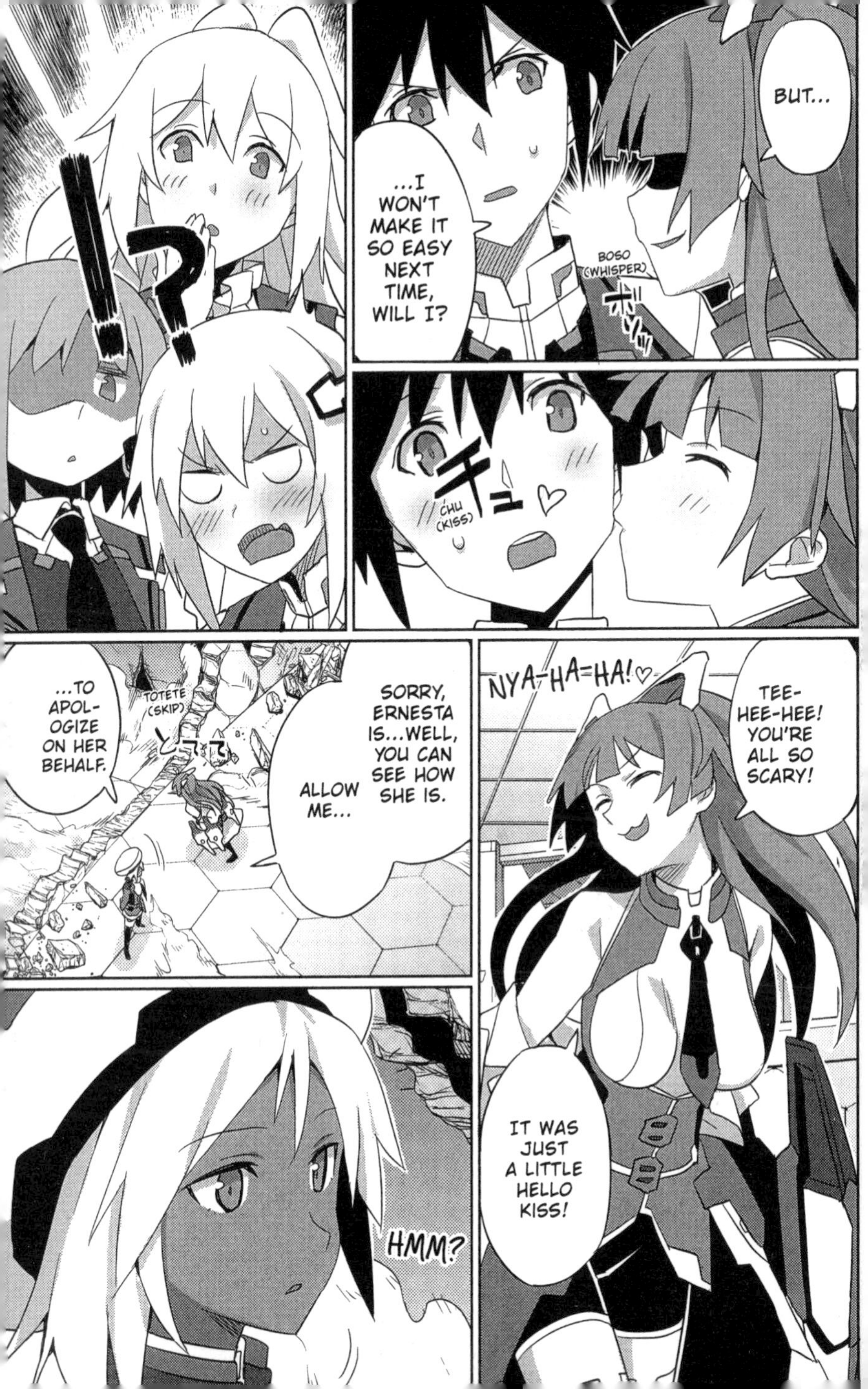
BUT...
...I WON'T MAKE IT SO EASY NEXT TIME, WILL I?
BOSO (WHISPER)
CHU (KISS)
!?
NYA-HA=HA!♡
TEE-HEE-HEE! YOU'RE ALL SO SCARY!
IT WAS JUST A LITTLE HELLO KISS!
SORRY, ERNESTA IS...WELL, YOU CAN SEE HOW SHE IS.
ALLOW ME...
TOTETE (SKIP)
...TO APOLOGIZE ON HER BEHALF.
HMM?

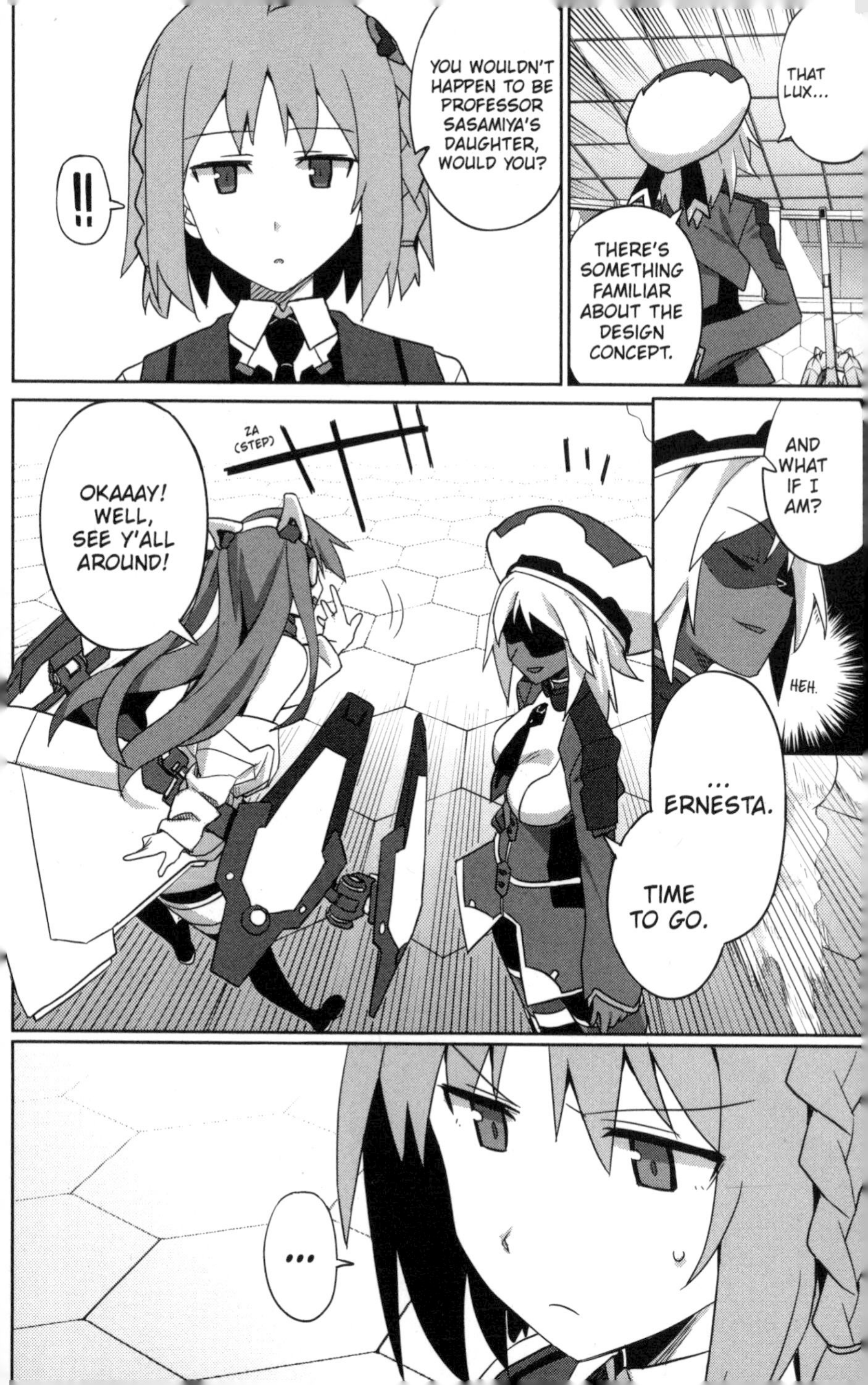
THAT LUX...
THERE'S SOMETHING FAMILIAR ABOUT THE DESIGN CONCEPT.
YOU WOULDN'T HAPPEN TO BE PROFESSOR SASAMIYA'S DAUGHTER, WOULD YOU?
!!
AND WHAT IF I AM?
HEH.
... ERNESTA.
TIME TO GO.
OKAAAY! WELL, SEE Y'ALL AROUND!
ZA (STEP)
...

—— TO BE CONTINUED...

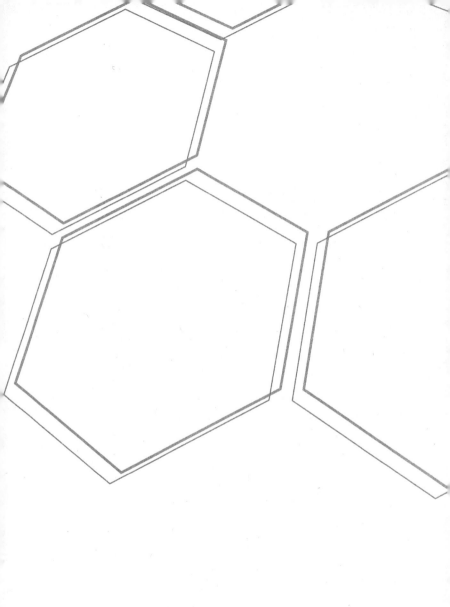

THE
ASTERISK WAR

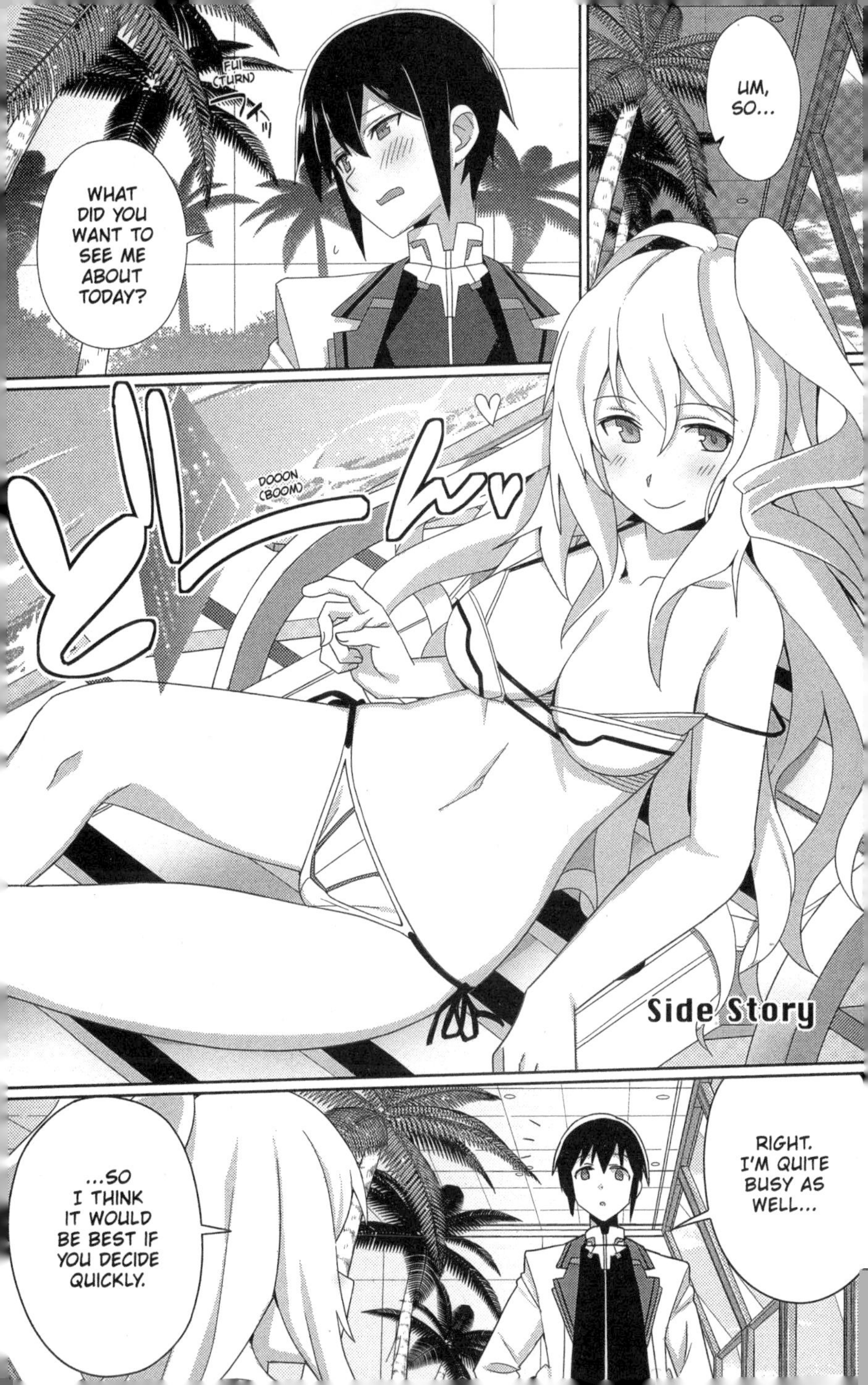
UM, SO...
FUI (TURN)
WHAT DID YOU WANT TO SEE ME ABOUT TODAY?
どーん
DOOON (BOOM)
Side Story
RIGHT. I'M QUITE BUSY AS WELL...
...SO I THINK IT WOULD BE BEST IF YOU DECIDE QUICKLY.

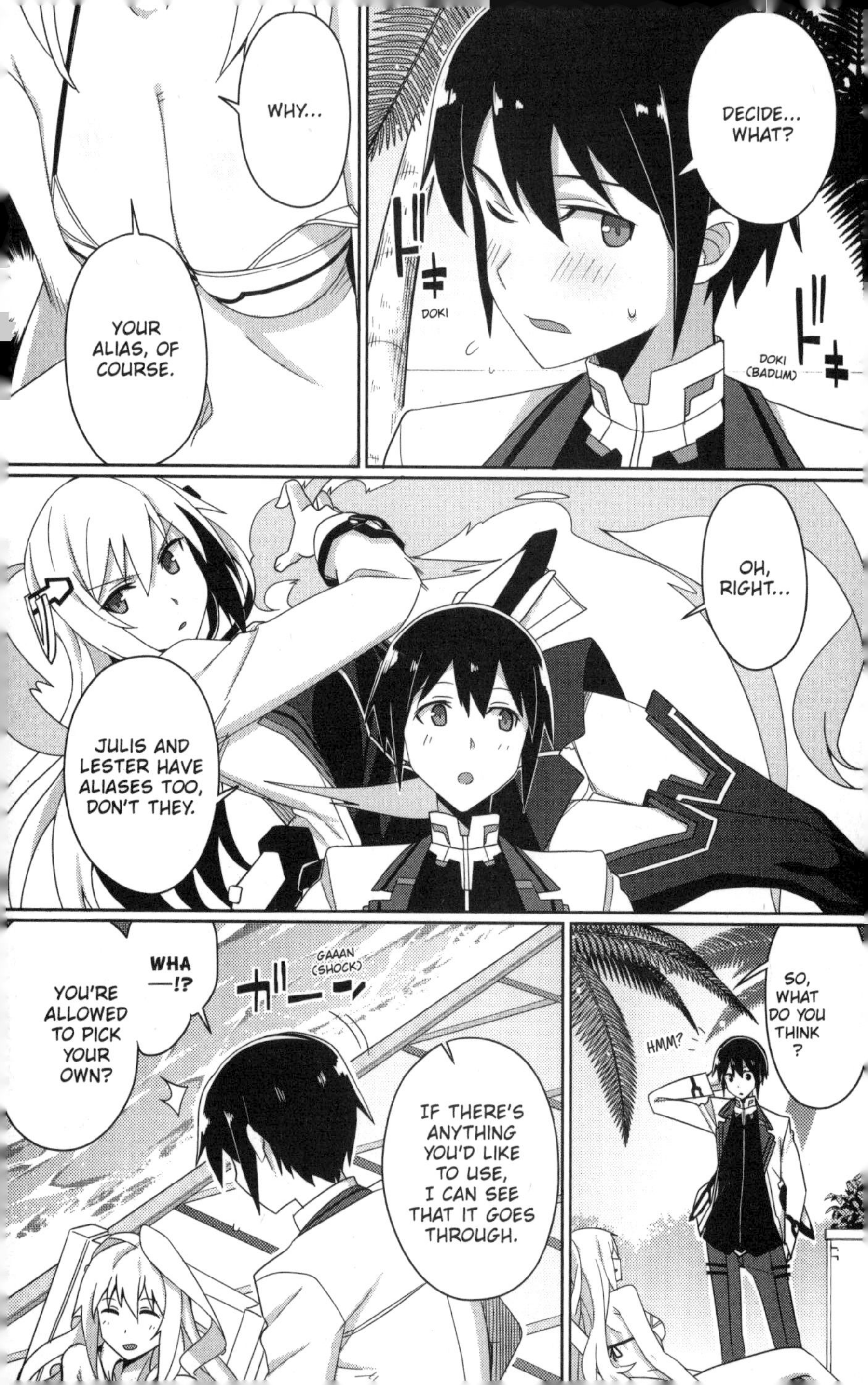
DECIDE... WHAT?
DOKI (BADUM)
DOKI
WHY...
YOUR ALIAS, OF COURSE.
OH, RIGHT...
JULIS AND LESTER HAVE ALIASES TOO, DON'T THEY.
SO, WHAT DO YOU THINK?
HMM?
IF THERE'S ANYTHING YOU'D LIKE TO USE, I CAN SEE THAT IT GOES THROUGH.
GAAAN (SHOCK)
WHA—!?
YOU'RE ALLOWED TO PICK YOUR OWN?

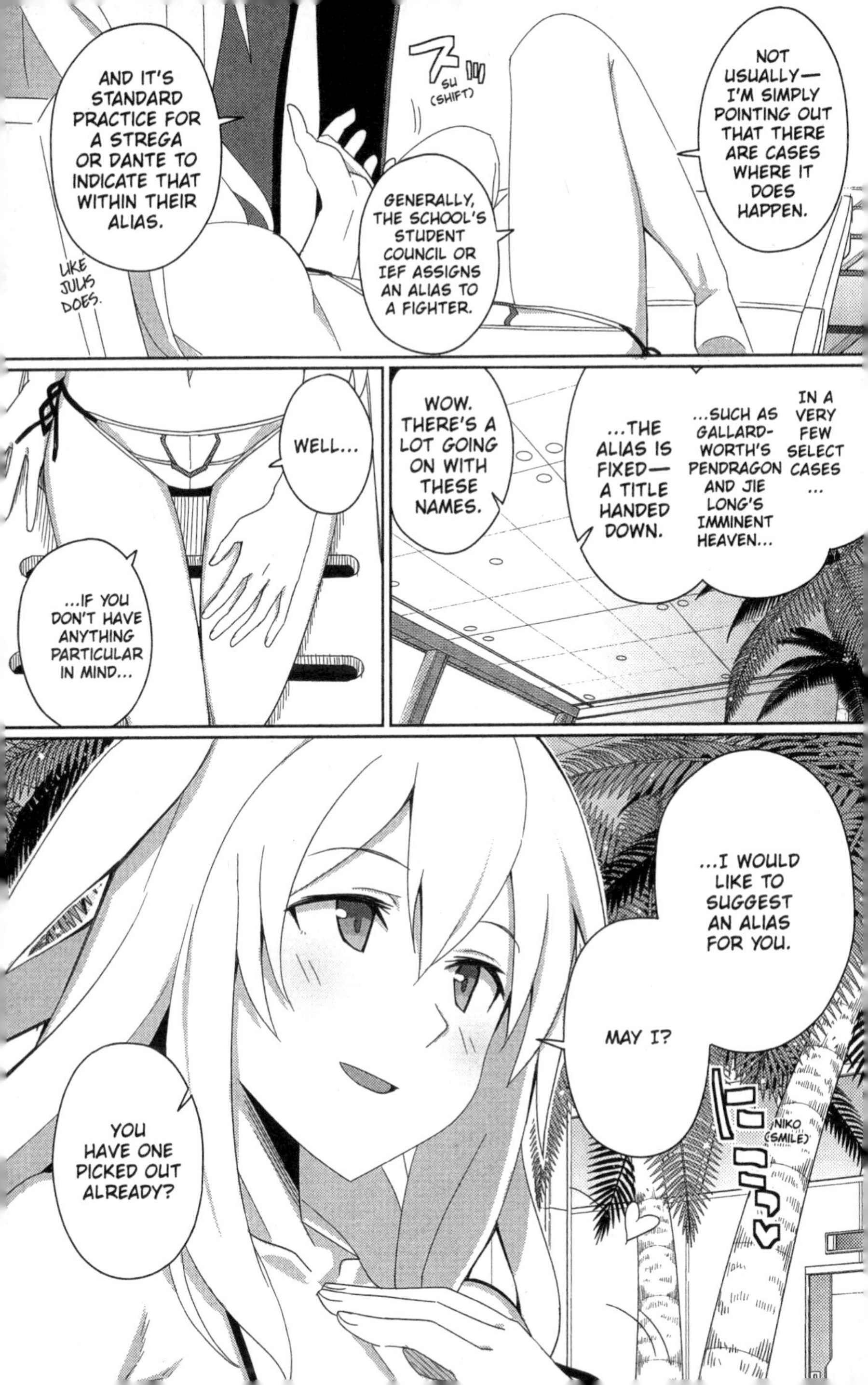
NOT USUALLY—I'M SIMPLY POINTING OUT THAT THERE ARE CASES WHERE IT DOES HAPPEN.
SU (SHIFT)
GENERALLY, THE SCHOOL'S STUDENT COUNCIL OR IEF ASSIGNS AN ALIAS TO A FIGHTER.
AND IT'S STANDARD PRACTICE FOR A STREGA OR DANTE TO INDICATE THAT WITHIN THEIR ALIAS.
LIKE JULIS DOES.
IN A VERY FEW SELECT CASES...
...SUCH AS GALLARDWORTH'S PENDRAGON AND JIE LONG'S IMMINENT HEAVEN...
...THE ALIAS IS FIXED—A TITLE HANDED DOWN.
WOW. THERE'S A LOT GOING ON WITH THESE NAMES.
WELL...
...IF YOU DON'T HAVE ANYTHING PARTICULAR IN MIND...
...I WOULD LIKE TO SUGGEST AN ALIAS FOR YOU.
MAY I?
NIKO (SMILE)
YOU HAVE ONE PICKED OUT ALREADY?

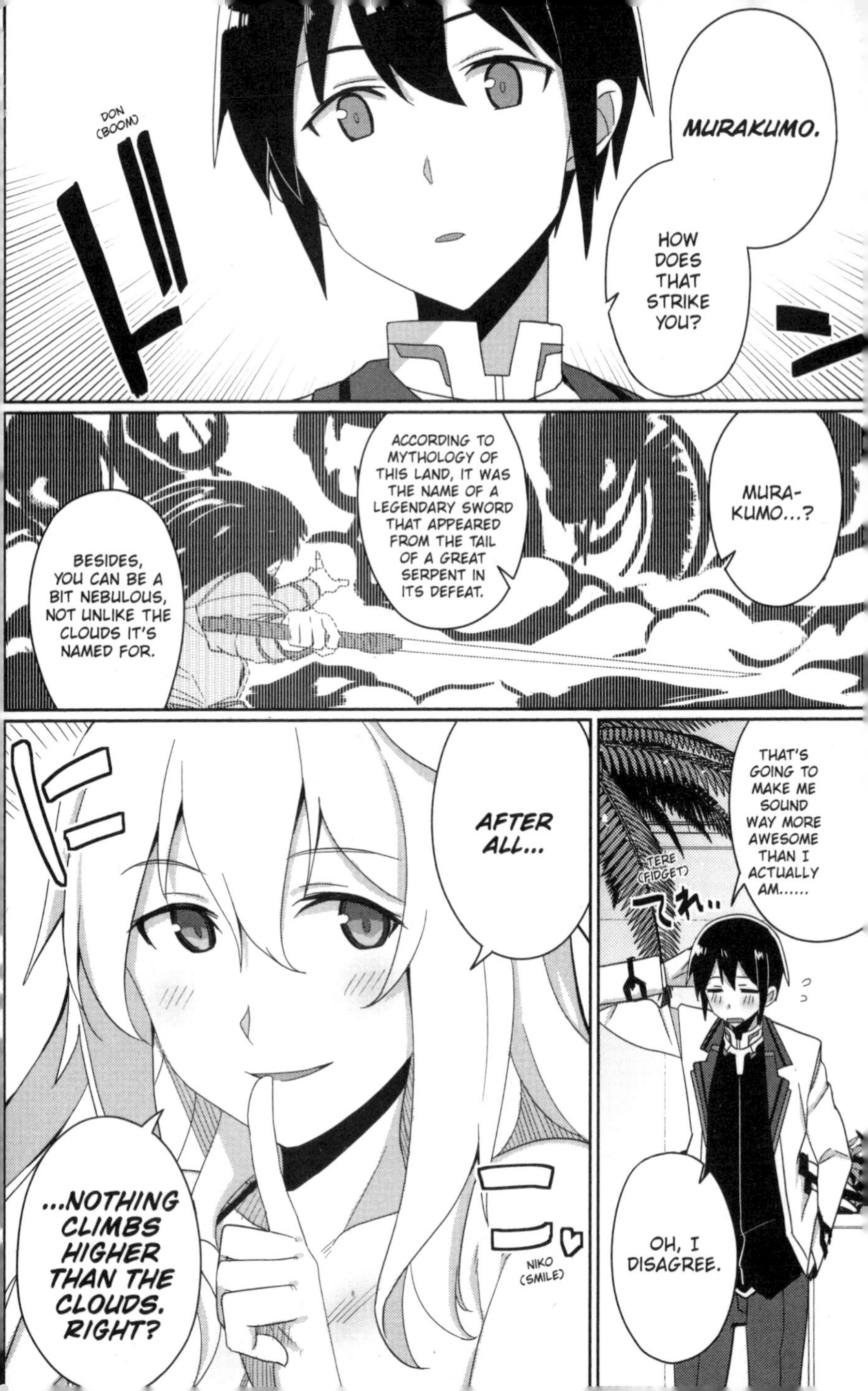
MURAKUMO.
HOW DOES THAT STRIKE YOU?
DON (BOOM)
MURA-KUMO...?
ACCORDING TO MYTHOLOGY OF THIS LAND, IT WAS THE NAME OF A LEGENDARY SWORD THAT APPEARED FROM THE TAIL OF A GREAT SERPENT IN ITS DEFEAT.
BESIDES, YOU CAN BE A BIT NEBULOUS, NOT UNLIKE THE CLOUDS IT'S NAMED FOR.
THAT'S GOING TO MAKE ME SOUND WAY MORE AWESOME THAN I ACTUALLY AM......
TERE (FIDGET)
OH, I DISAGREE.
AFTER ALL...
...NOTHING CLIMBS HIGHER THAN THE CLOUDS. RIGHT?
NIKO (SMILE)

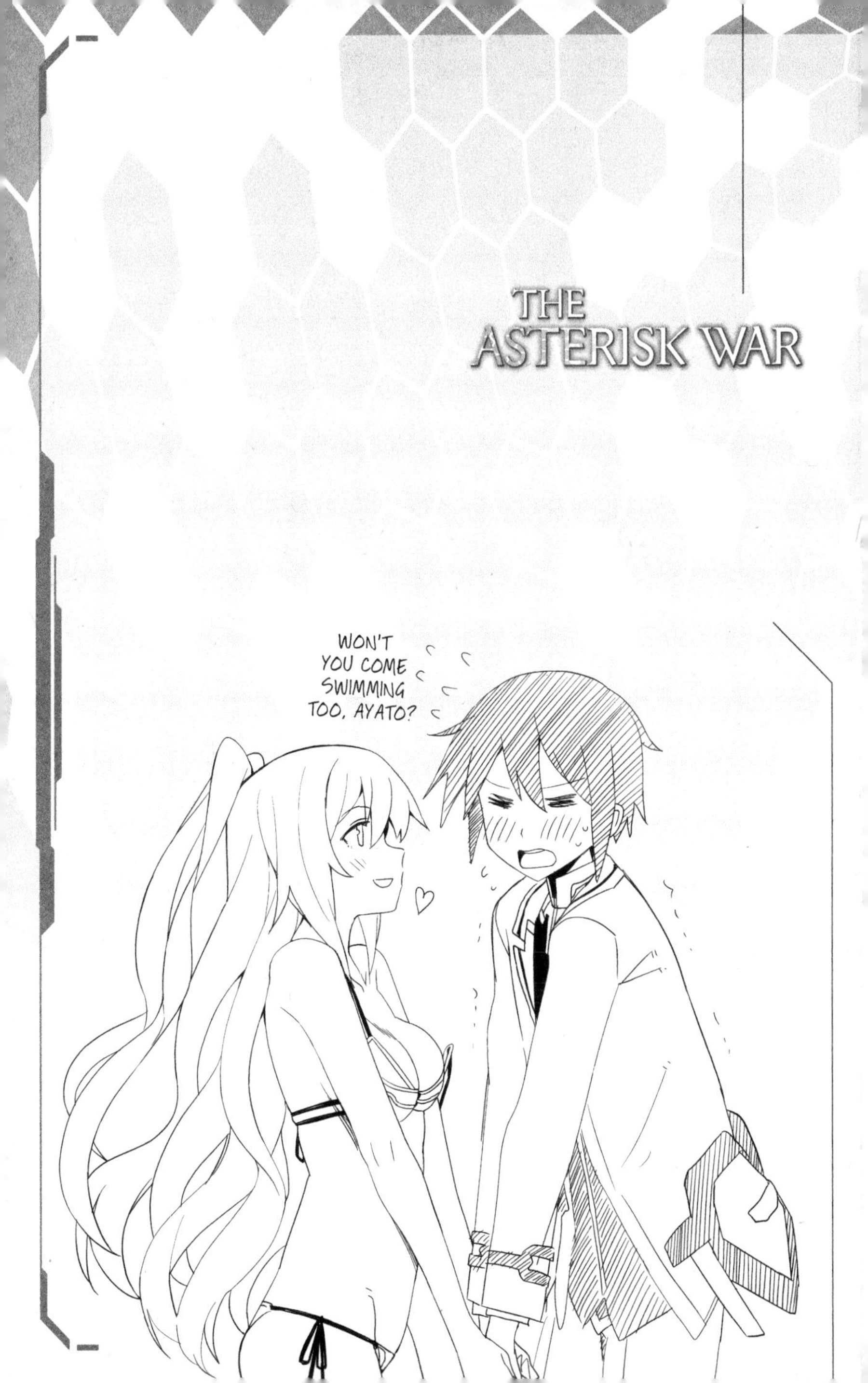
THE ASTERISK WAR
WON'T YOU COME SWIMMING TOO, AYATO?

THE ASTERISK WAR

Afterword

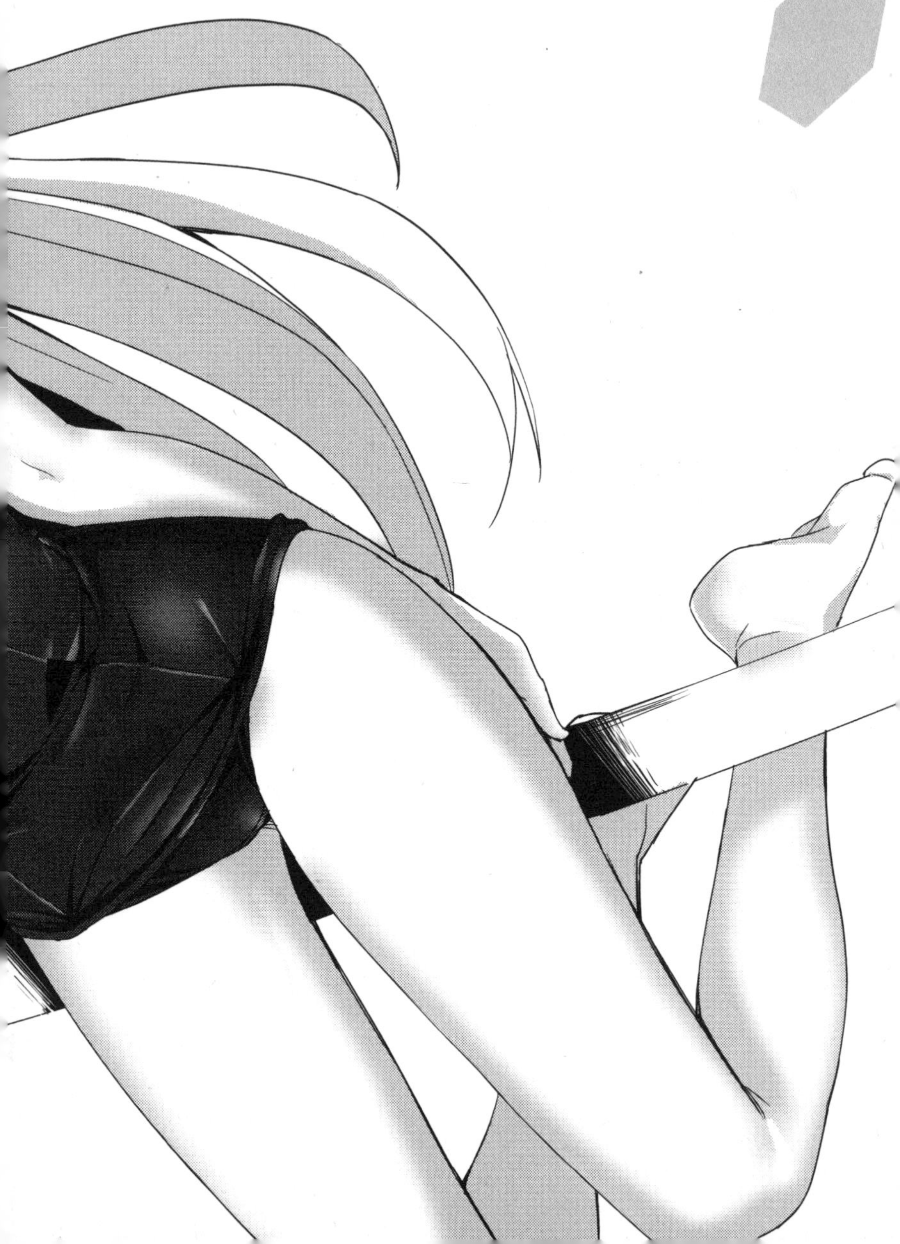

Hi, Ningen here. Good to see you again. Thanks to all your support, the third volume's out!

The anime is making progress too. I hope these books let you enjoy even more of the *Asterisk War* world.

Once again, I'm so grateful to Yuu Miyazaki-sensei and okiura-sensei, the original author and illustrator, to the *Comic Alive* editorial staff, to Shimada-kun, Jou Yukino-sama, and Maguro Koizumi-sama!

See you next time in Volume 4.

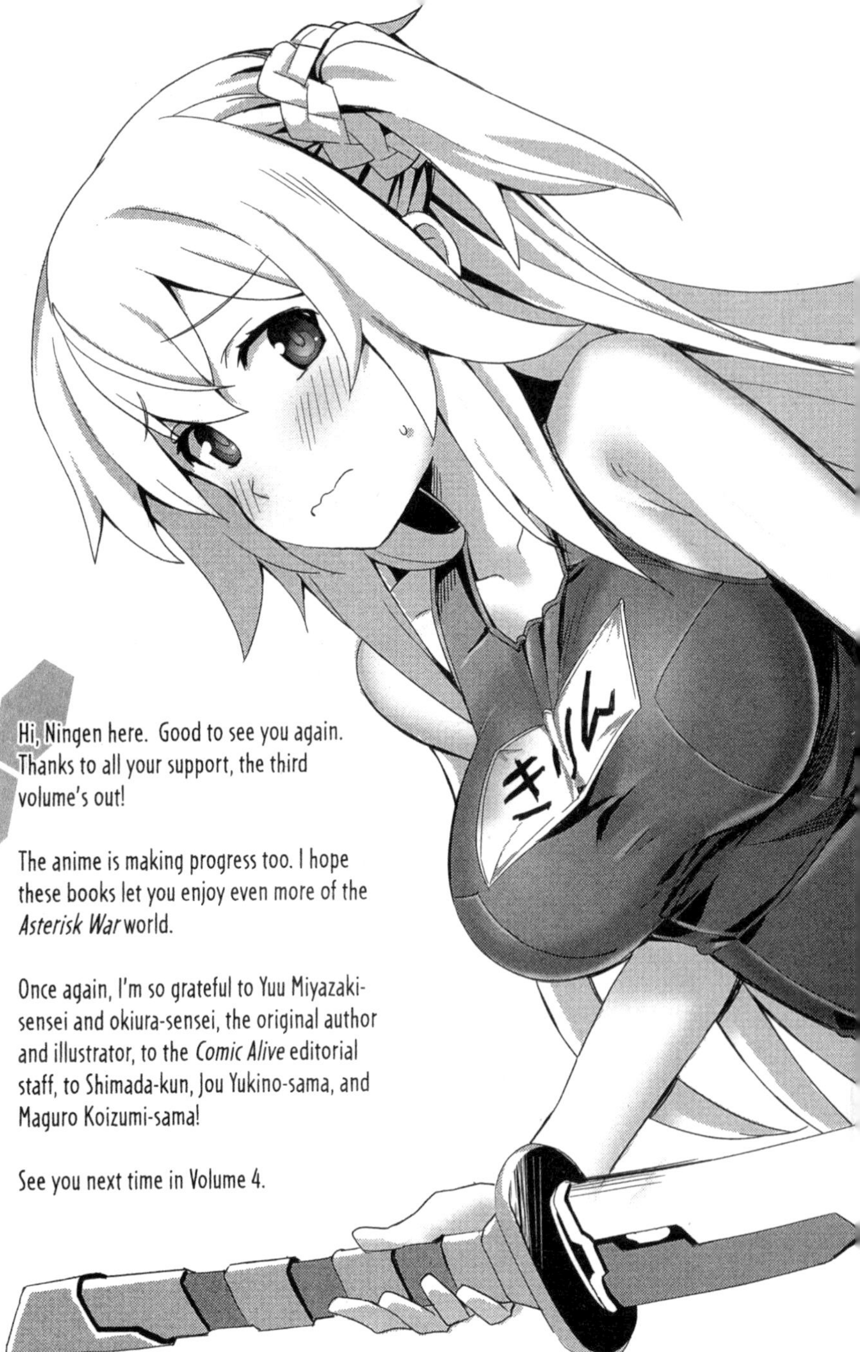
きりん

*SWIMSUIT: KIRIN

THE ASTERISK WAR {03}

Ningen
Original Story: Yuu Miyazaki
Character Design: okiura

Translation: Melissa Tanaka   Lettering: Phil Christie

THE ASTERISK WAR
© Ningen 2015
© Yuu Miyazaki 2015
First published in Japan in 2015 by KADOKAWA CORPORATION, Tokyo.
English translation rights arranged with KADOKAWA CORPORATION, Tokyo,
through TUTTLE-MORI AGENCY, Inc., Tokyo.

English translation © 2017 by Yen Press, LLC

Date: 11/7/17

GRA 741.5 AST V.3
Ningen
The asterisk war.

Yen Press is an imprint of Yen Press, LLC.
The Yen Press name and logo are trademarks of Yen Press, LLC.

The publisher is not responsible for websites (or their content) that are not owned by the publisher.

Library of Congress Control Number: 2016936539

ISBN: 978-0-316-50275-7

10 9 8 7 6 5 4 3 2 1

BVG

Printed in the United States of America